DIGGING *for* VICTORY

Gardens and Gardening in Wartime Britain

TWIGS WAY & MIKE BROWN

Sabrestorm Publishing

First published in the United Kingdom in 2010
by Sabrestorm Publishing
90, Lennard Road, Dunton Green
Sevenoaks, Kent TN13 2UX

www.sabrestorm.com

British Library Cataloguing in Publication Data
A catalogue record for this book is available from the British Library.

Designed and typeset by Annie Falconer-Gronow

ISBN: 978-0-955272370

Printed by Tien Wah Press

We would like to thank all those who kindly contributed their memories of wartime gardening.

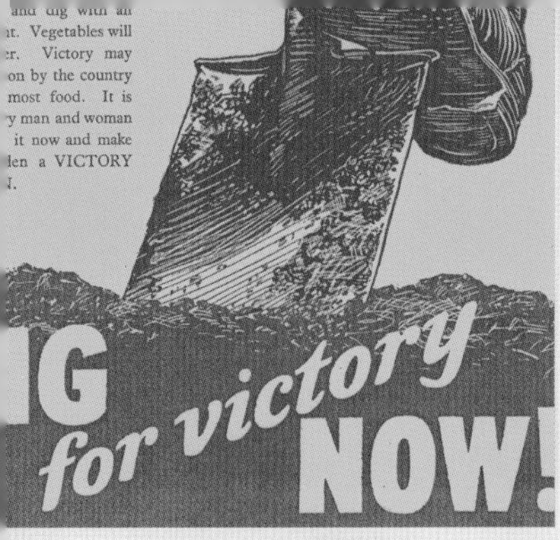
for victory
NOW!

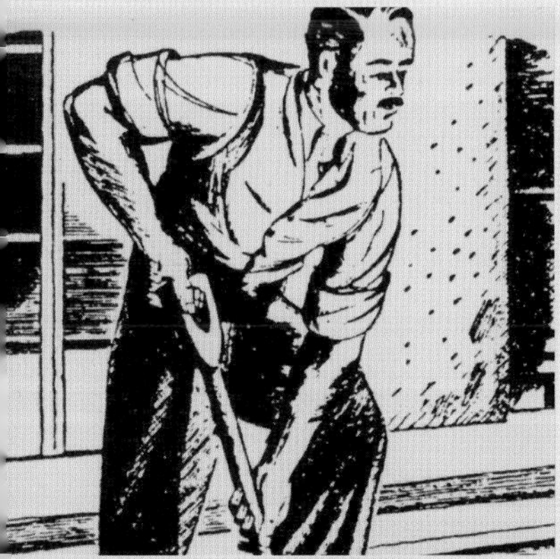

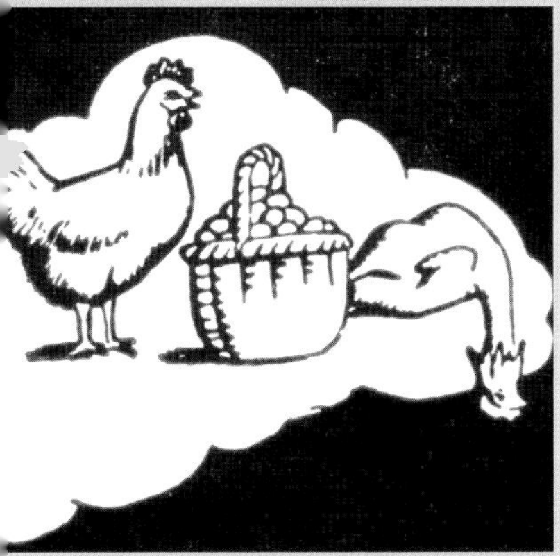

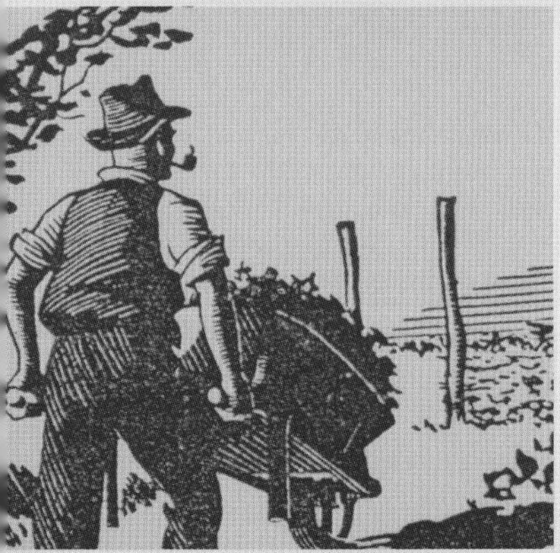

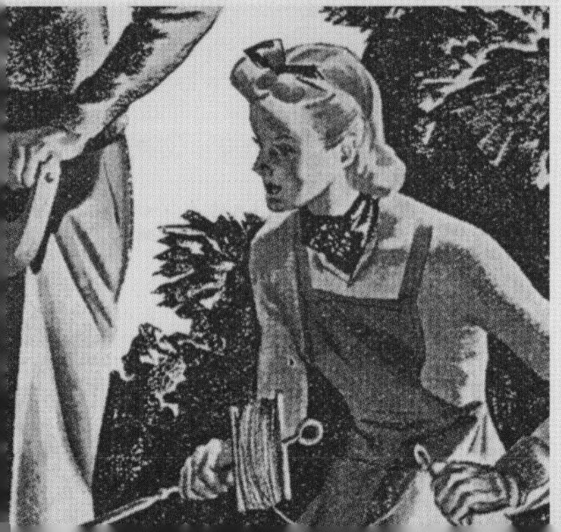

Contents

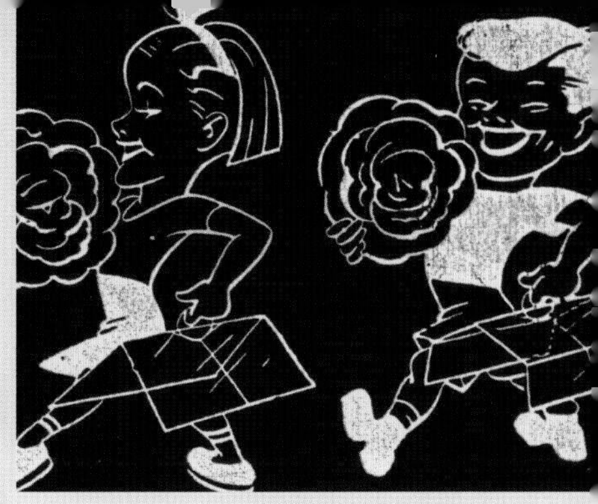

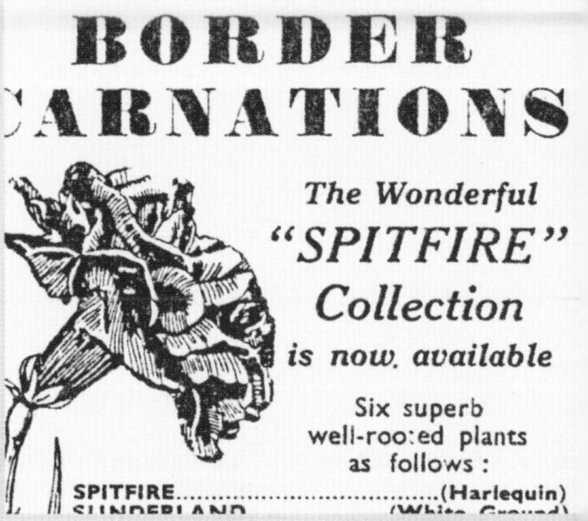
BORDER
The Wonderful
"SPITFIRE"
Collection
is now available
Six superb
well-rooted plants
as follows :
SPITFIRE.....(Harlequin)

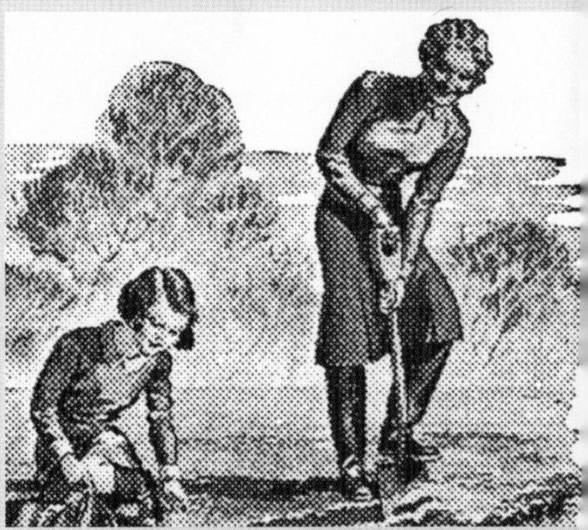

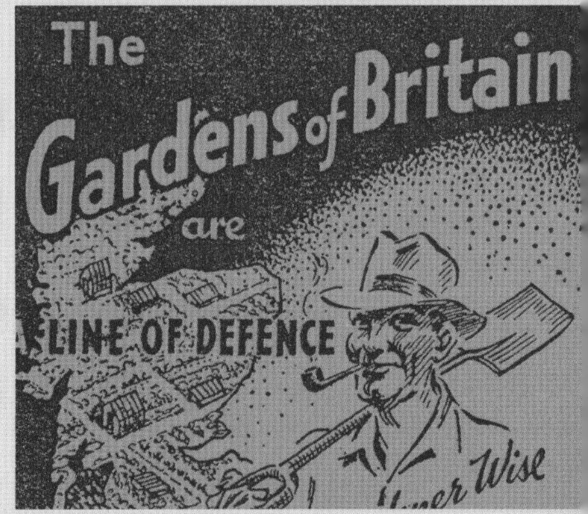
The
Gardens of Britain
are
LINE OF DEFENCE

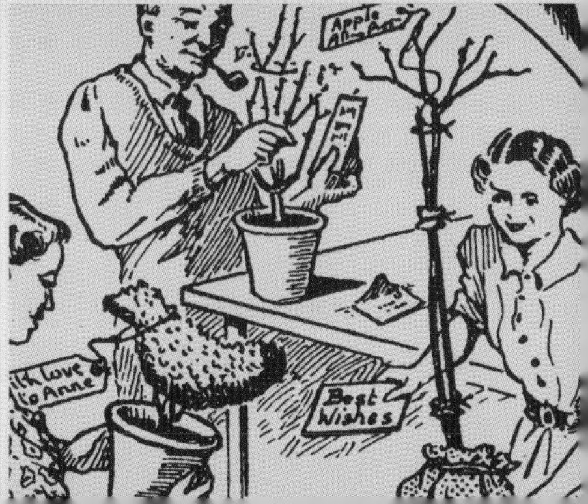
Best Wishes

The Gardens of Britain are A LINE OF DEFENCE

Gardener Wise says

GROW ALL THE FOOD YOU CAN, and the best ammunition for the Line of Defence is Dobbie's Dependable Seeds

Sow this specially priced G.C. COLLECTION OF VEGETABLE SEEDS

suitable for a small garden; will provide a full year's supply of Vegetables for 5 or 6 persons. 6/6 post free.

DOBBIE & CO. LTD.

Seedsmen, Dept. G.C. EDINBURGH 7

Secure our Catalogue at once before the stock is exhausted Contains many cultural hints

Introduction

During the spring and summer of 1939 a small group of gardeners met in secret to plan what was eventually to become the most successful campaign ever staged by the British government. The 'Dig for Victory' campaign was an ambitious attempt to make Britain self-sufficient in food in the war which many now saw as inevitable.

Britain was extremely vulnerable. In 1938 over 55 million tons of food had been imported into the country; over 90% of onions were imported, while almost all tomatoes came from Holland and the Channel Islands. A repeat of the tactics employed by Germany in the First World War was expected, with an assault on our merchant ships by German U-boat packs. Added to this was the need for shipping to carry only essential goods. In the words of the **Gardeners' Chronicle** on the outbreak of war, *'growing vegetables was a form of National Service'*.

Planning for war had been moving up through the gears throughout the 1930s. The ARP (Air Raid Precautions) Service had been set up as early as 1935, gas masks issued in 1938, and by September 1939 air-raid shelters had become a common sight. The Emergency Powers (Defence) Act was passed in August 1939, giving the government final powers to

make any regulation considered necessary for public safety and services, thereby setting up the legal framework for the future requisition of land and property. A register of country houses suitable for use as hospitals, schools and military bases was in circulation by autumn 1939. It was as part of these careful preparations for war that the government turned its attention to getting the nation to feed itself, literally Digging for Victory.

When war finally came on 3 September 1939 gardens became battlegrounds and gardeners enlisted in the allotment army. Slogans such as 'Beans as Bullets', 'Vegetables for Victory' and 'Cloches versus Hitler' emphasised the link between vegetable growing and the battlefield. 'Doing your Duty' included planting 'Victory tomatoes' and 'Home Guard potatoes'. Gardeners across Britain were exhorted to undertake their own struggle, and to 'Grow More Food', an uninspiring slogan which was rapidly to be replaced with the better-known 'Dig for Victory'. Horticultural societies around the country were encouraged to set up shows and meetings to encourage novice and amateur gardeners to respond to the campaign.

Encouraged, cajoled, instructed, and even exhorted from the nation's pulpits, men, women, and children all responded to the government's call to join the allotment army. Gardens went on 'war service', becoming Britain's 'Line of Defence', cropping plans her battle cry, and lawns went on the compost heap as the country as one dug for victory. Pilfering garden vegetables was punishable with hard labour, a recognition of the vital importance of the hard labour that had been spent growing them. Towns and villages competed with each other to produce mountains of marrows and to have the oldest allotment-holder. No stone was left unturned in an effort to feed the nation. **Garden Work** of 16 September 1939 told its readers that *'Once again we are at war with Germany. In the great conflict ahead of us, we who stay at home can play just as important a part as those in the firing line. We urge all our readers to make every effort to enlarge their cultivations of vegetable and fruit crops.'*

Although the vegetable garden and the allotment loom large in memory, flowers were not forgotten. As the **Gardeners' Chronicle** stated in the first week of the war, with admirable foresight, *'Spring-time will come as certainly as summer and winter and we may need the beauty of flowers when there may be much that is unbeautiful, pitiful and painful. Flowers inspire faith, hope, cheerfulness and courage and these we may need in large measure until brighter and more peaceful conditions are reached.'*

The individual efforts of families in suburban gardens and allotments were matched by production in large private gardens as the nation's gardeners pulled together to feed us all. In the national press gardeners started to be associated with phrases usually connected to the services. The 'allotment army' sprang into action, plant pests became 'the nation's enemy', and the vegetable garden was called the 'Maginot Line', at least for a short while. Tools were dusted off or newly purchased, and regarded variously with optimism or apprehension. Digging for Victory had begun!

The **Gardeners' Chronicle** of 9 September 1939 recommended that *'Everybody whose whole time is not engaged in other forms of national defence, and who has a garden or garden plot or allotment, can render good service to the community by cultivating it to the fullest possible extent. By that is meant not only getting the largest amount of produce from the soil, but also in keeping the ground in good heart for the war upon which we have entered may last a long time and therefore next year must be considered as well as this. Beside these essentials of war-time gardening is another no less important, that is preventing pests and diseases from damaging and wasting the produce, as so much is often damaged in the kindlier days of peace.'*

As the gardening press waited for the government's media campaign to swing into action gardeners stood poised with their spades in their hands; they did not have long to wait.

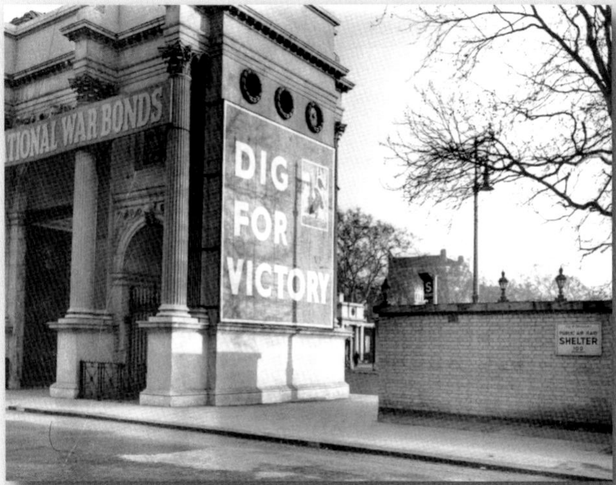
TIONAL WAR BONDS
DIG FOR VICTORY
SHELTER

Far Left
'The Gardens of Britain are a Line of Defence': A typical advertisement of the period from January 1941.
Left
Massive Dig for Victory poster in Westminster.
HMSO

The Minister of Agriculture says:

"To smallholders, allotment holders and those who have a reasonable sized garden, to those also who may be termed 'back-yarders,' you can help—help perhaps more than you realise—to feed yourselves and others. . . . The results of your work are of vital importance."

WAR-TIME GARDENING

By J. R. Wade, F.R.H.S.

This is the ideal book for all who are taking the Minister's advice.

Contents : Digging for Victory. Cropping on a System. On Growing Good Potatoes. Cabbage All the Year Round. Vegetable Marrows. Summer Spinach and Spinach Beet. Success with Onions and Leeks. Big Crops of Peas and Beans. The Culture of Celery. The Right Way with Tomatoes and Cucumbers. Lettuces and other Salads. How to Grow Root Crops. Grow More Fruit.

The outbreak of war: this present emergency

The first few weeks after the declaration of war were a tense but active time for those who were keen to get going on the Garden Front. Common sense, and the newly reborn Ministry of Food, insisted that the population would soon be grateful for all the vegetables it could get, and growing them at home was the only way of ensuring a supply for the family. Although the government's planned 'Grow More Food' bulletin was released as soon as possible, there were still anxious weeks when people were wondering what they should grow, and above all how much they needed to grow. Should they uproot their flowers or carry on as normal? The reporter for **Garden Work** wrote on 7 October 1939: *'I had occasion to make a short journey into Surrey on Sunday and everywhere there was evidence of the amateur gardener's determination to do his bit on helping the nation's food supply. I was interested to note that in practically every instance the plan was being adopted of extending the existing kitchen garden portion of the garden by taking in all or part of the lawn, leaving the decorative portion of the garden more or less intact. A very good plan, too.'*

With the outbreak of war coming in late summer /early autumn the main display in the flowerbeds were the popular Michaelmas daisies, accompanied by dahlias, chrysanthemums and golden rod. The weather that year meant that many gardens were a riot of autumn colours, pinks, bronze, purples, yellows and orange. Not everyone had the heart to rush out and cut down the precious display, but many set to with a will as soon as war was declared. Peter Blackburn lived in York with his parents in 1939; he recalls their efforts at the outbreak of war: *'Initially my father was at home, being over 37, and was keen to do his bit to help the war effort. He, with some help from myself, dug up a third of the back garden, which was devoted to flowers, thus extending the vegetable patch by 50%. Seeds and young plants were purchased or given to us by friends and relatives who lived in the area with large gardens and allotment plots.'*

In his suburban garden near London, the amateur gardener and garden writer Stephen Cheveley threw himself enthusiastically into the new campaign to Grow More Food. Cheveley had moved into his suburban house just a couple of years earlier, having previously struggled with gardens on the coast of North Yorkshire, and a swampy area in Berkshire. In peacetime, he had long ago abandoned all attempts to cultivate vegetables as being 'aesthetically jarring'. In his book, **Out of a Wilderness: A Week-end Garden**

Left

'Your Work is of Vital Importance' a message that would be repeated throughout the war years.

or 'semi' had a large garden by today's standards. Whatever the size the decisions were the same: the flower borders and lawn must go and vegetable growing was the order of the day.

Stephen Cheveley described how *'On a Saturday afternoon, early in September, my young son and I cleared the border. We cut off all flowers worth taking into the house; whole plants of chrysanthemums were executed, and they made a glorious bunch in a huge bowl in the hall. After the first unhappy twinges of regret we became keen on the job, and once the flowers were out of the way it didn't seem nearly so bad. The new chrysanthemums were lifted, and replanted close together in two rows at one end of the border. Here they will, at any rate, survive until*

Above

An immaculately rolled and trimmed lawn in the act of being sacrificed for wartime necessity.

Right

The front cover of *A Garden Goes to War*, by Stephen Cheveley, featured the author and his family in the process of digging up their lawn to convert to potatoes and root vegetables. It was one of the first books published on wartime gardening, and one of the last to feature a photographic cover before the onset of War Economy Standard Book Production.

Book, he had written, *'A small out-of-the-way piece of ground is planted with rhubarb, herbs and some-times a few marrows, otherwise there is no kitchen garden and the family vegetables come from the shops.'* At two-thirds of an acre, his was perhaps a rather larger garden than most, although many a detached

A GARDEN
GOES TO WAR
BY STEPHEN CHEVELEY

happier times return, and they can be restored to a more worthy position. The other plants were lifted bodily, their roots freed from soil by banging with the back of the spade, and taken to the compost heap.'

Being a garden writer, Cheveley insisted on testing the soil type under the lawn for its suitability for growing vegetables. Alas for the lawn, a series of small inspection holes proved the soil to be ideal, and further sacrifice was made. With most of the vegetables packed into the flower borders, with the hedges at the back clipped severely back to allow in light and air, the lawn was to be used for deep rooted crops and potatoes. Shuffling the old herbaceous and perennial plants around meant crowding them but, as Cheveley cheerfully remarked, *'they will not take any harm for a year or two . . . some day, when we can restore everything to its former beauty, it will be easy to increase the stock fairly quickly by dividing up these plants'.* 'A year or two' was the longest that most people could foresee the war lasting, although ensuring there would be plenty of winter greens for the winter of 1940/41 was an early concern.

The **Gardeners' Chronicle** argued that everybody who could should set about producing as much food as possible, even though they believed 'sea-borne supplies are not likely to be severely depleted by submarine attack'. Their argument in the first days of war was an economic one, the nation's budget being necessary for weapons rather than food. Most writers were less worried about salad crops such as tomatoes in the early days of war, and recommended that the traditional crops of carrots, parsnips, peas, swedes, beetroot, leeks, runner beans, broad beans, Brussels sprouts and savoys were the essentials, with flowers taking up

Above
Stephen Cheveley uprooting the flower border that was to serve as a vegetable bed for the duration of the war.

only the odd corners left uncropped. Potatoes, not widely grown previously as they were so easily available in shops, were to join this list as it became apparent that agricultural producers would have to concentrate on wheat. In addition supplies of onions were soon in short supply and were added to the list, while all winter greens were emphasised, in particular cottagers kale and curly kale, sprouting broccoli and cabbages.

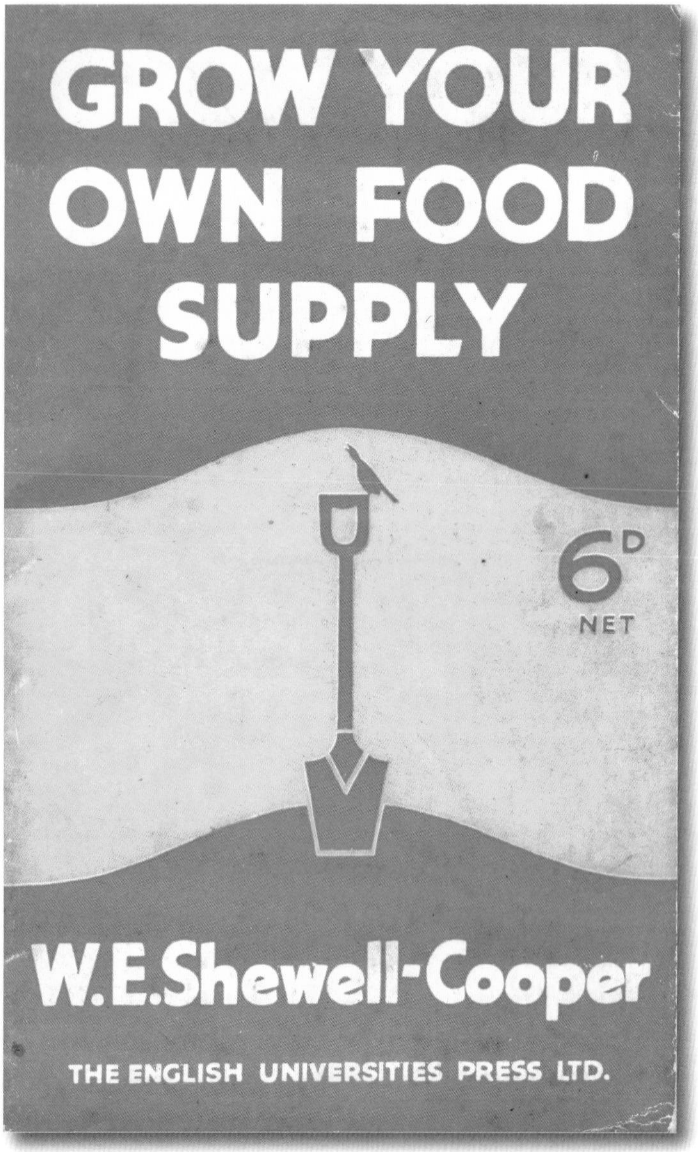
GROW YOUR OWN FOOD SUPPLY
6D NET
W.E.Shewell-Cooper
THE ENGLISH UNIVERSITIES PRESS LTD.

How much to grow was another puzzle; the gardening press attempted various calculations, most based on a family of three adults and two children, as many more families then had an adult relative such as a mother-in-law living with them. Including the basic vegetables and potatoes, most calculated that an area of 344 square yards would be needed, notably more than the 250 square yards of an allotment, with 160 square yards being taken up by potatoes (a crop of 8cwt). However the government's Grow More bulletin cut down the area used for potatoes to ensure that there was sufficient space for other vegetables, even within the 'average' plot.

First Strike: Grow More Bulletin No. 1

During the lead-up to war the government had prepared not only its strategy for military action, but also its plans for gardening, or rather for feeding the populace from their own home produce. Known during planning as the 'Grow More Food' campaign (later shortened to 'Growmore' and used in the naming of Growmore fertiliser, and a series of longer bulletins), the first Grow More bulletin was being prepared in the spring and summer of 1939. Drawing on the knowledge and experience of a number of people, including representatives of the Horticultural Education Association, the Grow More bulletin no. 1 was designed to inspire and educate the most novice of gardeners. It provided basic information on garden layout, soil preparation, sowing times, crop spacing and yearly rotational cropping in case the war continued past the first year. Unfortunately for the compilers of this first 'strike' in the government campaign, they had no idea at what time of year war would eventually be declared and so it was not possible to include any seasonal advice. Its eventual release date in September was, in many ways, the worst month possible for prospective gardeners. Too late to plant crops ready for that first winter, and too early to plant most spring crops, and released just as the days shortened and the weather worsened, the Grow More bulletin no. 1 must have lost some of its impact due to unfortunate timing.

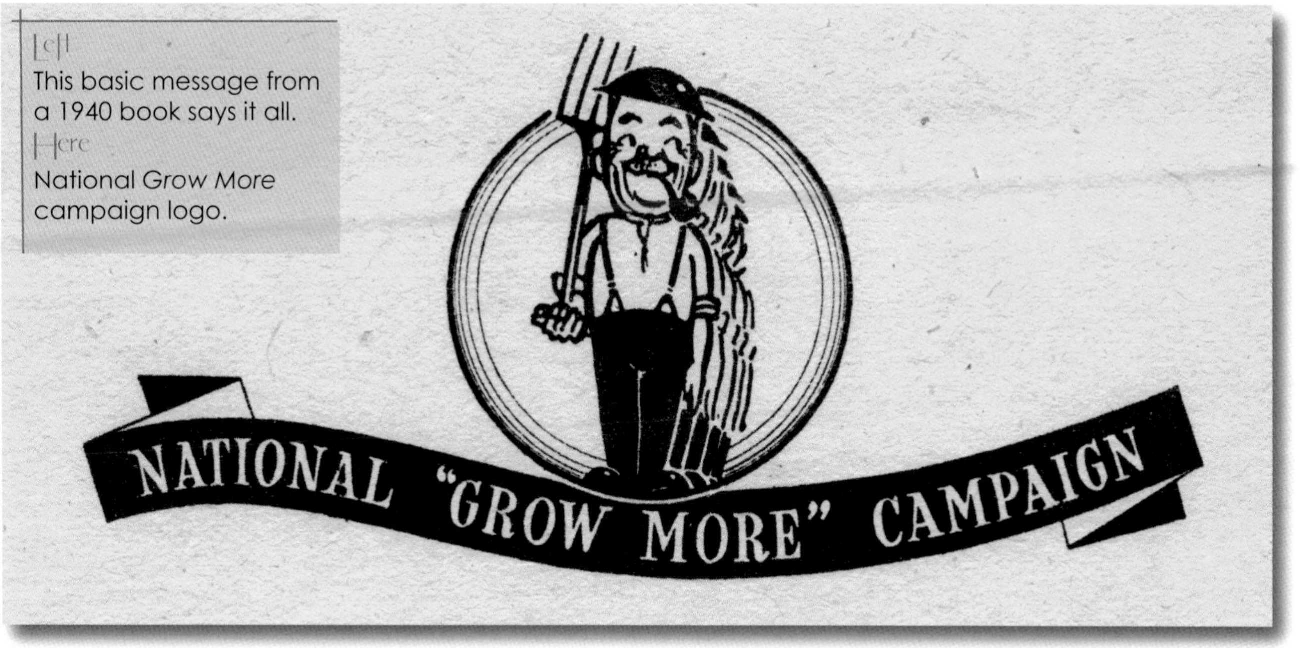
NATIONAL "GROW MORE" CAMPAIGN

Left
This basic message from a 1940 book says it all.
Here
National *Grow More* campaign logo.

Grateful though the general populace might have been for basic instruction, professional gardeners managed to find considerable fault with bulletin no. 1. 'Pernickety discussions' of the instructions in the bulletin occupied much space in the **Gardeners' Chronicle** throughout the winter of 1939/40. Cropping plans, spacing and even sowing times were subject to criticism, along with the 'small area' being given over to potatoes. Stung into answering the critics Mr Pearl (one of the compilers) replied in a letter to the **Gardeners' Chronicl**e of 6 January 1940: *'Obviously the official cropping plan differs widely from the peace-time cropping of many allotments, but if examined fairly it will be found to provide the basis for the production of those vegetables especially needed in war-time. For instance there will be an increased need for leafy, green vegetables and salads to take the place of imported oranges and other fruits of protective food value, particularly in the early months of the year. There is need here for an appetizing range of foods to supplement the eternal Cabbage. Broad Beans and similar protein-yielding seed vegetables may have to replace restricted meat and fish supplies. . . . The storage of certain vegetables with special protective food values may be mentioned. Frost tender crops and those of low food value or yield are hardly worthwhile under stringent war conditions, especially for the novice. Seeds of some popular vegetables or varieties may be difficult to get and others too uncertain in cropping to justify inclusion. Continuous heavy production from every available inch of ground is necessary, and the importance of the thorough rotation and cultivation implied in the three-year cropping plan will be obvious.'*

Tensions ran high between those who attempted to put together a generic guide to vegetable growing for the use of amateurs, and those who obviously felt the small bulletin should have contained all the knowledge and practice that might be gained in years of devotion to large, complex, and labour-rich productive gardens with recommendations according

to each local variation in climate and soil type. Supporting the compilers of the bulletin, Mr Bradnall of Grayshott Hall Garden, Hindhead, pointed out *'gardeners in private service have every opportunity and room for practising rotational cropping, but I wonder how we should carry it out if we had a garden the size of a standard allotment to do it in!'* His comment pinpointed one of the difficulties that beset the professional gardener in giving advice to the beginner. Fortunately there were men who were experienced in fitting their gardening into 'an allotment size plot' and one of these, Mr G.C. Johnson of Lewes, gave his whole-hearted approval to the bulletin as being *'a basis upon which any man can produce the maximum amount of the kinds of vegetables most required during the present war period. This was its purpose, and with minor adjustments to suit special conditions that may obtain in some districts, it fulfils its purpose.'*

Variations in diet, climate and soil types across Britain meant that no one plan was ever going to suit the whole country, and much criticism was also based on the differing needs of the northern and southern areas. The small quantity of potatoes was especially highlighted as meaning that the northerners' diet would be short-changed. Recommendations for potato planting were expanded as a response to the criticisms, reclaiming their more 'normal' proportion of space on the allotment. However the argument was still rumbling on through the letters pages of gardening magazines well into spring 1940, with technicalities about the planting distance of potato varieties being bolstered by sad predictions of a dearth of fish and chips due to the lack of a potato harvest. Mr F. Baker in a letter to the **Gardeners' Chronicle** of 27 January drew attention to this culinary factor in planting plans: *'The evacuation of children from vulnerable areas has proved that townsfolk value their "fish and chips" and may even regard them as an essential contribution to their gastronomic requirements and general happiness; and one cannot imagine them asking for fish and greens or fish and parsnips.'*

To the relief of those on both sides of the argument, and lovers of fish and chips, a revised edition of the bulletin was issued in January 1941, correcting some of the printing errors and attempting to satisfy the demand for larger areas to be devoted to potatoes. Alternatives to the government's 'official' allotment plan were being suggested in the gardening press throughout the war (and beyond!).

The winter of 1939/40 proved to be the worst for fifty years, and made the brave decision to recommend growing as much spinach and greens as possible look a poor choice, as even hardy winter cabbages froze to mush.

Garden Features under Attack: The Lawn and the Rock Gardens

Previously regarded with almost religious fervour by many suburban gardeners, the lawn was one of the main victims of the zeal for food-growing. Most suburban homes had a large expanse of flat lawn with small crazy-paving paths round the sides of the lawn, dividing it from the narrow flower borders. These borders were often too narrow to make practical vegetable beds, and without substantial effort the paths could not be moved. Therefore it was the 'empty' space in the middle that proved the obvious place for the vegetable plot. **Garden Work** of 12 April 1941 stated that: *'Lawns, pride and joy of amateur gardeners in peace-time, verdant carpets to set off gay blossoms, have naturally to come under the most searching consideration in these days when our national life may actually depend on the amount of foodstuffs we can raise at home. Desperate diseases call for desperate remedies, and it would undoubtedly be both prudent and patriotic if those who are maintaining very large lawns decided that part of the plots should be devoted to vegetable culture.'* Owners of substantial country homes also chose to dig up lawns rather than established flowerbeds, although often it was the tennis courts and bowling greens that suffered, being flat, often at a short distance from the house, and of an appropriate size.

However for many the sacrifice of a lawn was a sacrifice too far. Aware of the favoured place of the lawn in the nation's heart, in the same month that it had recommended digging up lawns, **Garden Work** rather confusingly gave instructions for the sowing and laying of new lawns during the wartime period. Not wishing to alienate any of its possible readers, it hinted that some might be able to fulfil their patriotic duty on an allotment or other patch of ground and leave their lawn untouched apart from constant weeding, mowing, renovating, manuring, levelling, and so on. *Whilst some of our readers will be sacrificing lawn space, there are sure to be others, maybe with large allotments for food production,*

Left
The winter of 1939/40 was the coldest for fifty years. Here evacuees enjoy themselves in the snow, but there was little enjoyment for gardeners that winter.
Below
The *Amateur Gardening Garden Lover's Calendar* for 1941 demonstrates the lasting affection for the rockery, complete with alpine planting.

Garden Lover's Calendar, 1941

who are enthusiastically developing a garden and who wish to establish a lawn from seed. In such cases the first three weeks in April mark the best period of the year for seed-sowing.' For those who did keep their lawns, mowing was soon to become a problem with the advent of petrol rationing. In Cornwall, Marjorie Williams, whose diaries and letters were later published as **Letters from Lamledra**, noted as early as 17 September 1939 that her gardener *'looks sadly at the unkempt tennis lawn. He cannot cut it any more as he has not the petrol for the mowing machine, and there is, besides, no-one to play. I want to borrow some sheep to put in there – quite as good as a machine.'*

One of the other popular elements of the 1930s and '40s garden was the rock garden. Variously constructed of everything from convincing rock with strata, to pieces of less convincing concrete and clinker, these were usually planted with a range of alpine plants or small creepers and pinks. On the outbreak of war garden writers were united in recommending that rock gardens should be allowed to remain in even the smallest suburban garden. Attempting to dig out the rocks and generally poor quality soil was regarded as not worth the effort. **Garden Work** continued to run articles on rock gardening throughout the war, in March 1943 instructing its readers on protecting their rockery plants against soil wash and cold, and recommending that a good rich covering of soil and sheets of glass (by then in short supply) should be continued until the end of the month.

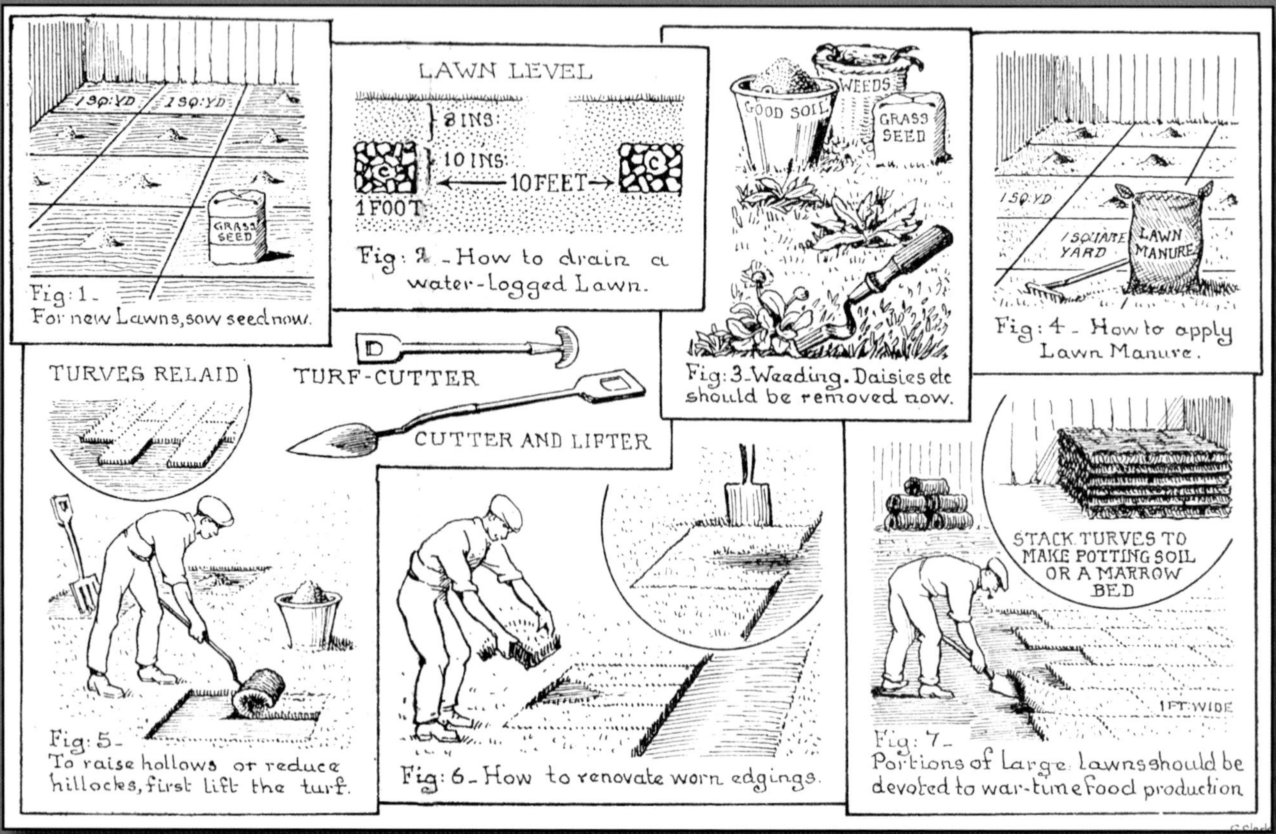
1 SQ: YD
1 SQ: YD
GRASS SEED
Fig: 1 - For new Lawns, sow seed now.
LAWN LEVEL
8 INS:
10 INS:
10 FEET
1 FOOT
Fig: 2 - How to drain a water-logged Lawn.
GOOD SOIL
WEEDS
GRASS SEED
Fig: 3 - Weeding. Daisies etc should be removed now.
1 SQ. YD
1 SQUARE YARD
LAWN MANURE
Fig: 4 - How to apply Lawn Manure.
TURVES RELAID
TURF-CUTTER
CUTTER AND LIFTER
Fig: 5 - To raise hollows or reduce hillocks, first lift the turf.
Fig: 6 - How to renovate worn edgings.
STACK TURVES TO MAKE POTTING SOIL OR A MARROW BED
1 FT: WIDE
Fig: 7 - Portions of large lawns should be devoted to war-time food production

Anderson Shelters

Anderson shelters were available to what the government considered 'vulnerable' homes from the end of February 1939. They presented proud garden owners with an immediate problem – how on earth to integrate the shelter into their garden design? Even after the outbreak of war, in a garden where the lawn was now vegetables and the rosebed given over to chickens, a large metal and earth shelter was bound to be a conspicuous object, and one which **Garden Work** described as not only an eyesore but also very noticeable from the air! The most obvious solution was to turn the shelter into a garden, making it, as the magazine enthused, *'a handsome feature of the landscape'*. As well as the obvious possibilities for shallow-rooted vegetables such as lettuce or marrows, the shelter might be made, rather ironically, into a lawn or planted with bulbs for the coming spring. Mr Lamb of Forest Gate did just that, with a mini-lawn and flowerbeds. Rockeries were also a popular way to disguise shelters, with alpine plants taking well to the shallow and sloping site.

Garden Work, in November 1939, suggested that: *'In addition to making extra provision for the growing of food, some of us have had to find accommodation for an air-raid shelter. Perhaps we are not too pleased with the result from an artistic point of view. They are rather a blot on the landscape. Here again the rose will help us beautify this ugly feature. Some of the ramblers will prove excellent for this. Planted each side of the shelter their rambling growths may be just laid over the soil covering the shelter. . . . If the war lasts long enough, . . . these roses will soon turn this unpleasant, if necessary,*

blot into a beautiful spot.' The rose varieties recommended were Alberic Barbier, Blush Rambler, Minehaha and Snowflake.

Food growing was however the priority and so most shelters boasted lettuces and marrows – the latter basking in their sloping sun-catching sites. Turning shelters into victory gardens was the sort of propaganda opportunity that the government did not miss, and images were soon available to the press of women tending the family dinner on top of the shelter. **Garden Work** in August 1940 described the shelter of Mrs Prendergast of Clapham: *'So far as Mrs Prendergast's shelter is concerned, she has economically selected to grow vegetables – as indeed many other enthusiastic amateur food producers are doing. And these are the dugout owners who are getting a joke out of Hitler's attempts to subdue the British spirit. . . . When one remembers the relatively trifling damage to our country's resources*

Left
Lawn making and renovation carried on despite the Dig for Victory campaign (instructions in Garden Work in 1941).
Above
This Croydon shelter appears to have been given a floral makeover.

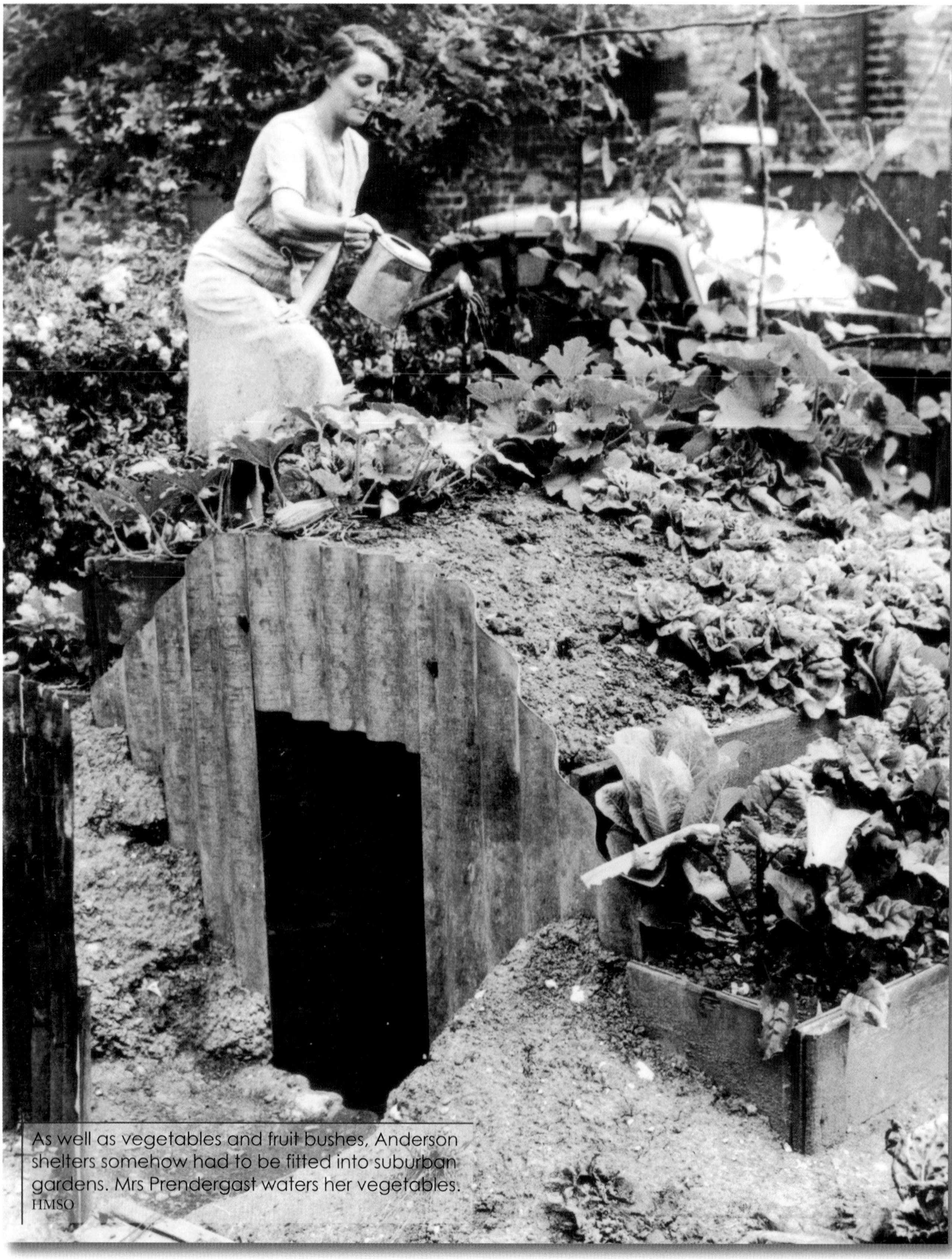

As well as vegetables and fruit bushes, Anderson shelters somehow had to be fitted into suburban gardens. Mrs Prendergast waters her vegetables.
HMSO

done by the raids that have taken place, and then reckons up the potential food-producing capacity of the hundreds of thousands of semi-buried shelters which the war has brought into existence, it is not difficult to suppose that the food produced could easily in importance exceed the property destroyed.'

Charms that Should Not Be Sacrificed

Not everyone threw themselves wholeheartedly into adapting their gardens for productivity. From the outset of the war there were garden owners who felt that their garden contained design or planting that should set it apart from the general campaign to turn lawns into potatoes. In October 1939 **The Times** carried a small piece outlining a scheme put forward by the Institute of Landscape Architects (ILA) to 'save' features of horticultural importance. Under the heading 'Charms that Should Not Be Sacrificed' it outlined the scheme, which had been approved by the Ministry of Agriculture: *'A panel of qualified advisors would help owners of gardens to adapt their gardens to wartime . . . while during wartime the kitchen garden will have to be given the first consideration, there are good reasons for continuing to obtain all the enjoyment possible from the ornamental parts of the garden. These, it is pointed out, represent the investment of so much capital and expenditure, of so much thought and care that it would be senseless to admit the gradual destruction of valuable property that might be saved by timely precautions. The panel of experts will, where desired, draw up schemes to ensure the best practical results in a garden as a whole, and so prevent the sacrifice of features of artistic and horticultural importance.'*

Make every yard of ground yield Food!
Beg, buy or borrow a spade and Dig for Victory. Not a yard of land must lie idle. To waste land is as bad as wasting food. Dig up your garden. Get an allotment. Grow vegetables that you can store, and keep your family provided for most of the year. Help yourself and help your country.
DIG for victory NOW!
Issued by the
MINISTRY OF AGRICULTURE & FISHERIES, LONDON, S.W.1

Unsurprisingly a fee was to be charged by the experts who would also 'guide' their clients on the difficulties of maintenance and labour while conforming with regulations. During September and October 1939, the ILA took out advertisements in the **Gardeners' Chronicle** promoting their services.

In the first few months of war even some notable garden advisers urged against digging up your peacetime garden. In a booklet written especially for Boots (**The Gardener's Chemist**) Cecil Middleton advised readers to leave their lawns undug, their rockeries in place, and their small front garden and narrow borders 'brighter and more cheerful than ever with your favourite flowers'. By 1942 he was admitting that 'Leeks, Lettuces and Leatherjackets' had to replace 'Lilacs, Lilies and Lavender', longingly adding that 'the harder we dig for victory the sooner will the roses be with us again'.

Feelings ran high among some garden owners; in a letter in the **Gardeners' Chronicle** in December 1939, Mr R. Cottam of Chelmsford became quite irate on the subject of the 'Wicked Destruction' of flowerbeds and borders: *'To my mind many irresponsible persons are still doing their best to get the owners of our beautiful English gardens "panicky".*

The small amount of produce that would be grown in flowerbeds surely is negligible and cannot replace the look of gloominess the Cabbages etc. make. . . . One can only hope, when the panel of professional gardeners is in full working order, we shall neither see nor hear any more of this tearing up of lawns, flower borders etc.'

My Garden, a rather upmarket gardening magazine aimed at those with gardeners as well as gardens, came down firmly on the side of the flowers. An article by D.J. Desmond grumbled that: *'They keep telling us to dig up our flowers and plant potatoes. To get busy and dig Spring cabbages instead of gillyflowers. Up with the grass and down with the borders. Rockeries to be dug-outs and the whole garden to be an allotment. I am a lazy gardener with a young family and a smallish garden, and only last year I converted what was supposed to be the vegetable garden into another lawn. And when Hitler and we came back from our holiday we had to face the issue. Should we plant potatoes? Should we be blacklegs and traitors if we left the garden in peace? Was Hitler worth it?'* The answer to all this soul-searching was apparently to consult the gardener (Jackson). Jackson flatly refused to dig up the lawn, or to put a 'dug-out' in the borders, and declared that flowers, not food, were to be the essentials of wartime life. For those readers of **My Garden** who felt the wartime spirit demanded extra vegetable growing a paddock or grass orchard was recommended as the ideal spot, avoiding any established garden features. 'Urgent zeal' was to be guarded against and discretion recommended where lawns and borders were concerned.

Stephen Cheveley also had his doubts about struggling with vegetable growing on soils that were not really up to the job: *'The soil most to be feared for growing vegetables is a really stiff clay, that lies wet and heavy in winter, and bakes to a brick-like consistency in the heat of summer. If you are cursed with this sort of land, then frankly it is a waste of time to attempt to grow vegetables. Leave it as it may be, under grass or whatever has succeeded in establishing. The other type of land that may cause difficulty is where there is little depth of soil to give sufficient foothold to vegetables . . . here again the idea of growing vegetables should be abandoned and the garden left as it is.'*

Even the most ardent food producers felt that flowers had an important role to play. The **Gardeners' Chronicle** of 9 September 1939 commented that *'flowers of all kinds play their part by brightening parks and gardens and bringing their cheerfulness into homes, hospitals and sick rooms. Therefore in places where the cultivation of foodstuffs would be either impractical or uneconomical, flowers should be cared for.'*

In the first weeks of the war the established horticultural societies seemed to withdraw rather than expand operations, offering support for the vegetable growers rather than the advocates of flowers and roses. The Royal Horticultural Society (RHS) cancelled its Great Autumn Show (due to be held on 13–15 September 1939), and all fortnightly meetings of the RHS were cancelled. The National Dahlia Society cancelled its annual exhibitions, and the Royal Botanic Gardens at Kew closed to the public. The RHS resumed some of its activities in the following March, when it was realised that the war was likely to go on for some time, and that its role in advising and encouraging gardeners was vital, although none of the large annual shows took place during wartime.

The Winter of 1939/40

Those victory gardeners who leapt to action in the first autumn of the war were to regret it by springtime. That winter was one of the most devastating and disastrous in living memory. The first three weeks in January were appalling, killing off most autumn-sown plants including even the toughest brassicas and cabbages. Official advice in the previous autumn to sow as much spinach as possible, to replace the vitamins usually provided by imported fruit, looked sadly misguided.

The freezing weather of winter 1939/40 did not encourage a rush of applicants for the roughly ploughed up parks and pasture. Many novice gardeners were horrified by the frozen mud they encountered on the newly created allotments. In fact there had been a disappointing take-up of new allotments during the first winter of the war. The existing gardening magazines found this disappointing and encouraged their readers to befriend possible novice gardeners, giving them advice. The disappointment in the gardening press also extended to criticism of the government for failing to provide sufficient propaganda! In late January 1940 the **Gardeners' Chronicle** made accusations that there was a *'defective ability in the propaganda line. . . . Only fatuous complacency can believe that we are already doing anything like so much as we ought to be doing. It is high time that our effort is made commensurate with our need.'* The magazine went on to suggest that all people

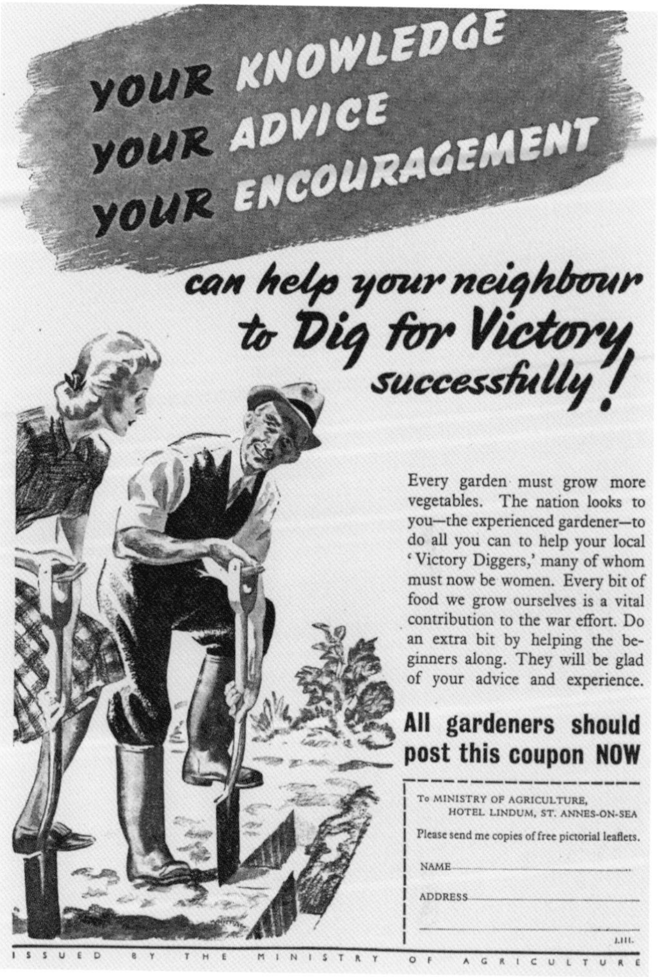
YOUR KNOWLEDGE
YOUR ADVICE
YOUR ENCOURAGEMENT
can help your neighbour to Dig for Victory successfully!
Every garden must grow more vegetables. The nation looks to you—the experienced gardener—to do all you can to help your local 'Victory Diggers,' many of whom must now be women. Every bit of food we grow ourselves is a vital contribution to the war effort. Do an extra bit by helping the beginners along. They will be glad of your advice and experience.
All gardeners should post this coupon NOW
To MINISTRY OF AGRICULTURE, HOTEL LINDUM, ST. ANNES-ON-SEA
Please send me copies of free pictorial leaflets.
NAME
ADDRESS
L.III.
ISSUED BY THE MINISTRY OF AGRICULTURE

who might be capable of leading the campaign for food production should be mobilised forthwith. Head gardeners, parks superintendents and county horticultural instructors should all be invited to a conference to establish a new campaign. Given the acrimonious exchanges in the pages of the **Gardeners' Chronicle** over the initial Grow More bulletin no. 1, it seems unlikely that such a conference would have been a harmonious or productive one. However reluctant, confused, or discouraged novice gardeners were in that cold first winter, in the following months and years almost everyone with any possibility of taking on a small plot was destined to become a 'victory gardener'.

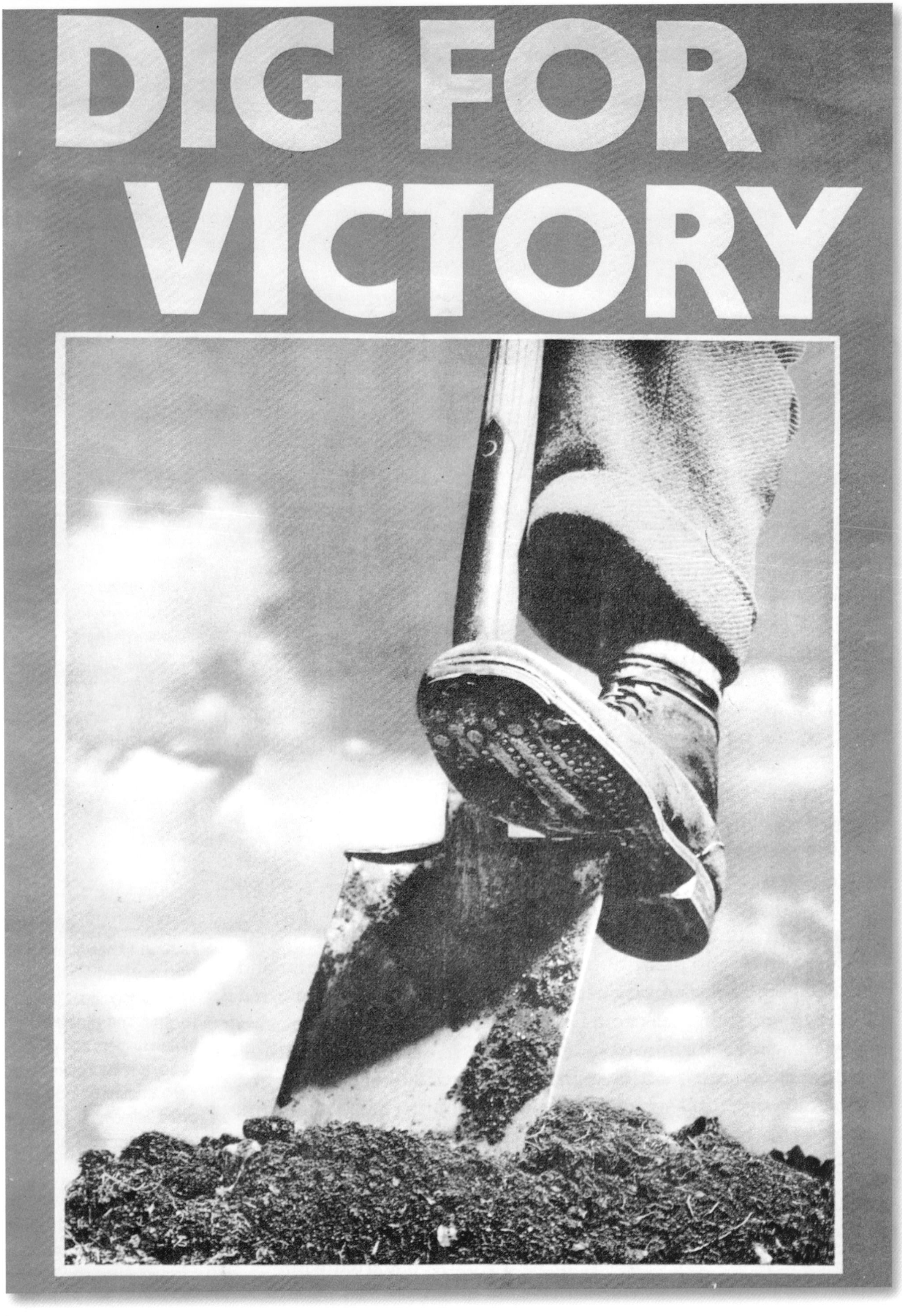
DIG FOR
VICTORY

The famous **Dig For Victory** poster. HMSO

Digging for Victory: the Campaign in full bloom

After the first month of the war, the initial flurry of equal amounts of activity and uncertainty in the gardening world began to settle down. While the earliest government pronouncements had merely emphasised the urgency of the situation, they were soon giving solid information backed up by regulations. Panic gave way to order as lawns gave way to vegetables. For the following five years, and well into the post-war period, the various ministries responsible for food production, information, and agriculture, together dispensed what they considered vital encouragement and guidance to the gardening populace. The campaigns were so successful that by the end of the war it was claimed that England's gardeners had produced 10% of the vegetables needed to feed the nation. They had done this by throwing themselves wholeheartedly into sacrificing their flowers, their lawns, and their precious 'spare time' to feed the country. However, the campaigns were not without their difficulties at the outset. The gardening press in particular was vociferous in calls for a Department of Food Production to co-ordinate the efforts of gardeners and producers everywhere, while the initial Grow More campaign had a faltering start with the media and public before settling down.

The government's food production campaign was initially named the 'Grow More Food' campaign; posters and pronouncements were accompanied by 'Grow More Food' bulletins. Alongside the eventually displaced 'Grow More', other slogans were trialled in the popular press. The **Gardeners' Chronicle** of 22 June 1940 thought that 'Go To It' might suit. *'We urge all who appreciate the need, possibly the dire necessity, of increasing food production, to "Go To It" once again. Individual and local collective efforts must combine, even at this late date, and make up for deficiencies in other directions.'*

Grow More Becomes Dig for Victory

Running side by side with the official 'Grow More Food' campaign for the first few months was the unofficial use of the phrase 'Dig for Victory'. This term had been in common use since it first appeared in public in newspaper articles reporting a speech given by the Minister of Agriculture, Sir Reginald Dorman-Smith, on 3 October 1939. It soon caught on with the public and was widely used in news-papers and advertisements. By March 1940 letters to the **Gardeners' Chronicle** referred to the need for everyone to Dig for Victory, and the London papers also adopted it. Having had a shaky first season dogged by criticism and poor weather, the Grow More Food campaign was in urgent need of

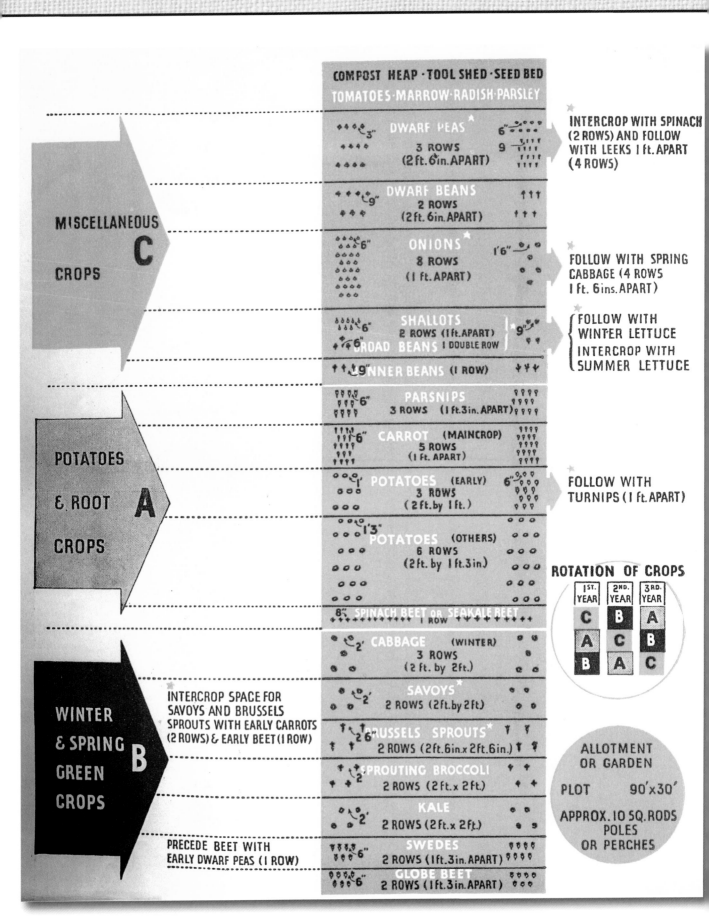

COMPOST HEAP · TOOL SHED · SEED BED
TOMATOES · MARROW · RADISH · PARSLEY

MISCELLANEOUS C CROPS

DWARF PEAS*
3 ROWS
(2 ft. 6 in. APART)

*INTERCROP WITH SPINACH (2 ROWS) AND FOLLOW WITH LEEKS 1 ft. APART (4 ROWS)

DWARF BEANS
2 ROWS
(2 ft. 6 in. APART)

ONIONS*
8 ROWS
(1 ft. APART)

FOLLOW WITH SPRING CABBAGE (4 ROWS 1 ft. 6 ins. APART)

SHALLOTS
2 ROWS (1 ft. APART)
BROAD BEANS 1 DOUBLE ROW

RUNNER BEANS (1 ROW)

FOLLOW WITH WINTER LETTUCE
INTERCROP WITH SUMMER LETTUCE

POTATOES & ROOT CROPS A

PARSNIPS
3 ROWS (1 ft. 3 in. APART)

CARROT (MAINCROP)
5 ROWS
(1 ft. APART)

POTATOES (EARLY)
3 ROWS
(2 ft. by 1 ft.)

FOLLOW WITH TURNIPS (1 ft. APART)

POTATOES (OTHERS)
6 ROWS
(2 ft. by 1 ft. 3 in.)

SPINACH BEET OR SEAKALE BEET 1 ROW

ROTATION OF CROPS

1ST. YEAR	2ND. YEAR	3RD. YEAR
C	B	A
A	C	B
B	A	C

CABBAGE (WINTER)
3 ROWS
(2 ft. by 2 ft.)

WINTER & SPRING GREEN CROPS B

INTERCROP SPACE FOR SAVOYS AND BRUSSELS SPROUTS WITH EARLY CARROTS (2 ROWS) & EARLY BEET (1 ROW)

SAVOYS*
2 ROWS (2 ft. by 2 ft)

BRUSSELS SPROUTS*
2 ROWS (2 ft. 6 in. x 2 ft. 6 in.)

SPROUTING BROCCOLI
2 ROWS (2 ft. x 2 ft.)

KALE
2 ROWS (2 ft. x 2 ft.)

ALLOTMENT OR GARDEN

PLOT   90' x 30'

APPROX. 10 SQ. RODS POLES OR PERCHES

PRECEDE BEET WITH EARLY DWARF PEAS (1 ROW)

SWEDES
2 ROWS (1 ft. 3 in. APART)

GLOBE BEET
2 ROWS (1 ft. 3 in. APART)

being rebranded and repromoted by 1940 and the government took the easy way out by officially adopting Dig for Victory as their new campaign title, one which was later described as the most successful campaign slogan of the war.

An important part of the new campaign was the new logo: a red circle around a black and white picture of a foot and spade caught in mid-action. The logo featured the left foot of Mr W.H. Mckie of Acton, London. Using the left leg on the spade was traditionally recommended for all right-handed gardeners as it was thought to 'balance' the body. This iconic symbol came to represent the whole campaign and appeared on all the Dig for Victory leaflets, whether about cultivation or not; even leaflets on food preservation or disease prevention featured the famous spade and foot. Campaign posters on the side of houses featured the foot 5 feet long! Grow More Food did not totally disappear. As a slogan it continued to be used throughout the war; Clay's Fertiliser regularly used it as part of their advertising, as did Sofnol. It was also used as the name of the famous 'Growmore' fertiliser issued by the government in 1942. Other slogans and catchphrases in use by 1942 included 'Don't Spare the Hoe', 'An Hour in the Garden Saves One in the Queue', 'It All Depends on Me', and in a desperate moment 'Dig to Survive'. The Mayor of Bradford even went as far as to claim 'Dig for Victory or Dig for Death' but understandably this did not catch on. In April 1942 the Minister of Agriculture's 'Dig for Victory and Dig for Dear Life' was slightly better reported in the press, but still had an element of desperation.

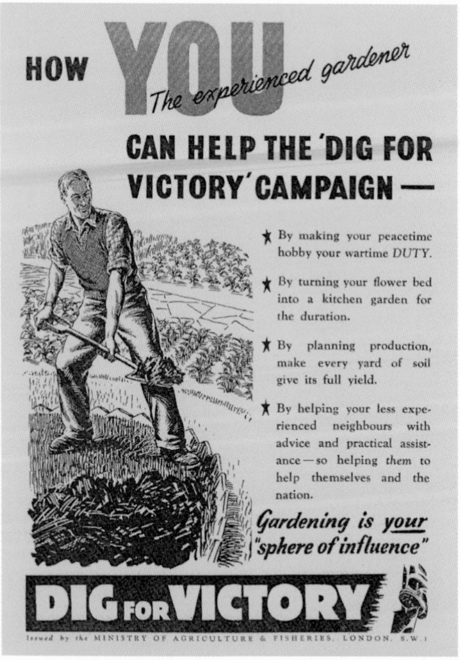
HOW YOU The experienced gardener
CAN HELP THE 'DIG FOR VICTORY' CAMPAIGN —
★ By making your peacetime hobby your wartime DUTY.
★ By turning your flower bed into a kitchen garden for the duration.
★ By planning production, make every yard of soil give its full yield.
★ By helping your less experienced neighbours with advice and practical assistance — so helping them to help themselves and the nation.
Gardening is your "sphere of influence"
DIG FOR VICTORY
Issued by the MINISTRY OF AGRICULTURE & FISHERIES, LONDON, S.W.1

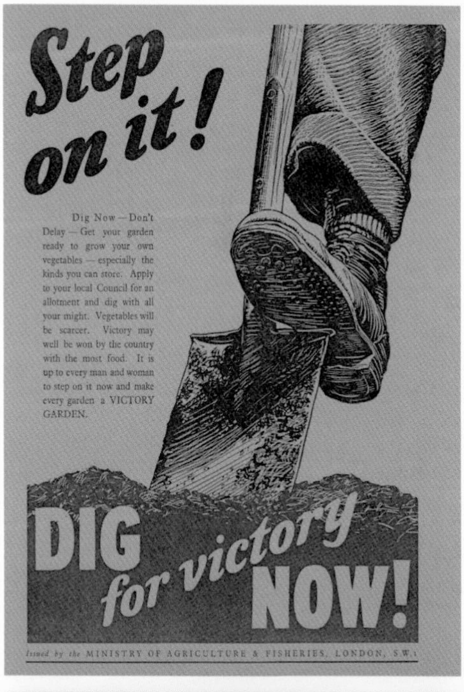
Step on it!
Dig Now — Don't Delay — Get your garden ready to grow your own vegetables — especially the kinds you can store. Apply to your local Council for an allotment and dig with all your might. Vegetables will be scarcer. Victory may well be won by the country with the most food. It is up to every man and woman to step on it now and make every garden a VICTORY GARDEN.
DIG for victory NOW!
Issued by the MINISTRY OF AGRICULTURE & FISHERIES, LONDON, S.W.1

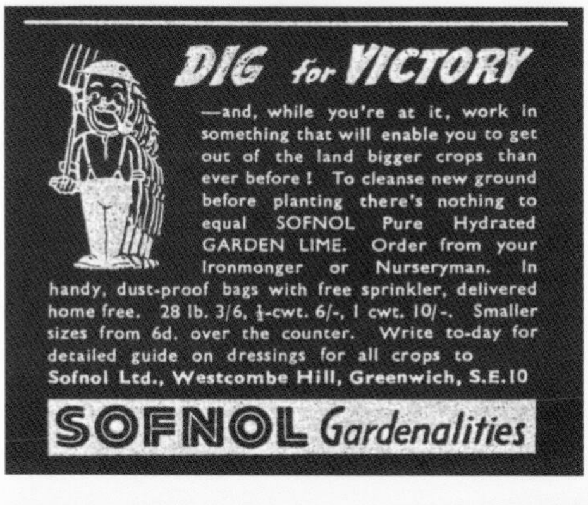
DIG for VICTORY
—and, while you're at it, work in something that will enable you to get out of the land bigger crops than ever before! To cleanse new ground before planting there's nothing to equal SOFNOL Pure Hydrated GARDEN LIME. Order from your Ironmonger or Nurseryman. In handy, dust-proof bags with free sprinkler, delivered home free. 28 lb. 3/6, ¼-cwt. 6/-, 1 cwt. 10/-. Smaller sizes from 6d. over the counter. Write to-day for detailed guide on dressings for all crops to Sofnol Ltd., Westcombe Hill, Greenwich, S.E.10
SOFNOL Gardenalities

Left

The very first plan for cropping an allotment or garden under the Grow More Food campaign. This was issued in October 1939.

Top

A Dig for Victory campaign poster from the *Gardeners' Chronicle*, November 1940.

Middle

This full-page advertisement in the *Gardeners' Chronicle* of 19 October 1940 was among the first to use the iconic foot and spade, although the phrase 'Dig for Victory' was first used by Sir Reginald Dorman-Smith in October 1939.

Below

An early example of the use of the Dig for Victory slogan. This advertisement dates from 28 October 1939.

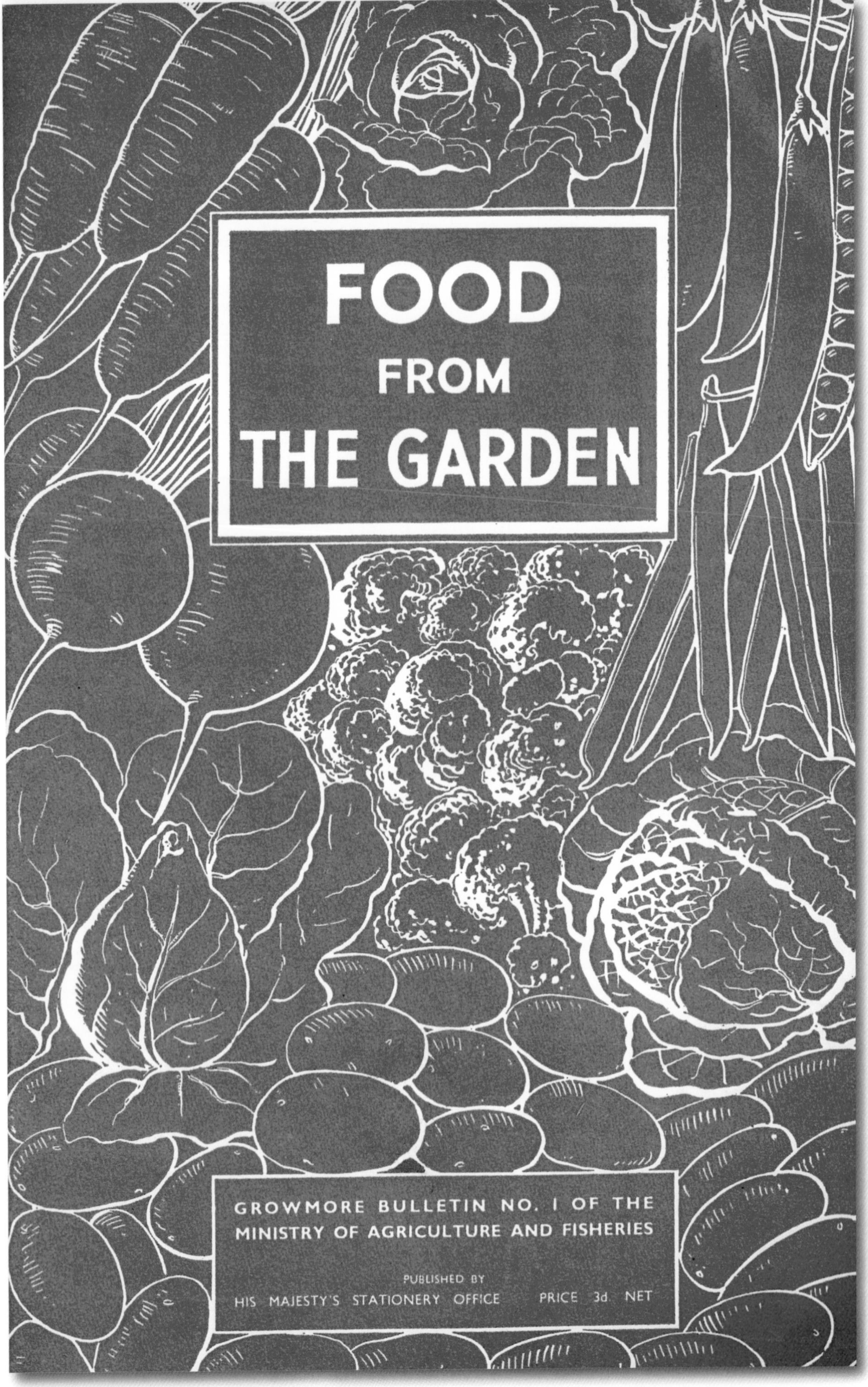

FOOD FROM THE GARDEN

GROWMORE BULLETIN NO. 1 OF THE MINISTRY OF AGRICULTURE AND FISHERIES

PUBLISHED BY
HIS MAJESTY'S STATIONERY OFFICE PRICE 3d. NET

Grow More bulletins were largely replaced by the 'Dig for Victory: New Series' leaflets from 1941, but remained available. These were more substantial than the new leaflets, and were sold for 3d or 4d each, whereas the new series were free. However, the more detailed advice was appreciated by some gardeners and in 1943 the government sold an estimated 55,000 bulletins, despite the easy and free availability of the smaller leaflets. There were four bulletins:

No. 1 'Food from the Garden' (first published October 1939)

No. 2 'Pests and Diseases in the Vegetable Garden' (1940)

No. 3 'Preserves from the Garden' (1940)

No. 4 'Fruit from the Garden' (1940)

Also available were 'War-Time Poultry Keeping'; a more substantial bulletin on 'Domestic Preservation of Fruit and Vegetables' for 1s 6d; and 'Tomatoes, their Cultivation, Diseases and Pests', originally written for the commercial market.

By the summer of 1940 the situation for food imports had rapidly deteriorated with the supplies from Holland and Belgium lost, and it became obvious that England might eventually have to be totally self-sufficient in its food production. This led to renewed efforts by the Ministry of Agriculture to promote the Dig for Victory campaign in the late summer of 1940. A new series of advertisements was issued in the press, encouraging everyone to do their bit. The first predictably showed a householder digging up a lawn, suggesting that everyone should turn their flowerbeds into a kitchen garden.

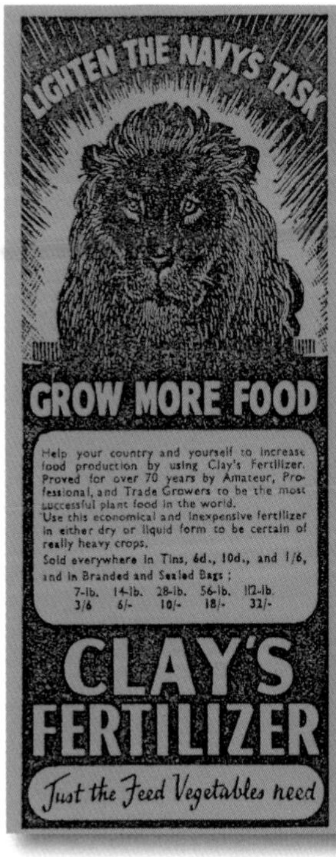
LIGHTEN THE NAVY'S TASK
GROW MORE FOOD
Help your country and yourself to increase food production by using Clay's Fertilizer. Proved for over 70 years by Amateur, Professional, and Trade Growers to be the most successful plant food in the world.
Use this economical and inexpensive fertilizer in either dry or liquid form to be certain of really heavy crops.
Sold everywhere in Tins, 6d., 10d., and 1/6, and in Branded and Sealed Bags;
7-lb. 14-lb. 28-lb. 56-lb. 112-lb.
3/6 6/- 10/- 18/- 32/-
CLAY'S FERTILIZER
Just the Feed Vegetables need

Dig for Victory leaflets (New Series) covered the following subjects:

1. Vegetable Production: Grow for Winter as Well as Summer (Cropping Plan for 10-pole Allotment or Garden)
2. Onions, Leeks, Shallots, Garlic
3. Storing Vegetables for Winter Use
4. Peas and Beans
5. Cabbages and Related Crops
6. Root Crops: Root Vegetables for the Small Grower
7. Manure from Garden Rubbish (How to Make a Compost Heap)
8. Tomato Growing is not difficult
9. How to Make Bordeaux and Burgundy Mixtures in Small Quantities
10. Jam and Jelly Making
11. Bottling and Canning Fruit and Vegetables
12. Seed Potatoes
13. Storing Potatoes for Food and Seed
14. Drying, Salting, Pickles, Chutneys
15. Potato Growing in Allotments and Gardens
16. Garden Pests and How to Deal with Them
17. Potato Blight
18. Better Fruit: Disease Control in Private Gardens
19. How to Sow Seeds
20. How to Dig

Left

'Food From The Garden' was the original Grow More bulletin no. 1. Sold for 3d each (as opposed to the later Dig for Victory leaflets which were free), they were more in the nature of booklets than leaflets. Although not recorded on the plan, the text recommended that marrows were planted 3 inches apart, one of several errors instantly spotted by the gardening press.

Above

This advertisement for Clay's fertiliser used the phrase 'Grow More' in June 1940.

21. Saving Your Own Seeds
22. How to Grow Small Fruits
23. Cropping Plan: Instructions for a 5-pole Allotment
24. Roof and Window-Box Gardening (issued in Spring 1944)
25. How to Prune Fruit Trees and Bushes (issued August 1944)
26. How to Use 'Cloches'

The leaflets were constantly reissued and updated and so early numbers often carry advertisements for supposedly 'later' leaflets in the series.

Digging by Instruction

A key part of the Dig for Victory campaign was the new series of leaflets on all aspects of productive gardening. Using the minimum amount of paper (soon in short supply) to get over the maximum information these were shorter than the original **Grow More** bulletins. The leaflets were easy to assimilate, practical, included useful illustrations and were, most importantly, free. With the aid of these any gardener, whether novice, experienced, amateur or professional, was expected to be able to produce an enviable range of fresh, and unrationed, vegetables. Some leaflets were in the form of 'posters' on the front, with short instructions and encouragement on the inside and rear. Mostly of four or six pages, they did not demand a lot of reading time or gardening experience.

Most popular were the leaflets which told you which crops to plant and where, and in particular the leaflet which included an application form for an allotment. Leaflet no. 23 was specifically addressed to those people who, for whatever reason, did not want to have a full-size allotment but opted instead for the newly available 5-pole plots (half the usual size), and this proved popular as wartime work responsibilities burgeoned, leaving less time for the plot. As more allotments were made available more Dig for Victory leaflets were distributed. They were sometimes linked to Pathé information films, shown in cinemas before the main news or feature; for example, leaflet no. 7 on 'manure from garden rubbish' was animated by a cartoon of Cecil Middleton, and leaflet no. 16 on garden pests also merited a Pathé feature.

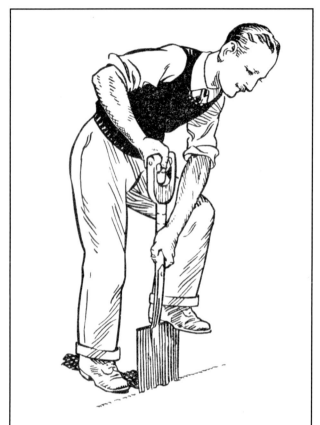

Figure 1 from the Grow it Yourself *Daily Mail Practical Instruction Book on Food From the Garden in War-Time*, demonstrating the use of the left foot. The description of the figure states that 'With body and leg thrust evenly balanced, the blade should be forced into the ground to its full depth'.

In June 1943 the **Gardeners' Chronicle** told its readers that *'Free or cheap advice is available* *in many forms to the public who grow their own vegetables and a pretty thorough enquiry last year suggests that allotment-holders and gardeners are not finding any difficulty in getting the information they need. Gardening notes in the Press and broadcast talks are the most popular sources of information, but leaflets and films play their part. . . . Many new producers who were questioned had also been advised by brother gardeners and "old hands". However more use might be made of the official advisory service.'*

In July 1943, the gardening press looked back on that year's campaign, using the numbers of requests for each leaflet as a guide to what was on the mind of the victory digger. Planning the allotment was the most popular of all with 14,000 applications for a leaflet (following an advertisement campaign in February of that year), while 9,000 had asked for information on planning a small plot. 'How to Sow Seeds' had attracted 10,000 people, and the leaflet on tomatoes had elicited 10,000 applications when it was advertised in May, with a guide to sowing and raising onions getting similar numbers. What was most astonishing about these figures was that, with the exception of the 'How to Plan a 5-pole Plot', all the leaflets had been available in the earlier years of the war and millions had already been distributed. That 23,000 people still needed to know how to plan a plot (of 10 or 5 poles) by June 1943 was either encouraging or disheartening depending on how the government looked at it.

Not everyone appreciated the endless distribution of leaflets and bulletins. As early as June 1940, George H. Copley wrote, '*The literature that emanates from the Ministry is singularly puerile.*

Quite early in the campaign my wife received a large bundle of leaflets urging her to dig for victory, and stating that if she needed more of these leaflets for distribution they could be obtained for the asking. She pretends to no horticultural qualifications, but she did distribute the leaflets. I received none, although all my life has been spent in gardens. I heard of a bed-ridden old lady of ninety who was also urged to dig for victory! I wonder how many of these leaflets were wasted.' By 1944 the number of wives and previously bedridden 90-year-olds cultivating their own plots might have forced Mr Copley to eat his own words, along with his wife's vegetables!

As Dig for Victory seeped into the subconscious mind of the entire population, manufacturers started to see it as an advertising slogan. Naturally, makers of garden tools and sundries, and seedsmen, were the first to embark on the endless round of '*Cloches against Hitler*', '*Mortlegg Tar Wash Holds Your Maginot Line*' and so on, but makers of products as diverse as nail polish, soap, whisky and Oxo were soon on the bandwagon. Advertising could be seen as a patriotic duty if it included reference to the government's campaigns. Some were easier to relate to the push for victory gardening than others. Oxo meat-flavoured cubes benefited from the rationing of meat, enabling housewives to make 'meat stew' from garden vegetables, but the links between whisky and gardening seem less obvious, at least in retrospect. Women's magazines also had a heyday advertising gardening gloves, hand creams and nail restorer for those with 'gardening hands'!

Despite the increased pace of the Dig for Victory campaign through 1940 and 1941, bad weather, bad backs, and general malaise meant that many of the new allotment sites enthusiastically created by local councils lay uncultivated at the end of 1941. In addition many lawns remained unturned and private gardens still boasted flowers instead of foodstuffs. The government found this sometimes unenthusiastic response to their campaigns disappointing. The nation should make more strenuous efforts or it would starve. In October 1942 the Mayor of Southport said: *'Every available inch of suitable land . . . must be devoted to growing vegetables especially for the winter of 1943/44. Encourage the able-bodied women and older children to play their part in the production battle. Standards of production must be raised and the slogan for next year is "Better Planning, Better Gardening, Better Crops".'*

In the meantime the gardening press was still arguing about exactly what should be grown. In November 1941 the **Gardeners' Chronicle** had reported that celeriac was now officially out (too difficult) and Jerusalem artichokes (unpopular but easy) were back in. Good King Henry, a traditional wild plant incredibly easy to raise, was to replace summer spinach, and marrows were more or less compulsory. Winter vegetables were still of prime concern to both the government and the housewife, and spring 1942 was dominated by adverts reminding people not of the coming summer, but the following winter. Leaflets full of advice and instruction were everywhere, and those few that had not received them were sure to be handed them by neighbours. People were urged to 'Dig for Dear Life' as well as for victory. Details on digging, manuring and seed potatoes were repeated endlessly, along with the invitation to send off for the Dig for Victory leaflet no. 20 'How to Dig'.

The fact that the leaflet telling people how to do the actual digging was not released until well into the campaign suggests that the Ministry of

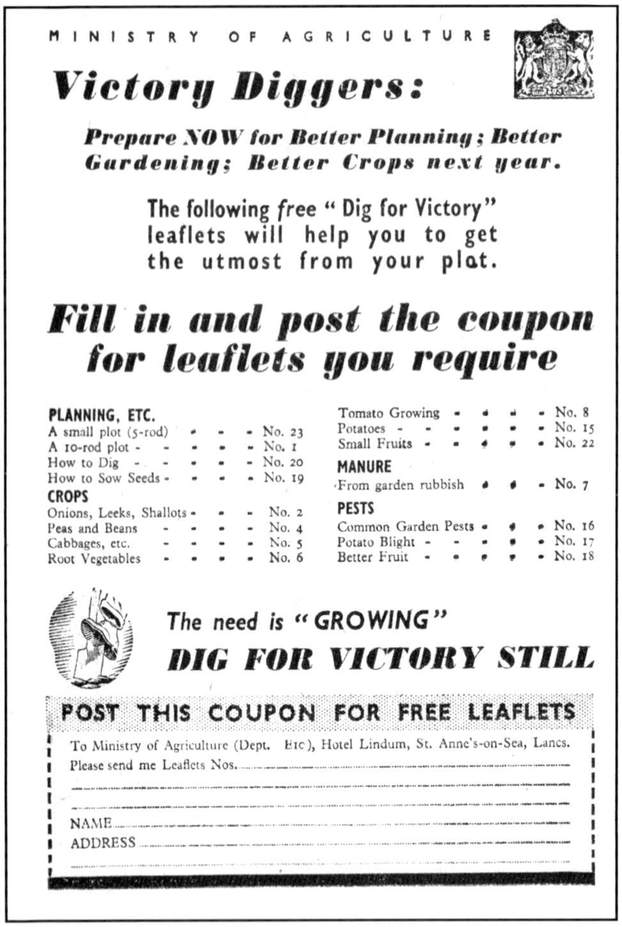
MINISTRY OF AGRICULTURE
Victory Diggers:
Prepare NOW for Better Planning; Better Gardening; Better Crops next year.
The following free " Dig for Victory" leaflets will help you to get the utmost from your plot.
Fill in and post the coupon for leaflets you require
PLANNING, ETC.
A small plot (5-rod) - - - No. 23
A 10-rod plot - - - - - No. 1
How to Dig - - - - - No. 20
How to Sow Seeds - - - - No. 19
CROPS
Onions, Leeks, Shallots - - - No. 2
Peas and Beans - - - - No. 4
Cabbages, etc. - - - - No. 5
Root Vegetables - - - - No. 6
Tomato Growing - - - - No. 8
Potatoes - - - - - - No. 15
Small Fruits - - - - - No. 22
MANURE
From garden rubbish - - - No. 7
PESTS
Common Garden Pests - - - No. 16
Potato Blight - - - - - No. 17
Better Fruit - - - - - No. 18
The need is "GROWING"
DIG FOR VICTORY STILL
POST THIS COUPON FOR FREE LEAFLETS
To Ministry of Agriculture (Dept. EIC), Hotel Lindum, St. Anne's-on-Sea, Lancs.
Please send me Leaflets Nos.
NAME
ADDRESS

Above
Throughout the war advertisements for the Dig for Victory leaflets resulted in hundreds of thousands of leaflets being sent out. The government kept records of how many responses each advertisement elicited. This example dates to late in the war when the new slogan 'The Need is Growing' was introduced.

Right
The Dig for Victory leaflet no. 1 (New series) steered people firmly away from the delights of peas and lettuce towards the virtuous path of year-round cabbages. The bulletin was re-issued several times over the course of the war.

Agriculture was not initially aware of how unfamiliar some prospective gardeners might be with basic techniques. It was only once the Royal Horticultural Society had published their fully illustrated **The Vegetable Garden Displayed** in 1941 that the government thought of using photographs in their own leaflet on digging. Some new victory diggers knew little about the use of tools, and found the sight of them bewildering and even daunting. H. Williams of Redruth wrote to the **Gardeners' Chronicle** of August 1942 to report that *'When the digger, the spade, hoe, rake, hook, shears etc came, they were all set out and I tried my level best to admire them. The shears and hoe were fascinating, but the digger and the spade were repulsive. I went out and dropped them in the hut and went for a walk. It is best to go at it in this way.'* For those people who shared this response to the sight of gardening tools, the government commissioned a short film, entitled, appropriately, **Garden Tools**, to be shown at various venues throughout the country. Once they had mastered the tools, a further film tackled **Garden Friends and Foes**; this concerned pests and diseases rather than the neighbouring allotment-holder. **Saving Seeds** was the subject of a third film in the series, aiming to make up for the increasing shortage of seeds.

By 1942 victory gardens were not restricted to public parks, homes and allotments. Bombsites, golf courses and even churchyards started to sprout vegetables. The Rev. G.R. Parkinson of St Mary's church in Halifax declared that, *'Naturally we would prefer to have flowers surrounding the Church, but food is much more important now, and so we are trying to do what we can in that direction.'* Bridgwater's Rugby Football ground was taken over for allotments, while at Hurlingham the Polo Ground was ploughed up and allotted out. London Transport's station flowerbeds were also put down to vegetables, with money prizes awarded to those who made best use of these small garden plots.

In 1943 the Ministry of Agriculture and Fisheries was still advising that 'There are many new Victory Diggers this year who are needing helps and tips'. Those that still had weed or flower filled gardens were looked on as traitors to the cause, and neighbours were encouraged to help each other or even report each other. The tone of the campaign became increasingly militaristic by 1943 with commands being issued, plans being laid, and armies of diggers mobilised. The **Gardeners' Chronicle** of March

DIG FOR VICTORY
Grow for Winter as well as Summer
THIS PLAN WILL GIVE YOU YOUR OWN VEGETABLES ALL THE YEAR ROUND
COMPOST HEAP · TOOL SHED · SEED BED
TOMATOES · MARROW · RADISH · PARSLEY
MISCELLANEOUS C CROPS
DWARF PEAS* 3 ROWS (2 ft. 6 in. APART)
INTERCROP WITH SPINACH (2 ROWS) AND FOLLOW WITH LEEKS 1 FT. APART (4 ROWS)
DWARF BEANS 2 ROWS (2 ft. 6 in. APART)
ONIONS* 8 ROWS (1 ft. APART)
FOLLOW WITH SPRING CABBAGE
SHALLOTS 2 ROWS (1 ft. APART)
BROAD BEANS 1 DOUBLE ROW
FOLLOW WITH WINTER LETTUCE
INTERCROP WITH SUMMER LETTUCE
RUNNER BEANS* (1 ROW)
POTATOES & ROOT A CROPS
PARSNIPS 3 ROWS (1 ft. 3 in. APART)
CARROT (MAINCROP) 5 ROWS (1 ft. APART)
POTATOES (EARLY) 3 ROWS (2 ft. by 1 ft.)
FOLLOW WITH TURNIPS (1 ft. APART)
POTATOES (OTHERS) 6 ROWS (2 ft. by 1 ft. 3 in.)
ROTATION OF CROPS
1ST. YEAR C A B
2ND. YEAR B C A
3RD. YEAR A B C
SPINACH BEET OR SEAKALE BEET 1 ROW
WINTER & SPRING B GREEN CROPS
CABBAGE (WINTER) 3 ROWS (2 ft. by 2 ft.)
SAVOYS* 2 ROWS (2 ft. by 2 ft.)
BRUSSELS SPROUTS* 2 ROWS (2 ft. 6 in. x 2 ft. 6 in.)
SPROUTING BROCCOLI 2 ROWS (2 ft. by 2 ft.)
KALE 2 ROWS (2 ft. by 2 ft.)
SWEDES 2 ROWS
GLOBE BEET 2 ROWS
PRECEDE BEET WITH EARLY DWARF PEAS (1 ROW)
ALLOTMENT OR GARDEN
PLOT ...... 90' x 30'
APPROX. 10 SQ. RODS POLES OR PERCHES
ASK FOR COPY OF PLAN AND 'DIG FOR VICTORY' LEAFLET No. 1 or write for free copies to Ministry of Agriculture, 55 Whitehall, London, S.W.1

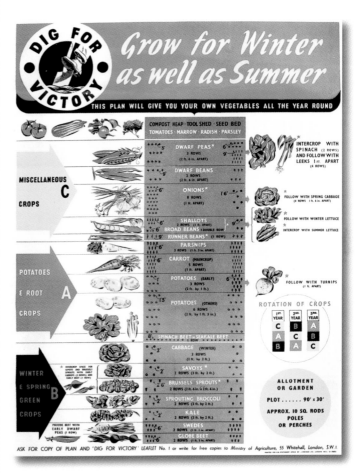

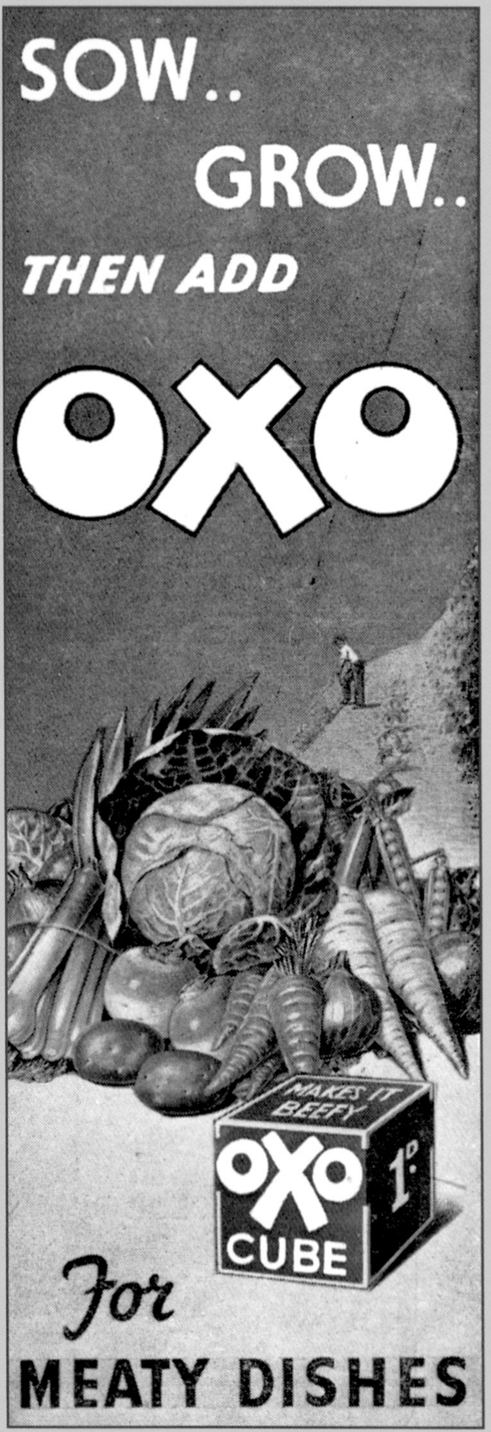
SOW..
GROW..
THEN ADD
OXO
MAKES IT BEEFY
OXO CUBE 1D.
For
MEATY DISHES

1943 told its readers that '*"Plan Your Cropping" is one of the battle commands issued from Whitehall to the vast army of Victory Diggers in England and Wales. It is being repeated by a sixteen sheet poster, advertisement, word of mouth and leaflets broadcast in every town and many rural areas.*' During the summer and autumn of 1943 over 130,000 people wrote in for the leaflets that formed the backbone of the Dig for Victory campaign, an indication of the success of the government's approach. The fact that by 1944 there were still people in need of the leaflets was slightly more worrying, although the main thrust of the campaign by then was to prevent backsliding, as the demands on people's time to perform other duties made it increasingly difficult to keep up the vegetable plot.

In an effort to maintain morale and revive any flagging gardeners, a series of new slogans was brought into action in the spring of 1943. The first of these was 'Better Planning – Better Cropping' (or the rather more long-winded 'Better Planning, Better Gardening, Better Crops'). This reflected the government's concern that people were just gardening anyhow, with no forward planning or rotation of crops over the years. Having discouraged potatoes at the outset of the war, and then done a U-turn the following year, the Ministry of Agriculture and Fisheries now decided that home gardeners were growing too many potatoes, possibly because they were relatively easy to grow, harvest and store. The 'Potato Pete' campaign aimed at housewives had been too successful, and many

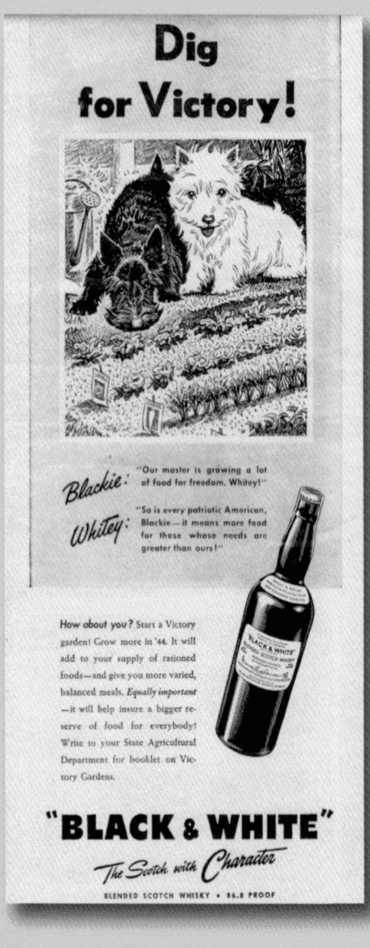
Dig for Victory!
Blackie: "Our master is growing a lot of food for freedom, Whitey!"
Whitey: "So is every patriotic American, Blackie — it means more food for those whose needs are greater than ours!"
How about you? Start a Victory garden! Grow more in '44. It will add to your supply of rationed foods—and give you more varied, balanced meals. Equally important —it will help insure a bigger reserve of food for everybody! Write to your State Agricultural Department for booklet on Victory Gardens.
"BLACK & WHITE"
The Scotch with Character
BLENDED SCOTCH WHISKY • 86.8 PROOF

Left
Sow, Grow, Then Add Oxo became yet another wartime 'catchphrase' for those facing long-term meat rationing.

Right
Black & White Whisky also used Dig for Victory – here in an American advertisement. The Americans were also busy digging up their back-yards.

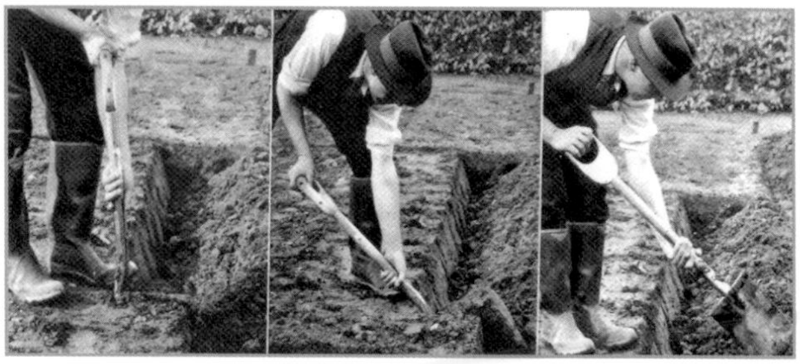

had turned half of their vegetable patch over to this essential food leaving them, in turn, short of greens. Frustration with conflicting decrees from on high resulted in a demand for 'a clear clarification of the potato issue' before the rest of the cropping plan could proceed. One month later, an advertisement by the Ministry of Agriculture and Fisheries replied with the following guidance: *'You know the importance of good digging and wise planning. But there are many newcomers to vegetable growing that don't. So keep an eye on them and help with advice when you think they need it. Chat about the crops they plan to grow. Warn them against growing too much for summer at the expense of winter vegetables. Don't let them grow too many potatoes.'*

From now on the numerous demonstration plots that had sprung up in every public park and in places like Kew were instructed to plant few, if any, potatoes. Brussels sprouts, savoys, kales and cabbages were to be the order of the day until peacetime came, with lettuces and marrows as light relief. Needless to say most allotment-holders ignored the instruction, sticking as ever to the rewarding forests of potato plants in their impressively ridged trenches. According to the **Gardeners' Chronicle** of February 1943, *'cottage and allotment gardeners alike cling religiously to their potato patch, and no amount of government assurance as to the widespread availability of potatoes in shops will make them give it up'.*

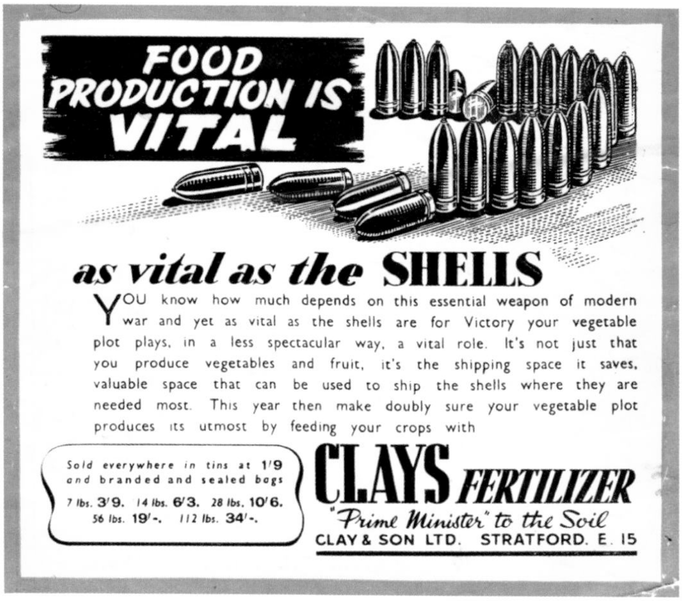
FOOD PRODUCTION IS VITAL
as vital as the SHELLS
YOU know how much depends on this essential weapon of modern war and yet as vital as the shells are for Victory your vegetable plot plays, in a less spectacular way, a vital role. It's not just that you produce vegetables and fruit, it's the shipping space it saves, valuable space that can be used to ship the shells where they are needed most. This year then make doubly sure your vegetable plot produces its utmost by feeding your crops with
Sold everywhere in tins at 1/9 and branded and sealed bags
7 lbs. 3/9. 14 lbs. 6/3. 28 lbs. 10/6. 56 lbs. 19/-. 112 lbs. 34/-.
CLAYS FERTILIZER
"Prime Minister" to the Soil
CLAY & SON LTD. STRATFORD. E. 15

Left

An illustration from Dig for Victory leaflet no. 20, this photographic sequence illustrated 'Simple digging where there is no turf'. It included instructions on preparation for digging, stance, and action. A separate series of photographs dealt with 'bastard trenching' – the term used for the technique of digging ground covered with turf.

Above

'Food Production is Vital, as Vital as the Shells', another catchphrase of the Dig for Victory campaign used by Clay's Fertiliser.

Digging Despite it All: the elderly and the infirm

As the campaign to get everyone growing progressed, there was an increasing emphasis on which city or village could claim the oldest and the youngest allotment-holders, who had been digging for longest, or who battled against the greatest infirmities. The gardening press faithfully reported items sent in from around the country while the local press tried to outshine their rivals. A few examples give just a flavour of these claims to digging fame: in March 1943 'an old age pensioner from Doncaster' aged 88 was cultivating an allotment of 1,500 square yards (approximately five times the normal size). This definitely beat the aged Luton allotment-holder who had been reported in the **Gardeners' Chronicle** one year earlier as *'taking on his second allotment'*. In Sheffield, about thirty allotment-holders were said to be over 80 years of age, and some of them had been cultivating allotments well before the previous war. A man of 78 in Carnarvon not only had two allotment plots but, according to his neighbours, 'does it really well'! All of these were in turn trumped by Mr E. Beaumont who at 90 grew all his own vegetables on his allotment in Norwood. But surely the final word went to John Johnson of Romsey (Hampshire) who had worked in his garden until he was 100; although as he died aged 104 in 1944 he rather ironically had just missed gardening through the Dig for Victory campaign, being forced to give up gardening just as it started. Mr Johnson still merited an honourable mention however, as setting an example to others who had not yet reached their century.

Disabled victory diggers also merited special comment: Mr J.W. Birchall of Barnes (Middlesex) was one of the first to apply for an allotment on the new wartime plots there despite being blind. He was said to have set such a good example with his productivity and neatness that the plots on the site were renowned throughout the county. Mr W.J. Collins and a friend both suffered from having lost legs, but still did their bit by sharing an allotment plot between them, and Mr W. Jeffries who had lost an arm in the previous war also kept an immaculate garden.

Women, and in particular the aged or widowed, were also held up as examples to the general public. An unnamed widow looking after three children under 14, an evacuee boy, and an aged mother, was featured in press releases by the Ministry of Agriculture in May 1942. Knowing nothing of gardening before the war she had produced all the food her extended family needed on her two allotments and garden by using the government's Dig for Victory leaflet no. 1. What the unnamed widow should have done of course was put her children to work growing

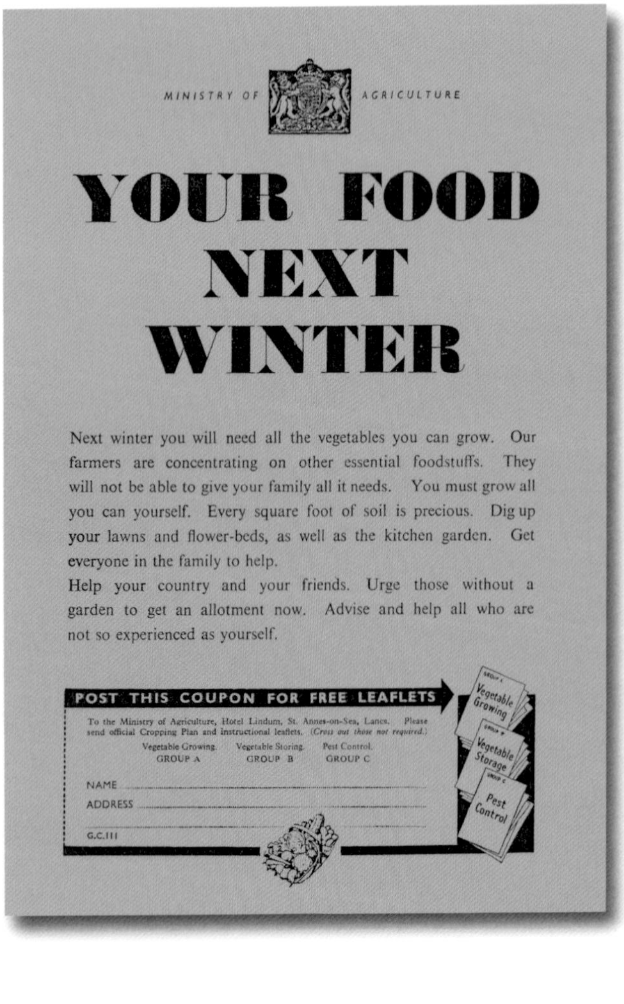
MINISTRY OF AGRICULTURE
YOUR FOOD NEXT WINTER
Next winter you will need all the vegetables you can grow. Our farmers are concentrating on other essential foodstuffs. They will not be able to give your family all it needs. You must grow all you can yourself. Every square foot of soil is precious. Dig up your lawns and flower-beds, as well as the kitchen garden. Get everyone in the family to help.
Help your country and your friends. Urge those without a garden to get an allotment now. Advise and help all who are not so experienced as yourself.
POST THIS COUPON FOR FREE LEAFLETS
To the Ministry of Agriculture, Hotel Lindum, St. Annes-on-Sea, Lancs. Please send official Cropping Plan and instructional leaflets. (Cross out those not required.)
Vegetable Growing. GROUP A
Vegetable Storing. GROUP B
Pest Control. GROUP C
NAME
ADDRESS
G.C.111
Vegetable Growing
Vegetable Storage
Pest Control

Left
'Your Food Next Winter.'
Right
Even the most basic techniques of digging and sowing were valuable skills which should be passed on to aspiring new victory diggers.

Your help is Vital!

Carry on with the good work. You grow all the vegetables you can. Encourage your neighbours to do the same. Get them digging now. Show the "new chum" how to do it. Tell him what to grow. Your gardening experience is a national asset. In your own and your country's interests use it to the full.

HELP THE NATION TO

DIG for VICTORY

Issued by the MINISTRY OF AGRICULTURE AND FISHERIES, LONDON, S.W.1

the vegetables – but no-one mentioned that. Mrs Wheatcroft, wife of the famed rose grower, appears to have gone one better, digging up her flower garden and producing enough food for her family of nine! By the end of 1943 in order to earn a place in the 'allotment news' a plot-holder had to be over 90 and either disabled or female. Mrs G. Hunt of North Petherton managed two of these (being a widow 'aged over 90'), as well as gaining second place in a local allotment competition. The Women's Institutes encouraged women to take over allotments and vegetable gardens when their husbands left for service or extended duty hours on the Home Front. The WI urged them not only to grow vegetables and fruit but also to make jam, preserve and bottle, raise hens, collect herbs, preserve eggs, and rear pigs.

Many gardens became positive cornucopias of fruits and vegetables flourishing under the women of the household: on the **BBC People's War On-Line** the well-known wartime cookery and government food expert Marguerite Patten describes her mother's wartime garden as *'An abundance of produce. There were apple and plum trees plus a small pear tree, a long line of black, red and white currants (delicious raw), with gooseberry bushes, raspberries and loganberries. The Royal Sovereign strawberries were our pride and joy. Beans were great favourites so through the months we picked the broad and French and runner varieties, also lots of peas. There were plentiful supplies of onions to give flavour to wartime dishes, leeks, potatoes, carrots, turnips and parsnips. For some reason we did not grow swedes. Throughout the months there were various green vegetables – kale and spinach being favourites, plus a good range of herbs. The cos lettuce and tomatoes were so plentiful we could present some to friends. When it got dark we retired to the kitchen to bottle fruits – including tomatoes – and make jam and chutney when we had saved sufficient food from our rations. Wartime gardening was hard work but very satisfying and productive.'*

The more food you could produce from the garden the better the family would eat, and the less time the busy housewife would have to spend in endless queues. With a plentiful supply of fruit and vegetables a family might even indulge in a little bartering – thus expanding the usefulness of their vegetable garden or hen coop. In **The Wartime Kitchen and Garden**, Jennifer Davies recorded the memories of Margaret Clark of Burnham, Buckinghamshire, who remembered her family

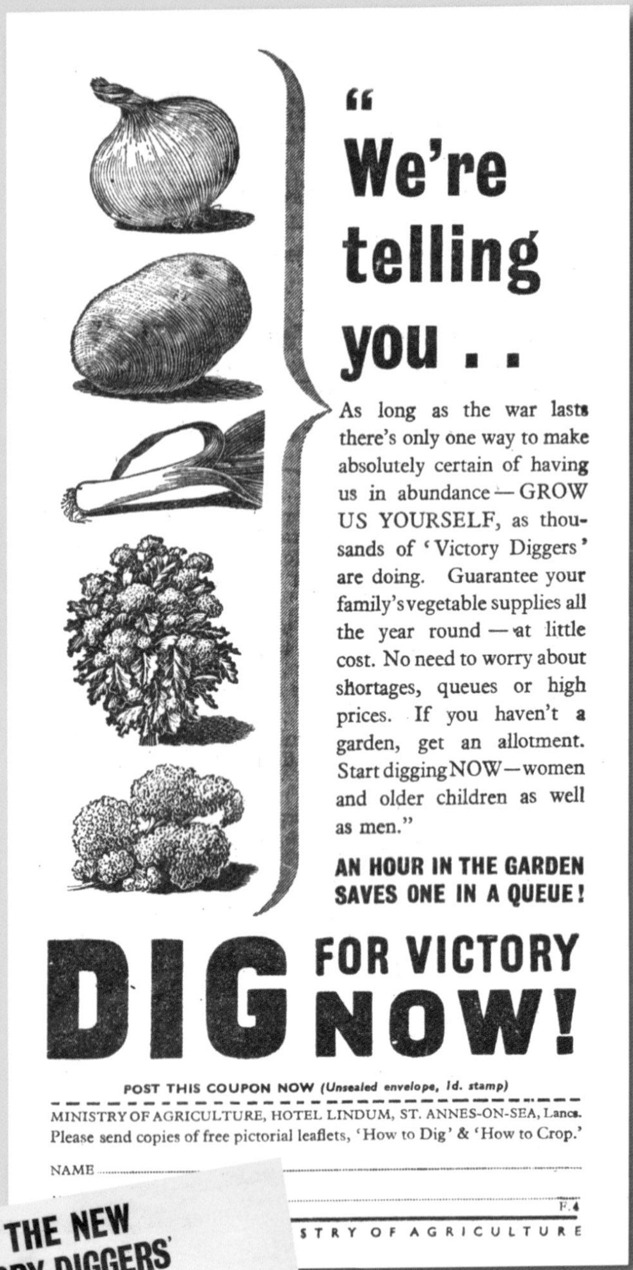
"We're telling you . .
As long as the war lasts there's only one way to make absolutely certain of having us in abundance—GROW US YOURSELF, as thousands of 'Victory Diggers' are doing. Guarantee your family's vegetable supplies all the year round—at little cost. No need to worry about shortages, queues or high prices. If you haven't a garden, get an allotment. Start digging NOW—women and older children as well as men."
AN HOUR IN THE GARDEN SAVES ONE IN A QUEUE!
DIG FOR VICTORY NOW!
POST THIS COUPON NOW (Unsealed envelope, 1d. stamp)
MINISTRY OF AGRICULTURE, HOTEL LINDUM, ST. ANNES-ON-SEA, Lancs.
Please send copies of free pictorial leaflets, 'How to Dig' & 'How to Crop.'
NAME
F.4
STRY OF AGRICULTURE

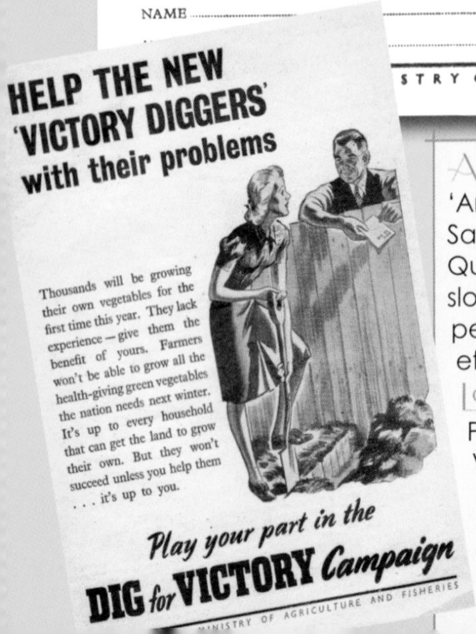
HELP THE NEW 'VICTORY DIGGERS' with their problems
Thousands will be growing their own vegetables for the first time this year. They lack experience—give them the benefit of yours. Farmers won't be able to grow all the health-giving green vegetables the nation needs next winter. It's up to every household that can get the land to grow their own. But they won't succeed unless you help them . . . it's up to you.
Play your part in the DIG for VICTORY Campaign
MINISTRY OF AGRICULTURE AND FISHERIES

Above
'An Hour in the Garden Saves One in the Queue' – yet another slogan to encourage people to greater efforts.

Left
Part of the 'New Victory Diggers' campaign.

bartering fruit and vegetables for fish, while even services could be 'purchased', with family doctors receiving eggs and fruit instead of fees.

Prisoners of War Dig for Victory

Perhaps the most surprising participants in the Dig for Victory campaign were the prisoners of war. Across Germany and Italy Allied prisoners of war were encouraged to create gardens in their camps providing themselves with both an occupation and relief from a poor and monotonous diet. To assist them the Royal Horticultural Society sent parcels of flower and vegetable seeds under Red Cross labels to camp leaders. From a relatively small beginning in the spring of 1942, the campaign expanded and soon both new and experienced gardeners in the camps were spending time brightening their surroundings and improving their diet.

With the aid of British seedsmen, the Ontario Horticultural Association and the Canadian Prisoners of War Relatives' Association, 1,000 packets of seeds were sent to internees in German POW camps in the summer of 1944. Letters from the grateful recipients paint a wonderful picture of vegetables flourishing in the most unlikely settings. In one camp 5,000 tomato plants were grown in addition to onions, leeks, carrots, beet, ridge cucumbers, lettuces and vegetable marrows. Flowers were also included in the seed supplies and a colourful mix of poppies, cornflowers, godetias, larkspur, marigolds, gypsophila, zinnias and asters must have brought comfort. *'Flower seeds have been used to great benefit in beautifying the camp and to maintain a profusion of blooms on the graves in the military cemetery*', wrote one internee. Gardener-soldiers took charge of work detachments and gardening helped the time pass as well as providing fresh food and colour. Soon examinations in gardening were being made available in some of the more 'relaxed' POW camps. In 1943 the gardening press was able to include lists of those who had passed the prestigious RHS examination while in camp. Among those obtaining passes under what must have been some of the most difficult of circumstances were Capt. C. Follick of Oflag IX A/H, and Sgt Alan Francis-Clare and Private Arthur William Jeyes in Stalag XX. In Stalag 383, ten people passed, with Sgt Arthur William John Souster gaining silver medals. Opportunities for actual gardening must have been restricted at Oflag VII B, as Capt. Arthur MacIntosh Hilton had to have the practical exam deferred until 'after the war' despite passing the theory (written) paper.

While they no doubt received great satisfaction from their gardening, most prisoners would have been happy to give it up. In September 1944 the **Gardeners' Chronicle** reported a letter from one gardening POW in Germany: *'Although we are planning our spring cropping for 1944, we feel justified in hoping we may not be here to harvest all the crops.'*

Above
Tom Lee, aged 82, was one of the oldest allotment-holders at the site in Acton, Middlesex. He was featured in a campaign by the Ministry of Information to try and get more elderly people out on to allotments. HMSO

Right
With ever more men joining the forces, or working in the Home Guard, ARP, fire watching, and so on, the job of tending the nation's allotments fell increasingly on women.

Potato Pete's recipe book

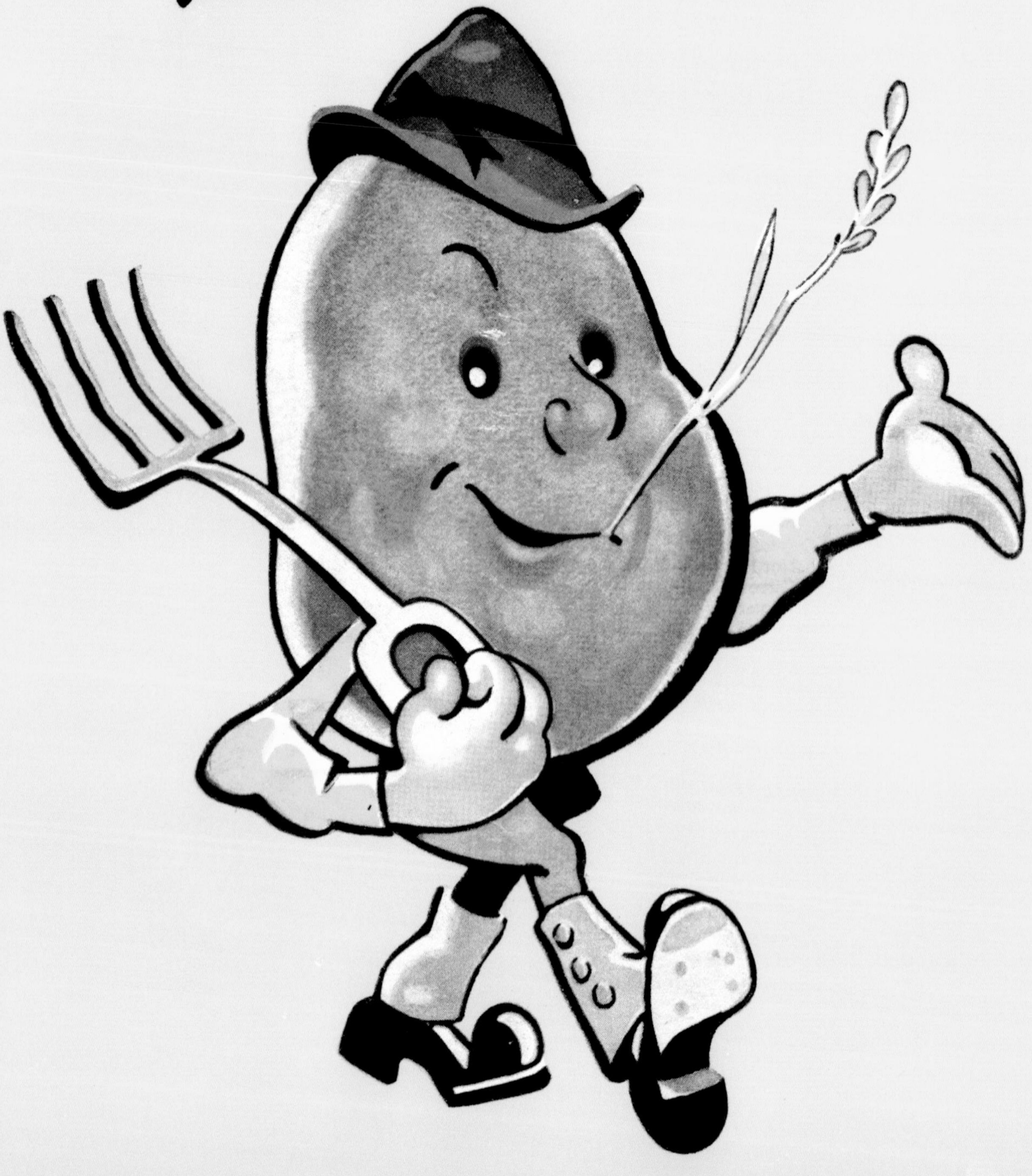

Dig for Victory: the crops

Grow More What?

The main thrust of the Grow More and Dig for Victory campaigns was to make families as self-sufficient in food as possible. In working out what vegetables (and fruits) would best fulfil this aim the government and its horticultural advisers had to bear several things in mind: the ease with which novice and amateur gardeners could grow the particular crop, how resistant it was to pests and diseases, whether a year-round diet could be achieved with the combination recommended, and whether the housewife would be able and confident to use it in preparing family meals. The 1940s diet was rather conservative and did not include many of the European-influenced dishes that were to become popular in the 1960s and '70s. Garlic was still regarded with suspicion, onions, although popular, were eaten 'despite the after-taste', aubergine, peppers and courgettes almost unknown, and salad stuffs restricted to the basics of lettuce, cucumber and tomato.

In addition to bearing in mind these restrictions, the government had to try to balance vegetables that were carbohydrate-heavy with those that provided vitamins and minerals. By 1942 they were also trying to discourage the use of wheat and encourage potatoes (a policy later changed) as these were recommended as a rich source of energy, providing a substitute for cereal grains, while carrots provided vitamin A and sweetness. Vitamins were little understood by the population in general although by the end of the war most people had got the hang of vitamins A and C, thanks to the media campaigns for 'Dr Carrot', and the issue of rose-hip syrup.

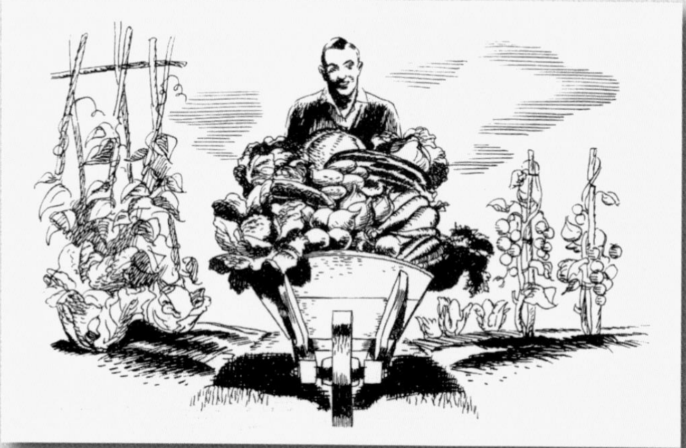

At the time of the release of the first of the new series of Dig for Victory leaflets the government's main concern was that there would not be sufficient food for the winter months, with people concentrating on the

Above

Every victory digger's dream, as depicted on a wartime garden guide.

Left

Potato Pete had his own cookbook and advertising campaign. He was a creation of the Ministry of Food and Lord Woolton, who coordinated their campaigns with the Ministry of Agriculture.

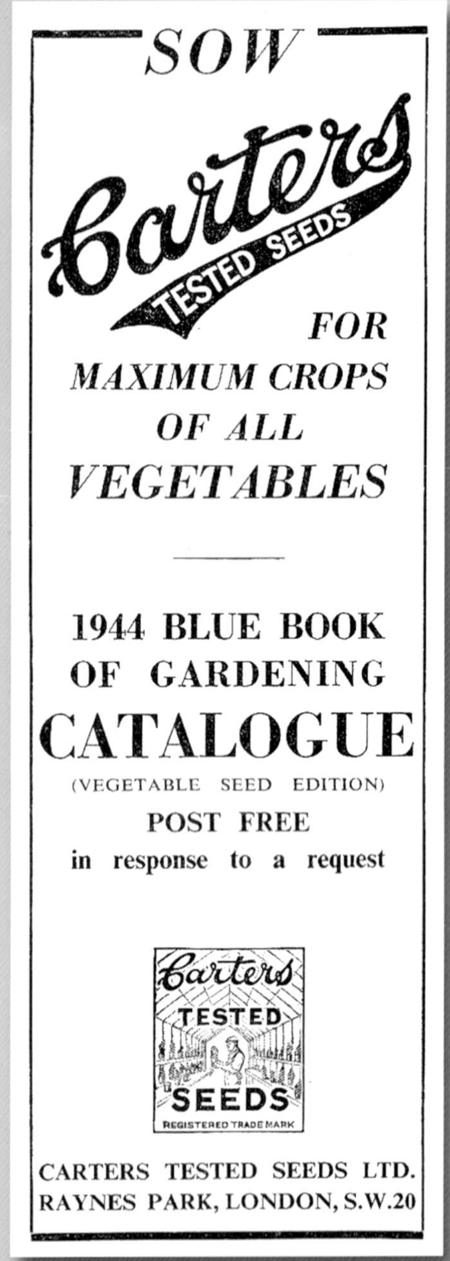

SOW

Carters

TESTED SEEDS

FOR
MAXIMUM CROPS
OF ALL
VEGETABLES

1944 BLUE BOOK
OF GARDENING
CATALOGUE
(VEGETABLE SEED EDITION)
POST FREE
in response to a request

Carters
TESTED
SEEDS
REGISTERED TRADE MARK

CARTERS TESTED SEEDS LTD.
RAYNES PARK, LONDON, S.W.20

Above
During the war, vegetable
catalogues were supplied
free, but customers had to
pay for flower catalogues.

quick and easy summer crops such as lettuces, and so the leaflet included not only dates of sowing and planting, but months when the crops might be eaten. With the heading 'Grow for Winter as well as Summer', vegetables such as savoys, sprouts, kale, leeks and parsnips were highlighted as 'health giving vegetables in Winter'. Most of these crops needed considerable forward planning, and some benefitted from transplanting, making them less attractive to novice gardeners. The leaflet stated that if the table of planting that accompanied it was followed, sufficient crops could be raised in an area of 90 x 30 feet to feed a family of five. It recommended the following vegetables as the best combination for providing year-round supplies: broad beans, dwarf beans, haricot beans, runner beans, beet, broccoli (sprouting), Brussels sprouts, spring cabbage, winter cabbage, cabbage for cold districts, early carrots, maincrop carrots, kale, leeks, summer lettuce, winter hardy lettuce, marrows, onions, parsnips, early peas, peas (other), early potatoes, maincrop potatoes, radishes, savoy, shallots, summer spinach, winter spinach, spinach beet or seakale beet (according to taste and climate), swedes, tomatoes, turnip tops and turnip roots. The very first Grow More bulletin had also recommended planting more leafy green vegetables and salads to 'take the place of imported oranges and other fruits'. It was the food value rather than the taste which one presumes made them successful substitutes!

Many people followed the advice, although some added their own favourites. Marie Mainwaring recalls that *'In Swindon we lived in a rented terraced house with a back garden. Part of that space was taken up by a large shed and also by a small lawn. My father thought that that was a waste of space, so with the permission of the landlord the tree and the grass were banished. We did have some blackcurrant bushes and some raspberry canes but the veg had to have priority. Potatoes, onions, root vegetables, peas, broad beans, runner beans, lettuces, radishes and beetroot were grown. New to us was asparagus.'*

Some home produce was also suitable for being stored for use over the difficult late winter and early spring months, using clamps or simply left in the ground, and these crops were particularly valuable; leeks for example could be left in through the hardest frosts, as could parsnips, while carrots could be lifted and stored. Getting people to actually grow the 'right' balance of winter foodstuffs was however a challenge which the government was to face throughout the war.

Potatoes

Potatoes were to be one of the backbones of the wartime diet, providing bulk carbohydrates and vitamin C. One of the most memorable cartoon figures of the wartime campaign was 'Potato Pete' who promoted potato eating through cookbooks, posters, cartoons, nursery rhymes and even his own song (sung by Betty Driver). Traditional nursery rhymes were given a 'Potato Pete' makeover to get the message through to housewives and children to eat more potatoes and less bread:

> THERE WAS AN OLD WOMAN WHO LIVED IN A SHOE.
> SHE HAD SO MANY CHILDREN SHE DIDN'T KNOW WHAT TO DO.
> SHE GAVE THEM POTATOES INSTEAD OF SOME BREAD,
> AND THE CHILDREN WERE HAPPY AND VERY WELL FED.

The original Grow More bulletin had recommended that a much smaller area of the allotment or garden be given over to potatoes than might normally be the case. The Government was concerned that the plan should provide sufficient greens to overcome winter shortages and replace the vitamins usually available from fruit. However they soon realised that potatoes were filling, warming, easy to grow, and easy for the housewife to cook. The **Gardeners' Chronicle** of 10 August 1940 commented that *'It appears that those responsible for increased food production are now stressing the vital importance of producing storable root crops, and more particularly potatoes, rather than on devoting an unduly large proportion of land to the cultivation of Brassicas. The experience of last winter indicates that too great a reliance of green vegetables may prove equally disastrous as the reliance on the so-called impregnable Maginot Line.'* As imported wheat started to fail, potatoes were once again accorded a prime place on the allotment. Inevitably there was a delay between the rise in demand and supply, and the price of potatoes soared. The traditional Sunday lunch of 'meat, potato and two veg' rapidly became meat and two veg.

A rush in demand for potatoes led to problems with obtaining seed. Seed potatoes were the subject of lively debate throughout the war and the shortage of seed potatoes led to use of non-certified seed stock by many amateur growers. Desperate gardeners cut their seed potato into two or four rather than using one seed potato per new plant. Some people even recall trying to use the waste or peel from potatoes rather than actual seed potatoes. Home gardeners and the government were soon at odds over seed potatoes. 'Inferior seed' was thought by the government to be resulting in poor yields and they blamed the home producer for everything from wart disease to potato blight, not to mention weakling tubers. The Ministry of Food encouraged all growers to buy from certified seed stock, despite difficulties in obtaining these. The best stock, certified as Class 1, came from Scotland or Ireland. English or Welsh seed potato could also be Class 1, but only if especially authorised under a wartime scheme. A further subdivision of Class 1 covered English grown potatoes which were only one generation away from their Scottish or Irish ancestors. Class 2 covered all other potatoes that were authorised to be sold. In addition to being sold by class, seed potatoes were sold according to variety, size, dressing, and with or without official certification against wart disease. Britain was divided into 'protected' and 'unprotected' areas from wart disease, and different regulations applied depending on which you were in! The wonderfully named 'Wart Disease of Potatoes Order' was passed in 1940 and outlined the different areas. Needless to say, just planting some old potatoes that Fred on the neighbouring allotment had given to you was severely frowned upon in official circles, but was frequently done.

Do you remember when the headlines said—
"No potatoes for this Sunday's joint"
While thousands of housewives enjoyed another little grumble, the wiser families who had dug for victory enjoyed their Sunday joint with all the potatoes and other vegetables they wanted. Learn from experience. To be sure of the family's vegetables, you must grow them yourselves—women and older children as well as men. If you haven't a garden, ask your Local Council for an allotment. Start to
DIG FOR VICTORY NOW!
POST THIS COUPON NOW (Unsealed envelope, 1d. stamp)
TO MINISTRY OF AGRICULTURE, HOTEL LINDUM, ST. ANNES-ON-SEA, LANCS.
Please send me copies of free pictorial leaflets, "How to Dig" and "How to Crop"
NAME
ADDRESS
B.99
ISSUED BY THE MINISTRY OF AGRICULTURE

By late October 1942, the **Gardeners' Chronicle** was reporting that *'The most extravagant luxury in the garden is the first-early potato; the crop is not fit to lift in the average garden until the second week in July, and averages only one and a quarter pounds per root at that period. I should recommend only one or two rows of first earlies, followed by a second-early heavy cropper, and the rest to be late keepers such as Majestic.'*

Of course the spread of diseases such as wart disease or blight could endanger a whole region's supply of potatoes, but there were varieties available that were resistant to the diseases, such as Arran Pilot, Majestic, Kerr's Pink, Arran Victory, Arran Pink, Arran Comrade, Arran Banner, Gladstone, or Dunbar Standard. Arran varieties dominated the market and were well known and trusted. The Ministry of Agriculture encouraged home growers to stick to the large commercial names, and not to try out varieties bearing uncommon names, tempting though they might be. One problem was that many of the heavy-yielding, disease-resistant potatoes were not as tasty as the older varieties. In 1943 McGill & Smith Ltd of Ayr

Above
As even potatoes became in short supply it was up to everyone to ensure their own stock.

(Scotland) bred what was to become one of the best-known wartime potatoes: Home Guard. A cross between Doon Pearl and Cummock, it gave a very early crop with a high yield. It was immune to wart disease, although susceptible to blight. But what made it so popular was undoubtedly its name!

Storage of large quantities of potatoes was either done in a shed or a clamp, and some versions of Dig for Victory leaflet no. 13 (Storing Potatoes for Food and Seed) had diagrams of how to construct a clamp, although it warned against problems of pilfering. Clamping overcame the problems encountered by housewives of suddenly having to find room to store large quantities of vegetables.

At national level, farmers were encouraged to plant an extra 4–500,000 acres of potatoes. In 1940, a quarter of the newly ploughed-up pasture and parkland was laid down to potatoes. Being a good 'breaking-in' crop they were excellent for such areas. However, the increased demand meant additional worries about the seed stock, and gardeners were increasingly competing against farmers for their seed potatoes. New allotment-holders also found potato crops useful for breaking up their new plots, but their crops suffered from a lack of manure. Potatoes are a 'hungry' crop and ideally need farmyard manure and fertiliser, which was of course in short supply.

I was front-page news a year ago . . . more precious than gold to those lucky enough to get a pound of me. That was because you relied on having me brought to you from abroad. Yet, if women and older children, as well as men, are sensible enough to Dig for Victory now, you can have me ALL THE YEAR ROUND for only the cost of a packet of seeds . . .

YOU SEE, I AM ONE OF THOSE CROPS YOU CAN STORE

DIG FOR VICTORY NOW!

★ ★ ★ If you haven't a garden, ask your Local Council for an allotment. Send NOW for Free pictorial leaflets "HOW TO DIG" and "HOW TO CROP" to Dept. A.103, Ministry of Agriculture, Hotel Lindum, St. Annes-on-Sea, Lancs.

ISSUED BY THE MINISTRY OF AGRICULTURE.

Above
Onions were destined to be one of the first casualties of war.

Onions

Onions were one of the first vegetable casualties of the war. Before the outbreak of war over 90% of onions had been imported, mainly from Spain and France. By the spring of 1941 onions were so scarce that they were almost impossible to buy. During the first years of war onion salt was the nearest many families got to onions, unless they grew them themselves. For the housewife this shortage was a disaster, as onions were added to a wide variety of dishes to add flavour, although often cooked for so long that the actual onion was indistinguishable. Many found the aftertaste of onions objectionable and most often they were used in gravies, stews and casseroles with strong-tasting meat. As meat supplies dwindled the onion took over for flavouring. It was not surprising then that growing these valuable vegetables formed the focus of the government's second Dig for Victory leaflet. At least 75,000 of these leaflets were initially published, with details of appropriate varieties which would store well over the long winter months. In fact storage rather than taste seems to have been the main criterion in choosing which varieties to grow.

Onions had traditionally been thought of as 'difficult' for the amateur grower in England, and more trouble than they were worth, especially as they had usually been in such plentiful supply from abroad. As shortages set in, **Garden Work** encouraged its readers to 'have a go' with onions. They were actually less work than potatoes, not needing ridging up. A rush for onion seed meant that many of the most popular varieties were unavailable in 1940 and 1941 and so the Dig for Victory leaflet no. 2 gave a long list of alternative strains. Foremost among these were White Spanish, Rousham Park Hero, Improved Reading, Nuneham Park, Banbury, Danvers Yellow and Ebenezer. It is interesting to note how many of these had obviously been developed in the large kitchen gardens of English country houses, Rousham Park Hero and Nuneham Park among them. Red onions were traditionally less popular but the nurserymen had developed several strains including Unwin's Reliance, Sutton's Solidity, Carter's Autumn Queen, Carter's Long Keeper, and Carter's Flagon. There were also the wonderfully named James's Long Keeping and Red Wethersfield.

Unfortunately onions do not do well in newly broken-up ground and so those taking on new allotments often had poor crops at first until the soil could be made into a finer firm tilth. Deep trenching was recommended, preferably the previous autumn, leaving the weather to pulverise the soil. A rather demanding

mix of weathered soot, wood-ash, dried blood, steamed bone flour and sulphate of potash was suggested as an ideal soil preparation – with nitrate of potash as an ongoing fertiliser through the summer. Early sowing in boxes was recommended as producing maximum plants from minimum seeds, with outdoor sowing needing about 1oz of seed for 100ft of seed drill. Due to shortages and war economy the Dig for Victory leaflets did not consider using onion 'sets' which became far more common in the following decades as being much

Below
Food production at Knighton-on-Teme, Worcestershire, 1943. HMSO

less trouble and effort. Shallots (also called scallions) were planted as bulbs, as was garlic, for those few who could take the exotic flavour of the latter! The thinnings from some varieties, such as Nuneham Park or White Spanish, might also be used as an early spring onion in salads. For those that still shied away from onions, either in the ground or on the plate, there were always the rather more traditional English leeks.

Where onions were grown successfully on allotments they were often the victims of pilfering, a serious problem by 1942. Although serious looters were usually caught with bags or even sacks of onions a casual 'thief' might think he could get away with taking just one onion, but he would have been wrong. One East London man was fined £1 in July 1943 for being caught red-handed with just one onion, and fined another 10s for trespassing on the allotment to take it. The onion in the case was valued at 2d!

Leeks

Leeks are a traditional British vegetable, happy with the poor weather, easily left in the ground during frost, and available through that difficult January–March period. They had been grown since the medieval period and were always a staple of the peasant and monastic diet. **Garden Work** magazine of April 1941 described them as *'a grand vegetable, easily grown from April and May sowings – a crop that can be planted out on ground cleared of early potatoes or early lettuces, and one that improves with frost, and being lifted from the ground, like parsnips, only as required for use, requires no winter storage.'*

No wonder the government took every opportunity to promote them. Although the long varieties were popular for show, the short-necked thick varieties were best for general cultivation, and Dig for Victory leaflet no. 2 recommended London Flag, Musselburgh and The Lyon. They were however a plant that needed planning, with sowing in March and May of one year giving crops from the following December through to the March of the next year. For many a novice gardener forward planning for crops a year in advance was something new, and many failed in the first year. This caused panic at the Ministry of Agriculture which warned of a glut of lettuces and marrows and not enough winter vegetables such as leeks. A Pathé newsreel depicting a man feasting in summer and dying in winter emphasised the need to plan ahead if you too were not to be caught out by Father Time. Leeks, the Ministry said, were the perfect solution to that winter 'gap'. Blanching, which could be achieved by earthing-up, the use of paper collars or even drainpipes, produced a long white 'stem'. Prizetaker was a popular leek for blanching, although for most victory gardeners time was too short for wrapping leeks in paper collars!

As with the onion pilferer, there were unexpected dangers for leek growers: the **Gardeners' Chronicle** of 19 August 1944 reported that *'Mr F.A. Secrett, adviser on vegetable production to the Ministry of Agriculture, has told Herefordshire farmers how a 4 acre crop of leeks disappeared overnight. The land was near the rugby ground at Twickenham, and a few days before Mr Secrett intended to lift the crop, Wales played England. When he visited his leek field the day after the match, every plant had vanished.'*

"**Who's next?**"

—says the Sprouting Broccoli

Onions, tomatoes and potatoes have all disappeared from time to time. Health-giving green vegetables may also become scarce, unless you grow them yourselves — women and older children, as well as men. Make sure of your family's supply of greens all through the year from your garden.

DIG FOR VICTORY NOW!

★★★ *If you haven't a garden, ask your Local Council for an allotment. Send NOW for Free pictorial leaflets, "HOW TO DIG" and "HOW TO CROP" to Ministry of Agriculture, Dept. C.103, Hotel Lindum, St. Annes-on-Sea, Lancs.*

I S S U E D   B Y   T H E   M I N I S T R Y   O F   A G R I C U L T U R E

Above
Were green vegetables the next to become scarce? The government played on people's worries to get them planting their own winter greens.

Right
Cabbages and kale featured heavily in all government instructions, or 'hints', to victory diggers.

Cabbages and Savoys

Cabbages and savoys of all kinds, plus Brussels sprouts, cauliflower, broccoli and kale were the government's favourite vegetables of the war, providing vitamins through the summer and winter and a ready supply of greenstuffs. That they were the favourite of children is less likely! With the aid of a large quantity of manure, a sprinkling of lime and some protection against the dreaded club root, cabbage crops could be had winter, spring and summer. According to government recommendations, as much as a third of the vegetable garden was to be set aside for these valuable green crops. Club root was to be controlled by 'mercuric chloride' or 'corrosive sublimate' – although as a poison this had to be handled carefully. Popular varieties of cabbage included the wonderfully named Clucas Roundhead, Ormskirk Late Green and Omega. Flower of Spring, Harbinger and Early Market could be sown in July or August for cropping the following spring. Sprouting broccoli, ready in April and May, would supplement greens at this period. Snow's Winter White and Veitch's Self-Protecting were popular. 'Snow' was a famous head gardener of the Victorian period.

Kale (also known by its traditional name of borecole) was disease resistant and would grow in poorly prepared soils. This made it ideal for new allotments. Cottagers Kale was also well known for continuing to regrow small side sprouts even once the main leaves

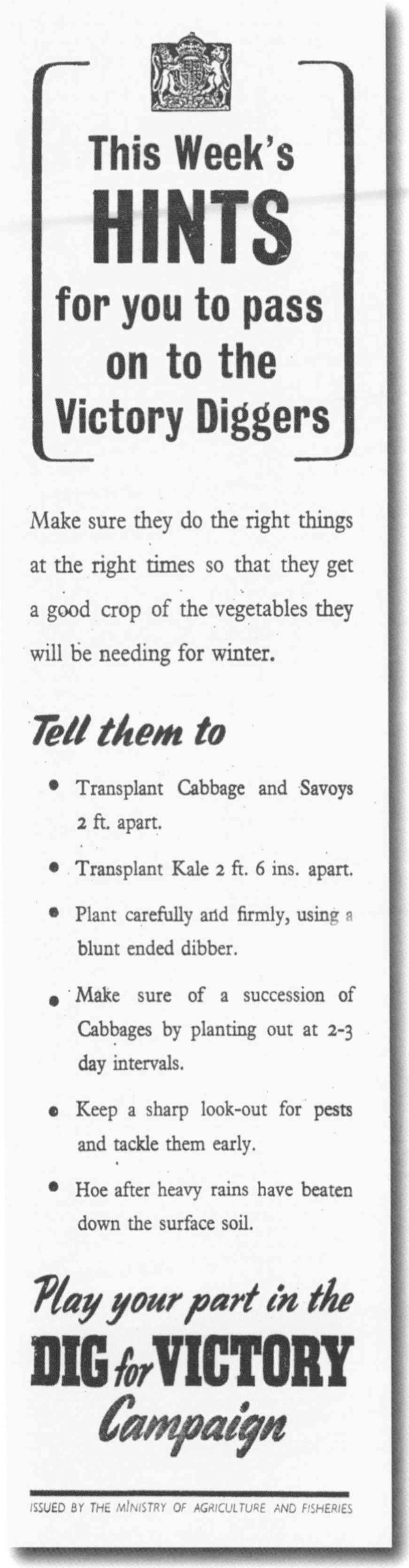

This Week's
HINTS
for you to pass
on to the
Victory Diggers

Make sure they do the right things at the right times so that they get a good crop of the vegetables they will be needing for winter.

Tell them to

- Transplant Cabbage and Savoys 2 ft. apart.
- Transplant Kale 2 ft. 6 ins. apart.
- Plant carefully and firmly, using a blunt ended dibber.
- Make sure of a succession of Cabbages by planting out at 2-3 day intervals.
- Keep a sharp look-out for pests and tackle them early.
- Hoe after heavy rains have beaten down the surface soil.

Play your part in the
DIG *for* VICTORY
Campaign

ISSUED BY THE MINISTRY OF AGRICULTURE AND FISHERIES

had been cut. Its name was redolent of the generations of poor cottagers that had relied on it to see them through the winter. Dwarf Green Curled was more suitable for those trying to cram their vegetables into a small garden rather than an allotment.

Cauiflowers

Cauliflowers could be demanding and were not ideal for the wartime garden. They could be difficult to get to heart-up, and Dig for Victory leaflet no. 5 on Cabbages and Related Crops stated that *'Cauliflowers give best results in districts where extremely hot summers and dry soils are not experienced, and in soils which have been dug deeply and enriched with manure. If these conditions are not possible, it is a waste of time and space to attempt this crop.'* Among those that did grow cauliflowers, Veitch's All Year Round was the most common dwarf variety with small heads, suitable for the smaller family, but with supplies of this variety running short by 1942, most gardeners grew Veitch's Autumn Giant, which produced large heads, popular in peacetime for its success in garden shows. Both varieties had been developed by the Veitch family, Victorian nurserymen and seeds suppliers.

Spinach

Spinach was promoted by the government as one of the most useful vegetables to grow. Rich in vitamins and easily digestible, it grew readily and was available in all seasons. Summer spinach was recommended for cropping between rows of peas, while perpetual or winter spinach (or spinach beet) could survive the worst of winters, although the appalling winter of 1939/40 had proved a challenge even to this hardy vegetable. Spinach could also be grown as a 'catch-crop' between other crops which took longer to reach maturity such as sprouts and cauliflowers, a technique increasingly recommended as the war continued. As ever, a dressing of good garden fertiliser was recommended to ensure sturdy and plentiful growth.

In fact, the only problem with spinach was that many families didn't like it! In the USA, children were enticed into eating the dark green pungent-tasting vegetable by promises of unlikely powers in the cartoon Popeye.

Beans and Peas

" Maybe I am! But it's better than being a blinkin' pessimist!"

Increasing difficulties with providing sufficient meat and dairy proteins resulted in the government encouraging garden writers and correspondents to promote planting of beans, peas and broad beans. The population in general were not as aware of different nutritional values of foods in the 1940s as they are now, and so discussions of different vitamins, carbohydrates and proteins left many confused and wondering why beans made good substitutes for

meat. Haricot beans and French dwarf beans had not been traditional crops in Britain, and only broad beans, runner beans and peas (not including mange-tout) were usually grown. People were encouraged to eat the outside 'haulm' of both the dwarf and runner bean as well as the actual bean as a 'protective food' full of starch. Peas and beans could be stored out of season as dried or salted. Salted runner beans were a long-lasting memory of the war for many, especially when insufficiently rinsed before serving.

Recommended varieties of broad bean in the gardening press included Giant or Four-seeded Windsor for spring sowing, while Dig for Victory leaflet no. 4 (Peas and Beans) printed in 1942, recommended Broad Windsor and Early Long-pod as the easiest beans to grow, demonstrating yet again the divergence between government advice and the traditional gardening press. Not everyone was familiar with growing broad beans: *Worried because his broad bean flowers were turning black, an amateur picked them all off and took them to Manchester's allotment demonstrator for advice. It took some time to persuade him that the flowers are naturally black and white'* (report in July 1943's **Concerning Allotments**).

Peas had long been a mainstay of the small-holder's vegetable plot. Taller sorts of peas available included Pilot and Gradus, although anything needing support, became less popular as the war went on. The shorter varieties of peas had distinct advantages once sticks, string and indeed any kind of support, became in short supply. Meteor, Superb and Forerunner were recommended as first earlies, with the traditional English Wonder, Little Marvel and Kelvedon Wonder slightly later. A main crop might be made up of Senator, Onward, and Advance Guard; the last two suitably stirring military names. In 1942 Onward, Foremost, Early Bird, Pilot, Duplex and Admiral Beatty were all in short supply and Dig for Victory leaflet no. 4 that year had to suggest alternatives. This was made doubly complex by the need to balance the shortage of short varieties with the shortage of sticks for the readily available tall varieties! Sugar peas, although sweet, were unsuitable for wartime production as they were often attacked by birds and mercilessly stripped.

John Hampshire in **The War-time Week-end Gardener** was echoing the belief of many when he wrote: *'Scarlet Runners are, I think, the gardener's standby and his favourite crop. Their gay flowers make a brave show at the bottom of the garden, they are prolific, and with very little care and attention they give him a good crop of a vegetable which is always a firm favourite.'* Varieties such as Rentpayer had been developed specifically for their heavy cropping, making them ideal for wartime use. Runner beans such as Scarlet Emperor, Sutton's Exhibition, Prize Winner, and Best of All were also in short supply in 1942. Pinching out the tops of runners was suggested as a way of getting round the need for the 6–8ft pole supports normally used. In peacetime some optimistic gardening books had even suggested 9ft sticks would be needed. Getting sufficient manure for runner beans was a difficulty, as they are hungry plants and do best with a trench of good manure.

Although broad beans and peas were common on vegetable plots before the war haricot beans were little planted in Britain, although popular in France. The government had tried to encourage people to grow Dutch brown beans in the First World War, but for some reason bean cookery had not been popular here in the way it was in the rest of Europe. The varieties recommended by the Ministry of Agriculture during the Second World War had mostly originated in mainland Europe, including Comtesse de Chambord, Dutch Brown and Ne Plus Ultra. **The Times** of 8 January 1940 wrote, *'The best haricots to grow are those with small, well flavoured beans. Their value is high because they can be eaten in three stages – the pods when sliced, the beans when partially mature like green peas, and the dried beans in winter, when they may be used for soups and to supplement meat in stews, etc. In France Purée Musar is a favourite thick soup. It is made when the haricots are in the second*

Left
Despite shortages of bean sticks runner beans were always popular.
Below
Instructions on the cultivation of celery in *Garden Work* were accompanied by a cartoon showing exact width and depth of trenches.

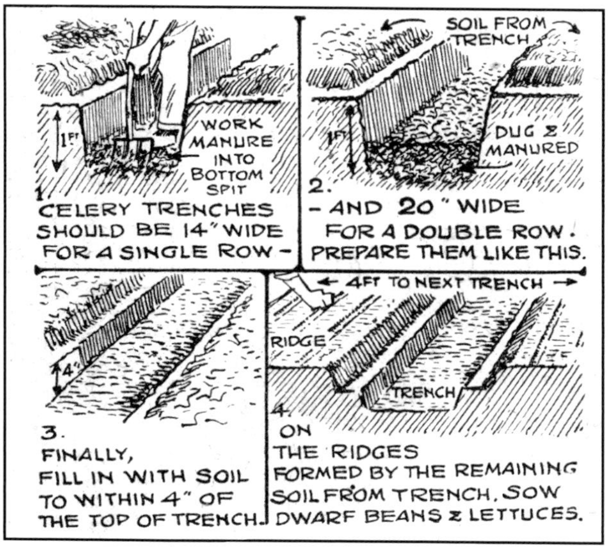
1FT
WORK MANURE INTO BOTTOM SPIT
1. CELERY TRENCHES SHOULD BE 14" WIDE FOR A SINGLE ROW –
SOIL FROM TRENCH
1FT
DUG & MANURED
2. – AND 20" WIDE FOR A DOUBLE ROW. PREPARE THEM LIKE THIS.
4"
3. FINALLY, FILL IN WITH SOIL TO WITHIN 4" OF THE TOP OF TRENCH.
4FT TO NEXT TRENCH
RIDGE
TRENCH
4. ON THE RIDGES FORMED BY THE REMAINING SOIL FROM TRENCH, SOW DWARF BEANS & LETTUCES.

stage and the soup consists of cooked pods and beans rubbed through a sieve and enriched with yolk of egg. The pick of these haricots are the Pea bean, the Dutch brown bean, Comtesse de Chambord, and the Jersey bean. Pea bean – not as the name suggests a hybrid of a pea and a bean – is a most prolific haricot with pods of such delicious flavour that it has been described by a well-known epicure as the pick of the hardy vegetables.'

Celery

Celery was widely thought of as 'difficult' for the novice, demanding blanching by earthing up or forcing. This did not stop **Garden Work** recommending it to its readers, although the detailed and lengthy instructions on trenching, banking, breaking subsoil, manuring with hops and horticultural peat, adding bonemeal and sprinkling salt, planting on, and covering up must have put many off. A correspondent to the **Gardeners' Chronicle**, W.S. Sharp of Durham, argued in January 1940 that celery was almost a mainstay of the northern diet: *'In many northern counties a tea-table is not considered complete without cheese and celery accompanying it',*

and should be considered an essential of the garden. He also noted that some of the vegetables common in London and the south were relatively unknown in the north; Jerusalem artichokes, spinach, sprouting broccoli, scarlet runner beans, kohl rabi, celeriac, salsify and seakale were all, according to him, almost unsaleable in the Durham area.

Almost two years later the argument was still rumbling on, with the **Gardeners' Chronicle** of 22 November 1941 noting that *'Opinion is divided on the question of celery in war-time and the pros and cons are certainly worth consideration. . . . Celery does not yield a large amount of food, but as a set off against that it is to be remembered that food which people like is always good for them because they like it. It sets the salivary and gastric juices going.'*

Carrots, Parsnips, Swedes and Turnips

Root crops were a standard of all victory gardens, and all traditional dinners! 'Meat and two veg' usually included at least one root crop, and parsnips, carrots and swedes in particular were common casserole and stew ingredients. Carrots best suited light and sandy soils and, to prevent forking, they had to follow a crop which had not been highly manured. Rotating crops was some-

Left
An alternative to traditional celery or celeriac was the American self-blanching or summer celery. Less easy to obtain, it needed thorough soil preparation and a temperature of 60°F to germinate. Here it is being grown in Miss Rohde's nursery in Reigate, Surrey. Note the female workers.
Right
Most gardeners grew a relatively small selection of basic vegetables.

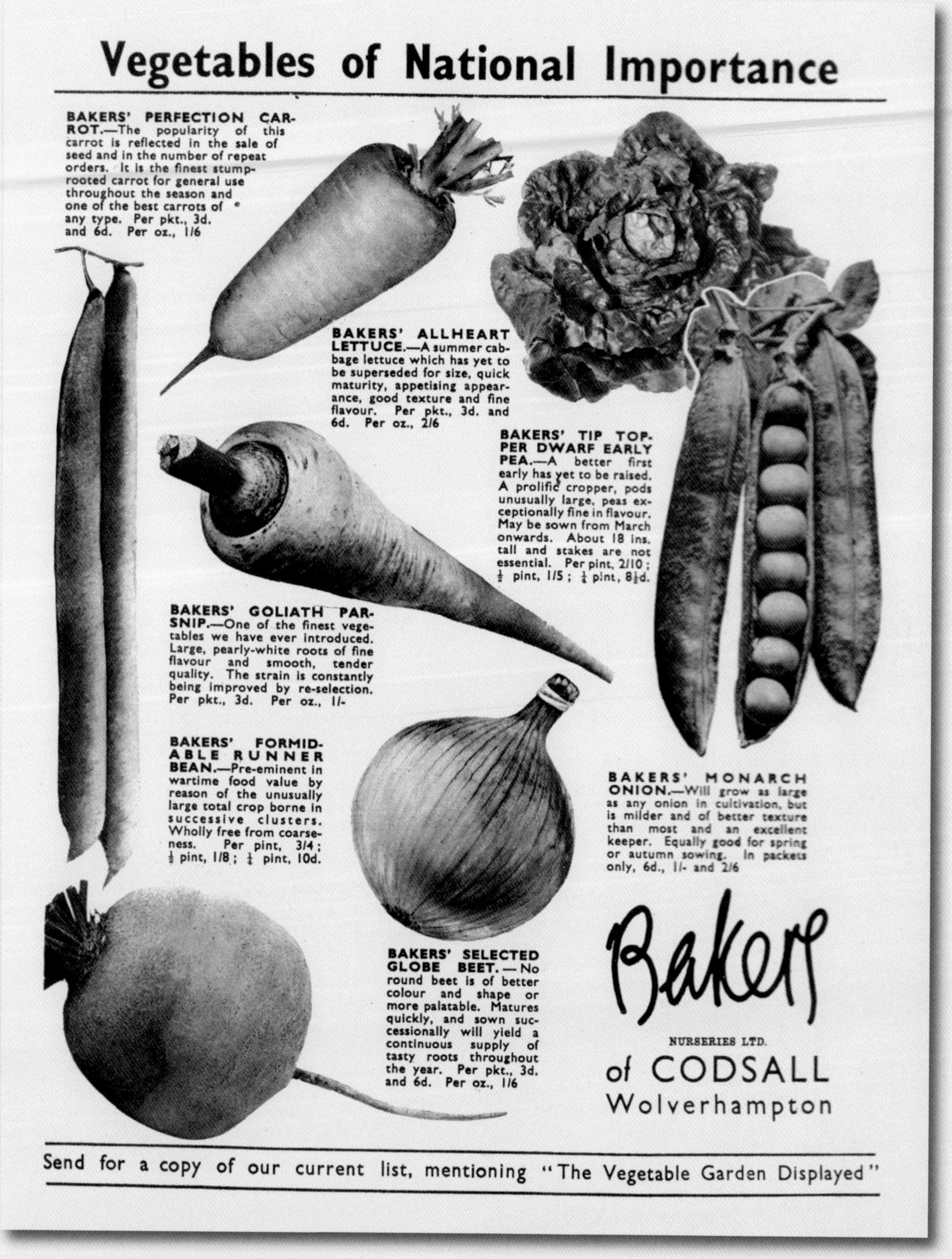
Vegetables of National Importance
BAKERS' PERFECTION CARROT.—The popularity of this carrot is reflected in the sale of seed and in the number of repeat orders. It is the finest stump-rooted carrot for general use throughout the season and one of the best carrots of any type. Per pkt., 3d. and 6d. Per oz., 1/6
BAKERS' ALLHEART LETTUCE.—A summer cabbage lettuce which has yet to be superseded for size, quick maturity, appetising appearance, good texture and fine flavour. Per pkt., 3d. and 6d. Per oz., 2/6
BAKERS' TIP TOPPER DWARF EARLY PEA.—A better first early has yet to be raised. A prolific cropper, pods unusually large, peas exceptionally fine in flavour. May be sown from March onwards. About 18 ins. tall and stakes are not essential. Per pint, 2/10 ; ½ pint, 1/5 ; ¼ pint, 8½d.
BAKERS' GOLIATH PARSNIP.—One of the finest vegetables we have ever introduced. Large, pearly-white roots of fine flavour and smooth, tender quality. The strain is constantly being improved by re-selection. Per pkt., 3d. Per oz., 1/-
BAKERS' FORMIDABLE RUNNER BEAN.—Pre-eminent in wartime food value by reason of the unusually large total crop borne in successive clusters. Wholly free from coarseness. Per pint, 3/4 ; ½ pint, 1/8 ; ¼ pint, 10d.
BAKERS' MONARCH ONION.—Will grow as large as any onion in cultivation, but is milder and of better texture than most and an excellent keeper. Equally good for spring or autumn sowing. In packets only, 6d., 1/- and 2/6
BAKERS' SELECTED GLOBE BEET. — No round beet is of better colour and shape or more palatable. Matures quickly, and sown successionally will yield a continuous supply of tasty roots throughout the year. Per pkt., 3d. and 6d. Per oz., 1/6
Bakers
NURSERIES LTD.
of CODSALL
Wolverhampton
Send for a copy of our current list, mentioning "The Vegetable Garden Displayed"

thing explained in the Dig for Victory leaflets and, with an eye on the possible length of the war, new gardeners were encouraged to consider rotation. Short (stump) rooted carrots were best for amateurs as they were less likely to fork and could be lifted early. Main crops included Scarlet Intermediate and St Valery. As ever there were gardeners who still wanted to grow crops for show – and for those only the longest carrots would do! Special holes 2–3ft deep were created with crowbars and the hole filled with especially light and sandy soils. An armed guard was mounted in case of the dreaded carrot fly and combinations of crude naphthalene, along with the 'usual' weathered soot, creosote and powdered calk, potash, and bonemeal, were all recommended.

Parsnips were an easier crop than carrots, although again shorter varieties such as Empire Globe were more suitable for newly opened ground. Salsify might be grown alongside other root crops by more adventurous gardeners, giving a taste that was said to resemble oysters. It could be left in the ground until wanted, even in the most severe weather, like parsnips. Swedes were popular and wartime recipes included using the green tops in salads and stews. Purple Top and Bronze Top were the main swedes grown.

To encourage almost year-round production of turnips, seeds were sown under cloches or frames as early as February while outside sowing went on as late as July or early August, with Early Snowball and Golden Ball popular turnips. When asked 'What are the most difficult vegetables to grow?' at the 'Dig for Victory' Brains Trust at Portsmouth, Mr Tom Hay, ex-superintendent of royal parks and well-known BBC broadcaster, replied that, on the whole, cauliflowers and turnips were.

Tomatoes

Given the shortage of glass-housing, timber, and glass, during the war the strong emphasis placed on tomato growing might seem surprising. However, many suburban gardeners had greenhouses in place from before the war, used for growing chrysanthemums and asters for show, or indoor cucumbers. At the beginning of the war some gardeners were able to maintain a little heating in the greenhouse and could start early sowings in March, but most had only unheated glasshouses at best and had to await late April or early May. In contrast to onions, which were then usually bought as seed, it was recommended that tomatoes be bought as plants from the nurserymen, which, if they were to be placed outdoors, then needed hardening off in frames or cloches. Outdoor growing was worthwhile in the south and Midlands, but ripening proved difficult further north and plants often suffered from mould and blight.

The fact that the government urged as many people as possible to attempt to grow tomatoes despite the difficulties faced in ripening, and in avoiding whitefly, leaf mould and blight, was a sign of how important they regarded the health-giving tomato. Even green tomatoes could be used in chutneys and pickles, and Dig for Victory leaflet no. 8, 'Tomato Growing is Not Difficult', pointed out that many of the immature fruits could be brought to ripen in darkened drawers and cupboards in spare bedrooms. The most popular tomato

Drawing by C. F. Tunnicliffe

HOW GREEN *is your* GREENHOUSE?

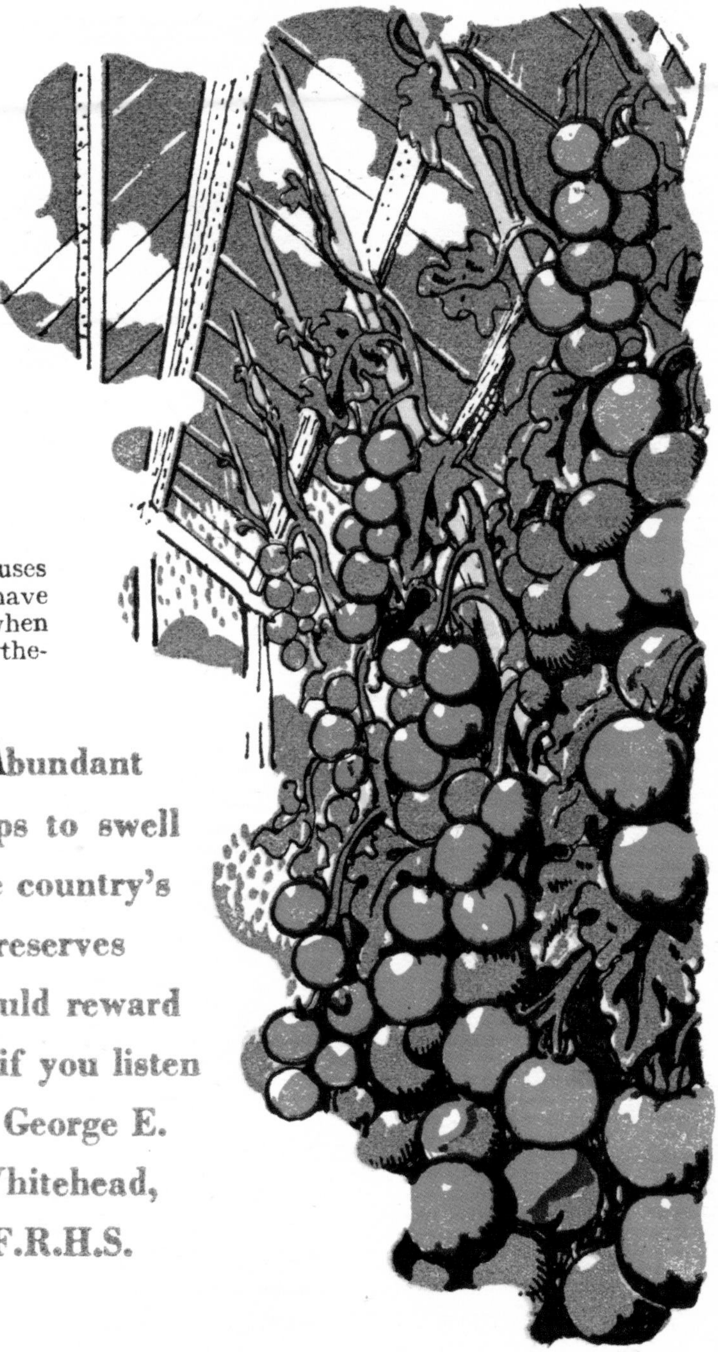

I FEEL reluctant to write about greenhouses because people not fortunate enough to have one are apt to become envious, or bored, when they see an article upon this subject. Nevertheless, they shall be my theme this month because there are so many greenhouse owners who are not growing as much forced food as they ought. It is no exaggeration to state that half the number of small greenhouses dotted about and within the small gardens of Britain are depressing affairs. At this time of year, these places of neglected opportunities contain a few starved, unhappy plants, some dirty, empty pots, some broken deck-chairs, a few miserly remnants of some outdoor crop, such as onions, and hosts of energetic wood-lice, or spiders with cobwebs complete. The last word that should be applied to such a place is "green"—unless it denotes the scum or moss adhering to the glass roof. How to make the greenhouse really green must be the problem of every owner who has not solved it already.

Abundant crops to swell the country's reserves should reward you if you listen to George E. Whitehead, F.R.H.S.

Green or red tomatoes were a valuable crop (Advertisement in *Good Housekeeping*).

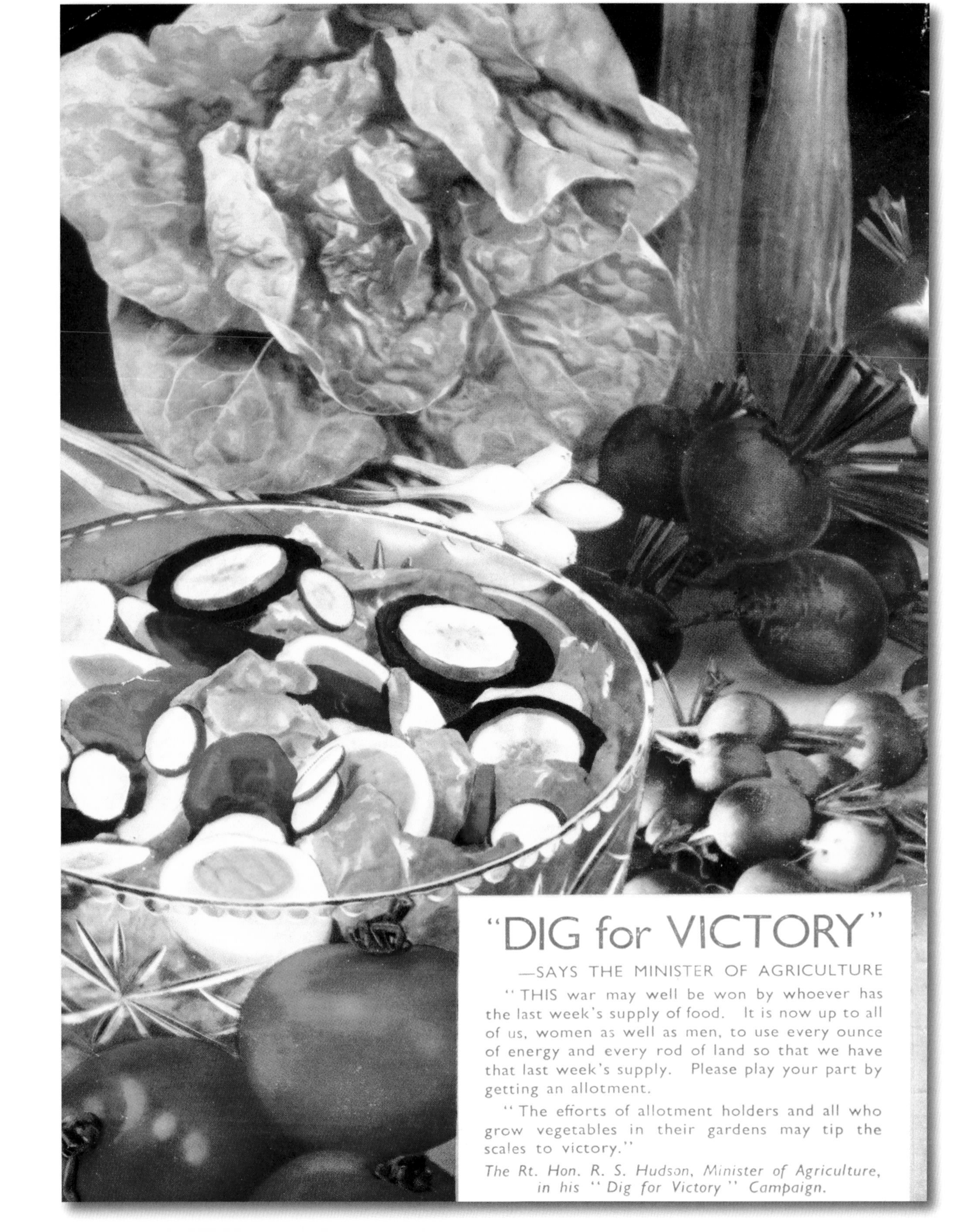
"DIG for VICTORY"
—SAYS THE MINISTER OF AGRICULTURE
"THIS war may well be won by whoever has the last week's supply of food. It is now up to all of us, women as well as men, to use every ounce of energy and every rod of land so that we have that last week's supply. Please play your part by getting an allotment.
"The efforts of allotment holders and all who grow vegetables in their gardens may tip the scales to victory."
The Rt. Hon. R. S. Hudson, Minister of Agriculture, in his "Dig for Victory" Campaign.

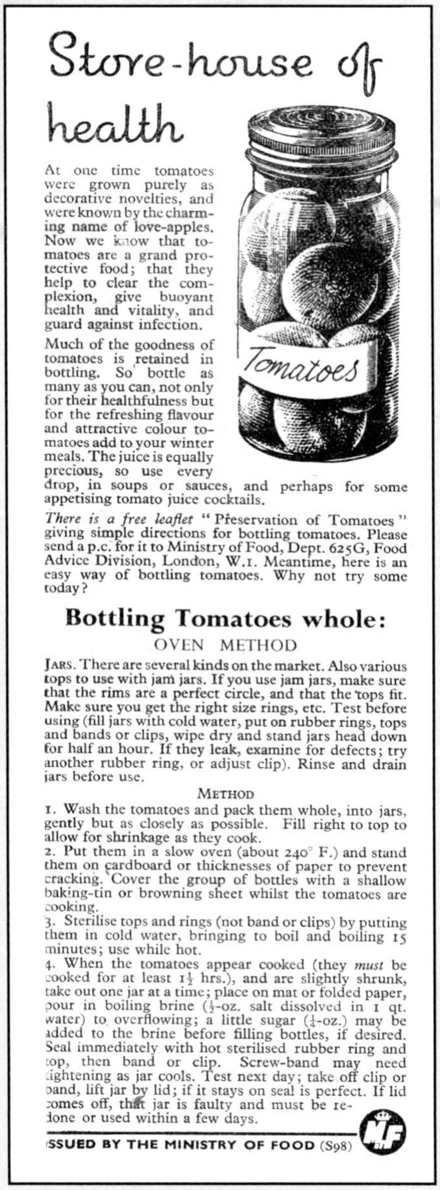
Store-house of health
At one time tomatoes were grown purely as decorative novelties, and were known by the charming name of love-apples. Now we know that tomatoes are a grand protective food; that they help to clear the complexion, give buoyant health and vitality, and guard against infection.
Much of the goodness of tomatoes is retained in bottling. So bottle as many as you can, not only for their healthfulness but for the refreshing flavour and attractive colour to-matoes add to your winter meals. The juice is equally precious, so use every drop, in soups or sauces, and perhaps for some appetising tomato juice cocktails.
There is a free leaflet "Preservation of Tomatoes" giving simple directions for bottling tomatoes. Please send a p.c. for it to Ministry of Food, Dept. 625G, Food Advice Division, London, W.1. Meantime, here is an easy way of bottling tomatoes. Why not try some today?
Tomatoes
Bottling Tomatoes whole:
OVEN METHOD
JARS. There are several kinds on the market. Also various tops to use with jam jars. If you use jam jars, make sure that the rims are a perfect circle, and that the tops fit. Make sure you get the right size rings, etc. Test before using (fill jars with cold water, put on rubber rings, tops and bands or clips, wipe dry and stand jars head down for half an hour. If they leak, examine for defects; try another rubber ring, or adjust clip). Rinse and drain jars before use.
METHOD
1. Wash the tomatoes and pack them whole, into jars, gently but as closely as possible. Fill right to top to allow for shrinkage as they cook.
2. Put them in a slow oven (about 240° F.) and stand them on cardboard or thicknesses of paper to prevent cracking. Cover the group of bottles with a shallow baking-tin or browning sheet whilst the tomatoes are cooking.
3. Sterilise tops and rings (not band or clips) by putting them in cold water, bringing to boil and boiling 15 minutes; use while hot.
4. When the tomatoes appear cooked (they must be cooked for at least 1½ hrs.), and are slightly shrunk, take out one jar at a time; place on mat or folded paper, pour in boiling brine (½-oz. salt dissolved in 1 qt. water) to overflowing; a little sugar (¼-oz.) may be added to the brine before filling bottles, if desired. Seal immediately with hot sterilised rubber ring and top, then band or clip. Screw-band may need tightening as jar cools. Test next day; take off clip or band, lift jar by lid; if it stays on seal is perfect. If lid comes off, that jar is faulty and must be re-done or used within a few days.
ISSUED BY THE MINISTRY OF FOOD (S98)

varieties were Ailsa Craig, Evesham Wonder, and Ideal, the last two suitable for outdoor cultivation, but the demonstration allotments at Kew also grew Best of All, Essex Wonder, Harbinger, Market King, and Stonor's Progress. In the summer of 1943 the tomatoes on the Kew allotment plot were said to attract more interest and visitors than the giant water lily, banana plants or oranges.

Market gardeners were also under pressure to produce as many tomatoes as possible, replacing some of the 3 million tons that had been imported from the Channel Islands, Holland and the Canary Islands before the war. Regulations meant that over 90% of commercial nursery glasshouse space had to be used for tomatoes for up to six months of the year. Glasshouses at country house gardens were also requisitioned for tomato growing – often ousting venerable vines or labour-intensive peaches.

Growing 'salad stuffs', about which the government was so cautious in case it resulted in a summer glut, usually meant lettuces and tomatoes, and perhaps a cucumber (although some people avoided these as they gave 'wind'). Market gardeners were not allowed to devote glasshouse space to cucumbers and anyone found 'harbouring a cucumber' could be taken to court and fined. Even outdoor ridge cucumbers were frowned upon by the government as they took up space for a vegetable with little nutritional value. Needless to say many home gardeners ignored the advice.

As early as the autumn of 1939 **Woman** magazine was advising its readers that *'Salads will be scarce this winter so I advise you to lose no*

Above
Tomatoes were classified as a 'protective food' due to their vitamin content. Eaten raw they contain vitamins A, B1, B2 and C. They were also easy to preserve through bottling.
Left
Despite encouragement in articles in magazines such as *Woman*, salad vegetables in most households focused on tomatoes and lettuce, with eggs if you kept hens.
Right
Marrows had never before been the centrepiece of so many meals. They could also be used as substitutes in jams and flavoured with meat stock as a 'mock' meat.

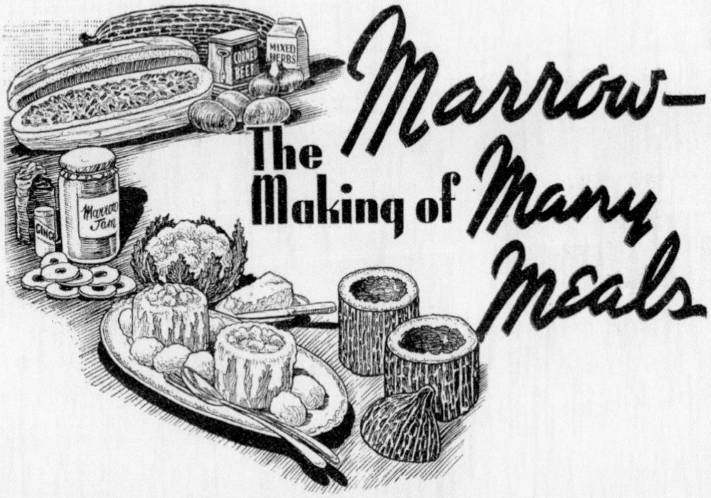
Marrow–
The Making of Many Meals
CORNED BEEF
MIXED HERBS
Marrow Jam

time about sowing corn salad, winter lettuce, mustard and cress, radishes and onions. These will give you a good variety for the salad bowl. The onions will not, of course, develop roots for cooking, but their green tops should serve both for salads and for soups.'

"Is it all right now Henry?"
"Yes, not even scratched"

Vegetable Marrows

'Among voluminous writings on wartime vegetables little has been said regarding Vegetable Marrows, and yet, under present conditions they provide one of the most valuable crops, and one that, for time and labour expended, gives a very satisfactory return. Good strains of Long Green and Long Cream are good for general cultivation. But Rotherside Orange and Custard are extremely good,' said the **Gardeners' Chronicle** of 2 May 1942.

Although the gardening press didn't devote a lot of space to the cultivation of marrows, this reflected the lack of difficulty in growing them more than a lack of enthusiasm among growers. Marrows had always been a source of pride at horticultural shows, and despite official discouragement of 'the largest vegetable'- type competitions, marrows still became the focus of many an amateur gardener's ambitions and pride. With relatively shallow roots and a need for constant watering, marrows were often planted on top of the air raid shelter, where they could be constantly tended.

what does your garden grow?
GOOSEBERRIES!
.. serve them with
BIRD'S
CUSTARD
and use less sugar
EAT more fruit and eat it with Bird's Custard. That is the way to save on sugar, and that is the way to add nourishment to meals. For BIRD'S CUSTARD is easily digested GOODNESS. And, of course, there's the famous extra-special flavour of BIRD'S CUSTARD to persuade children to take their daily quota of milk.
BIRD'S CUSTARD AND JELLIES

Fruit

Fruits (in particular soft fruits and bush fruits) were to form an essential part of the wartime garden, replacing not only the imported bananas and

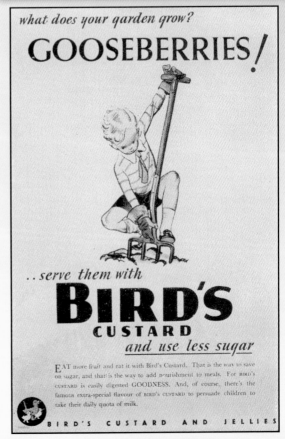

oranges of the pre-war period, but also substituting for sweets and chocolate for the sweet toothed. Shortages of fruit of all kinds resulted from restrictions on imports, as not just oranges, but also pears and even apples had previously been imported. However the government did not include fruit trees or bush fruits in the plot plan in its Grow More and Dig for Victory bulletins. Fruit trees of course need several years to mature before they produce fruits, and also require permanent space. In the first months of the war few people were willing to admit that hostilities would last long enough for trees to come to maturity. Even bush fruits might need a couple of years and it was not until 1942 that Dig for Victory leaflet no. 18 addressed 'better fruit' and disease control on fruit crops in private gardens. As leaflet no. 18 said, *'Fruit grown in private gardens is an even greater asset in wartime than it is in peace. Supplies from overseas can no longer be depended upon and gardeners are therefore urged to do everything possible to ensure bigger and better crops from their trees and bushes.'* In order to achieve this a strict and frequent regime of spraying was recommended, concentrating on apples, pears and plums. Leaflet no. 25 on pruning covered a wider variety of fruits, including blackberries, loganberries, raspberries, blackcurrants, redcurrants, gooseberries, plums, damsons, cherries, apples and pears. Renovation and rejuvenation of old and neglected fruit trees and bushes was dealt with in the hope that some gardeners might have old trees that just needed some care and attention in order to start producing fruits once more.

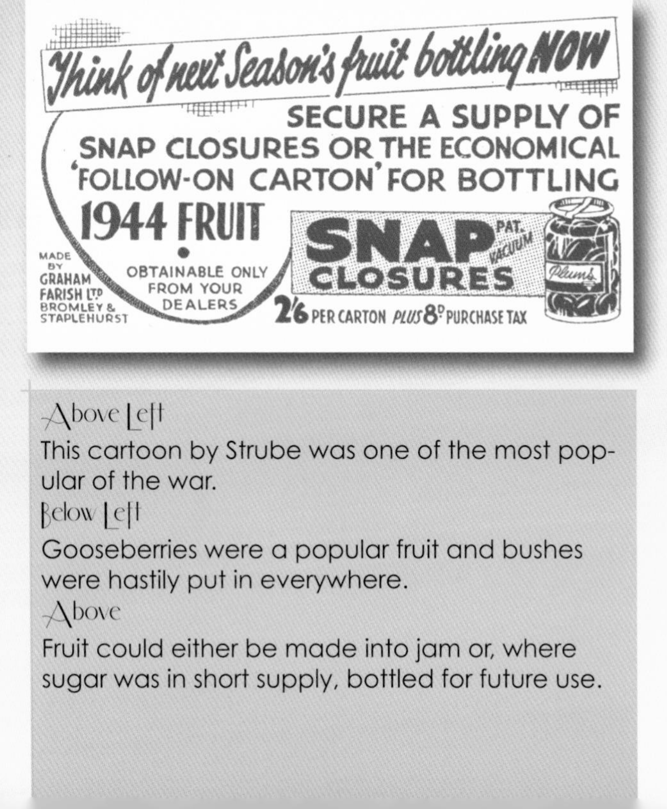
Think of next Season's fruit bottling NOW
SECURE A SUPPLY OF SNAP CLOSURES OR THE ECONOMICAL 'FOLLOW-ON CARTON' FOR BOTTLING
1944 FRUIT
MADE BY GRAHAM FARISH LTD BROMLEY & STAPLEHURST
OBTAINABLE ONLY FROM YOUR DEALERS
SNAP CLOSURES
PAT. VACUUM
Plums
2/6 PER CARTON PLUS 8D PURCHASE TAX

Above Left
This cartoon by Strube was one of the most popular of the war.
Below Left
Gooseberries were a popular fruit and bushes were hastily put in everywhere.
Above
Fruit could either be made into jam or, where sugar was in short supply, bottled for future use.

Maintaining production of tree fruits was still a concern by May 1943, when the Head of the Department of Pomology at Plant Protection Ltd in Yalding (Kent) took out a whole page in **Garden Work** to explain the topic more fully. Although he acknowledged the important role of manures and pest control, what he was mainly concerned to explain was the tricky matter of pollination and fertilisation. Failure to crop was all too often due to lack of suitable cross-pollinators when the plants had originally been put in. Unfortunately his learned explanation of the roles of diploids, triploids, and cross-incompatibility probably went right over the head of many of the readers of **Garden Work**, which was aimed at the novice and amateur. Part of an 'Expert Advice Series' (this was no. 13), it was also backed up by a special leaflet (rather confusingly called leaflet no. 4), for which the bewildered fruit grower could send off. The same edition of **Garden Work** included an article on pests of apples and

pears featuring such delights as the codlin moth, sawfly, nicotine wash and lead arsenate. The plum crop of 1940 was a record one, with a surplus above estimates of 20,000 tons, so perhaps the pests had not had it all their own way.

So as not to waste this bumper fruit harvest an extra sugar ration was issued. The Ministry of Food booklet, **The Market Square**, described what happened: *'The first wartime soft-fruit season arrived and means had to be devised for granting additional supplies of sugar. Two methods were tried; in the first place those who had their own supplies of fruit were granted 6 lbs. per ration book or three-quarters of the weight of fruit, whichever was the less. A little later any applicant was granted an extra 2 lbs. of sugar per ration book on the strength of a declaration that it was to be used for jam making. Neither of these proved to be a very happy method and neither was repeated.'*

Strawberries, that traditional fruit of an English summer, had been provided in the 1930s by acres of nurseries in Kent and Essex. In order to ensure early and consistent supplies, acres of glasshousing had been created. With wartime restrictions in place the strawberry growers had to convert to vegetables, as strawberries were not considered nutritious enough to merit the glass and labour. The government also avoided any mention of strawberries in their cropping plans for private gardeners – despite the popularity of the fruit and the ease with which it could be grown. When short of even home-grown fruit, swedes, parsnips and carrots from the vegetable plot were recommended as ideal substitutes, along with marrow jam.

Unusual and Different Vegetables

Kale and leeks, onions and savoys, broad beans and peas, rhubarb and potatoes; the planting plans envisaged by the government did not extend beyond the most standard diet and hoped-for high-yielding vegetables. It was left to the more adventurous garden writers and seedsmen to extend the gardener's horizons. Missing from the recommended planting schemes were crops that were thought of as either less useful or more difficult to grow. Garlic for example was not initially included in the victory garden scheme, although it appeared in the Dig for Victory leaflet (no. 2) alongside onions, leeks and shallots. By 1943 garlic itself was reaching prices as high as a guinea a pound, from a pre-war price of 3d to 6d a pound, due to the impossibility of importing it from the Mediterranean. The ease of importation before the war, combined with a series of poor summers, had meant that along with the onion, home production had sunk very low and so prices quickly shot up in 1940.

In **Uncommon Vegetables: How to Grow and How to Cook**, garlic was described in rather dubious terms: *'Garlic as a flavouring has enjoyed very little popularity in this country. In fact it is usually regarded as the worst feature of Mediterranean cookery. Now that it is so scarce the general public is learning to appreciate it. In cookery it is useful in any dishes made with mutton, which it renders more palatable. And most thick vegetable soups are improved by the addition of a little garlic.'*

Jerusalem artichokes were generally avoided at mealtimes as they had a well-known side effect of causing of flatulence, although Arthur Brooke, the

Left
Kohl rabi was widely recommended as an easily grown 'catch crop', especially useful as a root crop where turnips would not grow, but many housewives were reluctant to use it. The small green leaves could either be eaten or dug back into the ground as green manure.

well-known wartime allotment writer for **Garden Work** was prepared to give them a try. He told his readers to restrict the tall sunflower-like heads in order to get larger tubers, but didn't comment on the wind. Other less adventurous eaters recommended the Jerusalem artichoke as a shelter for other plants or a screen for unsightly sheds or refuse heaps on the allotment. The crop could be 'lifted as desired' although one gets the impression that this was infrequent at best!

Globe artichokes were also grown for their decorative value as much as their role on the plate. In June 1942 the **Gardeners' Chronicle** commented that *'Although the Globe Artichoke cannot be considered by any stretch of imagination to be an indispensable wartime vegetable, yet for those who seek something suitable and useful for planting in the most cherished and prominent part of the floral*

domains, this handsome and imposing perennial stands unrivalled. It has been somewhat surprising to note that the Globe Artichoke has never been so generally appreciated in this country as it is in France . . . as is well known to former visitors to that at present unhappy country.'

Kohl rabi was another crop that many people were unfamiliar with. In 1943 **Garden Work** suggested that it would make an excellent substitute where there was difficulty in growing turnips. The early white variety, and the later green, were described as 'being very palatable' if used before they became overgrown. Storage was easy and seed readily available, so the government made some efforts to introduce it into the nation's diet, but with little success.

Although asparagus was discouraged by the government, it was still often grown by amateur gardeners, especially in the home garden, tucked away from the prying eyes of allotment societies or pilferers. **Garden Work** advised its readers that: *'Although asparagus is not amongst the vegetables recommended for growing in wartime, those with space to spare may wish to plant a new bed, an operation that should be carried out during the next week or so. . . . Two-year-old crowns take longer to become established than three-year-old crowns, but they are more reliable and should provide supplies the first year after planting.'* This delay in getting a

"WANTED! men and women to grow nutritious MUSHROOMS for WAR TIME FOOD SUPPLIES"

Grow them in your cellar, spare shed, garage, barn, greenhouse, or open garden without interfering with your production of other vegetables. You can make beds that will yield continuous crops worth from 1/6 to 3/6 per lb, according to season. (An area 10 ft. by 10 ft. will yield 200 lbs.)

NO MANURE REQUIRED. The old-fashioned way of making beds with stable manure is now a thing of the past. The new method we show you is revolutionising the industry.

NOW is the time to start. Send to-day without obligation for FREE 32-page book "Mushroom Growing for Profit in War Time" and details of NOMURE Manureless Method of growing. (Enclose 1½d. stamp to cover cost of postage, etc.)

BRITISH MUSHROOM INDUSTRY Ltd.

(Dept. T 27), BEDFORD CHAMBERS, COVENT GARDEN MARKET, LONDON, W.C. 2

WRITE TODAY FOR *free* ILLUSTRATED BOOK

Above
For the adventurous gardener mushrooms were a crop that could be raised from 'kit'. Fortunately 'no manure was required'.

crop was one of the reasons the government did not encourage asparagus, the other being the luxury nature of the crop, taking up considerable space year-round for a relatively small harvest. It was also expensive to start growing. In April 1940, ten 3-year-old crowns cost 17s 6d; this at a time when enough vegetable seeds to feed a family of six for a year were advertised for 2s 6d.

In spring 1942 America sent its own contribution to the Dig for Victory campaign and over 2,500 allotment societies received vegetable seeds from the USA. These included varieties unknown in England, but welcomed by many. The Bridgwater Allotment Association, for example, received twenty-seven hundredweight of seeds including seventeen different types and varieties. Thirty-six thousand packets were distributed as part of the West Country allocation. Sweet corn, then little known in England, was frequently included in these seed donations.

In September 1943 the **Gardeners' Chronicle** recommended the aubergine: *'People who have travelled a great deal often tell us of the delights of Aubergines served as a vegetable in a variety of ways by continental chefs. From the description of these varied dishes it would seem that Egg-fruits can be used much as we use tomatoes. In pre-war days it was not uncommon to see a well-grown batch of Egg Plants in the larger private establishments.'*

One of the most adventurous garden writers of the period was Eleanour Sinclair Rohde whose book on uncommon vegetables was published in 1943. Herbs, old world roses, and Shakespearean plants were the topics usually favoured by this writer, and some of her vegetables were uncommon not just for wartime Britain but for any part of Europe. Mange-tout peas, orach, and cardoons were not usually seen in Britain at this time, although they were common on the other side of the channel, but tree onions, currant tomatoes, Chilean marrows and Chinese artichokes were practically unknown even in the more adventurous and high status gardens of Europe! The introduction to the 1942 Carter's Seed Catalogue agreed with Eleanour Rohde's adventurous approach: *'Where plenty of land is available, the growing of uncommon Vegetables is to be commended, as these provide a welcome change to the more usual kinds.'*

By 1943 the nation was desperate (or at least the garden writers were) to bring variety to its increasingly monotonous wartime diet. **Garden Work** recommended Rohde's book and highlighted artichokes, pokeweed, celeriac, scorzonera, petit pois and Chilean marrows for the more adventurous gardener and cook. As **Garden Work** indicated, *'It is unlikely that market growers will be growing such lines but there are many amateurs who may like to adventure in pastures new.'* Portugal cabbage (also known as couve tronchuda) was also recommended, being in flavour something between cauliflower and seakale. Its appearance, a glaucous green with a remarkably thick stalk, was less prepossessing. Seeds for these vegetables were only available through specialist nurseries, such as that of Eleanour Sinclair Rohde herself. The nation as a whole was becoming slightly more adventurous, and **Garden Work** included chicory, endive and dandelion in their 'seeds to sow this month' section for May 1943. Endives were not widely popular but about 2,000 tons were imported annually before the war. Barbe-de-capucine was the variety recommended for chicory, but it was noted that seeds of this and of dandelion were difficult to obtain. The standard lettuce salads of Webb's Wonderful, Giant White, Nonsuch and Feltham King were much easier to obtain, if less exciting. Steamed rampion roots, from a member of the harebell family, and purslane soup were perhaps rather too exotic for most wartime cooks; indeed Miss Rohde herself admits to not yet having tried the purslane soup, based on an 18th-century recipe.

Seakale, usually planted as thongs but also available from seed, was featured in **Garden Work** too, despite not being considered an essential wartime vegetable, and needing a level of constant attention and preparation that many novice gardeners would have found difficult. Usually blanched, it had been a Victorian and Edwardian delicacy, springing from the days of walled gardens staffed by an army

Above
Celeriac was one of the 'uncommon vegetables' that was described as previously unpopular in the garden and kitchen. Due to shortages in labour during wartime it gained popularity by being quicker and easier to raise than celery, which usually needed blanching.

of labourers. Growing it, and indeed cooking it, was not so common in the 1930s and '40s. One bemused correspondent wrote to ask whether the hard shells on the seeds of seakale needed to be removed before sowing, and was told that it was actually part of the seed and should be left on. Starting with seed was a long process, however, as plants sown in one year would only start to form crowns for transplanting in the following spring, and a further year or more would be needed before any crop could be taken.

Aware that the production of these more unusual vegetables might cause confusion and even dismay when they made their eventual appearance in the kitchen, Miss Rohde included helpful hints for recipes and cooking in her book. Chicory and cheese pie, fried Chinese artichokes, Jerusalem artichoke fritters, and okra in hollandaise sauce were all urged as adding variety to the wartime diet. Some of the recipes must have been compiled before the outbreak of war, or at least the onset of rationing, as they included substantial amounts of butter, cheese and sliced oranges. Those households desperate enough to try golden thistle for the first time in their vegetable plot were most unlikely to have the required cream to make the recommended golden thistle soup and the olives and parmesan cheese necessary for garlic soup *à l'Italienne* were almost impossible to obtain. A letter to the **Gardeners' Chronicle** in January 1940 had recommended lettuce, banana and watercress salad with an orange juice dressing in case of a shortage of lettuce and encouraged others to experiment with fruits in salads. These experiments would have proved short-lived if carried out, as fruits and orange juice were soon unavailable.

HERBS

A 2d. Packet of most of these is enough for an ordinary garden. A large number of Medicinal Herbs will be found in the Flower Seed General List.

7814	Angelica, h.p.
7816	Anise, h.a.
7818	Balm, h.p.
7820	Basil, Sweet,* h.h.a.
7822	Basil, Bush,* h.h.a.
7824	Borage, h.a.
7826	Burnet, h.p.
7828	Caraway, h.b.
7832	Coriander, h.a.
7836	Dill, h.b.
7838	Fennel, Sweet, h.p.
7842	Horehound, h.p.
7844	Hyssop, h.p.
7846	Lavender, h.p.
7848	Marjoram, Sweet,* h.p.
7850	Marjoram, Pot,* h.p.
7852	Pennyroyal, h.p.
7854	Pot Marigold, h.a.
7860	Rampion, h.p.
7862	Rosemary, h.p.
7864	Rue, h.p.
7866	Sage,* h.p.
7868	Savory, Summer,* h.a.
7878	Thyme, Winter,* h.p.
7880	Wormwood, h.p.
7886	Dandelion, h.p.
7894	Valerian, h.p.
7896	Belladonna, h.p.
7900	Opium Poppy, h.a.

* Herbs which are invaluable as flavourings for many dainty dishes.

Abbreviations are described at commencement of Flower Seeds.

Some of the crops that people attempted were not just unusual but foolhardy. A Mr or Mrs Brown from Leicester, writing to **Garden Work** in 1941, had become so desperate about the lack of sugar for making jam that s/he proposed planting sugar beet for home use and extracting the syrup. The writer was anxious to know how many beet seeds would be needed to eventually obtain sufficient syrup for 40lb of jam, and how exactly the syrup could be extracted. The editors replied that although there would be no difficulty growing the sugar beet, the extraction in a normal household kitchen would be 'a tedious procedure even if it proved successful, which is doubtful'. Ingenuity had for once failed to win the day and Mr/s Brown was forced to face sugar rationing with the rest of the population.

Herbs

Herbs were another area where 1940s Britain was largely conservative in comparison with other European countries. Parsley, mint, sage, rosemary and thyme were the standard herbs – often reduced to parsley, mint and thyme in the vegetable bed, with rosemary and sage plants sometimes appearing in borders. In 1941 **Garden Work** recommended that its readers include lemon thyme, common thyme, tarragon, marjoram, mint, sage and chervil, although it also suggested they might like to order other herbs from advertisers in its own magazine. As Eleanour Rohde commented 'most people conjure up a vision of a dull little patch of Parsley, Mint, Etc'; in fact flowers such as bergamot and hyssop, lavender and chives were ideal border plants. Included in her book were traditional but little-used herbs such as alecost, bergamot, purslane and pennyroyal, as well as ones that had survived into modern usage such as garlic, mints, chives and angelica. Her recipes also veered between the wartime practical (mint jelly, mint and onion stuffing) and the less achievable under wartime conditions (mint and orange jelly, sorrel sauce with roast duck). 'Mock' coffee made with dandelion root was something that many people recall using during wartime when the real thing became hard to get. In fact ground roast dandelion root was still used to bulk out coffee in many Eastern European countries until recently. Miss Rohde was careful to recommend only small pinches of the herb pennyroyal in her recipe for pennyroyal eggs, undoubtedly knowing that one of its main medicinal properties is as an abortifacient, although it was also used to cure headaches. Herbs were not only grown for culinary, but also for medicinal purposes; Lord Woolton himself had declared the garden as 'the nation's medicine chest'.

Tobacco

Tobacco was grown in gardens and allotments during the war, providing some relief from the high taxation and shortage of cigarettes. It was not on the government's recommended list of food crops, but seed became readily available once demand was established. This was not to be confused with the popular annual flowering tobacco plant (*Nicotiana affinis*), which was recommended for bringing colour and scent to a garden, although one suspects that a few novice gardeners sent for some 'nicotiana' expecting something rather different from the colourful display they eventually raised! Although legal to grow tobacco, it was illegal to dry and smoke it. Needless to say many gardeners did just that, disregarding both the legal niceties and the generally low quality of home-produced 'baccy'. Fines were relatively rare as most consumption was in the home, but some were caught and prosecuted for defrauding the nation of tax and producing tobacco without a licence.

Left
List of herbs available from Ryders' seed catalogue, 1941 (code: h.a. – hardy annual, h.p. – hardy perennial, h.b. – hardy biennial and h.h.a – half-hardy annual).

Put your best face forward...

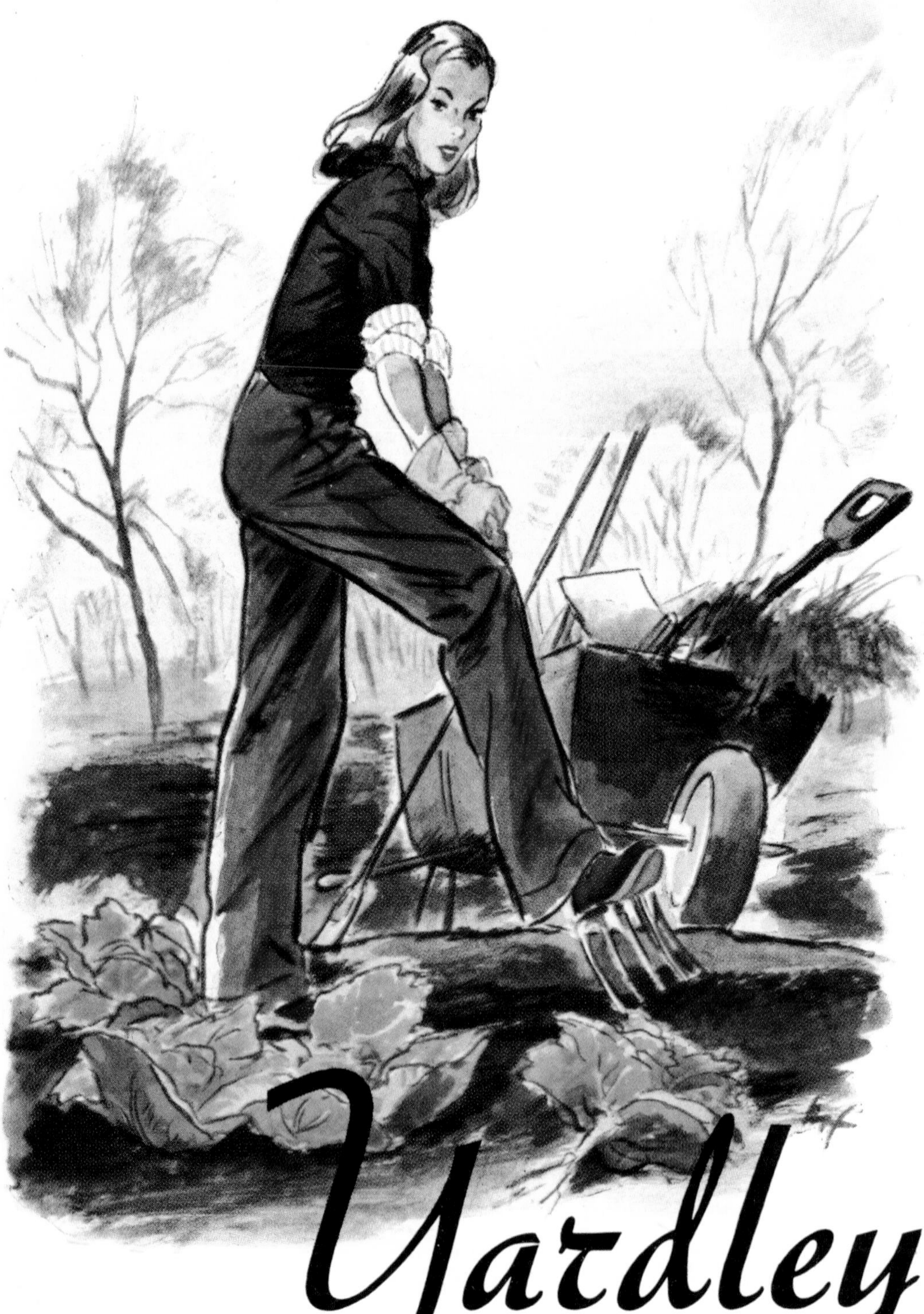

Because the loveliness they give seems truly natural, Yardley beauty-things are more precious today than ever.

Remember, they still have all the qualities you know and trust.

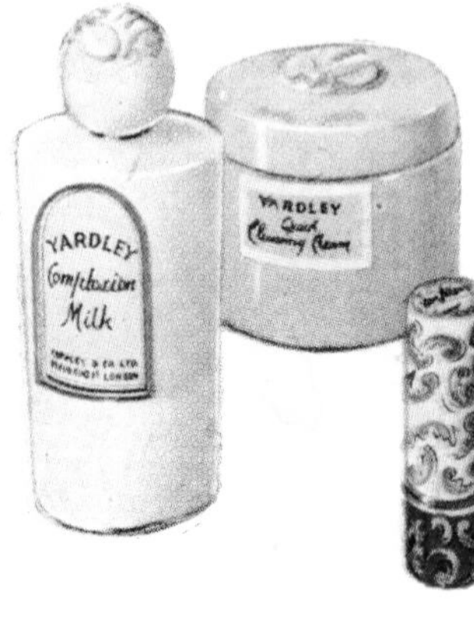
YARDLEY
Complexion Milk

Yardley

✱ *If you have any war-time beauty problems write to Mary Foster, the Yardley Beauty Consultant. She will be very glad to help.*

33 OLD BOND STREET · LONDON

The allotment army

Allotments and the 'Allotment Army' soon became the backbone of the Dig for Victory campaign, producing food that was to be vital if the war was to be won and the nation fed. In December 1939 the **Gardeners' Chronicle** wrote: *'During the war it is the duty of every able-bodied person who has the necessary time and land, to grow sufficient vegetables for his or her own family. . . . It is the duty of every parish council, urban council or county borough to provide land for allotments for all those who require land.'* An 18th-century innovation, allotments had played a vital role in the First World War. When the Kaiser had threatened to starve Britain into submission, allotment-holders had rapidly been recruited as patriotic producers, and allotment numbers had risen to nearly two million. In the postwar period, interest, and allotment availability, had fallen dramatically, so that they numbered about 8–900,000 by 1939. On 3 October 1939, Sir Reginald Dorman-Smith, Minister of Agriculture, announced that the government would be making available 500,000 new allotments as part of the Grow More Food campaign. It was calculated that these extra plots would feed a million adults and one and a half million children for eight months of the year. Under this scheme, the Ministry of Agriculture encouraged local authorities to search for land that was either unused or used unproductively, and to compulsorily

Left
Yardley used this very modern-looking woman on her allotment plot in their advertisements in *Good Housekeeping*.
Above
A view of wartime allotments.

rent it for an agreed agricultural rent. This land would then be turned into allotments for the duration of the war.

The government's aim was to have at least one allotment for every five households, although some towns far surpassed this. By the spring of 1945 Thetford in Norfolk had one allotment for every two households, and Sittingbourne (Kent) was not far behind with 2,000 allotments between 5,000 houses. In August 1943, Mr R. Hudson (Minister of Agriculture) was able to declare that *'It may not be easy to define what an allotment is, but it is like an elephant, you recognise it when you see it'*, and by the end of the war it was estimated that more than half of all working-class families were 'Digging for Victory' either on an allotment or in their own garden.

Provision of Allotments

The response to the government's 'call to plot' was immediate. Everywhere green and pleasant land turned brown as areas of pasture and lawn were ploughed for the first time in decades, in some instances the first time in hundreds of years. Previously sacrosanct playing fields were turned overnight into 10-pole plots waiting to play their part in the home front war. Local and town councils ploughed up parks and commons as well as playing fields and school plots. Take-up of new plots was generally good, especially in the traditional areas of allotment cultivation: the Midlands and north-west England, and around the manufacturing towns. Dennis Robbins remembers helping on his father's allotment: *'During the war, Mitcham Borough Council used the Figges Marsh Recreation Ground as allotments. This was a very large area stretching from the Streatham Road, Mitcham, to the borders of Tooting, and the area consisted of some 1,000 to 1,500 allotments. My father, Mr William John Robbins, had an allotment free of charge and I, being a young and energetic 10-year-old, helped him dig, sow seeds, thin, weed and transplant seedlings in aid of the Dig for Victory campaign. My mother, Edie Robbins, would barter fresh vegetables and eggs to neighbours in exchange for clothing coupons.'* Within just a week of the government announcement that new allotments were to be made available, an area of 8 acres had been allocated as 'residents' productive gardens' in Tunbridge Wells, the plots had been cleared and spadework already commenced, with low rents encouraging take-up. **The Times** was so inspired by this early example that they suggested that similar schemes

Above
New allotments being dug in a London park.
Right
Many of the London squares were dug up for allotments, ousting their previous privileged inhabitants. This cartoon by Fougasse shows the changes wrought by the wartime campaign.

be set up on golf courses, with members clubbing together to form golfing allotment societies! By summer 1940 the traditional 'allotment' counties of Yorkshire and Lancashire already had 62,000 and 34,000 allotments respectively, despite early confusion as to who one should apply to in order to get one (some articles recommending the National Allotments Association, others the local council). The rush for seeds and tools evidenced much enthusiasm that first autumn and winter.

In September 1940 a further 500,000 people were urged to become part of the Allotment Army and to join what was by then the Dig for Victory campaign. Mr R.S. Hudson (who had replaced Sir Reginald Dorman-Smith as Minister for Agriculture in May 1940) urged that *'by next spring the total number of allotments in Great Britain would be two million',* and added that *'if we could get the number of allotments in this country to three million, we could be certain that six-hundred-thousand adults and nine-million children would be amply supplied with green vegetables during the greater part of the year'.*

By February 1941 over 1.3 million copies of the Dig for Victory leaflet, which included an application form for an allotment, had been requested, and the campaign was well on its way. The number continued to increase throughout the war, with many corporations and councils pressurised into releasing

The Old-world Square—1

The Old-world Square—2

ornamental areas of public parks for allotments.

Not everyone was enthusiastic, however. In January 1940 it was reported that Accrington Corporation had reprieved the local parks from being ploughed up for allotments while they looked for ground elsewhere, and in spring 1940 the parks superintendent for Accrington was busy propagating ornamental plants as normal. Despite this initial reluctance in some areas, in time the number of allotments almost reached the three million enthusiastically predicted by Mr Hudson. Rents were typically 1s a pole (a 10-pole plot cost 10s), with tenancies usually of one year. Over 6,000 allotments were estimated to have been created in the London parks, including 30 acres at Bushey Park, and 4 acres at Greenwich Park. Pig clubs were also created at Battersea, Wimbledon, Wandsworth and King George's Square – all of course purely temporary. Sites on private land such as the royal parks did not guarantee tenancies after the end of the war as they had only been acquired under war emergency legislation. This lack of tenure was to cause difficulties later on in the war as plot-holders realised that it might not be worth planning for the next year. Inevitably this started to happen well before the actual end of the war.

Throughout the war the gardening press reported the number of new allotments created and the weight of produce coming from them. In Slough, for example, it was reported that over 1,600 allotments had been created in the first year of the war, spearheading the campaign for more allotments in the south-east of the country, while in Portsmouth the number of pre-war allotments, 1,784, was almost doubled to a total of 3,384. By February 1941 the Royal Borough of Windsor had over 1,300 allotments, Heston and Isleworth (Middlesex) had 3,360 (one for every seven households), Gravesend had 1,150, and Cardiff over 3,000 wartime allotments (in addition to normal peacetime allotments). By the next month it was said that Harrow had bettered Cardiff, with 3,315! The number of allotments rose every year throughout the war, as each city and parish competed with its neighbour for numbers of plots and foodstuff produced. In 1941 Kettering had 2,000 plots producing £15,000 worth of food, while Walthamstow had 2,500 allotments – or in their own unique term 'food plots'. Newcastle managed 5,000 allotments by May 1941, but Sheffield topped this with 9,000 at the same date. The **Gardeners' Chronicle** in December 1944 estimated that the average annual value of the food produced by allotment-holders in Britain during the war was £17,250,000.

Allotment societies, usually overseeing one or two sites depending on the number of plots per site, were a vital part of the organisation and administration of sites. The National Allotment Society had been set up in 1930 and coordinated 600 affiliated local societies. After the outbreak of war in 1939 the number of societies leapt to 1,800 and by 1941 this had further increased to 2,300. The government used the National Allotment Society as a conduit for giving instruction, encouragement, organisation and even grants to its local societies. During the war the National Allotment Society received £1,500 a year to help it form and encourage new societies. **Garden Work** in March 1943 reported

" My Commando son thought he'd help me on the allotment—but it's been too much for him ! "

that *There are no fewer than thirty-eight allotment associations at Newport (Mon.). Last year the Corporation supplied their Victory Diggers with many thousands of plants of tomatoes, leeks, onions, brassicas; seeds; stable and artificial manure, and nearly 4,000 bundles of pea sticks and bean rods.'* By the end of the war there were nearly 4,000 affiliated associations representing some 1,500,000 allotments, other allotment sites being overseen by railway companies, the church or private landowners.

As the war progressed conscription and war-work meant men had less time for the allotment; the Vicar of Witham in Essex, the Rev. B.E. Payne, arranged short services for allotment-holders early on Sunday to try to free up the afternoon for the allotment, but there were still too many calls on many men's time. The government tackled this by encouraging women to take on their own allotments, or at the very least cultivate their husband's plot. By October 1942 over 10,000 women had taken up wartime allotments in England and Wales. Middlesex alone had 1,650 female allotment-holders and Finchley had more than any other borough in the

country (550). Yorkshire was second to Middlesex with 1,200 women plot-holders in the county.

Although the allotment campaign was country-wide, as ever the national press gave prominence to the efforts of Londoners. Public parks, royal parks, as well as the Tower of London moat became home to patriotic plot-holders. Every green space, from the small London squares like St James's to the huge open spaces of Battersea Park, was marked out and handed over to allotments. As the war progressed, bombsites were also cultivated, a very visible method of propaganda. Bombsite allotments were a favourite subject of Pathé newsreels with the obvious overtones of triumphing over adversity. Some cities that had suffered badly from the blitz

Left
Allotmenters-holders were constantly encouraged to feel that their contribution was as worthwhile as that on the fighting front, and at least as hard.

Above
Even the moat at the Tower of London was used for allotments, with the lucky plot-holders having some of the richest soil ever! HMSO

also had a high percentage of women plot-holders, often utilising bombsite gardens. The Bethnal Green allotments were the most famous of the bombsite vegetable plots. Four hundred workers, plus members of the Young Farmers Club – all children under sixteen – ran a series of smallholdings on these large sites. Pigs, poultry, rabbits and even a Nubian goat joined the rows of potatoes and onions flourishing among the ruins. In an attempt to encourage the numbers of new allotment sites in bombed areas, the Queen visited the Bethnal Green allotments in June 1943, praising the work of children like Ernest Gander, who was in charge of the allotment pony and the Nubian goat. Playing to the media the goat ate two Red Cross Onion Scheme leaflets in front of the royal party.

Allotments were also set up at workplaces and around newly established service quarters by firemen, ARP workers, and others. **Garden Work** of 20 March 1943 reported that: *'The Guild of Ex-Patients of Guy's Hospital, London, SE1, is doing a grand job of work in its wide appeal for fresh vegetables, several tons of welcome produce being received last year. Allotments Associations in many parts of London are joining in the effort. Parcels of vegetables for Guy's (collected daily) may be left at the First Aid Post, Platform 10, London Bridge Station.'*

To provide a very practical guide on what your allotment should look like throughout the year, model allotments were created in many public areas. The most famous of these was at Kew Gardens. After closing briefly on the outbreak of war, Kew had reopened and became a popular holiday attraction during the war. The model allotment at Kew was created in January 1940, based on the first of the Ministry of Agriculture's Grow More bulletins. Regular talks were given at the site, attracting local allotment-holders from the Kew, Richmond and Barnes Allotments Associations. As the allotment campaign became widespread the allotment became a focus of interest and brought more visitors to Kew, with a head demonstrator, Miss P. Cornwell, on site to give advice and answer questions. Two demon-

stration plots were also laid out in Hyde Park; officially opened by the Minister of Agriculture on 5 December 1940 (although actually dug the previous autumn), the superintendent of the park gave talks on gardening techniques. Even London Zoo had a 10-pole plot featuring tomatoes grown from seeds sent over from America. In summer 1940 London Zoo put on a National Wartime Utility Exhibition, which featured specimen wartime back gardens, complete with cloches to help extend the growing season. Demonstration plots on allotment sites and public parks often met with an unexpected degree of interest from experienced gardeners and allotment-holders who were keen to see if their own plots were better than the model one. The **Gardeners' Chronicle** of 21 September 1940 reported that: *'In many localities demonstration plots have been maintained on the allotments site by the local authorities with a view to assisting holders in arranging their own crops etc. So far as the produce is concerned, this has not always had the desired results, and the professional gardeners responsible for the demonstration plots have had to submit to a certain amount of raillery because their crops were not always superior.'*

In his book, **Wartime Gardening with Mr Middleton**, the nation's favourite gardener admitted that: *'The older I get the more I realise how difficult it is to give advice on cropping an allotment; allotments and gardens are individual things, not all alike, any more than people's tastes are, and you can't generalise or lay down any one example scheme to be applied to all allotments. It's no use, for example, including parsnips in the cropping plan if you don't like parsnips. On my table I have quite a number of different leaflets showing how to crop an allotment;*

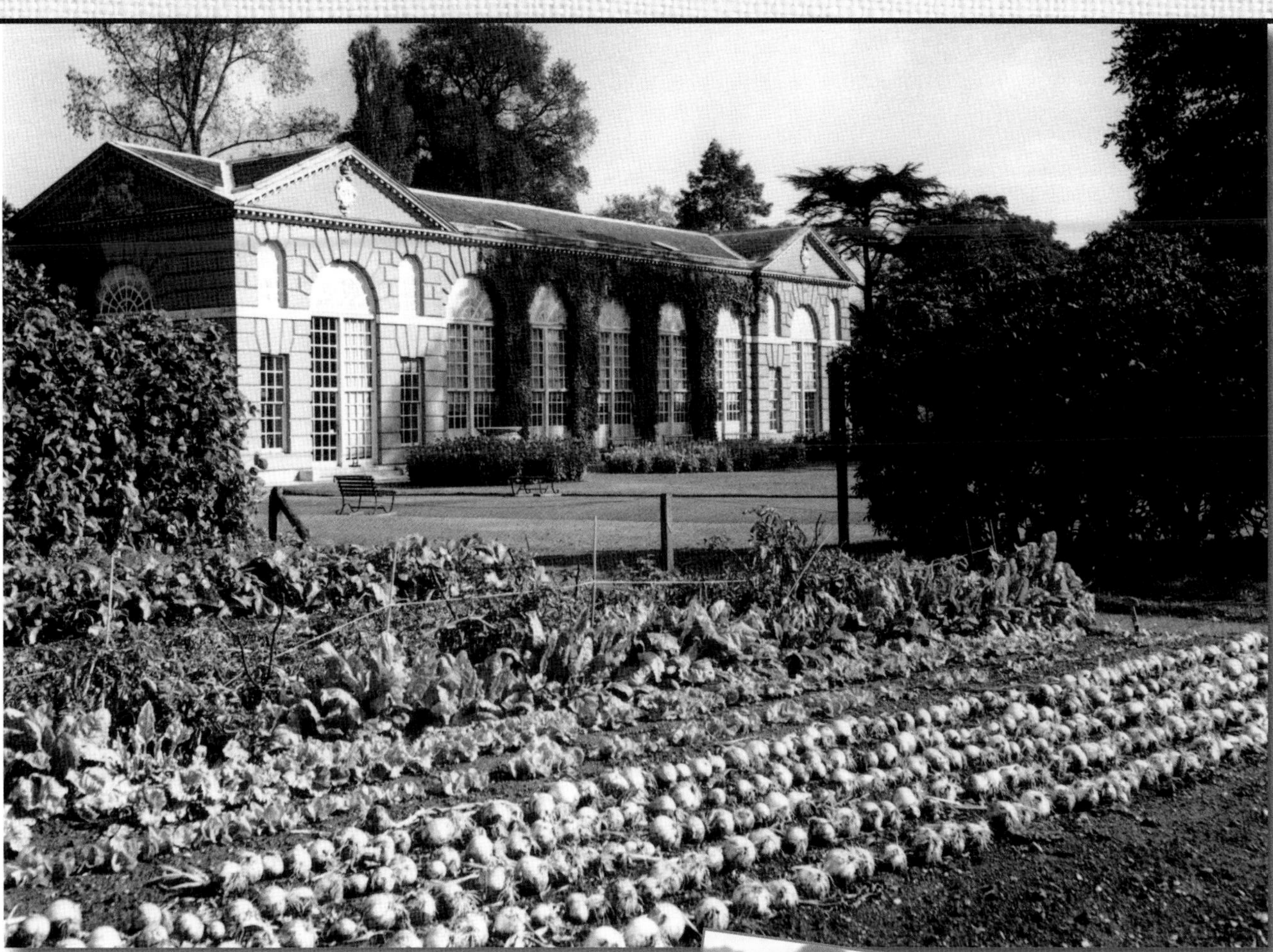

they are published by various authorities, and although they differ a good deal in detail, they are all good, and I have no fault to find with them, but I do suggest that you shouldn't slavishly follow them in every detail. So many people, I find, religiously copy these ideas and then they find they have grown a lot of things they don't want.'

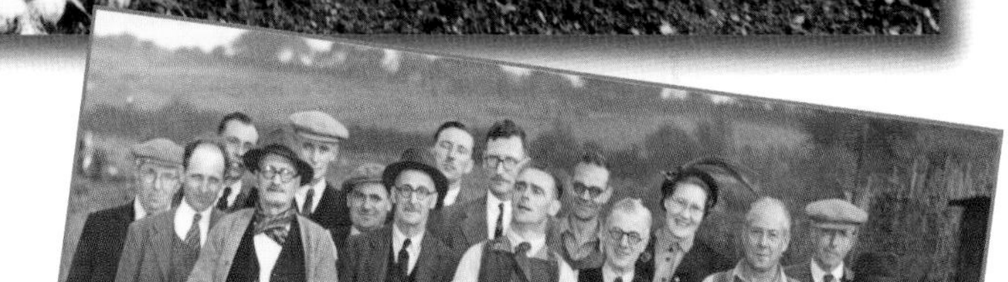

Allotment News

All the gardening magazines and local papers patriotically reported on the achievements of allotment societies and even individual allotment-holders as well as giving hints on allotment cultivation. Sent in by proud society secretaries these enumerated quantities of crops grown, equivalent money saved,

Above Top
Model allotment in front of the orangery at Kew Royal Botanic Gardens. HMSO
Above
Standing proudly to attention these plotholders show off their potato crops. THE GARDEN MUSEUM

These members of the Darby and Joan War Workers in Manuden, Essex, carried out work on the farm as well as on allotments. Mary Hannah Debnam is shown with her husband Hubert (both aged 67).HMSO

new members recruited, and even numbers of pea sticks sold! There was so much allotment news that there was simply not enough room to include it all despite some magazines giving an entire page to coverage of the home front efforts. The 12 April 1941 edition of **Garden Work** contained news items on surplus crops at Petts Wood Allotment Society (Kent), 400 new allotment-holders in the city of Worcester (bringing the total number to 2,000), a review of school allotments in Breconshire, discussion of the expanded powers of the Battersea Rise Allotment Society, and highlighted the achievements of Mrs McGarry of Blackburn who *'last year worked three allotments simultaneously, all on virgin land'*. In 1943 the same magazine carried encouraging news on the 'longest held' allotment: this was held by Mr H. Lunn, a retired

Southern Railway driver, who had cultivated the same railway-side allotment for 29 years.

To encourage even greater efforts the Ministry of Agriculture announced in June 1940 that it had created an award scheme for those who were making best use of their plot for food production. *'Certificates of Merit, signed by the Minister of Agriculture and Fisheries, are to be awarded to allotment-holders whose plots, in the opinion of the judges, are best cultivated to produce a continuous supply of the most suitable vegetables throughout the year. Every allotment entered for the competition will be visited twice by the judges who will give points for cultivation, rotation, planning, compost heap, control of weeds etc.'*

The certificates were so popular that in 1941 the Ministry of Agriculture received over 10,000 entries for the award of a Certificate of Merit. Of those 4,000 reached the required standard of 'efficiency' and were awarded certificates. In Bridgwater alone 791 entries were sent and 148 certificates awarded. West Bromwich gained 146 awards and Mitcham (Surrey) 139. In 1941, the National Allotments Society issued Dig for Victory badges at 3d each for allotment-holders to wear to show that they were 'doing their bit'.

By 1942 conscription and pressure of duties on the home front in the ARP and other organisations meant that the government was increasingly trying to attract women, children and the elderly on to allotments. Over 700,000 old age pensioners were recorded as doing their bit for the war effort, joining the many Darby and Joan War Workers working on allotments or farms. *Concerning Allotments* reported in November 1944 that, *'A gift of 500 packets of seeds from American Old-Age Pensioners* to Launceston (Cornwall) Allotments Association was gratefully appreciated. Some of the seeds went to blind allotment-holders.'

Children usually helped out on their parents' allotments – although some remember it slightly differently! Harold Taylor recalls that *'When war was declared I was 13¼. I do not exactly remember the date, but with my father we opened up our first allotment on land which had been used by Riding Stables horses. This was in Chichester, Sussex. From what I remember I did all the digging and my father turned up to do the planting. The ground was double dug in order to bury the turves at the bottom. Later we opened up another allotment not far away on ground which had also been used by the stables'.*

Bombs, Burglars and Dogs: Hazards of the Plot

Tales of bombed allotments with potatoes scattered far and wide have taken on the status of legend – or myth! However, it did happen. Even the *'Digger for Victory who Shares his Doubts and Difficulties'*, who wrote every week in **Garden Work** was on the receiving end; an outsized bomb left a crater on his plot 20ft deep and 35ft across, at least according to him. As he said, *'it looks like a real wartime allotment now'*! There was still some allotment left, although all top-dressed with a fine clay subsoil, and a nearby 5-pole plot was available to replace the plot that had been lost, at least until there was a chance to put some fresh hardcore and soil into it.

Norman Cattell remembers a plane coming down on the allotments in his North London suburb. The local park had been turned over to allotment plots for local residents, all tended with much care and enthusiasm. *'One day a transport plane, probably on its way to or from the local Hendon aerodrome, crash-landed in the park, skidding over several allotments as it did so. An elderly gentleman arrived hot-foot at the news and, told he was not allowed onto the site, replied to the special constable on-duty, "Never you mind about that, just you take that there aeroplane off my 'taters'." It was to become a catch-phrase for all the local lads for the rest of the war! Although the plane itself had done relatively little damage to the allotments, the emergency and recovery crews that came to recover it totally devastated the precious crops. Amazingly for such a built up area there were no fatalities, other than the potatoes!'*

Man's best friend was often the allotment-holder's worst enemy: 'Pompey', in a letter to the **Gardeners' Chronicle** of 10 August 1940, wrote: *'The almost daily complaints I receive as to damage done by dogs to allotments in urban areas indicate that drastic penalties ought to be inflicted on those careless people who allow their dogs to trespass on cultivated land. Unfortunately this trouble is such that some allotment-holders are almost driven to resign from the new army of gardeners because of the damage done on their plots.'*

Despite the patriotic status of the plot-holder, not everyone saw growing vegetables as the quickest and easiest method of getting them. Pilfering was inevitable when vegetables were increasingly difficult to get and gardens and allotments were so public. Stealing from allotments was taken very seriously – several judges took the view that it was on a par with looting. At the start of the war sentences were rarely more than a fine or seven days imprisonment, but by the autumn of 1942 punishments had become more severe. A man who stole 3lb of onions from an allotment was sentenced to a month's hard labour at Wimbledon, while in St Helen's that year a man who stole eightpennyworth of the same crop only avoided prison by the fact of his being 73 years old. In Yarmouth a man was sent to prison for a month for stealing a shilling's worth of onions from a garden, while in 1941 a man found stealing onions and potatoes from a railway allotment in Penryn was sentenced to two months hard labour. In 1942 Watford Corporation offered a £5 reward for information leading to the prosecution of allotment pilferers and at Hemel Hempstead was a reward of £1 for the capture of thieves and trespassers.

MINISTRY OF AGRICULTURE
WAR TIME CAMPAIGN
GROW MORE FOOD
1941
Certificate of Merit
Awarded to
WILLIAM STEVENSON
who cultivated a plot of land to the best advantage and so made a valuable contribution towards the Nation's effort to grow more food in time of war
Mayor of Chingford
Chairman of Allotments Committee
MINISTER OF AGRICULTURE AND FISHERIES
Omnia Vincit Labor

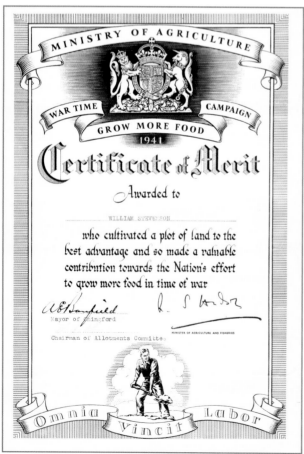

Merely trespassing on an allotment site cost a culprit £3 at Birmingham Police Court in August 1943. The **Gardeners' Chronicle** reported in March 1944 that *'An allotment-holder in Luton has a watch that keeps perfect time, and its price was six cabbages. He went to his plot one dark evening to cut some greens and found they had gone, but the cabbage-fancier had left his watch behind!'*

It was not just men who were caught making off with foodstuffs. In Hampstead two women were fined £1 each for stealing runner beans that hung over a bombed site. With all the news of pilfering and trespass it was not surprising that some allotments set up special patrols to catch thieves. Some sites employed 'plot watchers' for a small fee, or took it in turns to stand duty themselves. In Brighton, a collaboration between the Chief Constable and the Allotments Superintendent resulted in allotment-holders being enrolled as special constables for allotment patrol. Only two of the allotment societies took up the offer – but it did stop the pilfering. Even eager allotment constables might not have noticed the transgression of a Cambridge allotment-holder who carried out the heinous crime of carting away the turf from his allotment. What he should have done of course was dig in the turf as a valuable 'fertiliser'. For his lack of knowledge he was fined 5s costs at the local court.

In summer 1940 regulations on the sale of produce from allotments were relaxed, and the National Allotment Society ran voluntary schemes to sell excess produce either to local people or on to the trade, although it was still largely expected that a good neighbour would give away any perishable extras – or at the very least barter them.

Allotment gardening was not all unalloyed joy and healthy exercise as portrayed by the government and National Allotment Society. The gardening press had always carried a selection of advertisements for cough mixture, rheumatism ointment, and remedies for back pain. Risks from the widespread use of nicotine- and arsenic-based killers were added to during the war by the fast developing assortment of pesticides and herbicides. John Stoney in his **Fruit and Vegetable Preserving and Wartime Gardening** advised that *'Club root can be controlled by treating the plants with mercuric chloride or corrosive sublimate. It is a poison and must be treated as such. Mercuric chloride, from which the liquid is made, can be purchased from any chemist who knows you.'* Additional wartime hazards included barbed wire and old bits of metal and junk on long unclaimed land.

For many a novice gardener the first enthusiastic day spent digging resulted in a week of aches and pains, and traditional double digging and bastard trenching on pasture or grassland areas added to the strains. For John Rutherford the first memories of allotment digging were back-breaking: *'We had an allotment plot, one of about twelve that had been allocated at the edge of a school playing field, the turf being placed at the bottom of each row as the land was "reclaimed". It was a back-breaking task. I remember a pick being used at one stage. The site, about half a mile from home, had no storage facilities so we had to carry all the tools there each time; it probably looked like a scene from the Peasants' Revolt.'*

This memory of a daily trek highlights another problem; in **Digging for Victory: Wartime Gardening with Mr Middleton**, the author pointed out that: *'In the urban and industrial areas the allotment movement has grown to such an extent that in some places the difficulty now is to find land to satisfy the demand, and some enthusiastic gardeners I know of have to travel long distances after the day's work to get to their allotments. This is a great pity, but I suppose it can't always be avoided. Taking it all round, I think the large industrial centres are pulling their weight very well. It seems to me that we ought now to look to the country villages to get a move on and produce far more food than they have ever done before, not merely for themselves, but also for those who are unable to grow anything.'*

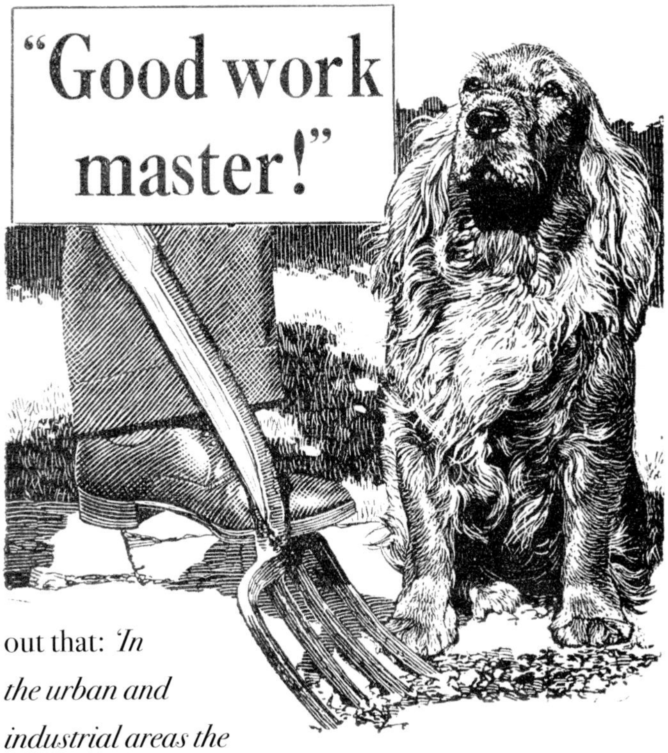
"Good work master!"

Left
Certificate of Merit Awarded to William Stevenson in 1941 for his part in the Wartime 'Grow More Food' campaign.

Above
An idyllic scene: man and his best friend, but dogs were not always an allotment-holder's best friend, and nor was his master – stealing from allotments became a real problem.

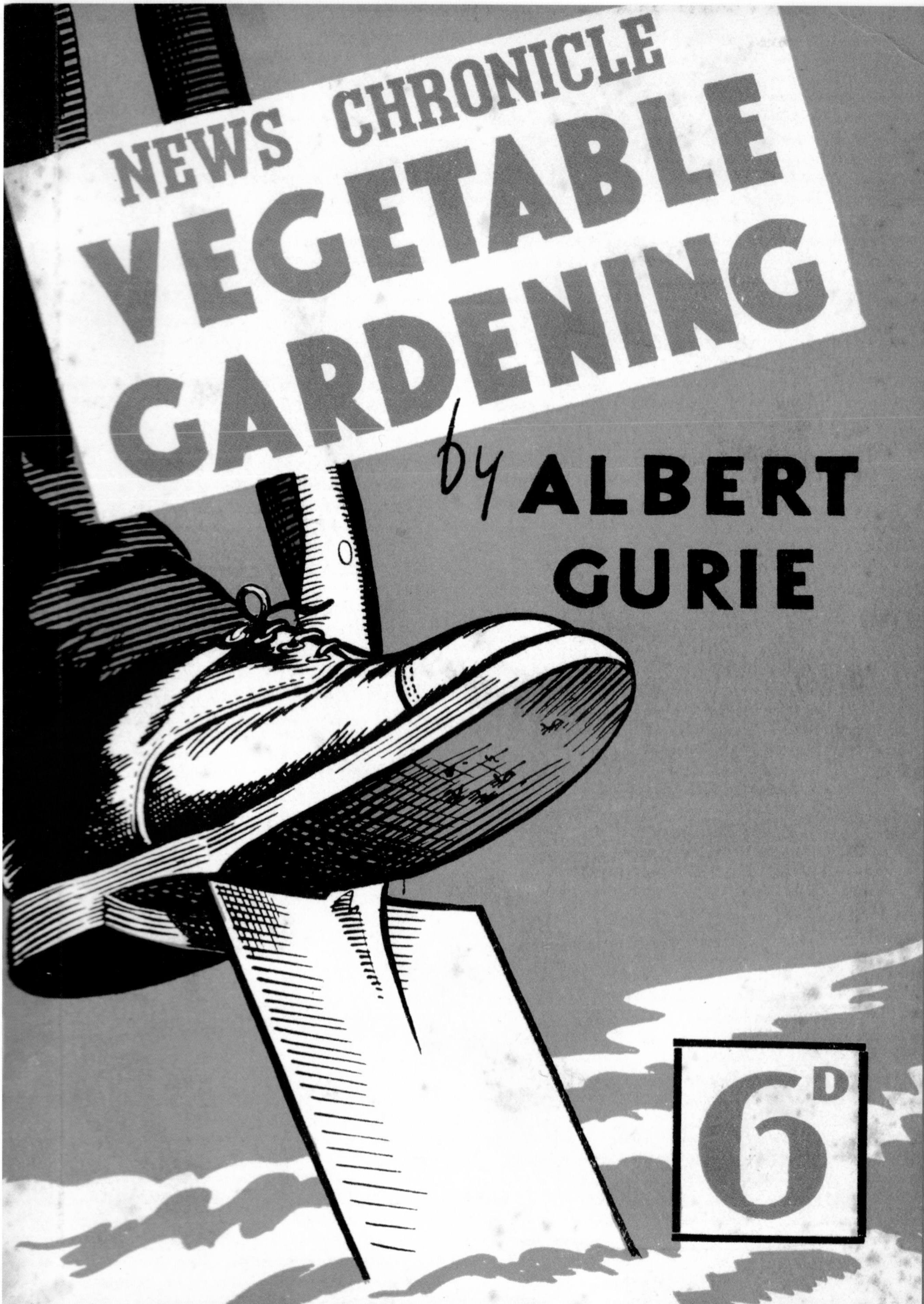
NEWS CHRONICLE
VEGETABLE
GARDENING
by ALBERT
GURIE
6D

Gardening by instruction: the role of the media

" So your advice, Mr. Compost, is—don't sow them too late or too early ? "

War on the home front was fought not only with forks and spades, but with print and broadcasts. Exhortations to Dig for Victory were accompanied by seemingly endless propaganda on why you should be doing it, how to do it, what to do it with, who else was doing it, and how successful other people were being in doing it.

As the war years wore on and the government became more accomplished in its role as the nation's gardening conscience, so did the media. Taking as their starting point the numerous Dig for Victory leaflets and government pronouncements, producers of books, radio programmes and even films promoted the gardening message. Instructed, encouraged, and as the years passed even coerced, into gardening, the nation responded by flocking to the newsstands and bookshops. Of course, this being wartime, the media were not totally independent and the messages they put out were very much 'guided' by the government. Nevertheless the programmes and books were extremely popular, especially among novice victory gardeners.

BBC Radio (In Your Garden, Radio Allotment, Brains Trust)

The Second World War was the first in which public radio broadcasts were to play a major role. BBC radio services began in 1922 and daily broadcasts were available from 1929. Competition from American and Independent broadcasting was intense in

Left
Newspapers, as well as gardening magazines, brought out their own 'readers' guides' to wartime vegetable gardening. On this cover the spade user appears to be using his right foot, rather than the left foot preferred on the Dig for Victory leaflets.

Above
Advice on gardening had never seemed so valuable as it was in the 1940s. The media hung on every word.

the 1930s, but the outbreak of war brought an end to this. On 1 September 1939, the 'Home Service' replaced the earlier national and regional channels and for the rest of the war the airways carried programmes to 'entertain and educate' those on the home front.

Perhaps the most famous and best-remembered radio gardening programme during the war years

Above
Listening to the wireless was a family event during the war. From the declaration of war to the announcement of VE and VJ day, all information came via the BBC. HMSO
Right
The Radio Gardener, Mr Middleton, was to become one of the most familiar voices (and faces) of the war.

was **In Your Garden**, presented by Cecil Middleton. Broadcast weekly from 1934 onwards, **In Your Garden** had had a firm following before the war. At the outbreak of war it was briefly taken off the air as the new Home Service channel was introduced. However the government soon realised the benefit of having Mr Middleton, 'the wireless gardener', dispensing their advice for them. The Ministry of Agriculture's proposal for reinstating **In Your Garden** suggested *'It would be very helpful to us if he [Mr Middleton] could get across the stuff we shall be putting out for the guidance of gardeners.'* This Mr Middleton duly did, but in his own inimitable style; informal and chatty, with a great deal of sly humour and a certain empathy with the benighted and hard-

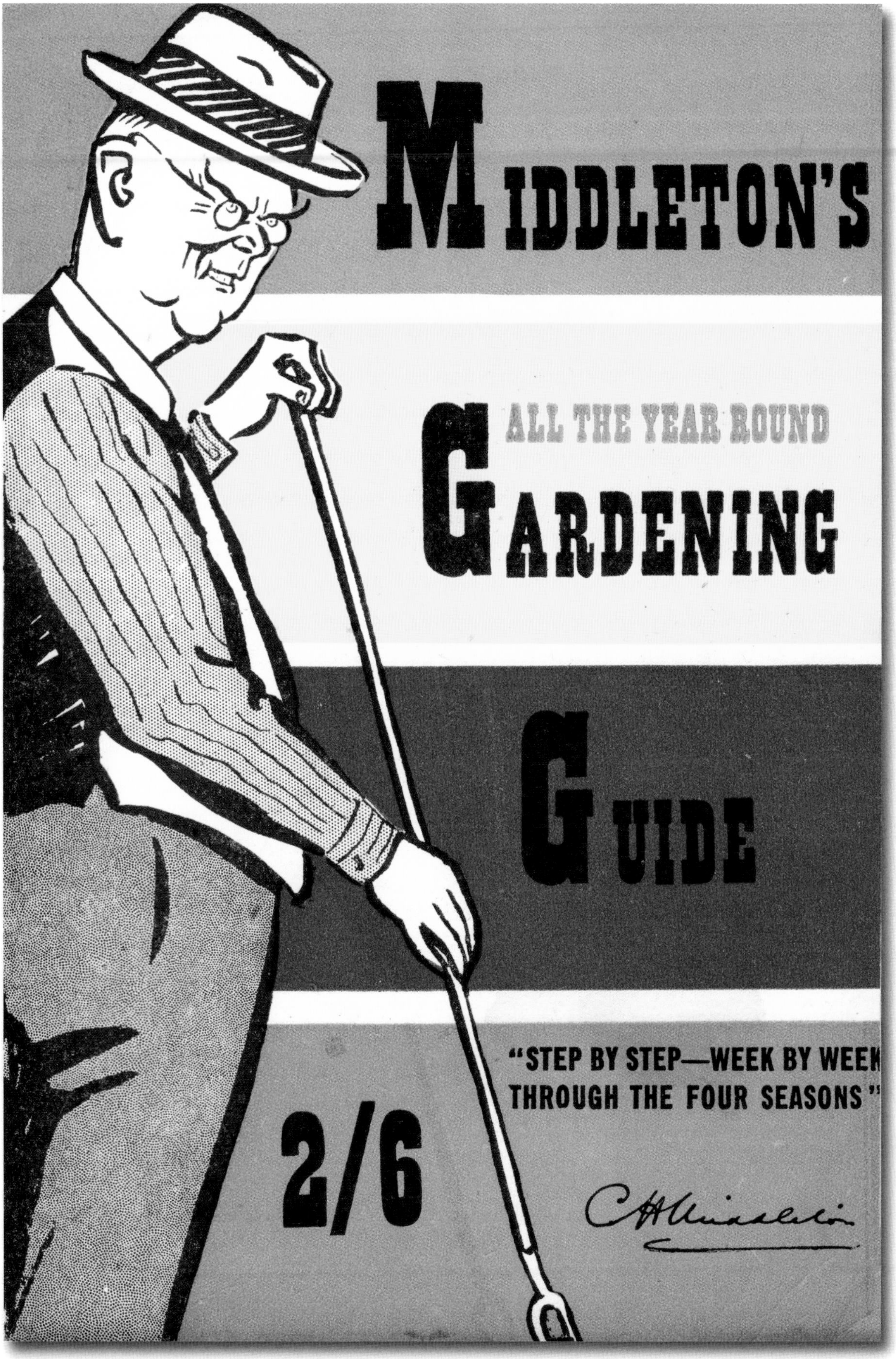
MIDDLETON'S
ALL THE YEAR ROUND
GARDENING
GUIDE
"STEP BY STEP—WEEK BY WEEK
THROUGH THE FOUR SEASONS"
2/6

pressed amateur gardener. He addressed the listeners as if they were close friends, and continually referred to his own gardening failures and successes. References to the weather (usually poor), and pests (usually voracious), provided both Mr Middleton and the unsuccessful gardener/listener with a sense of shared burdens and companionship as well as a series of excuses. Here is Mr Middleton on 'Potatoes, Bugs and Other Things' from **Digging for Victory: Wartime Gardening with Mr Middleton**: *'I wonder how many of you have sprayed your potatoes this year? I'm afraid we didn't get much suitable weather for the job after early July, and a good many of the crops must have been missed. It's no use talking about it now, of course. I only mention it because I was looking over some allotments the other day and saw an example of the good results of spraying. I wish you could have seen it.'* 'The Spring Hustle' in April 1942 expressed the same sense of 'muddling along': *'There are so many jobs to be done just now that it is difficult to know which to tackle first. We lost a good deal of time earlier on, when we ought to have been digging and preparing, owing to severe weather, and now some of us are like the cow's tail, all behind. But that need not worry us; as I have said often before, we should never garden by dates; and if the spring happens to be late, then we must be late too.'*

As well as gardening tips and a stock of ready excuses Mr Middleton also shared some of his home life, adding to the illusion of personal friendship. Here he shares his return to his suburban home with his readers and listeners, giving them a picture of rather touching garden dereliction: *'I expect I shall be later [with potato planting] than most of you, because I have recently returned to my suburban home, which was out of action for a time, and I'm trying to restore order in a very neglected back garden. I have packed the remaining rose bushes fairly close together along the back of the border, and a few of my choicest flowering plants that I don't want to lose; and I'm digging up most of what I used to call the lawn. It consists largely of weeds, moss, and bare patches rather than grass, so I'm burying it all rather deeply, together with an accumulation of ancient rubbish and lawn mowings which has been there since the year before last. . . . It looks a bit of a pickle at the moment but I hope to get it shipshape and planted before the end of this month.'*

In Your Garden was broadcast on Sunday afternoons, throughout the war, eventually gaining 3.5 million listeners. In 1940, 9 million radio licences were issued, so the programme captured about a third of the entire audience! Middleton's broadcasts were so successful that they were published as books, which were republished in 2008. Mrs Pat Ashby from Bedford recalls that, like so many others, *'I listened regularly to Mr Middleton's gardening talks on the radio, bought his little instruction books and used National Growmore recommended by him for allotment-holders. I was so proud of my achievements.'*

In 1942 the BBC announced a new programme aimed specifically at allotment-holders. **Radio Allotment** proved to have enormous appeal although it never rivalled Mr Middleton. The radio plot was a real one, located in a west London square, and needing the same preparation and tending as those around it. Recording 'on location' gave the presenters an opportunity to provide up-to-the-minute comments on weather and pests, as well as the latest government advice. The broadcasts began with the initial preparation and sowing and followed the experiences of many new allotment holders.

Tending, or at least broadcasting from, the plot was the responsibility of Wynford Vaughan-Thomas (otherwise a war correspondent and friend of Dylan Thomas) and Raymond Glendenning (known mainly for his sports commentaries). The final members of the team were Stewart MacPhearson, an ex-undertaker's apprentice who became known as the BBC 'Voice of the Year' for his work on broadcasting from the air during battles, and Michael Standing. It was this combination of excellent commentators, rather than any professed gardening knowledge, which made the programme such a success. Their lack of gardening knowledge also appealed to other novices. On one occasion, in a strange coming-together of

Left

Ferranti radios could not be bought during the war as output was restricted, but that did not stop them being advertised. *In Your Garden* was one of the programmes chosen to promote the importance of radio.

Below

A cartoon from the *Radio Times* suggests that it was the BBC female staff that actually kept the allotment in production while the men broadcast.

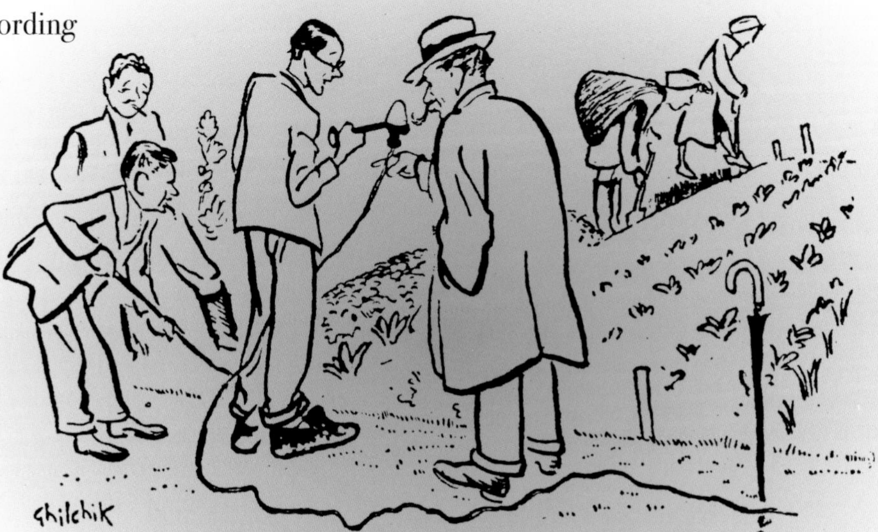
Ghilchik

'RADIO ALLOTMENT' comes on the air again today at 1.15. Above is Ghilchik's impression of some of the O.B. team at work. In the centre Tom Hay is instructing Michael Standing, Director of Outside Broadcasting.

the airwaves, Wynford Vaughan-Thomas inter-
viewed Mr Middleton at the annual horticultural
show at Weston and Weedon Lois, the distinctively
named Northamptonshire village where Mr Middleton's father had been head gardener. The gates
of the Weston and Weedon Lois allotments now
contain a memorial to Mr Middleton.

Other one-off gardening programmes also
appeared, often in the popular early-evening slot,
with advice on specific topics such as digging.
In 1940 the BBC even produced a play called
Digging for Victory. This heartening tale followed
a hero who had commenced digging only with the
outbreak of war, but had soon risen to the status of
acknowledged expert among the local allotment-
holders. This rise had been accomplished, it said,
with the sole aid of the government's Dig for
Victory leaflets. The final lines were designed to
encourage others to follow his example and go:

'BACK TO THE LAND – AND IF YOU ARE ABLE,
CONTRIBUTE A SPROUT TO THE NATIONAL TABLE.'

The **Brains Trust** also covered gardening
questions, drawing on both radio celebrity gardeners and members of the RHS committee. A general
'any questions' programme, the **Brains Trust**
became a long-running series from 1942 onwards
after a single edition in January 1941 (entitled 'Any
Questions?') proved hugely popular. Copycat
'Gardening Brains Trust' evenings based in local
halls became a popular feature of the Dig for
Victory campaign.

Instruction on growing was inevitably followed
by instruction on cooking, and **In Your Garden**
was soon joined by **The Kitchen Front**, broadcast
at 8.15am from Tuesday to Friday. Lord Woolton
himself appeared on the programme, alongside the
cookery writers Ambrose Heath and Marguerite
Patten as well as the popular Doris and Elsie
Waters. **The Kitchen Front** was also heavily influ-
enced by government policy on food growing, with
Lord Woolton at the Ministry of Food suggesting
suitable topics. In 1943, for example, lack of bread
flour meant that the government needed an emphasis
to be put on potatoes, resulting in a rush of potato-
based recipes, while in January of that year a glut of
green vegetables resulted in the Ministry ordering
a talk on cooking swedes to be cancelled and one
on using green vegetables substituted.

Films and Newsreels

Although television broadcasting ceased for the
duration of the war, newsflashes and information
films were created for cinema audiences. After a brief
shutdown at the declaration of war, cinemas soon
reopened to audiences desperate for light entertainment and an opportunity to 'get away from it all'.
Served up with the popular musicals and feature
films were a series of 'shorts', including government
information 'flashes', as well as the newsreels.

The Ministry of Information commissioned a
range of short films to reiterate the messages of the
Dig for Victory leaflets. For example, Dig for
Victory leaflet no. 1 (on planning for year-round
vegetables) was brought to life in a rather avant-
garde sketch. The film opened with a man sitting at
a table, which is disguised as a vegetable patch.
Knife and fork in hand he asks for his dinner.

Right

This is a 'still' from the Ministry of Information film *'Blitz on Bugs'*, a cartoon that was voiced over by the nation's favourite gardener, Mr Middleton. Such short films were a common addition to wartime cinema bills.

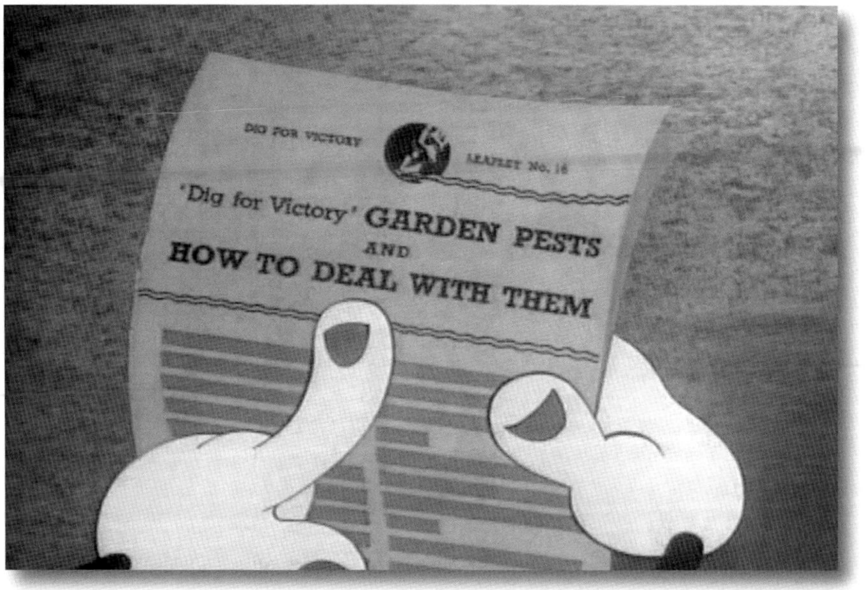
DIG FOR VICTORY
LEAFLET No. 16
'Dig for Victory' GARDEN PESTS
AND
HOW TO DEAL WITH THEM

Father Time, acting as a waiter, serves him his summer vegetables on the 'table' of soil, and stands by for the winter order. Father Time asks several times for the 'winter order', but none is forth-coming. In the next scene snow and ice appear on the table and despite calling for the waiter, the man is given no food to eat, as he has not given his order in advance. He crawls on to the table/plot in a desperate attempt to find food, and eventually dies. Father Time reappears to lay a lily on the corpse, before warning the audience of the dangers of not planning for your winter food.

A second film features a bizarre assortment of elderly army and navy officers failing to give direction for a battle, which they inevitably lose. The moral again was that one must plan ahead in life. The propaganda messages of these unusual little 'plays' may well have eluded many in the cinema audience, and certainly future Ministry bulletins and sketches became rather more straightforward. Popular among these were cartoons voiced by well-known gardeners such as Mr Middleton. **Blitz on Bugs** showed pests wearing enemy uniform invading by air, land and underground before being exterminated by an insect spray. The voice of Mr Middleton ended the cartoon saying, '*Tackle the Pest, Tackle Him Early, Dig for Victory Leaflet no. 16 Tells You How*'. Another cartoon demonstrated the basics of plant food, using a cross-section through a compost heap 'factory'. In the spring of 1942 a new **Dig for Victory** sound film was circulated in cinemas, sometimes accompanied by a supplementary short on the difficulties and dangers encountered by the Navy. Short newsflash items highlighted 'true life' stories such as blind allotment-holders 'doing their bit', children planting vegetables in London's East End, a livestock-filled backyard in Hoxton, and beans growing in a bombed basement.

Plant Protection Ltd produced a series of five colour films, the first entitled **A Garden Goes to War** to demonstrate the basic techniques of digging, planting and storing. These were said to be enormously popular, with 1,200 people in an Ilford air-raid shelter giving the films an enthusiastic reception one Christmas, although it might be argued that they were a captive audience. In London over 200 members of the Home Guard turned up to watch these instructional films when they were shown in the local area. By the end of 1942 the series

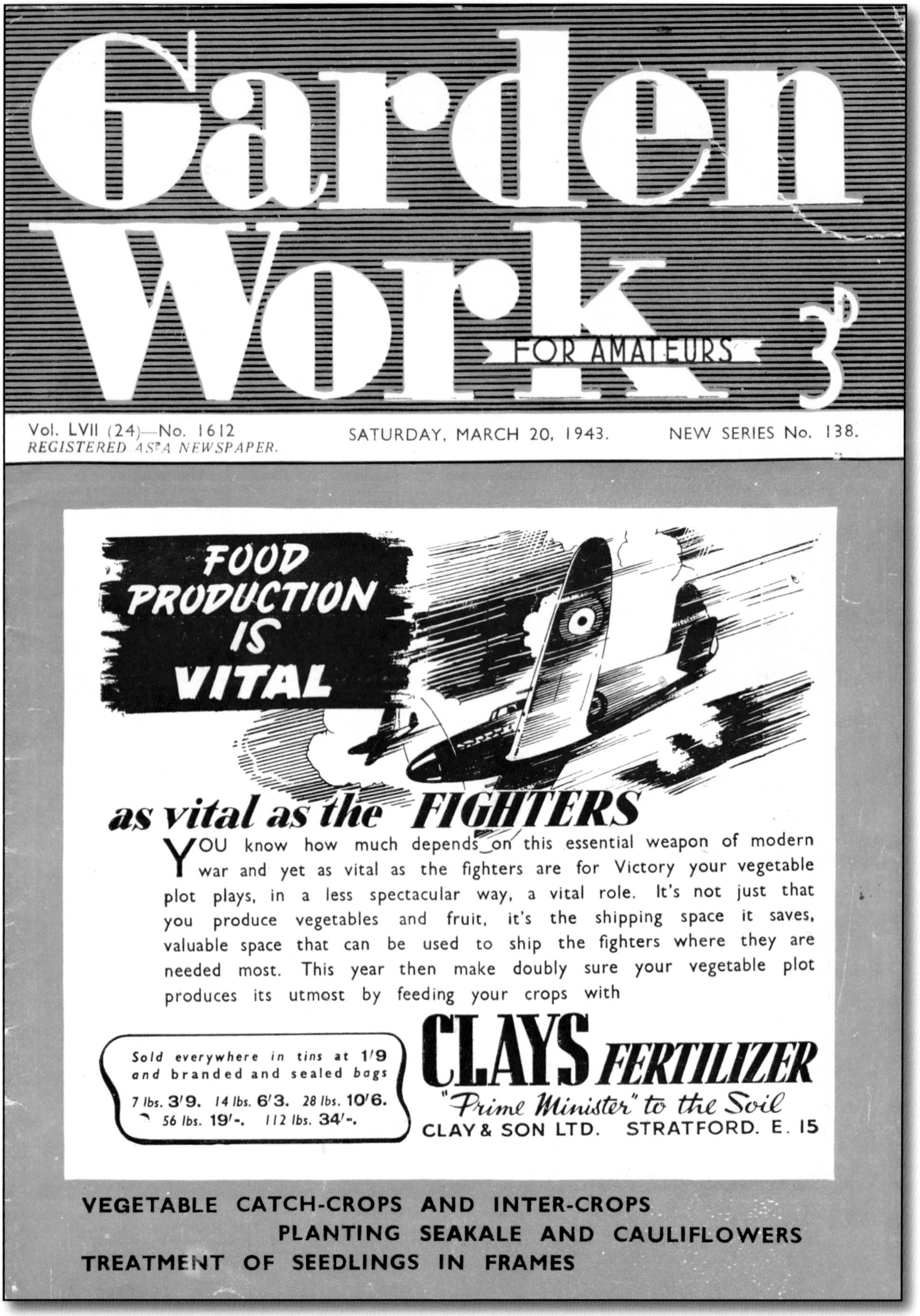

Garden Work
FOR AMATEURS

3d

Vol. LVII (24)—No. 1612 SATURDAY, MARCH 20, 1943. NEW SERIES No. 138.

REGISTERED AS A NEWSPAPER.

FOOD PRODUCTION IS VITAL

as vital as the FIGHTERS

YOU know how much depends on this essential weapon of modern war and yet as vital as the fighters are for Victory your vegetable plot plays, in a less spectacular way, a vital role. It's not just that you produce vegetables and fruit, it's the shipping space it saves, valuable space that can be used to ship the fighters where they are needed most. This year then make doubly sure your vegetable plot produces its utmost by feeding your crops with

Sold everywhere in tins at 1/9 and branded and sealed bags
7 lbs. 3/9. 14 lbs. 6/3. 28 lbs. 10/6. 56 lbs. 19/-. 112 lbs. 34/-.

CLAYS FERTILIZER

"Prime Minister" to the Soil

CLAY & SON LTD. STRATFORD. E. 15

VEGETABLE CATCH-CROPS AND INTER-CROPS
PLANTING SEAKALE AND CAULIFLOWERS
TREATMENT OF SEEDLINGS IN FRAMES

of Plant Protection films were becoming so popular that four new films were added, with a fifth one on 'common mistakes by amateurs' apparently eagerly awaited. One film was devoted entirely to raising onions and leeks. In addition to these 'on location' films, the Royal Horticultural Society produced a series of short educational films for the Ministry of Agriculture, with commentary by Roy Hay.

Gardening Magazines

Despite severe restrictions on paper, printing and postage, gardening magazines were produced in their millions during the war. With so many novice gardeners, and the need for even experienced gardeners to produce more, these magazines and gardening columns in newspapers and magazines flourished. Whether you were a novice or an old hand, housewife or husband, a reader of **The Times** or the **Daily Express**, gardening expertise was coming your way. There was a magazine title catering for everyone from the complete amateur to the experienced professional, from the allotment-holder with little spare money or time to those who could indulge themselves with glasshouses full of orchids and who employed gardeners to look after them.

One of the most popular gardening magazines was **Garden Work for Amateurs** (usually just known as **Garden Work**). First published in 1912 it was aimed at the gardener of a small suburban plot. In the pre-war years its gardening advice concentrated on rockeries, lawns, dahlias, alpines, greenhouse plants, herbaceous borders and annual bedding. A special section for 'Lady Readers' gave recipe ideas to help 'use the vegetables your husband produced on the vegetable plot or allotment'. Lady readers were not expected to do much of the gardening themselves, although they might potter in the borders.

On the outbreak of war **Garden Work** started to concentrate on the productive rather than the decorative aspects of gardening, although its beloved rockery articles continued through the long war years. Articles referred frequently to the latest Dig for Victory leaflets and the magazine also carried advertisements by the Ministry of Agriculture. At only 3d a week it was an ideal supplement to government information bulletins. In case you had missed the message, the commercial advertisements it carried also frequently referred to government campaigns. For the first year of the war the front cover even carried a cartoon of 'this week's tasks on the allotment', before being replaced by a long-running series of patriotic advertisements by Clay's fertilisers. Inside, the regular feature 'On the Home Front' told of gardeners' efforts all round the country, detailing numbers of new allotments set up, community and village produce associations, and collections made for Wings for Victory weeks and the Red Cross Agricultural Fund. Advice in **Garden Work** was usually practical. Articles during the war covered vegetables, fruit, manure, allotment tasks, catch-cropping, and pests

Left
A typical front page of *Garden Work* during the war. This advertisement for Clay's fertiliser reminds readers that food production is vital, as vital as the fighters. Clay's took front page advertisements on *Garden Work* for several months, taking over this privilege from a cartoon of current jobs in the vegetable garden and allotment.

Amateur Gardening
ANNUAL

for
1943

3/6 NET

and diseases. There was a small section on 'The Amateur's Greenhouse', focusing on dahlias, tender perennials and bright annuals, but this was clearly less important than vegetables. 'Readers' Questions', however, covered a wider range of topics, from heavy soils to growing flowers, from sludge manure to treatment of decorative winter cherry pot plants, and from cabbage gall weevil to sweet peas with no scent. The range of questions suggest that the Victory campaign occupied only part of their readers' gardening time!

Other magazines offering advice to the amateur gardener included **Home Gardening**, **Amateur Gardening** and the **Gardeners' Chronicle**. In January 1940 the latter wrote: *'It is perhaps only natural that beginners are sometimes reluctant to discuss their gardening problems, but if a little tact is employed the most reticent will discuss them at some length once he has sufficient confidence in your ability to advise him in a straightforward manner.'*

Not all garden magazines and newsletters during the war were aimed at the novice gardener or the practical producer. **My Garden: an Intimate Magazine for Garden Lovers** had been launched in 1934 and was aimed at the upper middle-class gardener. The magazine showed little interest in Dig for Victory or other practical campaigns, and continued to cater for the lover of snowdrops, the specialist in dahlias, and those who preferred their fruits ornamental rather than edible. That the war was going on around it was evidenced mainly in the advertisements, where Jackman & Sons' clematis nurseries were forced to rub shoulders with **Webb's Guide to Planning Your Wartime Garden**. Drummond's Perfect Alpines shared a page with 'Spring Onions,' the story of a man who had been changed by war from a banker to a smallholder. One regular contributor did provide articles on their 'Duration' garden (for the duration of the war), a smallholding which appeared to be battling against officialdom at all levels. Other contributors told of rather less serious struggles to get the leaves swept off their lawns and their borders tidied without the aid of the usual gardening workforce. In a letter to **My Garden** in December 1942, B.T. Barber wrote: *'I was interested in your remarks about working gardeners in the October issue of* **My Garden**. *My own gardener, who left to join the forces, is just such another good fellow, and knowing that I am now, owing to war conditions, absolutely without help, he never fails to come and give me most of his time when he is home on his regular spells of seven days' leave.'* 'The Nursery Directory', included in the December 1942 edition, tended to reinforce the stereotype that it was the working classes that were Digging for Victory, while those with larger gardens and purses to match continued to purchase rhododendrons, roses, rock plants and rare shrubs!

Garden Advice in Newspapers and Magazines

If you were not committed enough to buy a gardening magazine, there was still plenty of advice on offer

Left
Amateur Gardening continued to publish its popular annuals for most of the war years. Its usual colour images of overflowing herbaceous borders were replaced with single pots or vases of flowers.

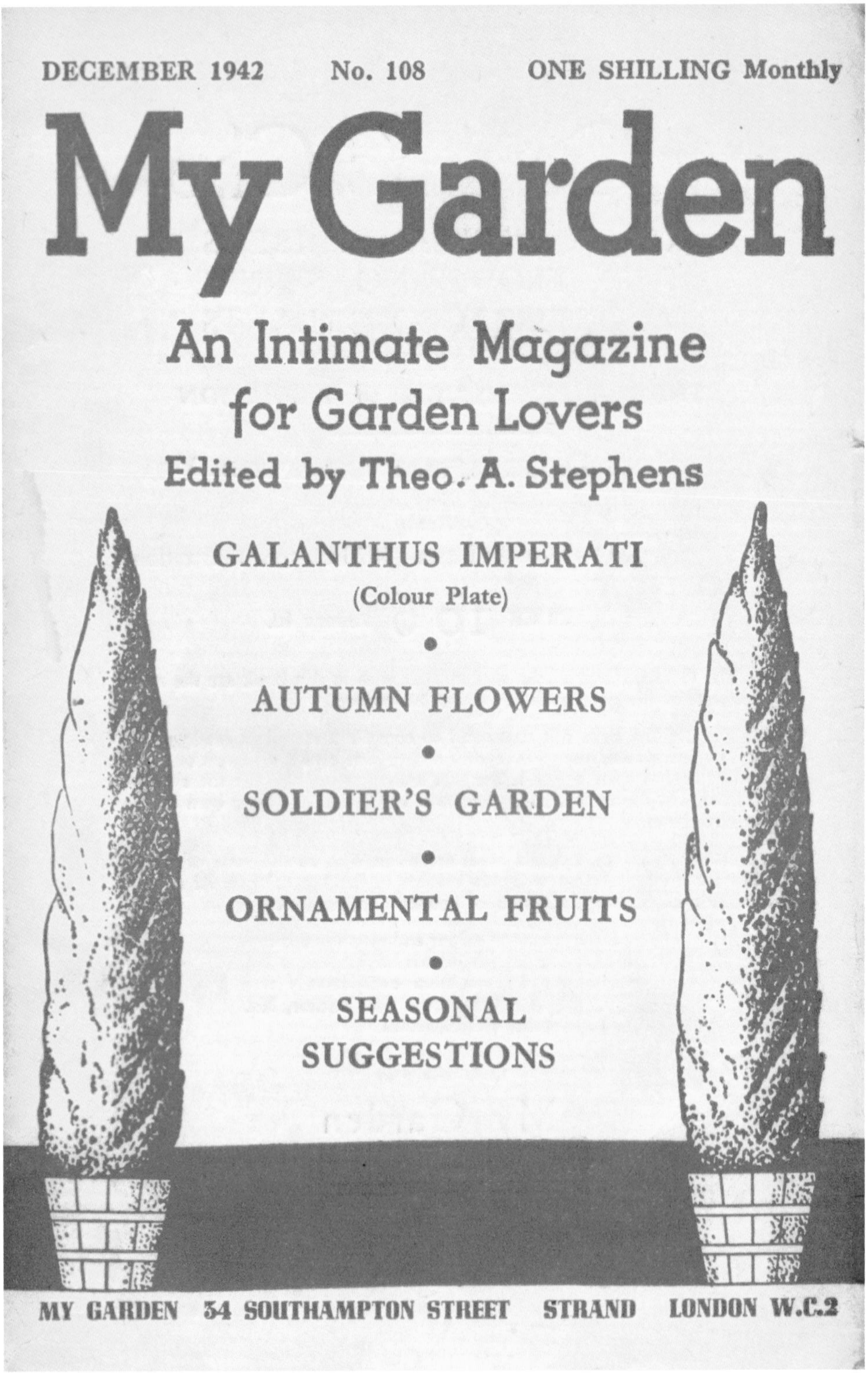
DECEMBER 1942 No. 108 ONE SHILLING Monthly
My Garden
An Intimate Magazine for Garden Lovers
Edited by Theo. A. Stephens
GALANTHUS IMPERATI
(Colour Plate)
AUTUMN FLOWERS
SOLDIER'S GARDEN
ORNAMENTAL FRUITS
SEASONAL SUGGESTIONS
MY GARDEN 34 SOUTHAMPTON STREET STRAND LONDON W.C.2

Above
The December 1942 edition of *My Garden*, featuring articles on *Galanthus imperati* (a variety of snowdrop), and ornamental fruits. The 'Soldier's Garden' was a philosophical piece by N. Courtman Davies dwelling on the role of the flower garden in times of peace.

in your daily paper or other 'household' magazines. The **Daily Express** had the delightfully chatty Cecil Middleton, the **Daily Mirror** employed the very practical E.T. Brown, while Percy Izzard gave gardening advice to readers of the **Daily Mail**. Stephen Cheveley, gardening expert for **The Times**, found himself called upon less frequently as **The Times** did not carry a daily or weekly column, contenting itself with occasional articles and comment. Cartoon strips were also popular, such as 'Adam the Gardener' in the **Sunday Express**, which continued into the 1960s. All the gardening experts repeated the current government 'line', as well as giving topical tips, gardening calendars and answering readers' questions. Differences were in style, rather than content. In addition to the daily papers, almost all periodicals managed to squeeze gardening in somewhere. **Woman** had its own gardening expert and a calendar of gardening operations from 1941, and was typical of women's magazines in intro-

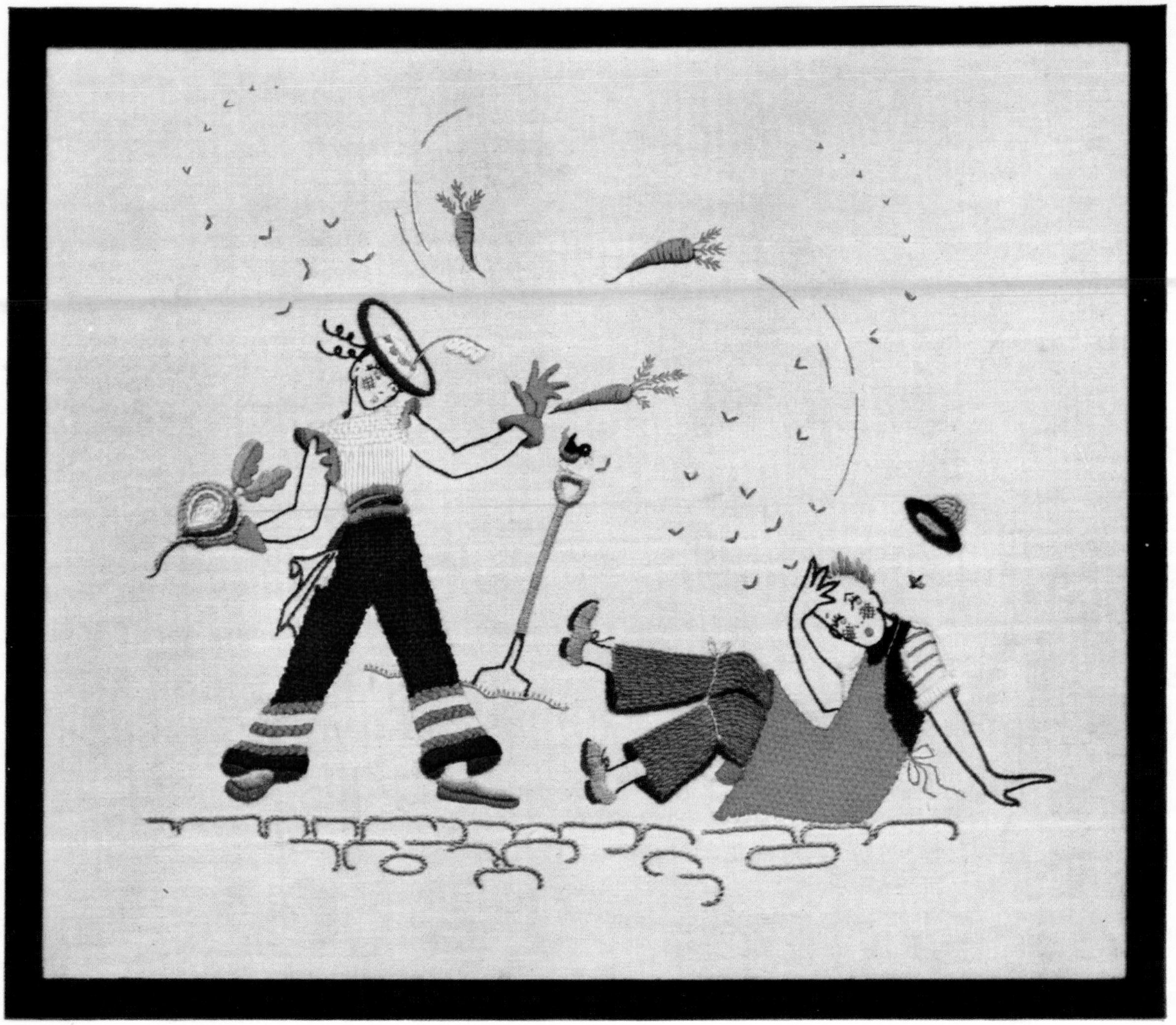

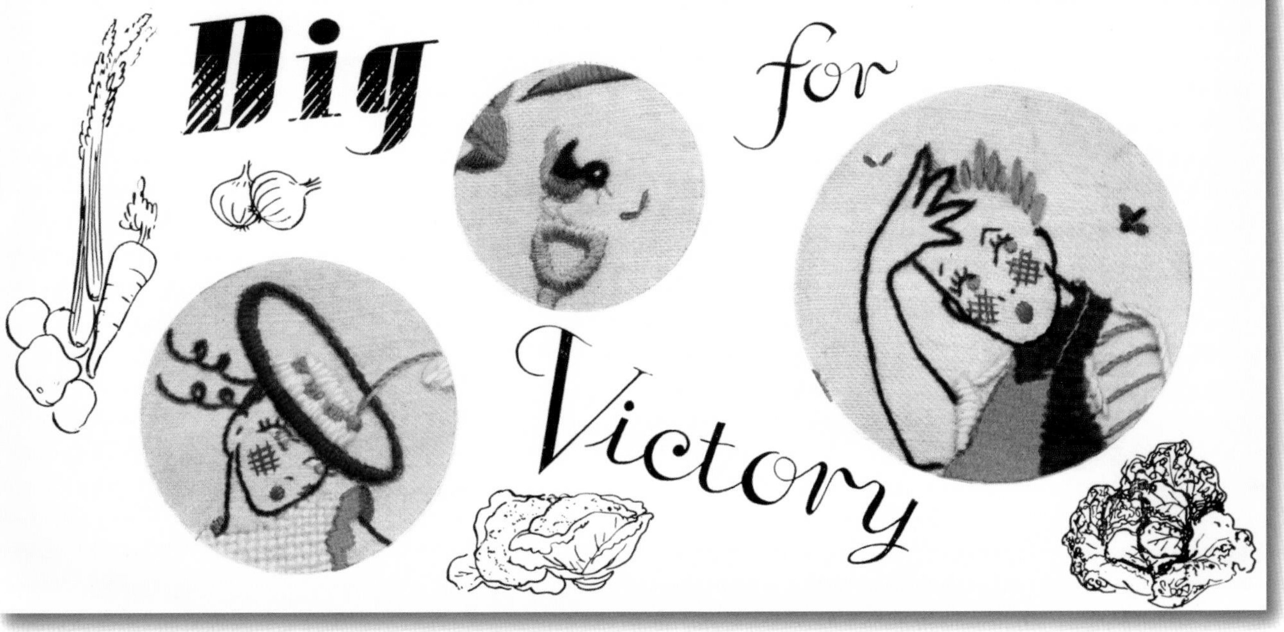
Dig for Victory

This unusual embroidery pattern from *Stitchcraft* magazine of July 1941 reflected the popularity of the new campaign.

ducing the Dig for Victory campaign into its cookery and recipe sections. With so much government advice available on the important role of vitamins and carbohydrates in daily food, periodicals such as **Good Housekeeping** urged the housewife to dig for the sake of her own and her children's health. Advertisements also took advantage of the new gardening scope of the magazines, linking traditional beauty products to women's new roles. Even hobby magazines included articles on building hutches, making garden tools, or embroidery. The **Boy's Own Paper** and **Girl's Own Paper** included projects for the garden and things to help in the Dig for Victory campaign.

Books

If you felt in need of more advice than magazines and radio programmes could give, then you might buy one of the many books that came out on wartime gardening. By the 1930s and '40s reading and book buying were no longer the preserve of the middle and upper classes as they had been at the beginning of the century, and despite restrictions on paper and printing, books were now an automatic choice for those who needed advice and encouragement. Some of those who leapt into print in the first months of the war have already been featured. Writers such as Stephen Cheveley (**A Garden Goes to War**, published in January 1940), Cecil Middleton (**Your Garden in Wartime**, 1941) and Richard Sudell (**Practical Gardening and Food Production in Pictures**, 1940), were to give invaluable practical advice to novice and experienced gardeners alike. Cecil Middleton was well

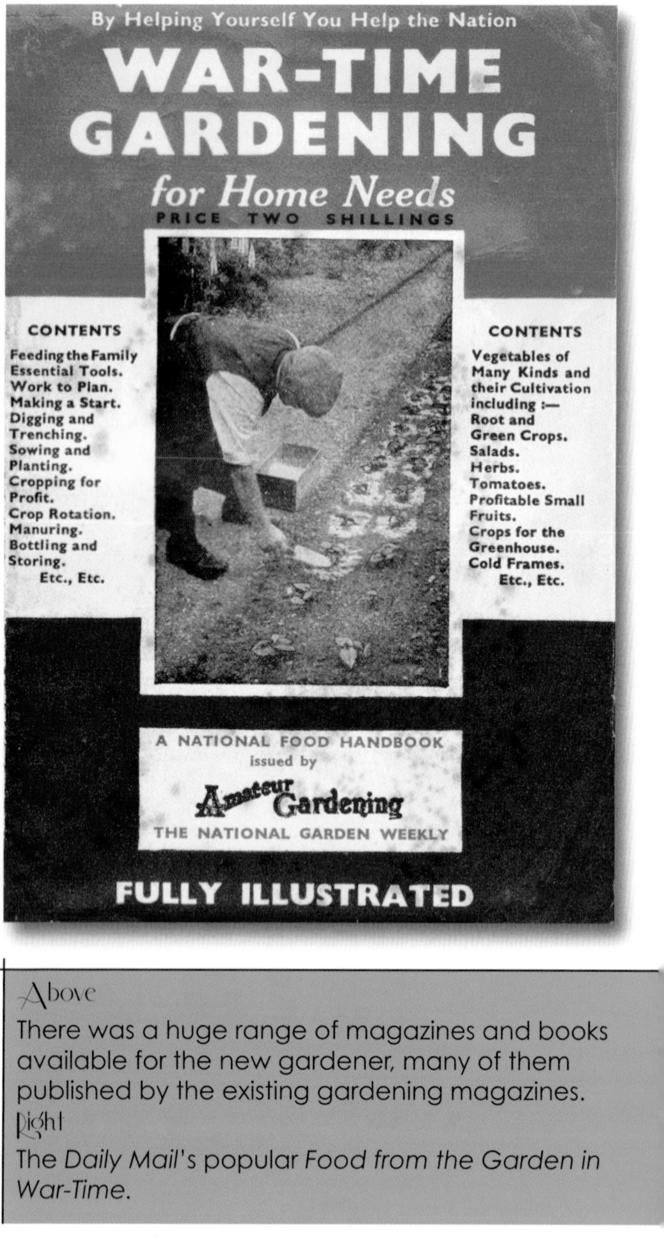
By Helping Yourself You Help the Nation
WAR-TIME GARDENING
for Home Needs
PRICE TWO SHILLINGS
CONTENTS
Feeding the Family
Essential Tools.
Work to Plan.
Making a Start.
Digging and Trenching.
Sowing and Planting.
Cropping for Profit.
Crop Rotation.
Manuring.
Bottling and Storing.
Etc., Etc.
CONTENTS
Vegetables of Many Kinds and their Cultivation including :—
Root and Green Crops.
Salads.
Herbs.
Tomatoes.
Profitable Small Fruits.
Crops for the Greenhouse.
Cold Frames.
Etc., Etc.
A NATIONAL FOOD HANDBOOK
issued by
Amateur Gardening
THE NATIONAL GARDEN WEEKLY
FULLY ILLUSTRATED

Above
There was a huge range of magazines and books available for the new gardener, many of them published by the existing gardening magazines.
Right
The *Daily Mail*'s popular *Food from the Garden in War-Time*.

known as a writer as well as a broadcaster, having published through the 1930s with popular titles such as **Colour All the Year in My Garden** (1938), **Winter-flowering Plants for Outdoor Borders** (1937), **Mr Middleton Talks about Gardening** (1935) and **More Garden Talks** (1936). Appearing in Pathé newsreels, on the radio and in a newspaper column he could lay claim to being the first real gardening 'multi-media personality'.

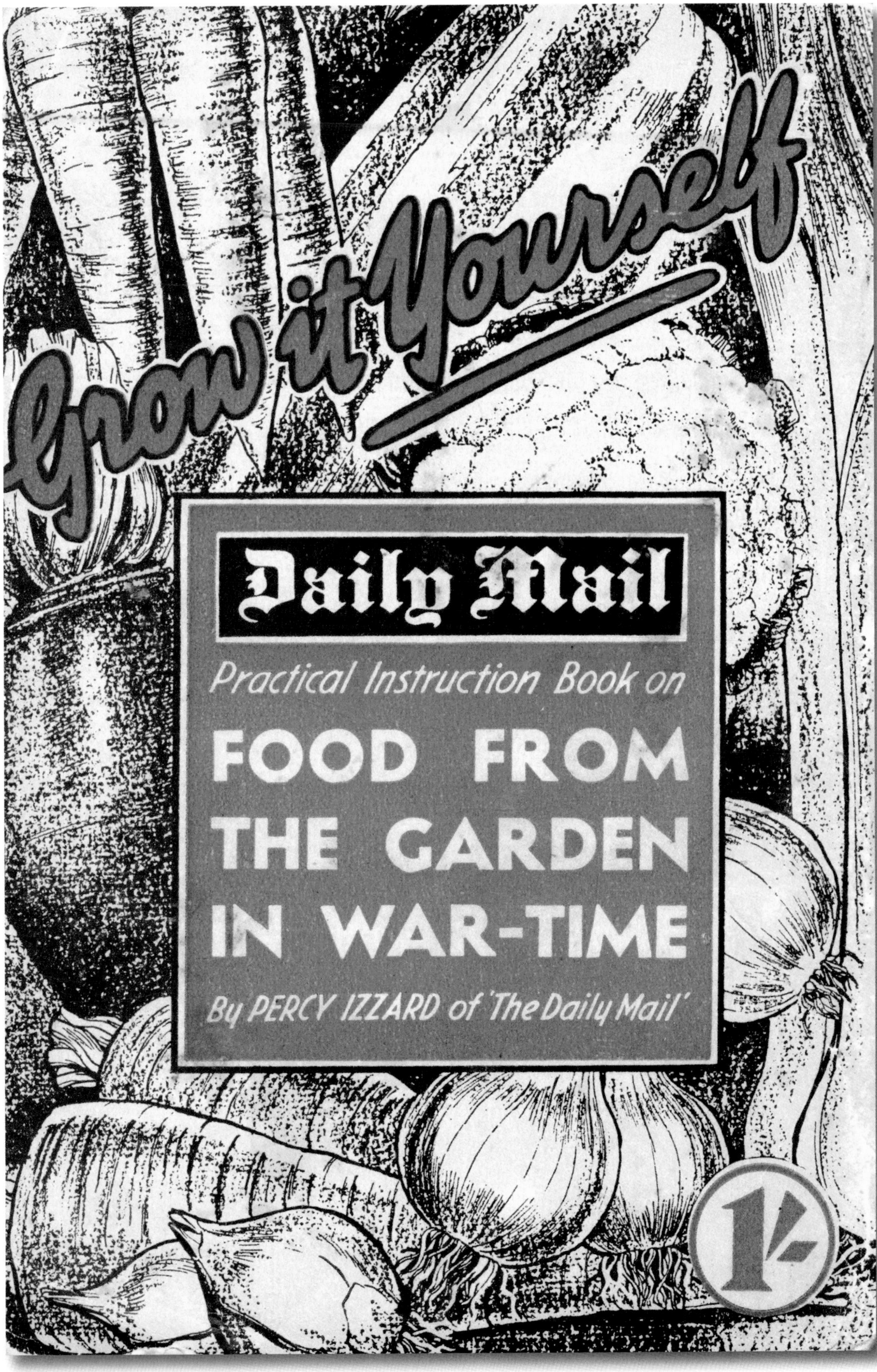
Grow it Yourself
Daily Mail
Practical Instruction Book on
FOOD FROM THE GARDEN IN WAR-TIME
By PERCY IZZARD of 'The Daily Mail'
1/-

Stephen Cheveley had his own burdens to carry in regard to lawns, but his description of digging up the immaculate turf in his garden of just under an acre may not have inspired much fellow feeling from suburban gardeners, whose small lawns often bore more resemblance to Mr Middleton's weedy patch. He was quick off the mark however with his book **A Garden Goes to War**, which was written literally as the government campaign was getting organised, and managed to make it to press only a couple of months after war broke out. So immediate was his response that he pre-dated the slogan 'Dig for Victory' and instead tried to rouse amateur and novice gardeners with the government's original call to 'Grow More Food'.

Once the campaign was properly under way there was no end of books giving advice, and by autumn 1940 the victory gardener was spoiled for choice. Almost all were aimed at the complete novice, with pictures of spades and forks and detailed descriptions of how to use them. W.E. Shewell's popular **Grow Your Own Food Supply** was usefully accompanied by **Cook What You Grow** written *with the aid of his wife*, Irene. **Make Your Garden Feed You** showed a woman gardener on the cover, but was ironically written by a man, E.T. Brown, gardening expert for the **Daily Mirror**. **How to Grow Food** (1940) by Doreen Wallace was one of the few gardening books written by a woman. Agnes and Beatrice Miall, who wrote **Gardening Made Easy** were also well qualified to instruct the gardener, Beatrice having qualified for the Diploma in Horticulture at Reading University. John Hampshire managed to pack all essential wartime gardening into the few spare hours that many people had, in **The Wartime Week-End Gardener**, and the **Daily Mail** competed with **Grow It Yourself** by its gardening correspondent, Percy Izzard. The books were almost uniformly pocket sized, and to the point – typically 90–150 pages. Shortage of paper and printing facilities meant that they were rarely illustrated, some carrying the approved stamp for 'War Economy Standard'.

Perhaps the best-known of all the wartime gardening books was Richard Sudell's **Practical Gardening and Food Production in Pictures**. Originally produced in the first months of the war, Sudell's book was superbly timed and ran to several editions during and after the war. The main selling point was the extensive use of illustration, including photographs of each procedure; this made the book ideal for novice gardeners. When it was published the book was advertised everywhere, including in periodicals such as **Woman**. Originally written before the outbreak of war **Practical Gardening** devoted chapters to laying out decorative gardens, lawns and alpine walls. But for the wartime gardener it was the sections on 'How to Adapt Your Garden in Wartime' and 'Allotment Gardening', that were of most interest. Richard Sudell also had time to add chapters on keeping poultry and rabbits, and preserving foods.

Following on from Sudell's pioneering work, the Royal Horticultural Society published a step-by-step photographic guide to what to do in the vegetable garden throughout the year. Published in May

Right
A much used and worn copy of *The Vegetable Garden Displayed*, this edition was 1s 3d, rather than the original 1s.

Second Impression

The Vegetable Garden displayed

1/3
Postage 3d

Royal Horticultural Society, London

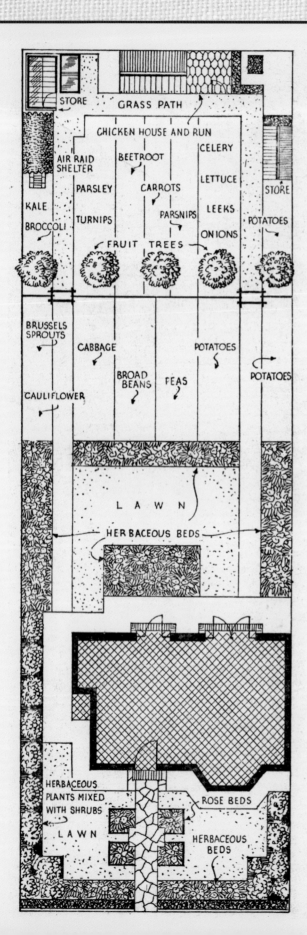

STORE
GRASS PATH
CHICKEN HOUSE AND RUN
CELERY
AIR RAID SHELTER   BEETROOT
LETTUCE
PARSLEY   CARROTS   STORE
LEEKS
KALE   TURNIPS   PARSNIPS
BROCCOLI   ONIONS   POTATOES
FRUIT TREES

BRUSSELS SPROUTS
CABBAGE   POTATOES
BROAD BEANS   PEAS   POTATOES
CAULIFLOWER

L A W N
HERBACEOUS BEDS

HERBACEOUS PLANTS MIXED WITH SHRUBS
ROSE BEDS
L A W N
HERBACEOUS BEDS

1941, **The Vegetable Garden Displayed** was based on a series of photographs taken at its gardens at Wisley in the previous year. **The Vegetable Garden Displayed** became an instant hit. Only 1 shilling in its first edition (with 3d extra for postage) it recorded every moment in the life of the vegetable, from seed sowing, to tying in, to first picking. 'Trustworthy varieties' were highlighted, along with harvesting and storing tips and pest control. So successful was the publication that in 1947 it was translated into German to help that country's starving civilian population get back on their feet.

For many gardening novices **The Vegetable Garden Displayed** lasted not only through the war but through a lifetime of gardening. Surviving copies are often dog-eared and scribbled on, with pencil notes on crops and plans. Wartime paper shortages meant that eventually the price went up in stages to 2s a copy, but it was still reported to be the best-selling RHS book ever by the end of the 1940s.

At the same price as **The Vegetable Garden Displayed** was **Grow It Yourself – the Daily Mail Instruction Book on Food from the Garden in Wartime'**. This was aimed at the beginner not just in vegetable gardening but in any kind of garden work. It hoped to assist those who had been making modest efforts at home but now felt impelled to do more, those whose 'spirit is willing to join in this great campaign but whose knowledge is weak'.

Adapting your garden to wartime needs from Richard Sudell's *Practical Gardening and Food Production in Pictures*. The proposals are to double the area of vegetable production by substantially reducing the lawn area.

Although many books claimed to be aimed at the novice gardener many lost sight of this ideal novice after the first few pages, but **Grow It Yourself** actually kept him (or her) in their sights. Chapter 1 was devoted to *'some words commonly used in describing gardening operations. Some you will find in the following pages; others may be used by gardening friends who see your work and offer advice'*. Fortunately for the reader the envisaged 'gardening friends' appear to have stuck to technical advice rather than derogatory comments! Among the words explained are spit, friable, ball, leggy, stagger, harden off, humus, brassicas, and pinch – a selection which, it must be admitted, might be open to some misinterpretation by the novice. In subsequent chapters the author went on to define 'bastard trenching' (a favourite of wartime writers), and seed bed. Dealing clearly with the what, why, how, when and even where, this was an excellent introduction for the novice who completed their education in the final chapter by learning about downy mildew and 'finger and toe' disease (a picturesque alternative name for club root).

Although most of the wartime gardening writers were men (as indeed had been the case before war broke out), there were one or two notable exceptions. Eleanour Sinclair Rohde, the specialist in unusual herbs and vegetables, was already an established writer in the 1930s. She concentrated on the popular overlap between horticulture and history, publishing books on old English gardening, anthologies of garden writing from previous centuries, and

ONION PLANTING.

1. Pricking out seedlings raised under glass.
2. Box of seedling Onions ready for planting out.
3. Planting out in rows 12 inches apart, plants 6 inches apart.
4. Bed of Onions in summer growth.

Above
This page of photographic instruction on onion propagation is typical of the thoroughness of *The Vegetable Garden Displayed*.

Below
The *Daily Mail Grow It Yourself* book really was for novices. In this figure they demonstrate how to hold and use a spade.

'recipes from olden days'. In 1940 she published a book on **Culinary and Salad Herbs: Their cultivation and food values**, including a handy collection of recipes to help those who were unused to using herbs beyond the 'standard' parsley, thyme and mint. A year later she produced **Uncommon Vegetables and Fruit and How to Cultivate Them**, still with the emphasis on the more adventurous gardener and cook. **The Wartime Vegetable Garden** was perhaps more mainstream, dealing with types of vegetables that might just have made it into the government Dig for Victory leaflets, and in 1944 **Vegetable Cultivation and Cookery** was aimed at those still unconvinced.

Publications on how to Dig for Victory had become so popular that libraries held exhibitions of the books that were available. Highgate Public Library in London was among the first to put on a display, in August 1940, including in the exhibition encouraging letters from Cecil Middleton. As well as printed material the library displayed seeds, and pictures from BBC programmes on food production. Newport Public Libraries published a pamphlet accompanying another Dig for Victory exhibition in February 1943. It was not the libraries' purpose to advise on actual cultivation, but they felt that it was imperative that everyone should make the most of whatever cultivation space they had by reading about gardening methods. Unsurprisingly their first recommendations were the books by Mr Middleton, followed by anything coming from the seed merchants Messrs Sutton and Sons, and the much respected, pre-war garden author H.H. Thomas. Eleanour Rohde was commended for her 'garden of herbs', while tomatoes and mushrooms would be covered in specialist booklets by Ravenscroft and Defrie. It is rather surprising to see books on grapes, peaches, nectarines and melons alongside the numerous books on British weeds and vegetable foes, but perhaps a sense of pride in the libraries' holdings was creeping in, as the next paragraph deals with books on the then novel method of hydroponics (raising plants without soil), and the possible advantages of planting by the moon. Pigs, poultry, bees and rabbits were also covered by books in the Newport Public Libraries' holdings, although they admitted that 'the literature on the pig is not very prolific', and resorted to drawing attention to Charles Lamb's classic essay on 'Roast Pig' and a Ministry of Agriculture and Fisheries **Report on the Marketing of Pigs in England and Wales**. Completing the overview of the libraries' relevant holdings, they added some recommendations for books on shooting, cooking, making non-alchoholic drinks, and even physiotherapy for gardeners' back pain. All residents, plus members of the services and the Women's Land Army, were encouraged to go and consult the books in the Newport libraries, although prospective gardeners were warned that 'Bailey's monumental three-volume **Encyclopaedia of Horticulture** was for reference only and could not be borrowed.

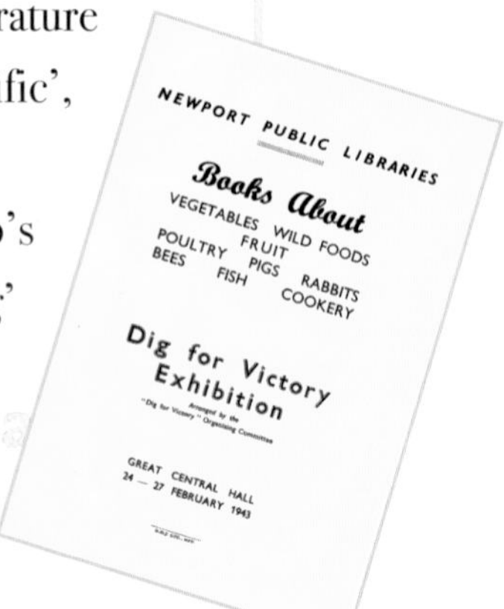
NEWPORT PUBLIC LIBRARIES
Books About
VEGETABLES WILD FOODS
FRUIT
POULTRY PIGS
BEES FISH RABBITS
COOKERY
Dig for Victory Exhibition
GREAT CENTRAL HALL
24 — 27 FEBRUARY 1943

Talks and Lectures (and War Ag)

A further source of inspiration and encouragement were the talks given by prominent local gardeners and head gardeners. **Garden Work** reported in May 1943 that *'During the war, parks superintendents in all districts have worked very hard to enlighten Victory Diggers. As one example, the head of Blackburn's parks has appeared 155 times on public platforms, and one can well imagine the countless questions he has been called upon to answer.'* Some of these talks were billed as local versions of the popular radio programme, the **Brains Trust**. Panels were usually made up of local parks superintendents and head gardeners, but the most popular included representatives of the Royal Horticultural Society, Plant Protection Ltd, or even radio celebrities. The RHS provided free speakers for anywhere in the country as part of their contribution to the war effort. Freddy Grisewood, a radio celebrity, was one of the most sought-after Brains Trust panellists, as of course was Mr Middleton!

The **Gardeners' Chronicle** of November 1940 even reported that *'Ministers of Religion are being supplied with plenty of biblical texts and quotations, and are asked to use their best endeavours, by means of sermons, to increase food production, which may well be one of the decisive factors for ensuring victory'*. Almost 5,000 of these 'Some Notes for Sermons' were distributed in the hope that local authorities might persuade local clergymen to make use of them. Religious instruction and cultivation tips combined must have made for some eccentric sermons!

The work of the parks superintendents, brains trusts, allotment and horticultural societies and the media was supplemented in a more official way by the county-based War Agricultural Committees, with their roving 'War Ag' advisers. These gave advice on all horticultural matters (despite their agricultural title). Accompanied by cookery advisers, they toured their counties dispensing the latest information and advice. Some even did demonstration work, or offered to lend a hand with tricky tasks such as pruning. Viola Williams, working as an assistant horticultural officer for the Wiltshire War Agricultural Committee, took on grafting fruit trees as one of her duties, as well as overseeing all the allotments in the county. In one village she recalls single-handedly grafting almost every tree. Women 'War Ags' often teamed up with the WI agricultural adviser, Elizabeth Hess, and the local WI federations, as this gave them the opportunity to deliver talks and advice to women who were taking on an increasing amount of the food production burden. Cookery demonstrations were also popular, although encouraging women to cook more of the 'unusual' vegetables, such as Kohl rabi, was an uphill task.

By the end of the war there can have been few people that had not heard a gardening programme on the radio, or spent an evening down in an air-raid shelter being regaled with a talk on brassicas and potatoes, and even fewer who had not a book, magazine or leaflet on Digging for Victory somewhere in their house or garden shed. The media had won its own war.

MANURES
FOR THE WAR-TIME GARDEN
S. B. WHITEHEAD, D.Sc.

*A Guide for the Conversion of
Garden and Household Refuse into Plant Food*

A NATIONAL FOOD HANDBOOK
ISSUED BY "AMATEUR GARDENING"

Winning ways with muck: manures & composts

'Worthwhile results in the great Growmore campaign cannot be expected from starved soil', claimed Sofnol, the providers of 'Victory' fertilisers, lime and their very own 'Peat-umus'. Never had dung seemed so desirable or fertiliser so fascinating. Constant cropping and necessary expansion on to poor soils led inevitably to low yields, and fertilisers and manures of all kinds became the focus of the nation's attention. Horse manure had for centuries been the backbone of the vegetable garden. Despite what one writer described as *'the remarkable development of mechanical transport with its consequent decline in horse-keeping and reduced production of stable-manure'*, many gardeners in the 1930s had been able to rely almost entirely on the 'natural product' and were convinced that animal manures were essential for soil nourishment and high yields. Although some gardeners and commercial producers had taken up the use of artificial manures and fertilisers, these were often considered a poor substitute for the 'real stuff', and some writers even considered them detrimental to health!

With the outbreak of war, manure supplies of any type were dramatically reduced. There were two causes of this; the vast increase in the area of land under cultivation meant that the demand for

Left
The front cover of S.B. Whitehead's *Manures for the War-time Garden* demonstrates his firm belief in the power of the compost heap made of garden and household rubbish.
Below
Sofnol advert, from *The Vegetable Garden Displayed*.

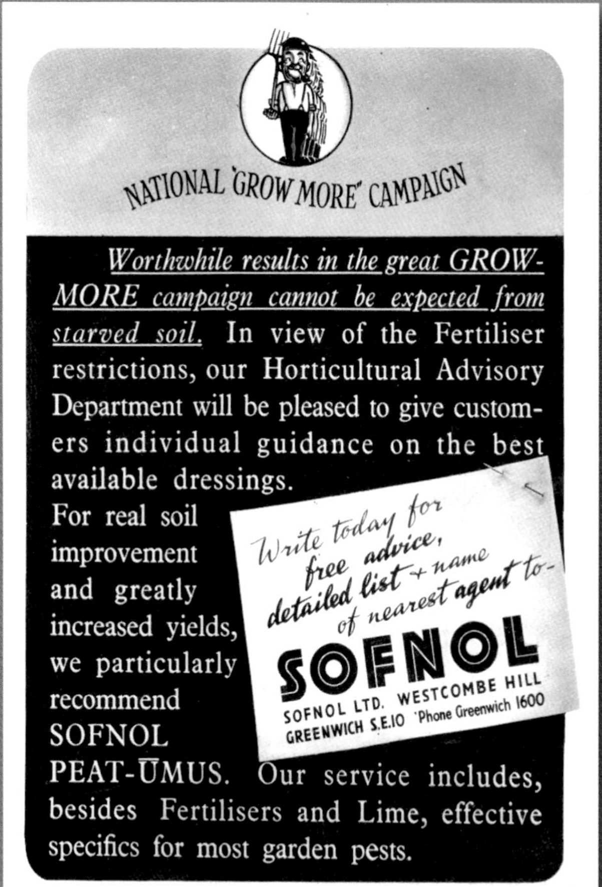
NATIONAL 'GROW MORE' CAMPAIGN
Worthwhile results in the great GROW-MORE campaign cannot be expected from starved soil. In view of the Fertiliser restrictions, our Horticultural Advisory Department will be pleased to give customers individual guidance on the best available dressings.
For real soil improvement and greatly increased yields, we particularly recommend SOFNOL PEAT-ŪMUS. Our service includes, besides Fertilisers and Lime, effective specifics for most garden pests.
Write today for free advice, detailed list + name of nearest agent to-
SOFNOL
SOFNOL LTD. WESTCOMBE HILL
GREENWICH S.E.10 'Phone Greenwich 1600

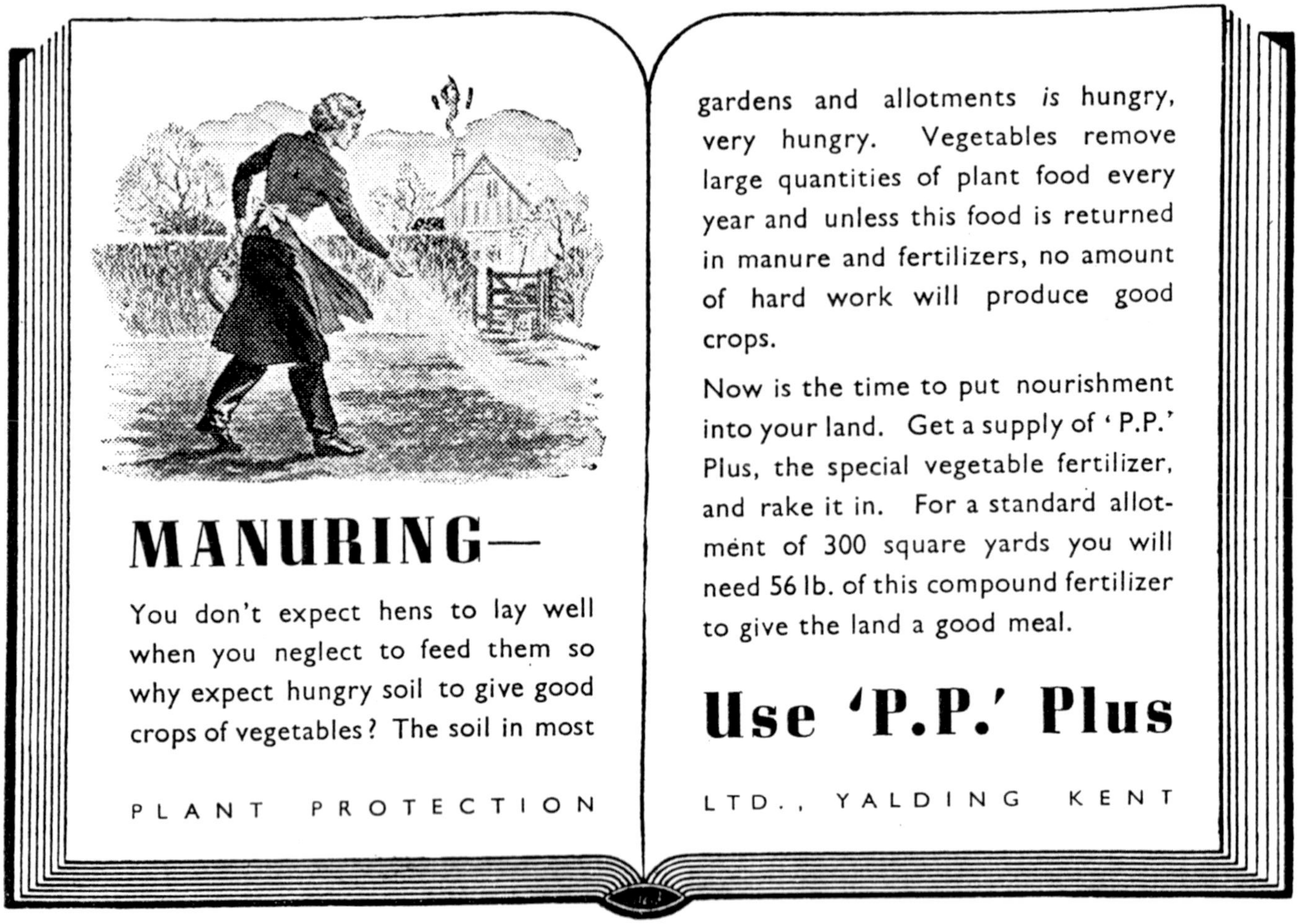
MANURING—
You don't expect hens to lay well when you neglect to feed them so why expect hungry soil to give good crops of vegetables? The soil in most
gardens and allotments *is* hungry, very hungry. Vegetables remove large quantities of plant food every year and unless this food is returned in manure and fertilizers, no amount of hard work will produce good crops.
Now is the time to put nourishment into your land. Get a supply of 'P.P.' Plus, the special vegetable fertilizer, and rake it in. For a standard allotment of 300 square yards you will need 56 lb. of this compound fertilizer to give the land a good meal.
Use 'P.P.' Plus
PLANT PROTECTION LTD., YALDING KENT

dung was high, while restricted animal feedstuffs meant fewer animals were being kept. Imports were also severely cut back; in the foreword to **Manures for the War-time Garden** A.J. MacSelf wrote: *'it has proved to be not always convenient or politic to rely entirely upon materials which must be brought from overseas or which, under conditions of emergency, may be required for purposes other than enriching the ground'.*

Farmers were given priority over gardeners for any substantial supplies, and gardeners were often reduced to using supplies from domestic livestock – hens and rabbits – and general garden rubbish. The situation was not resolved until the government stepped in with its own Growmore artificial fertiliser in 1942. Some new gardeners did not realise the need for manure at all, so campaigns had to be run to persuade them to 'feed the soil'.

Above

The idea of 'hungry soil' was a new one to many novice gardeners.

Right

A pig club. Not only were the pigs themselves of use, their droppings could be put to good use as manure. HMSO

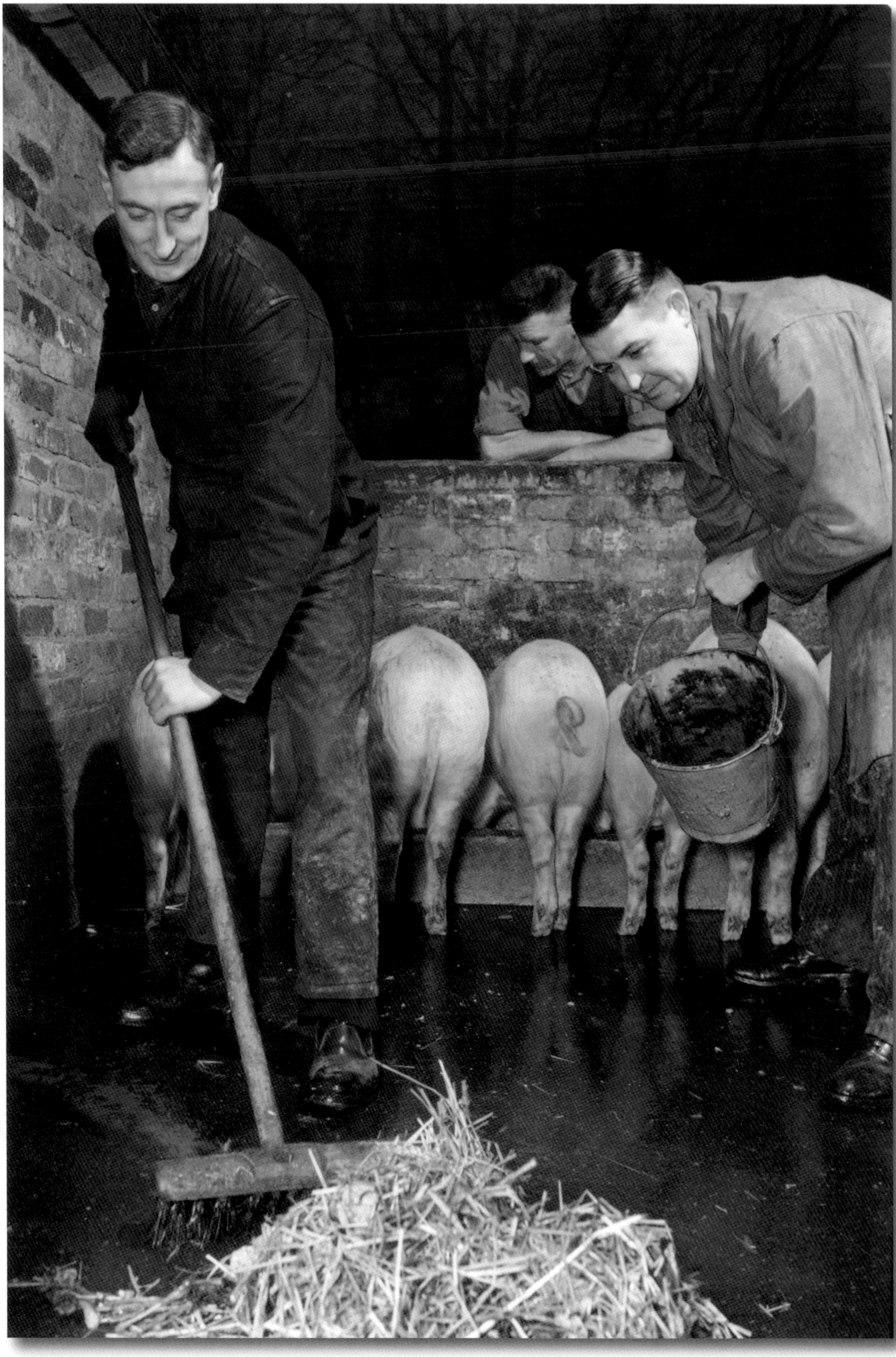

Animal Dung

Despite continued use of horses for deliveries of milk and other supplies, horse manure was soon in short supply. Marie Mainwaring (née Thomas) of Swindon recalls that *'The garden was occasionally treated to a feed of horse manure. Our baker and the coal-delivery man used a horse and cart and it was a case of whichever neighbour spotted it first in the street. The baker's horse also liked the privet hedge in the small front garden and when the iron railings were removed to help the war effort access became much easier.'* Children sent to follow the milkman in the hope of dung for the garden were often foiled by a dung bag, securely fixed to the rear end of the horse to ensure all supplies went back to the stables and could be used there or sold! *'Stable or farmyard manure is very difficult to obtain these days. It is however possible to advertise for it, especially if you live near a farming district'* (**The War-time Weekend Gardener**). In April 1941 James Cutting and Sons of Stamford in Lincolnshire were advertising Concentrated Stable Manure for 7s 6d. per hundredweight (carriage paid), and prices rose throughout the war.

One of the easiest manures to obtain during the war years was pig manure. With the government campaign encouraging as many people as possible to keep a (registered!) pig, there were more pigs in urban areas than ever before. Most streets boasted a pig bin for scraps even in the most urban of areas, and in return for leftovers schools and allotments could expect to gain pig manure for their vegetables from the local pig farmer or smallholder. The 'Pig Woman' and 'Pig Man' became familiar figures,

visited by a trail of wheelbarrows all hoping for their 'share'. The Pierrepont School for Girls in Nottingham sent all their school dinner and garden waste to the local pig woman, via a wheelbarrow pushed by pupils. The same barrow (and pupils) would come back full of pig muck. Although, as Mrs K.M. Price remembers, this had its hazards! *'We turned up the rather steep road with our smelly load, and reaching the bend … over went the barrow. Lily and me, well we just looked at each other and wished we'd never come. "What shall we do?" said Lily. "I'll go and ask at this house for a dustpan and we'll get it up." I opened the gate and went up to the front door. "Can I borrow your dustpan Missus, to clean the mess up?" I said. Well when she saw it she went berserk and no wonder, it looked worse out of the barrow. So I said, "Well if not we'll have to leave it here, and it's for our Dig for Victory as well".'*

With an increase in people keeping hens and rabbits, smaller droppings and animal bedding were available to many. Poultry and pigeon manure were too rich to be used direct and it was recommended that they be dried and then beaten with a mallet or hammer into a fine dust to be mixed with soil before being applied in small amounts. In Kensington, West London, 10 tons of pigeon manure were scraped from the inside of the roof of St John the Baptist Church and distributed to allotment-holders in the borough. Rabbit droppings were only of use if the bedding they came with was hay or peat; sawdust and wood shavings were described as injurious to the compost heap and to be avoided. One letter writer to **The Times** was anxious to receive government advice on the usage of rabbit manure and felt it was an area that

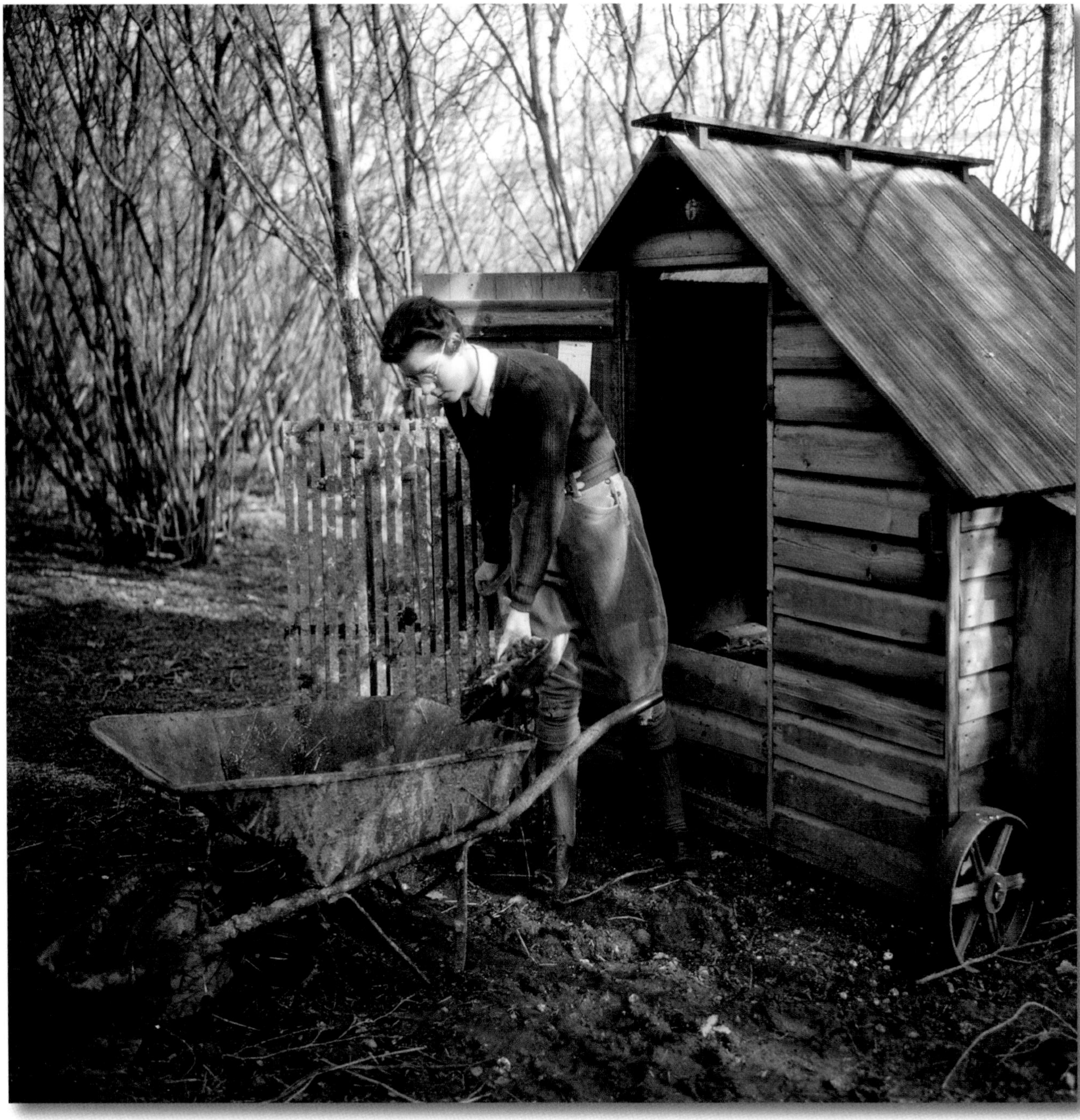

Above
A Land Girl mucking out a henhouse. Poultry droppings could be used in small amounts as fertiliser. HMSO

the bulletins and leaflets had much neglected!

The **War-time Weekend Gardener** obliged: *'Scrape the rabbit manure and the floor litter into a wide mouthed sack and store this in a cool place. When the sack is about half full, suspend it in a bath of water, preferably rain water, and use the liquid as* *a liquid manure when it takes on the colour of weak tea. Rabbit manure can also be stacked, mixed with the chicken droppings or stored in a sunk pit in the garden. The mixture will provide a valuable fertiliser if it is dug in during the annual digging.'*

Goat droppings were described as an extremely worthwhile manure, being a balanced mix – but more tricky to get hold of, especially if the goat was allowed free range in a field!

If the household had not joined in the victory livestock campaign then all was not lost. One man, for instance, desperate to improve his 'lumpy' clay soil, used boiler flue scrapings. Other unlikely additions to the panoply of general manures or fertilisers included 'shoddy', a waste product of the wool industry, 'screened dust' from household collections of domestic waste bins, bracken collected from the forests and heaths, and even hair cuttings and road sweepings. The latter two were utilised by the women's gardening school at Waterperry (Oxon). Shoddy was held to be particularly good for areas of light soil, as it decomposed slowly and released nitrogen organic compound. It was also available in increased amounts during the initial wartime period due to the military demands on the wool factories to make more uniforms. Screened waste on the other hand became less available as people learnt to 'make do and mend' and use every scrap of food or domestic waste rather than placing it in a bin.

A wide variety of household and other 'rubbish' was recommended for the compost heap by Stanley Whitehead in his book **Manures for the War-time Garden**. Rag and wool wastes from a nearby factory, vacuum cleaner dust, feathers, bracken, leather wastes, rabbit fur, blood, fish waste, ditch cleanings, soot, and even 'night soil' (human manure and urine, usually from chamber pots) were included in his list of suitable materials. Night soil had to be handled carefully and well composted before use, but as Whitehead pointed out 'habitation wastes' had been used by 'the peasants of China' for thousands of years. The experiences of gardeners and ex-army men who had worked abroad resulted in some increasingly bizarre suggestions to address the shortage of manures; worn-out clothing, ground-nuts, the outsides of palm trees, old thatched roofs, bracken roots and even the water-hyacinth plant (in the 1940s not yet the pest of Britain's waterways that it was to become).

Sludge manure, composed of the deposit from sewage settling tanks, was occasionally available and rich in nitrogen. It was best used on green vegetables but could be used on root crops and potatoes with caution, as it was believed to encourage wireworms. The Corporation of Plymouth created and sold a special 'Plymouth fertiliser' based on sewage sludge; advertised as *'eminently suitable for all gardening and farming requirements and also forming an ideal top dressing for lawns and grassland'.* 'Old hands', however, argued that sewage was not suitable for potatoes as they would end up strong and earthy tasting once cooked. The results of experiments in its use found that there were 'no regrets' among those who had used it and the flavour of the vegetables had not taken on the sewage. In Coventry, sewage sludge formed one of the 'exhibits' at a Dig for Victory exhibition in August 1944, where particulars of its make-up, the whereabouts of the sewage works, and even samples of sewage sludge were all on view. The exhibit was apparently very popular.

Hop manure was another popular alternative to animal dung. The hop industry was still in full swing in Kent in the 1930s and the by-products of the treatment and brewing process were widely marketed. Hop manure had a high humus content and therefore added body and texture as well as nutrients – although whether it could stand up to the advertisers' claims of 70–100% better gardening results than stable manure must have been debatable. In its marketed form hop manure was also cleaner and easier to handle than animal manures – which was an advantage when appealing to those whose commitment to victory digging was uncertain. Unfortunately by 1943 the hop industry had been severely curtailed, and combined with the growing popularity of hop manure, this resulted in severe shortages. 'Abol', one of the most popular hop manures, was forced to take out large advertisements in the gardening press announcing that 'Abol' hop manure now had so little hop in it that it was henceforth to be called just 'Abol' manure, deleting the word 'hop'. The makers claimed that the actual product was just as valuable for soil conditioning, but were not forthcoming as to what had replaced the all-important hops.

Top right

This advertisement for Wakeley's hop manure expects its readers to be familiar with the chemical constituents of fertilisers.

Bottom right

Adcompost was one of the main providers of hop manure. Note the man digging and the boy barrowing while a girl just 'stands around'! Women were only just making an appearance in commercial garden advertisements at this time, even though they featured regularly in government propaganda posters.

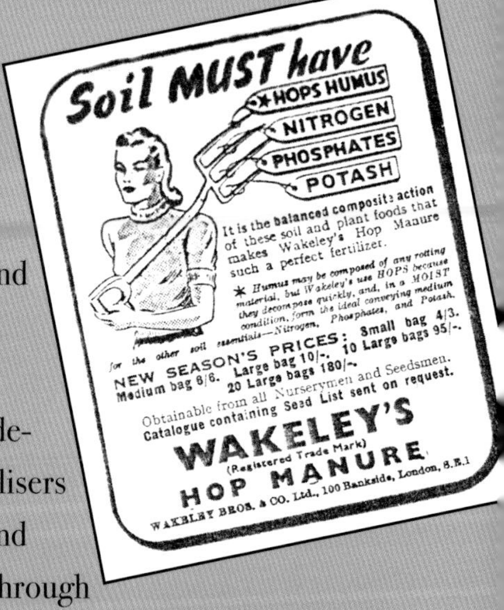
Soil MUST have
HOPS HUMUS
NITROGEN
PHOSPHATES
POTASH
It is the balanced composite action of these soil and plant foods that makes Wakeley's Hop Manure such a perfect fertilizer.
NEW SEASON'S PRICES: Small bag 4/3. Medium bag 8/6. Large bag 10/-. 10 Large bags 95/-. 20 Large bags 180/-.
Obtainable from all Nurserymen and Seedsmen. Catalogue containing Seed List sent on request.
WAKELEY'S
(Registered Trade Mark)
HOP MANURE
WAKELEY BROS. & CO. Ltd., 100 Bankside, London, S.E.1

Bonemeal of all kinds, along with scrapings of hoofs and horns, and fishmeal, were well-known additions to the gardener's arsenal of fertilisers and soil chemistry and remained available through the war, although in decreased supply. Blood, bone and fishmeal were known to be phosphate rich and were advertised as such. This caused instant confusion with amateurs flummoxed as to its relation to lime and the superphosphates then on offer. By 1943 amateurs were usually being recommended to stick to the National Growmore Fertiliser with its complete compounds of phosphates and nitrogens. Bonemeal also had the disadvantage of its unpleasant smell, and a nasty habit of attracting rats, foxes and other vermin. Soot was readily available in the 1940s when most houses still had coal fires, and was regarded as being extraordinarily beneficial for soil in all sorts of ways: improving texture, increasing fertility and also creating a darker coloured soil, which was believed to increase soil warmth. Soot might also be added to liquid forms of manure made with a mix of animal-based manure and nettles soaked in water. Lighter soot was thought to have the greater fertilising qualities, and

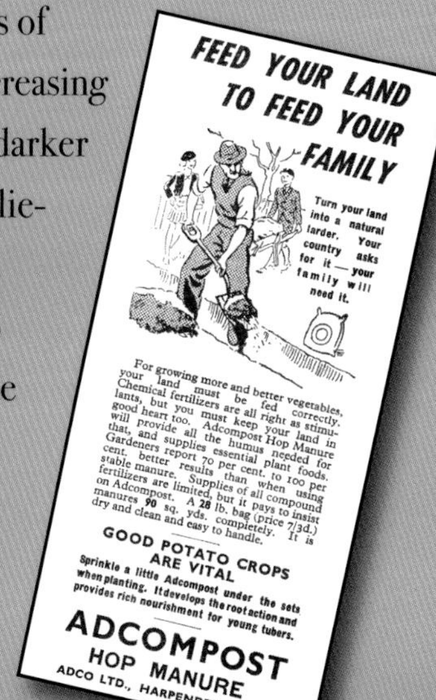
FEED YOUR LAND TO FEED YOUR FAMILY
Turn your land into a natural larder. Your country asks for it — your family will need it.
GOOD POTATO CROPS ARE VITAL
ADCOMPOST
HOP MANURE
ADCO LTD., HARPENDEN, HERTS

was recommended to be applied at a rate of seven pounds of soot per pole (an allotment usually being 10 poles). **Garden Work** magazine recommended soot especially for crops that required plenty of nitrogen, such as onions, lettuces and other green crops. Asparagus (where grown), cauliflowers, broccoli, Brussels sprouts and celery also benefited from an application of soot. Slugs and snails were said to avoid soot, which would give extra protection to young seedlings when it was applied along the rows. In fact soot seems to have been recommended for nearly anything! However the soot had to be stored for 2–3 months in a dry, open, area, before use. If used fresh it could actually be injurious and garden magazines always specified 'stale' soot or mixing the soot with other manures and digging it well in. Mixing the soot with household ashes was also bad for the soil, increasing porosity in some light soils without increasing goodness. Household ashes, a perennial problem as waste collections were cut back, were recommended for making paths rather than actually digging into the plot.

Green manure made an appearance in the Royal Horticultural Society's **The Vegetable Garden Displayed** as a way of keeping up the humus content of the soil, but was otherwise not widely used early in the war. Cecil Middleton suggested digging in turnip tops as green manure, although admitted that fitting in time for growing this type of manure was difficult. Prompt planting was essential if it was to be achieved in existing crop rotations. Other possible green manures included mustard, rape, vetches, clovers and tares, although some were not advisable if you were hoping to grow brassicas, a common crop in the Dig for Victory campaign.

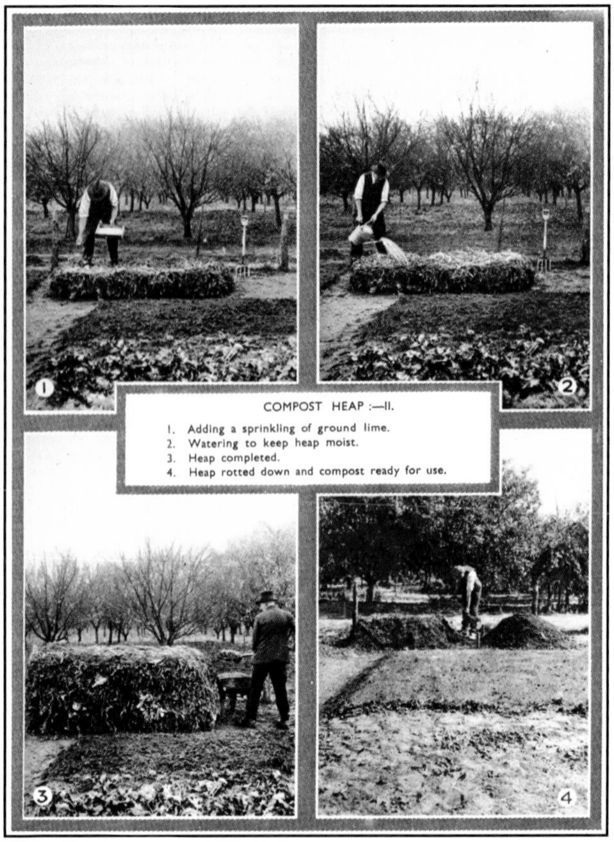
1
2
3
4

COMPOST HEAP :—II.

1. Adding a sprinkling of ground lime.
2. Watering to keep heap moist.
3. Heap completed.
4. Heap rotted down and compost ready for use.

Compost Heaps

In January 1940 **The Times** featured an article on natural and artificial manure. Not normally a paper one would have immediately thought of as a fount of knowledge on such a subject, its concern with such topics as manure was a sure sign of the widespread interest in such matters, as everyone got to grips with their new wartime garden. **The Times** considered the range of manures available to the

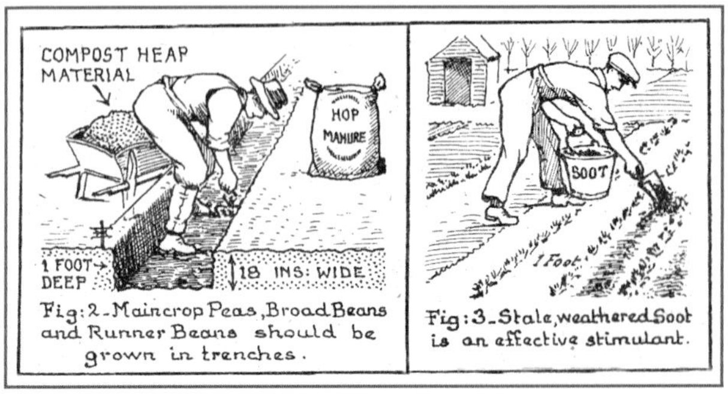
COMPOST HEAP MATERIAL
HOP MANURE
1 FOOT DEEP
18 INS: WIDE
SOOT
1 Foot

Fig: 2 – Maincrop Peas, Broad Beans and Runner Beans should be grown in trenches.

Fig: 3 – Stale, weathered Soot is an effective stimulant.

wartime gardener, and decided that in many instances the 'new' idea of the 'compost heap' might be ideal for amateurs. The compost heap had first become popular in India, where Sir A. Howard had trialled various combinations of content with great success. *'As straw manure has become scarcer and dearer, gardeners have had to turn more and more to chemical fertilisers. They have found, however, that whilst fertilisers alone stimulate plant growth, they do not fill the place of straw manure. That is because the chemicals contain no humus, that precious substance which, in the autumn decay of vegetation – leaves of all kinds, stems, stalks, husks and grass – is nature's annual contribution to the fertility of the soil.'* The article went on to argue that, although leafmould and horticultural peat might partly fill the void, 'science' must come to the gardener's rescue. In this case *'science was to appear in the shape of a compost heap'*.

The article continued: *'A domestic application of Sir A. Howard's well-known work in India, the compost heap combines humus and fertiliser. To it is consigned dead and dying vegetation of flower and vegetable garden, lawn mowings, weeds and vegetable refuse. . . . In its efforts to augment the home-grown food supply of the nation, the Ministry of Agriculture might well consider the issue of an illustrated leaflet showing unversed amateurs how to make and manage a compost heap in its simplest form.'*

Howard's work also attracted the attention of Stanley Whitehead, in his book on **Manures for the War-time Garden**, who argued that the techniques of organic soil fertility were better known in China and India than in the West. Whitehead claimed that thanks to Howard's work and that of the late Rudolf Steiner (now more famous for his educational work), *'every wartime garden can become self-supporting in the restoration and renewal of its fertility'*. Whitehead had been using compost on his own one-acre plot for six years before the war and claimed an abundance of healthful crops as a result. By 1941 compost heaps were springing up everywhere, and the

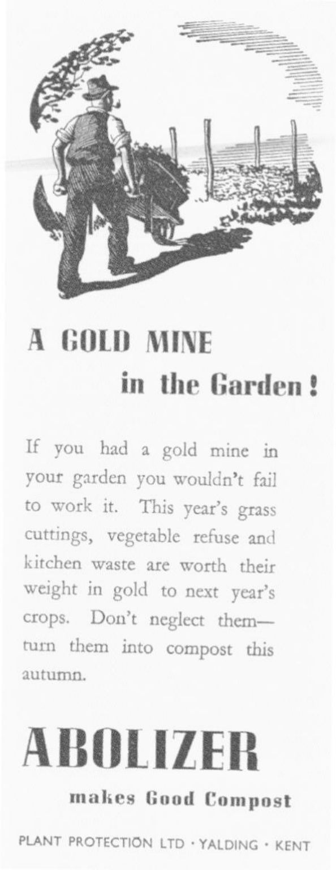
A GOLD MINE
in the Garden!
If you had a gold mine in your garden you wouldn't fail to work it. This year's grass cuttings, vegetable refuse and kitchen waste are worth their weight in gold to next year's crops. Don't neglect them—turn them into compost this autumn.
ABOLIZER
makes Good Compost
PLANT PROTECTION LTD · YALDING · KENT

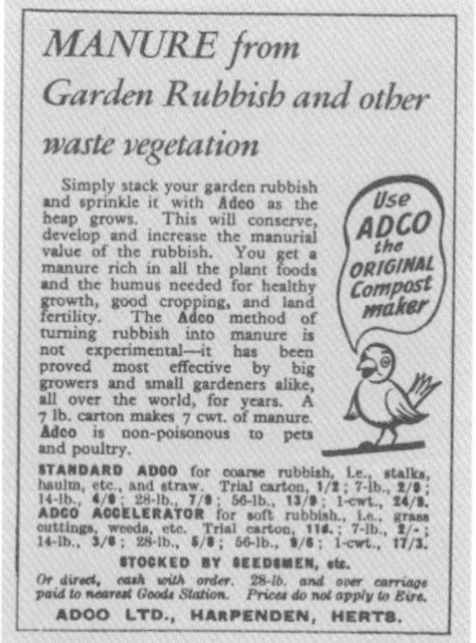
MANURE from
Garden Rubbish and other
waste vegetation
Simply stack your garden rubbish and sprinkle it with Adco as the heap grows. This will conserve, develop and increase the manurial value of the rubbish. You get a manure rich in all the plant foods and the humus needed for healthy growth, good cropping, and land fertility. The Adco method of turning rubbish into manure is not experimental—it has been proved most effective by big growers and small gardeners alike, all over the world, for years. A 7 lb. carton makes 7 cwt. of manure. Adco is non-poisonous to pets and poultry.
Use ADCO the ORIGINAL Compost maker
STANDARD ADCO for coarse rubbish, i.e., stalks, haulm, etc., and straw.
ADCO ACCELERATOR for soft rubbish, i.e., grass cuttings, weeds, etc.
STOCKED BY SEEDSMEN, etc.
Or direct, cash with order. 28-lb. and over carriage paid to nearest Goods Station. Prices do not apply to Eire.
ADCO LTD., HARPENDEN, HERTS.

Top left
How to make a compost heap, from the RHS's *The Vegetable Garden Displayed*.
Top right
Compost was regarded as second only to gold by many victory diggers.
Bottom left
Garden Work recommended the use of a wide variety of fertilisers and manures and included illustrated instruction in their use.
Bottom right
Adco also introduced an 'Original Compost Maker' to speed of the process of 'developing, conserving and increasing the manorial value of the rubbish'.

Royal Horticultural Society included instructions on making quick-maturing heaps in **The Vegetable Garden Displayed**. Dig for Victory leaflet no. 7 gave advice on the construction and maintenance of a compost heap, encouraging the manufacture of 'manure from garden rubbish'. The leaflet advised its readers that *By means of a compost heap, demanding neither much time nor labour, and little or no expense, all the vegetable waste of the garden can be turned into valuable manure. Leaves, grass cuttings, sods, lawn mowings, pea or bean or potato haulms, outer leaves or tops of vegetables, hedge clippings, weeds and faded flowers; in short any plant refuse green or otherwise, can be used for manorial purposes. Such a conversion of waste to good use, if widely adopted, can make a considerable contribution to the national effort for increased food production.'* It added that any left-over material that could not be composted should be burnt and the ashes dug into the plot. Bonfires however should be started early in the day in order to be extinguished by blackout time.

Trying to encourage even more gardeners into home composting (and home rubbish disposal!), the government also produced an animated cartoon to be shown by Pathé News. Dated May 1944, **Compost Heaps for Feeding** starred a cartoon Mr Middleton leaning on a garden gate. He described the importance of feeding your plants, and the way to make a compost heap, comparing the heap to a 'plant canteen'. Below him a cross-section through a heap showed small figures filling 'trolleys' with food and giving it to plant roots.

As the war progressed and manures became more restricted, with any available sources allocated to farms, 'gardening with compost' became a popular topic for articles and even books. In 1943 Frederic Charles King published **Gardening with Compost**, and in the same year Maye Emily Bruce produced **From Vegetable Waste to Fertile Soil, Quick Return Compost**. By 1945 it seemed most gardeners had been converted to using this valuable material, and the **Allotment and Garden Guide** for that year gave instructions in compost heap construction as a 'normal' part of the garden routine. For those who did not feel they could manage a compost heap, a fertiliser plus potash might be a substitute, but a poor one.

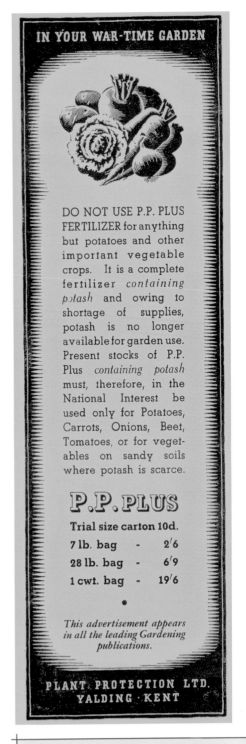

IN YOUR WAR-TIME GARDEN

DO NOT USE P.P. PLUS FERTILIZER for anything but potatoes and other important vegetable crops. It is a complete fertilizer *containing potash* and owing to shortage of supplies, potash is no longer available for garden use. Present stocks of P.P. Plus *containing potash* must, therefore, in the National Interest be used only for Potatoes, Carrots, Onions, Beet, Tomatoes, or for vegetables on sandy soils where potash is scarce.

P.P. PLUS

Trial size carton 10d.

7 lb. bag	-	2'6
28 lb. bag	-	6'9
1 cwt. bag	-	19'6

This advertisement appears in all the leading Gardening publications.

**PLANT PROTECTION LTD.
YALDING · KENT**

Above
Before the introduction of the government's Growmore fertiliser, other 'complete' artificial fertilisers were being made available. Plant Protection Ltd, based at Yalding in Kent, was at the forefront of the development of both pesticides and fertilisers.

Artificial Fertilisers

In addition to what were known as the 'organic' manures and fertilisers, there was a wide range of inorganic or mineral-based fertlisers (although the dividing line was not always clear in the advertising and discussions). Sulphate of ammonia, nitrate of soda, nitro-chalk, lime (in all its varieties), and sulphate of potash were the most popular. Professional gardeners were familiar with the use of all these, as were many amateurs, but for the novice they were confusing and often sounded dangerous and difficult.

Despite initial reluctance to change from animal manures, by 1944 a full range of artificial fertilisers was available to complement 'natural' fertilisers and composts. Fisons (originally founded in the 19th century) were at the forefront of artificial fertilisers. Whatever you were growing in your victory garden, Fisons had a fertiliser for you. Fisons' Granular Vegerite would 'give your vegetables a healthy start', Fisons' Ichthemic Guano would help boost the soft fruit crop, while the herbaceous border (making a return by this late stage of the war) would benefit from Fisons' Tomorite. Any area of the garden not 'covered' by this range of fertilisers would undoubtedly benefit from a liberal application of Fisons' improved hop manure.

However with manure in short supply and chemicals needed for war use, it was only a matter of time before artificial fertilisers were also restricted. In March 1941 it was announced that potash would no longer be available for general garden use; any fertiliser containing potash was reserved for essential vegetable crops such as potatoes, carrots and onions. Farmers were to have first call on what was available, with home gardeners rationed.

Although some gardeners took careful note of the suggested application methods and quantities of such essentials as nitrogen, phosphorus, potash, lime, zinc, cobalt, and so on, many others found they lacked both the chemical knowledge required and the dedication. While millions were willing to Dig for Victory, fewer were prepared to spend their evenings on advanced studies in soil chemistry. In January 1940 it was announced that: *'The following manure has been recommended by the Ministry of Agriculture for general use in vegetable growing, and it is easy to mix and apply:*

14lbs sulphate of ammonia; *14lbs steamed boneflour;*
28lbs superphosphate; *14lbs sulphate of potash.*

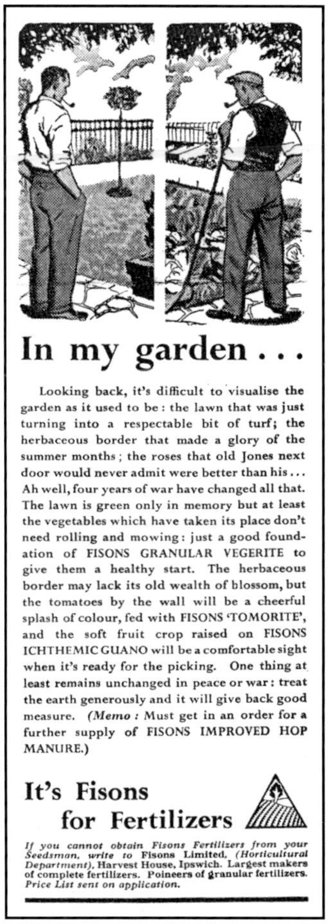
In my garden . . .
Looking back, it's difficult to visualise the garden as it used to be : the lawn that was just turning into a respectable bit of turf; the herbaceous border that made a glory of the summer months ; the roses that old Jones next door would never admit were better than his . . . Ah well, four years of war have changed all that. The lawn is green only in memory but at least the vegetables which have taken its place don't need rolling and mowing : just a good foundation of FISONS GRANULAR VEGERITE to give them a healthy start. The herbaceous border may lack its old wealth of blossom, but the tomatoes by the wall will be a cheerful splash of colour, fed with FISONS 'TOMORITE', and the soft fruit crop raised on FISONS ICHTHEMIC GUANO will be a comfortable sight when it's ready for the picking. One thing at least remains unchanged in peace or war : treat the earth generously and it will give back good measure. (Memo : Must get in an order for a further supply of FISONS IMPROVED HOP MANURE.)
It's Fisons for Fertilizers
If you cannot obtain Fisons Fertilizers from your Seedsman, write to Fisons Limited, (Horticultural Department), Harvest House, Ipswich. Largest makers of complete fertilizers. Poineers of granular fertilizers. Price List sent on application.

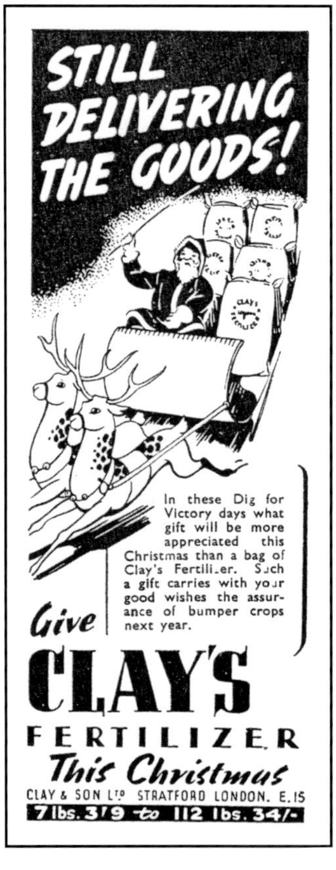
STILL DELIVERING THE GOODS!
In these Dig for Victory days what gift will be more appreciated this Christmas than a bag of Clay's Fertilizer. Such a gift carries with your good wishes the assurance of bumper crops next year.
Give
CLAY'S
FERTILIZER
This Christmas
CLAY & SON LTD STRATFORD LONDON. E.15
7 lbs. 3/9 to 112 lbs. 34/-

LIMING
No human being can live long without salt. No soil can produce good crops without lime. Most cultivated land should be limed every other year if it is to produce consistently good crops, and the best time to use lime is in winter and early spring.
Buy a bag of 'Limbux' hydrated garden lime to-day. It is cheap, easy to spread and will not burn your fingers or spoil your clothes. Spread it at the rate of ½-lb. per square yard on all land except that on which you intend to grow potatoes. Don't dig it in. If you dislike the snowy appearance of the garden after liming, rake the surface lightly. Lime will find its own level in the soil.
Use 'LIMBUX' GARDEN LIME
PLANT PROTECTION LTD YALDING KENT

Above

This 1942 advertisement for Limbux lime was placed in *Everywoman* magazine, marking the involvement of women in even the nitty-gritty of home food production.

Below

Hydrated lime was widely used to break up heavy soils, a typical problem on many new allotment sites. On light soils higher percentages of organic materials were recommended as well.

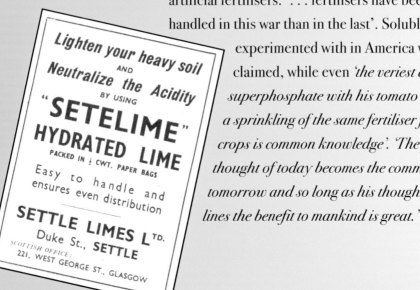

This mixture to be applied at three ounces per square yard or 5½ lbs per square rod.'

Faced with this sort of instruction it was no wonder many novices turned to ready-mixed fertilisers for their plot.

For these gardeners the government soon realised fertilisers would have to be provided that were easy, cheap, efficient and above all, readily available. National Growmore fertiliser was developed by the government in 1947 specifically for the Dig for Victory and Grow More campaigns. First made widely available at the very beginning of 1943, it contained a careful balance of nitrogen, phosphate and potash known as '7.7.7'. National Growmore could be obtained through the usual nurserymen and seedsmen, as well as through allotment societies and village food societies. But even this fertiliser was rationed. Only 3cwt of Compound (Growmore) fertiliser was allowed over 3 months without a special buying permit. In January 1945 private gardeners were allowed to buy 42lb of 'Growmore' (as it became known) and the Ministry of Agriculture Allotment and Garden Guide recommended *'that out of the 42lb of "National Growmore Fertiliser" that you might buy, you should set aside 2lb as a top dressing for spring cabbage. Or you can use sulphate of ammonia, applying it at the rate of one ounce per yard run. Lettuces and spinach would also benefit by a similar application. But keep the fertiliser off the leaves.'*

By the end of the war the gardening press was to enthuse over artificial fertilisers: '. . . fertilisers have been far more intelligently handled in this war than in the last'. Soluble fertilisers had been experimented with in America with much success, it was claimed, while even *'the veriest amateur now mixes a little superphosphate with his tomato compost'* and *'the value of a sprinkling of the same fertiliser for early and late sown crops is common knowledge'. 'The product of the scientist's thought of today becomes the common-place practice of tomorrow and so long as his thoughts are kept on such sound lines the benefit to mankind is great.'*

Lighten your heavy soil
AND
Neutralize the Acidity
BY USING
"SETELIME"
HYDRATED LIME
PACKED IN ½ CWT. PAPER BAGS
Easy to handle and ensures even distribution
SETTLE LIMES LTD.
Duke St., SETTLE
SCOTTISH OFFICE:
221, WEST GEORGE ST., GLASGOW

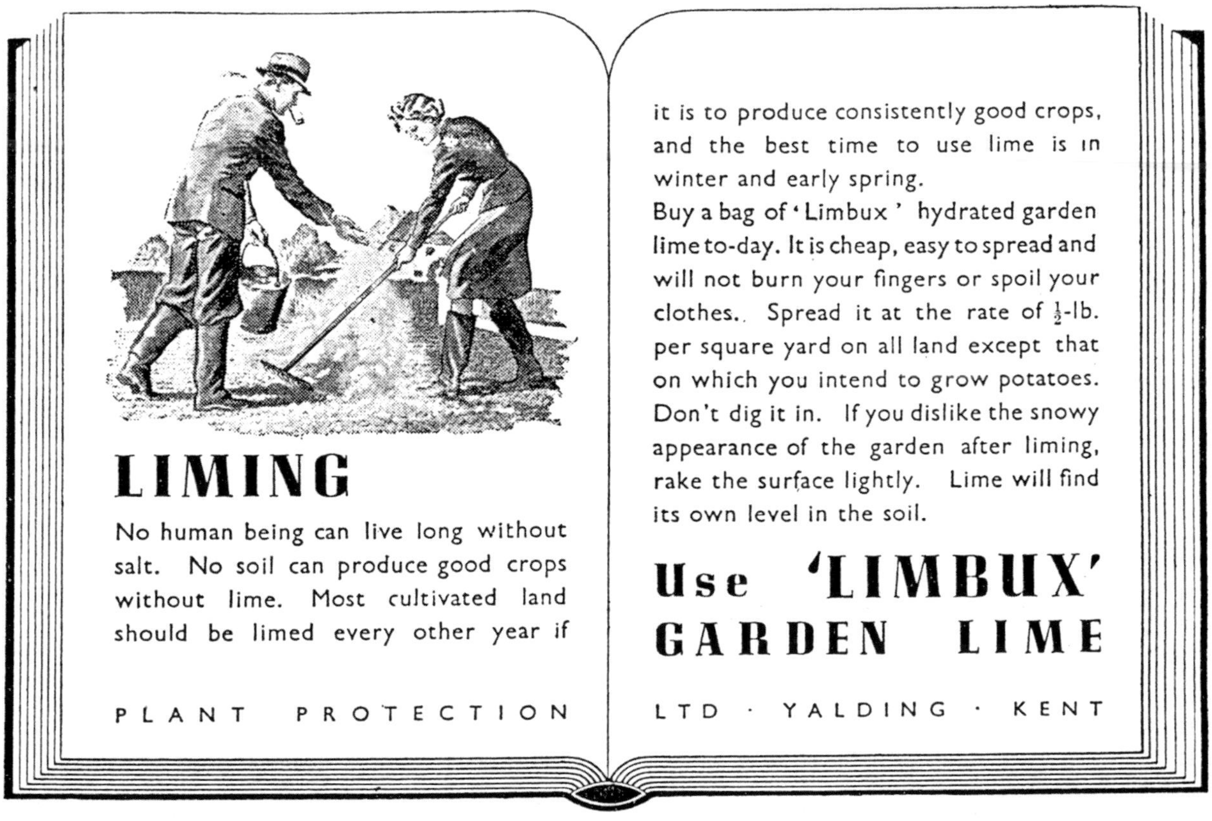

LIMING

No human being can live long without salt. No soil can produce good crops without lime. Most cultivated land should be limed every other year if it is to produce consistently good crops, and the best time to use lime is in winter and early spring.

Buy a bag of 'Limbux' hydrated garden lime to-day. It is cheap, easy to spread and will not burn your fingers or spoil your clothes. Spread it at the rate of $\frac{1}{2}$-lb. per square yard on all land except that on which you intend to grow potatoes. Don't dig it in. If you dislike the snowy appearance of the garden after liming, rake the surface lightly. Lime will find its own level in the soil.

Use 'LIMBUX' GARDEN LIME

PLANT PROTECTION LTD · YALDING · KENT

Above
Plant Protection Ltd led the campaign to use artificial fertilisers. This 1942 advertisement includes a woman, following the government's campaign for more female gardeners.

Lime

Lime, crucial for the release and take-up of other nutrients, was also recognised as an essential of wartime food production. Most gardening books recommended the use of lime both to control any acidity and to help break up heavy soils. Inevitably there was a consequent increased demand for lime, which promptly became in short supply! Lime was also recommended in agriculture rather than horticulture, with liming quantities recommended for farmers and smallholders in the government Grow-more (agricultural) leaflet no. 41. Yet again the farmers vied with the victory gardeners for supplies.

Amateurs and especially novice gardeners found lime a difficult topic. In 1941 a puzzled correspondent signing himself 'W.D. from Devon' wrote to **Garden Work** to ask: *'Please inform me whether superphosphate and superphosphate of lime are one and the same thing. If they are two distinct manures would you please explain their respective uses?'* Their comforting reply was that they were both the same and that he should apply it in spring at a rate of 2–3oz per square yard. The writer might justifiably also have queried the various trade names that lime appeared under. 'Setelime', Limex, Limbux, were all basically the same product under different trade names but guaranteed to confuse the novice gardener.

PESTS & DISEASES

IN THE

VEGETABLE

GARDEN

"GROWMORE" BULLETIN No. 2 OF THE
MINISTRY OF AGRICULTURE AND FISHERIES
PUBLISHED BY HIS MAJESTY'S
STATIONERY OFFICE

PRICE **4d.** NET

Fighting the enemy: pests, insects & diseases

Wartime gardening was not a peaceful affair. The victory gardener waged incessant warfare against a remarkably wide range of diseases and pests that attacked the home front garden. As the Humber Fish Manure Company pointed out in their May 1943 advertisement: *'By no stretch of the imagination can a gardener be described as a peaceful man. On the contrary, to him life is one long war, and when he isn't planning pincer movements on the caterpillars or encircling the slugs he is probably gassing something else.'* From moles to horses, rabbits to mice, wireworm to butterflies, aphids to fungus, gardeners were encouraged to trap, poison and spray their way to gardening success. Some pests could be 'regulated' for, with fines for letting dogs wander on allotments, but others had to be exterminated. Use of substances such as nicotine and arsenic had been widespread in larger gardens from the late 19th century, and were increasingly used by amateur gardeners in the 1920s and '30s. On the outbreak of war the government (and gardeners) determined to beat the pests with a combination of old-fashioned poison and 'modern' science.

Left
This 'Pests and Diseases' leaflet was one of the most popular of the government's selection.
Above
Garden pests – from *In Your Garden* by C. H. Middleton.

Identifying the Enemy

For novice gardeners the first step in destruction was successful identification. The difference between friend and foe was more difficult in the soil than the air. A confused reader wrote to **Garden Work** in May 1943 wondering whether the 'quick moving insects with an enormous number of legs' that he saw while spring digging were wireworm, and if so how to destroy them. The editor hastily informed him that these were in fact centipedes as wireworm only had three pairs of legs, and that he should on no account destroy the beneficial insects. Some gardening books tried to reinforce the image

BEWARE OF THESE !
HOUSE SPARROW
PIGEON
JAY

CENTIPEDE
FAST MOVING FRIEND
MILLEPEDE
SLOW MOVING ENEMY

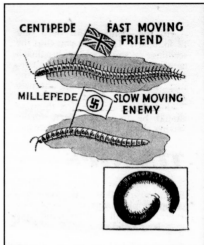

of friendly centipedes by illustrating them carrying English flags while their millipede 'foes' wore German helmets or carried German flags.

As ever the local Dig for Victory shows stepped in to help. At the 1940 Southport Flower Show exhibits included *'models and photographs of such pestilential evil-doers as Onion root fly, white fly of Tomatoes, Parsnip canker, large white cabbage butterflies, celery leaf-spot, surface caterpillars, cabbage aphis, Cabbage root fly, wart and scab diseases of Potatoes, and Carrot fly. Neatly typed descriptions and prescriptions were attached to each item in the exhibit.'* The Slough Wartime Horticultural Committee Allotment and Garden Week (1940) also had an exhibition devoted to what they called 'Hitler's Allies', including 'life-histories' of the more common pests and diseases. In January 1940, the **Gardeners' Chronicle** gave its readers an overview of some of the troublesome pests besetting the cabbage garden. First among these was the cabbage white butterfly, whose caterpillars reduce the leaves of cabbage to 'shot-shattered flags', followed by white fungal patches on leaves, turnip fly, cabbage gall weevil, and cabbage club root, traditionally known as finger and toe disease. Despite this wide range of potential pests and diseases the **Gardeners' Chronicle** felt that, on the whole, the cabbage tribe usually managed to 'hold their own in a world of trouble', as long as sufficient lime was added to the soil. Some gardeners were in need of very basic identification and knowledge; one Belfast woman claimed to kill every ladybird that she saw in her garden as she believed they ate her greens. In fact she was killing one of the gardener's best friends, as ladybirds eat greenfly and blackfly. A short newsfilm called **Garden Friends and Foes** issued in 1944 would soon put her right, although by then it may have been too late for her crops!

The **Gardeners' Chronicle** of December 1943 reported that: *'During the last week in July and the first in August this year, it is estimated that every day some 15,000,000 Cabbage White Butterflies crossed the Yorkshire coast on suitable days.'* They had most certainly come from the continent. The paper plaintively enquires whether there is no hope for farmers and gardeners: *'Must we go on fighting a losing battle against the caterpillars of these butterfly* *invaders? The most hopeful line of attack lies in international co-operation to swat the pest in its home country.'*

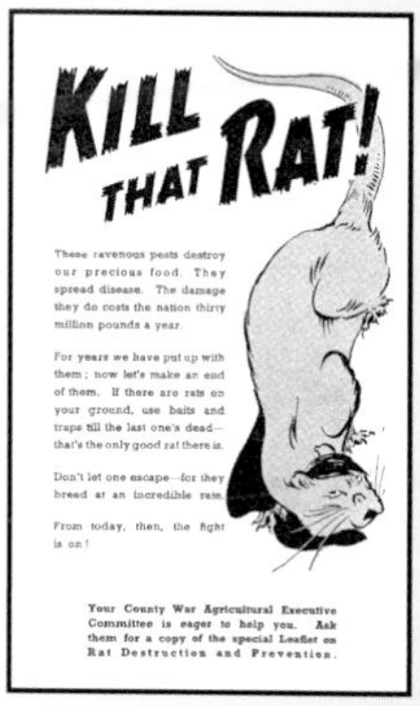
KILL THAT RAT!
These ravenous pests destroy our precious food. They spread disease. The damage they do costs the nation thirty million pounds a year.
For years we have put up with them; now let's make an end of them. If there are rats on your ground, use baits and traps till the last one's dead—that's the only good rat there is.
Don't let one escape—for they breed at an incredible rate.
From today, then, the fight is on!
Your County War Agricultural Executive Committee is eager to help you. Ask them for a copy of the special Leaflet on Rat Destruction and Prevention.

Rats, Cats, Dogs

Larger pests were not such a problem in terms of identification, although in terms of destruction they could equal any passing flock of butterflies. Rats were the main cause of concern for farmers and gardeners alike. Plundering stored seeds and grains, as well as crops in sheds and clamps, the rat was universally declared 'enemy number 1'. The presence of increased numbers of hens and rabbits in back gardens and on allotments meant that there was a ready source of food for the rats which ate both their food and occasionally the odd chicken or rabbit. Sheds full of stored carrots and onions proved a gourmet delight, and harsh winters which would normally have knocked back the population merely pushed them further into suburban areas. Unlike the wild rabbit there was not even a market for dead rats. Rat extermination campaigns were set up by the government, and Land Girls were sent on special patrol to kill as many farm rats as possible – not one of the most pleasant of their duties! Moles were also blamed for the destruction of gardens and allotments. At Gungrog school in Powys, the children were taught by the local mole catcher how to destroy the pests that were destroying their garden produce. House sparrows were also categorised as 'pests' and gardeners were encouraged to destroy all the nests and eggs they could find.

Although wild rabbits were much sought after as an ideal supplement to the meat ration, they were less desirable to the gardener. Allotments on areas of old pasture or parkland were particularly vulnerable. The new allotment correspondent for **Garden Work** found himself a victim to the depredations of a particularly persistent rabbit. Each week he described the rabbit's latest crimes, and his own counter-measures, until the eventual demise of the culprit:

'5 October 1940: I swanked about my spring cabbages, I invited a friend to come round simply that he might be impressed with my double trenching, I gloated daily over my Brussels sprouts. And then a rabbit found his way into the allotment. Much has been said and written about rabbits. At the present moment my own thoughts are too deep even for tears. A cold and bitter fury invades me every time I look at those sadly nibbled "Flowers of Spring". I know there is still time to replant spring cabbage, but I shall never cease to mourn my three-score that met with such untimely death.'

'12 October 1940: My sympathies used to be with Peter Rabbit, but I am now most definitely of the Mr

Far left
Bird pests, from the *Allotment & Garden Guide*, May 1945.
Left
Novice gardeners probably did not rely on millipedes carrying flags to aid identification! (*Allotment & Garden Guide*, April 1945)
Above
Rat destruction was regarded as a patriotic duty to be carried out by all farmers, gardeners and also by special patrols of the Land Army. Propaganda advertisements showed rats with a Hitler hairstyle and moustache.

Macgregor clan. Even a rabbit in the most bewitching little blue jacket would find me getting busy with a rake.'

In fact there was little that did not find its way to the unfortunate writer's plot. This sad tale was reported on 4 January 1941: *'Lately in a desperate attempt to stir up the egg laying capacity of my neighbour's hens they have been moved into a field adjoining my allotment. They have spent most of their time to date scratching and undermining the foundations of the old hedge, and one flew over into the allotment and destroyed more than a score of my Arctic King lettuce plants.'* Whether it was a result of

his lack of success on the allotment, or of his light and humorous touch, the column was obviously not to the taste of the more experienced garden hands, and was eventually replaced by the more usual 'old codger' type of allotment writer who had no truck with allusions to Beatrix Potter.

Even the famous Mr Middleton had trouble with pests. In **Digging for Victory** he wrote, *'Small suburban gardens have their limitations, what with the shade from trees and fences . . . and the depredations of cats and birds. My garden seems full of birds, starlings waddling about by the score, sparrows by the hundred and even seagulls are on* *visiting terms now. We fed the birds on the lawn for years and they don't seem to have forgotten it; they are glad to see us back again and now they seem to think that everything we put into the garden is intended for them alone. It's a bit discouraging, I admit, and I expect a good many of you are up against the same sort of problem.'*

Dogs were also a constant problem on allotments, and increasingly stringent measures were taken to keep them off the plots. Under the Defence Regulations of June 1941 any dog found trespassing on allotments would become liable to a fine of up to £5. This did not prevent an enthusiastic dog doing what was described as 'the Highland Fling' on a patch of onions recently transplanted by the London Mayor himself. In Sutton and Cheam allotment-holders were liable to be dispossessed if they took their dogs on to allotments, so no 'Highland Flings' there. Horses however were rather easier to catch; in Birmingham two men who rode on horseback over some allotments after they had already been warned of trespass said that a 5s fine would not hurt them. They took rather a different view of the fine when the magistrates instead fined them £10 each with £2 costs.

Insects and Diseases

After variously trapping, netting, poisoning or prosecuting the larger 'pests' on his plot, the gardener was left to deal with the more usual run of slugs, snails, insects, aphids, and diseases. Loss of garden crops caused by insects and diseases was a major concern for the Ministry of Agriculture, creating what they described as 'serious national waste'. A short Dig for Victory leaflet (no. 16) was issued on the subject of garden pests, and there was also a longer and more detailed Grow More bulletin available. Guidelines on diseases of fruit were covered in Dig for Victory leaflet no. 18, and separate advisory leaflets were also available on each of the different kinds of pests including such delights as gooseberry red spider (leaflet no. 305), and silver leaf disease (leaflet no. 246).

Slugs also beset the gardener, and again the allotment correspondent from **Garden Work** found himself the victim: *'Ever since the night when I went out with a friend and actually listened to the noise of a slug eating lettuce (. . . you need a large slug and a crisp lettuce for the effect to be really good), I have felt that no slug could really surprise me'* (23 November 1940).

The slug and snail took on the character of national villains as they munched their way through the lettuces and cabbages on which victory depended; soon no fate was held too terrible for them. In June 1940 the **Gardeners' Chronicle**

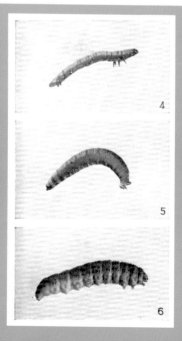

Left
Not all garden-life was the enemy – 'Garden Friends' from *In Your Garden* by C. H. Middleton.
Right
The wireworm, the leatherjacket, and the cutworm, from Grow More bulletin no. 2, 'Pests and Diseases in the Vegetable Garden'.

4

5

6

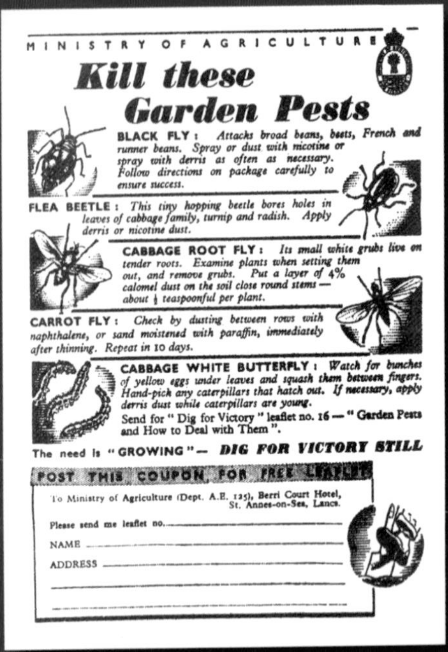
MINISTRY OF AGRICULTURE
Kill these Garden Pests
BLACK FLY: Attacks broad beans, beets, French and runner beans. Spray or dust with nicotine or spray with derris as often as necessary. Follow directions on package carefully to ensure success.
FLEA BEETLE: This tiny hopping beetle bores holes in leaves of cabbage family, turnip and radish. Apply derris or nicotine dust.
CABBAGE ROOT FLY: Its small white grubs live on tender roots. Examine plants when setting them out, and remove grubs. Put a layer of 4% calomel dust on the soil close round stems — about ¼ teaspoonful per plant.
CARROT FLY: Check by dusting between rows with naphthalene, or sand moistened with paraffin, immediately after thinning. Repeat in 10 days.
CABBAGE WHITE BUTTERFLY: Watch for bunches of yellow eggs under leaves and squash them between fingers. Hand-pick any caterpillars that hatch out. If necessary, apply derris dust while caterpillars are young.
Send for "Dig for Victory" leaflet no. 16 — "Garden Pests and How to Deal with Them".
The need is "GROWING" — DIG FOR VICTORY STILL
POST THIS COUPON FOR FREE LEAFLET
To Ministry of Agriculture (Dept. A.E. 125), Berri Court Hotel, St. Annes-on-Sea, Lancs.
Please send me leaflet no.
NAME
ADDRESS

Above
It was held to be a patriotic duty to kill pests.
Below
Spray, spray and spray again was the message put out by both government and advertisers.
Right
Bordeaux mix – Dig for Victory leaflet no. 9.

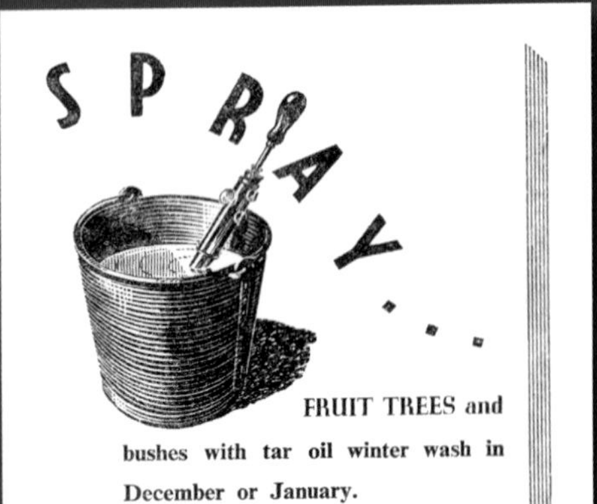
SPRAY...
FRUIT TREES and bushes with tar oil winter wash in December or January.
The wash that kills pests and leaves the bark clean and healthy is
ABOLENE
TAR OIL WINTER WASH
PLANT PROTECTION LTD · YALDING · KENT

recommended that: '*Pursuing the snail with copper sulphate in solution is a profitable evening's entertainment for the vindictive, and scattered aluminium sulphate in the track of the pest, or, better still, on its tail is effective, albeit somewhat laborious. Skewering them when these pests arrive in hordes, has its points, but messy ones and revolting to nice people.*' The anti-slug campaign was a military one, with talk of 'mopping up the advance guard' before they increase and multiply.

To combat the main culprits, slugs, wireworm, weevils, beetles and carrot fly, people were encouraged to use a basic 'kit' of the best known and easily applied pesticides; derris root, pyrethrum, nicotine, and metaldehyde. Most of these insecticides had been available for centuries, and their effects on both pests and gardeners were well known. Metaldehyde, so well known that it was usually referred to as 'meta', was used to kill slugs but was also dangerous to other small mammals and even children if eaten in sufficient quantities. Prior to the introduction of slug pellets, meta was generally used with moistened bran and left in heaps to attract them to the bait. By summer 1940 bran was in too short a supply and 'too precious to give to gastropods'. So experiments were carried out mixing meta, first with bread (also too precious and very liable to be eaten by children) and then dried lawn clippings.

Derris root was used as a dust on weevils and flea beetles and was relatively safe to all, except fish (and of course the weevils and beetles). Pyrethrum was also safe and widely used as an anti-vermin treatment around the house as well as in the garden. Nicotine was recognised as being very poisonous to humans and aphids alike, but it was still widely used in the fight against greenfly and whitefly. Whole greenhouses would be washed down with a mix of nicotine, soft soap and water. Users had to sign the 'Poisons Book' at the local chemist or hardware store in order to obtain the raw ingredients or preparatory mix. Frequent spraying was recommended for fruit bushes and trees. Tar oil, DNC (di-nitro-ortho-cresol), lime sulphur, and grease-banding

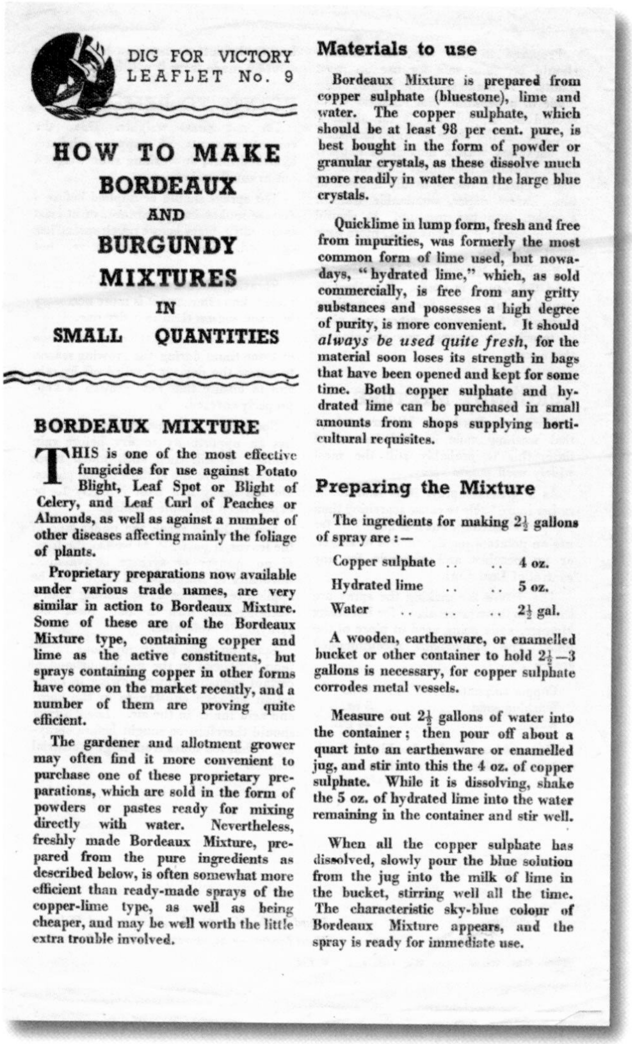

**DIG FOR VICTORY
LEAFLET No. 9**

HOW TO MAKE
BORDEAUX
AND
BURGUNDY
MIXTURES
IN
SMALL QUANTITIES

BORDEAUX MIXTURE

THIS is one of the most effective fungicides for use against Potato Blight, Leaf Spot or Blight of Celery, and Leaf Curl of Peaches or Almonds, as well as against a number of other diseases affecting mainly the foliage of plants.

Proprietary preparations now available under various trade names, are very similar in action to Bordeaux Mixture. Some of these are of the Bordeaux Mixture type, containing copper and lime as the active constituents, but sprays containing copper in other forms have come on the market recently, and a number of them are proving quite efficient.

The gardener and allotment grower may often find it more convenient to purchase one of these proprietary preparations, which are sold in the form of powders or pastes ready for mixing directly with water. Nevertheless, freshly made Bordeaux Mixture, prepared from the pure ingredients as described below, is often somewhat more efficient than ready-made sprays of the copper-lime type, as well as being cheaper, and may be well worth the little extra trouble involved.

Materials to use

Bordeaux Mixture is prepared from copper sulphate (bluestone), lime and water. The copper sulphate, which should be at least 98 per cent. pure, is best bought in the form of powder or granular crystals, as these dissolve much more readily in water than the large blue crystals.

Quicklime in lump form, fresh and free from impurities, was formerly the most common form of lime used, but nowadays, "hydrated lime," which, as sold commercially, is free from any gritty substances and possesses a high degree of purity, is more convenient. It should *always be used quite fresh*, for the material soon loses its strength in bags that have been opened and kept for some time. Both copper sulphate and hydrated lime can be purchased in small amounts from shops supplying horticultural requisites.

Preparing the Mixture

The ingredients for making 2½ gallons of spray are:—

Copper sulphate	4 oz.
Hydrated lime	5 oz.
Water	2½ gal.

A wooden, earthenware, or enamelled bucket or other container to hold 2½—3 gallons is necessary, for copper sulphate corrodes metal vessels.

Measure out 2½ gallons of water into the container; then pour off about a quart into an earthenware or enamelled jug, and stir into this the 4 oz. of copper sulphate. While it is dissolving, shake the 5 oz. of hydrated lime into the water remaining in the container and stir well.

When all the copper sulphate has dissolved, slowly pour the blue solution from the jug into the milk of lime in the bucket, stirring well all the time. The characteristic sky-blue colour of Bordeaux Mixture appears, and the spray is ready for immediate use.

were all considered essential to the war effort. Raspberries were also given dustings of derris against the maggots of the raspberry beetle.

By spring 1943 victory gardeners had taken to insecticides with such enthusiasm that there was a shortage of derris and nicotine. What little was available was being brought from the USA as part of the 'Lend-Lease' scheme. In the first instance all insecticides based on these chemicals were to be reserved for vegetables, not for flowers. But soon further limitations on quantities were necessary.

Bordeaux Mix

After the basic tool kit of derris, meta and nicotine (and a shotgun!), perhaps the most popular of garden treatments were Bordeaux mix and Burgundy mix. These were both used for the treatment or prevention of fungal diseases on foliage. Applications included leaf spot or blight on celery, leaf curl on peaches and almonds, and most importantly potato and tomato blight. Potato and tomato blight were serious problems, especially in damp summers and warm, damp autumns. On tomatoes, tell-tale dark brown blotches appeared first on the leaves and the stems, and then on the tomato fruits themselves. Often appearing just as the first tomatoes were beginning to ripen, entire crops were devastated within a matter of days. Even immature tomatoes, hurriedly picked and ripened at home, might succumb a few days later, leaving only a mass of stinking brown mush. Potato plants were the same, although the extent of the damage to the potatoes themselves would not be known until they were harvested. Even then some escaped detection and were put in storage – only to infect others. Before the intensive development of blight-resistant varieties, blight was one of the worst diseases that could affect a crop.

Bordeaux mix, as its name suggests, had originally been created in the vineyard areas of France to combat downy mildew and other fungal diseases associated with the Great French Wine Blight (actually caused by an aphid). The original mixture was of copper sulphate and lime, with the copper sulphate acting to prevent the germination of the downy mildew. Because the mix acts on germination it is best applied before the mildew strikes, although many gardeners recommended treatment several times during the season. Burgundy mixture was similar to Bordeaux mix, but used washing soda instead of lime. By the 1940s Bordeaux mixture could be bought in England as a powdered preparation ready to mix with water, although professional gardeners and keen amateurs preferred to mix the ingredients fresh themselves – and often tweaked the percentages of each component. In retrospect it seems quite incredible that the government was keen to encourage complete novices to handle and mix their own chemicals, using either lump quicklime or hydrated lime and the corrosive copper sulphates. In fact Dig for Victory leaflet no. 9 did warn that *'Spraying may prove injurious rather than beneficial in the neighbourhood of certain industrial towns, owing to interactions between substances in the spray and acid fumes in the air. Local advice should therefore be sought before spraying within ten miles from large industrial centres.'* However it went on to say that *'Prepared in this way, the mixture should be quite safe for use on most plants.'*

Drug Companies Join the War

By 1943 the war on pests had become almost as serious as the real war, and the gardening press carried as many advertisements for pesticides as for seeds. The government had encouraged research and development of a wide range of insecticides, sometimes offshoots from military research. By 1943 the rather suggestively named 'Corry Aids', established before the war, had a cure (or at least an instant death) for almost every type of pest, while Bailey's naphtha-lime single-handedly ensured pest-free plants. Mortegg (of Wheathampstead, Herts) ran a series of advertisements on the 'war' theme from the outbreak of war. Each of the adverts was headed 'Ministry of Mortegg Information' and each week there was a new 'war' theme. One memorable advertisement claimed that their tar oil products would help you hold your very own 'Maginot Line' against the pests, another reminded gardeners there was *'No Peace with Insect Enemies'*, and that *'The War (on Fruit Tree Pests) Must Go On'*. In the popular RHS **Vegetable Garden Displayed** advertisements for chemicals included Frederick Allen & Sons, based at the Phoenix Chemical Works, and Trenmans Hortico Limited, at the somewhat more lyrical 'Rivermead' in Sunbury on Thames.

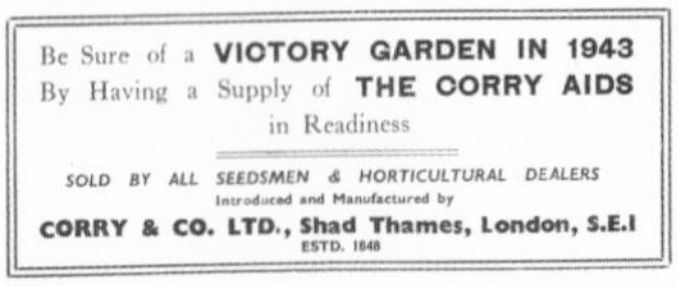
Be Sure of a VICTORY GARDEN IN 1943
By Having a Supply of THE CORRY AIDS
in Readiness
SOLD BY ALL SEEDSMEN & HORTICULTURAL DEALERS
Introduced and Manufactured by
CORRY & CO. LTD., Shad Thames, London, S.E.I
ESTD. 1848

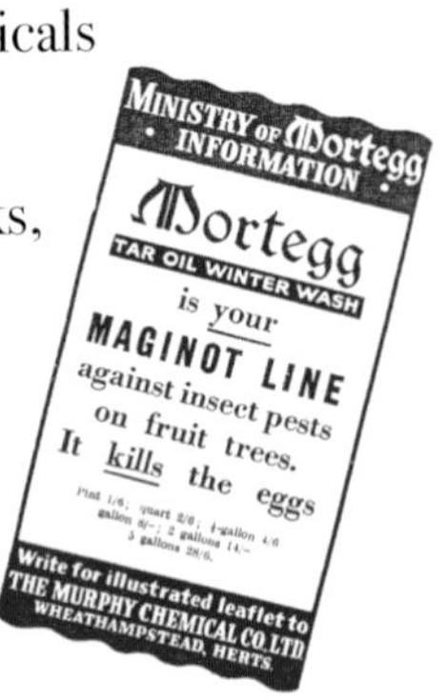
MINISTRY OF Mortegg INFORMATION
Mortegg
TAR OIL WINTER WASH
is your
MAGINOT LINE
against insect pests
on fruit trees.
It kills the eggs
Write for illustrated leaflet to
THE MURPHY CHEMICAL CO. LTD
WHEATHAMPSTEAD, HERTS.

Trenmans Hortico were typical in including among their products both old-fashioned *'Soluble Blood Crystals'* and eucalyptus oil spray (an insecticide and fungicide), and the rather more deadly naphthalene against potato worm. The latter came with a recommendation from Mr Middleton himself as 'Sure Death' for wireworm. For fruit trees or larger gardens, gardeners could purchase the Four Oaks 'Battle' pattern spraying machine, courtesy of Four Oaks of Birmingham. This particular sprayer appears to have rather fortuitously been named 'Battle' even before the outbreak of war.

Instant death and vengeance was not of course the final aim in the use of insecticides, although one could be forgiven for thinking that from a quick glance through the adverts! It was the impact on production levels that was of concern. Mathews Ltd, of Harold Wood, Essex, used the front cover of their 1943 seeds, potato, manures and insecticides catalogue to declare 1943 *'the year of Scientific Gardening to **Increase Production**'*. Frederick Allen & Sons advertised their 'Popular' brand of fertilisers and insecticides for every purpose: *'Most Effective for Soil Efficiency and Safe in Application'*, and readers were urged to send off for their booklet **Chemistry in the Garden** – essential, they claimed, for the *'extra food production required in war time'*.

With the intensification of chemical usage, Boots the Chemist became, for a while, 'the Gardener's Chemist' with Cecil Middleton writing specially for them. His typically soothing words were accompanied by 20 pages listing the necessary fertilisers and pesticides, insecticides, slug destroyer and tars. Alongside the specific 'cures' for greenfly, blackfly, woolly aphis, cuckoo-spit insect, scale and mealy bug, were general killers including 'naphthalene soil fumigant', worm destroyer, and nicotine in all forms.

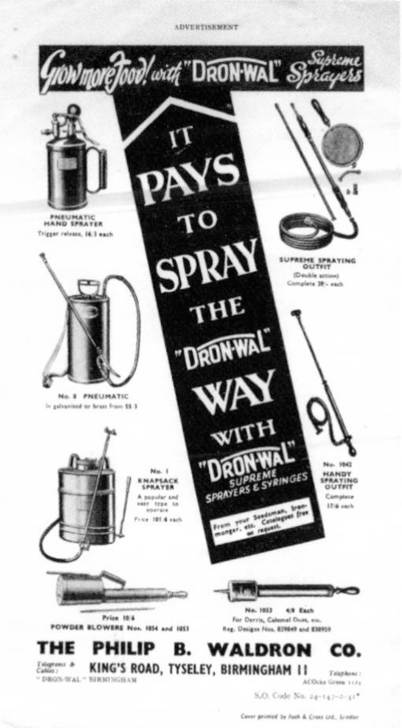
ADVERTISEMENT
Grow more Food! with "DRON-WAL" Supreme Sprayers
IT PAYS TO SPRAY THE "DRON-WAL" WAY WITH "DRON-WAL" SUPREME SPRAYERS & SYRINGES
From your Seedsman, Ironmonger, etc. Catalogues free on request.
PNEUMATIC HAND SPRAYER
Trigger release, 16/3 each
SUPREME SPRAYING OUTFIT
(Double action)
Complete 39/- each
No. 8 PNEUMATIC
In galvanised or brass from 55/3
No. 1 KNAPSACK SPRAYER
A popular and easy type to operate
Price 101/6 each
No. 1042 HANDY SPRAYING OUTFIT
Complete 17/6 each
Price 10/6
POWDER BLOWERS Nos. 1054 and 1053
No. 1053 4/9 Each
For Derris, Calomel Dust, etc.
Reg. Designs Nos. 829849 and 838959
THE PHILIP B. WALDRON CO.
KING'S ROAD, TYSELEY, BIRMINGHAM 11
Telegrams & Cables: "DRON-WAL" BIRMINGHAM
Telephone: ACOcks Green 1124

Far Left
'Corry Aids' included White Fly Death, Miracle Slug Death, pepper dust, and Wartime Derris dusting powder.
Left
The Murphy Chemical Co. used a range of war-related slogans.
Above
A range of garden sprayers available to gardeners in 1941.
Below
Anak products had an 'ak' cure for everything.

DDT

The need for artificial pest control spurred the chemical industry and although much of the arsenal of weaponry was not developed until the postwar period August 1944 saw the announcement of a *'Wonderful New Insecticide'*. Trialled originally in the USA, where *'every soldier carries a 2oz. pack of the new powder'*, this supposed gift to humanity was dichloro-diphenyl-trichloroethane, or DDT. Originally synthesised by a German chemist in 1874, the discovery had lain dormant until the American military had taken it up as an effective combatant against biting insects in North Africa and Italy. Its arrival into England was yet to be made officially, but with a shortage of traditional insecticides, such as pyrethrum, in 1944 it was being rushed through to manufacturers. The **Gardeners' Chronicle** of August 1944 hastened to tell its readers that *'Penicillin and DDT are two of the most wonderful discoveries made during the war period and both are for the healing of the nations and not their destruction'*.

In 1973 DDT was banned in the USA following an outcry on its appalling impact on wildlife and human health. By 1985 it was officially banned for agricultural use in most countries after being implicated in massive losses among birds and other wildlife.

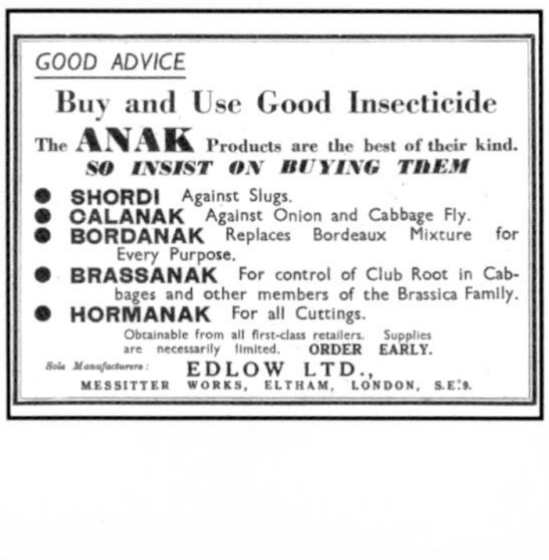
GOOD ADVICE
Buy and Use Good Insecticide
The ANAK Products are the best of their kind.
SO INSIST ON BUYING THEM
SHORDI Against Slugs.
CALANAK Against Onion and Cabbage Fly.
BORDANAK Replaces Bordeaux Mixture for Every Purpose.
BRASSANAK For control of Club Root in Cabbages and other members of the Brassica Family.
HORMANAK For all Cuttings.
Obtainable from all first-class retailers. Supplies are necessarily limited. ORDER EARLY.
Sole Manufacturers: EDLOW LTD.,
MESSITTER WORKS, ELTHAM, LONDON, S.E.9.

What Equipment Do I Need?

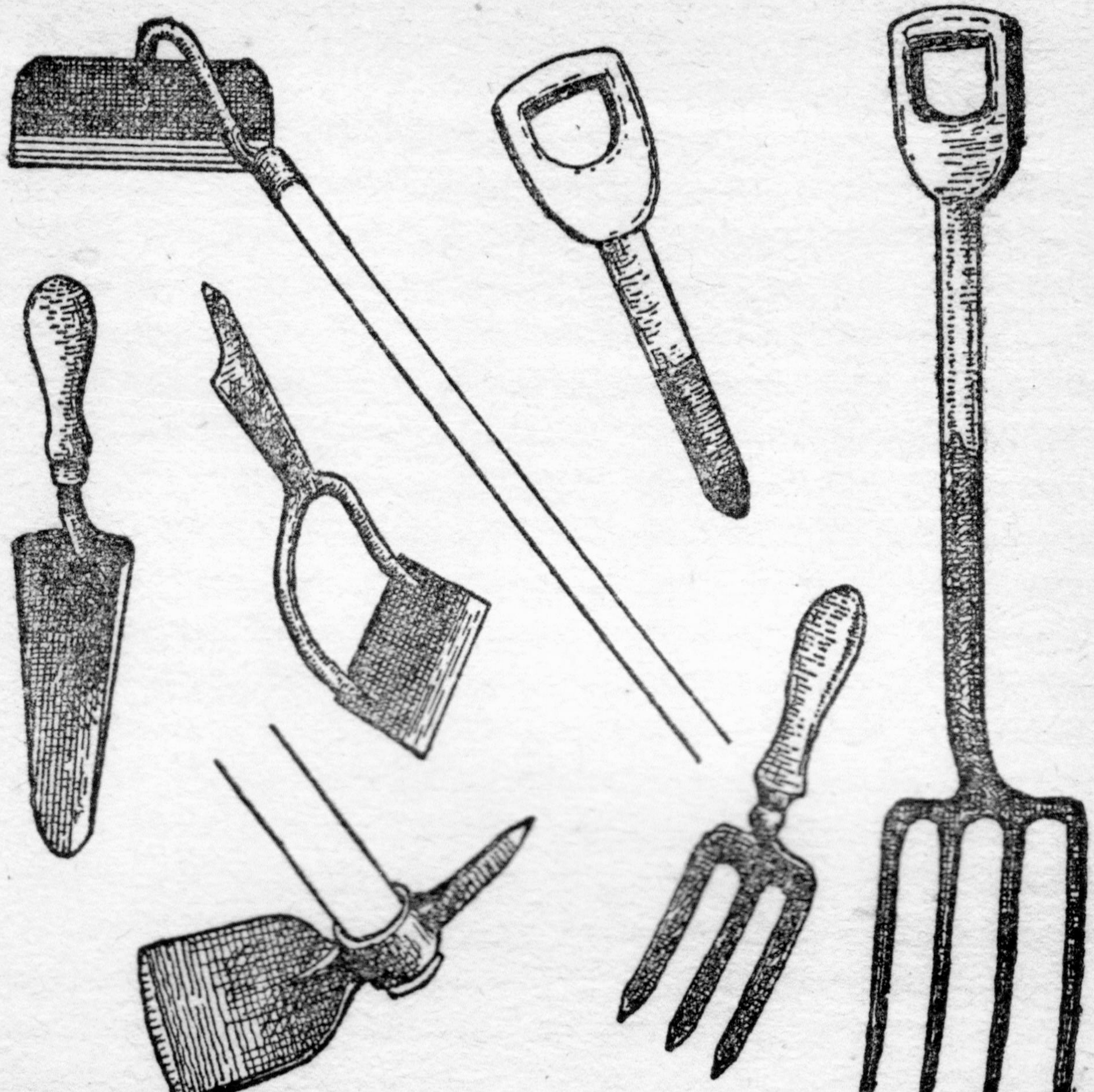

Some Useful Garden Tools.

The kinds shown are as follows: *Top left*, draw hoe; *top centre*, dibber; *right*, D-handled fork; *middle left*, trowel; *middle centre*, Dutch hoe; *bottom left*, mattock; *bottom centre*, hand fork.

Even the most basic tools had to be described to the novice gardener.

Weapons & techniques for the garden front

With a country full of first-time gardeners even the most basic of gardening tools and techniques had to be explained. Gardening books, otherwise sparsely illustrated, carried line drawings of tools you might need, ways to use them and of course advertisements for buying them, although by 1943 many tools were in short supply. 'Spade cultivation' (basically any sort of digging) was described in detail, usually favouring use of the left foot for right-handed people, and vice versa, as proudly shown on the Dig for Victory logo. This method was meant to prevent the body from unnecessary twisting. Deep digging over any plot to the depth of sub-soil was still the usual practice, and 'forking over' regarded as lazy and inadequate as preparation; wars, even in the garden, were won by armies with the right training, determination and equipment! Pre-war techniques and tools obviously had to be adapted to wartime situations – but in some cases adaptation had to take the form of abstinence as certain products became unavailable. Fertilisers were rationed for both commercial and domestic users (as explored in chapter 6), but restrictions were also placed on the use of timber and metals. Lawnmower production was also halted and by 1943 Shanks mower manufacturers were forced to advertise themselves as 'back soon': *For the time being production is suspended. But the day will come when those of us not already fortunate in owning a Shanks lawn-mower will be able to acquire this finest of mowers'.* As lawns had been dug up for vegetables the lack of mowers was not as disastrous as it might otherwise have been.

The Gardener's Weapons

All good gardens should start with the right tools, and wartime gardening was no exception. What was different, however, was the immediate shortage of all the essential tools. This was partly due to the rise in demand and, later in the war, to shortages of metal. It was recommended early on that allotment-holders share tools such as wheelbarrows and mattocks. Wooden wheelbarrows, standard until the 1930s, made a comeback as galvanised iron was difficult to obtain. Books usually differentiated between essential tools and others. In 1943, **Gardening Made Easy** stated that: *To do good gardening the right tools are essential. We can divide tools into two classes – those you must have if you are to do any gardening worth the name, and those which are very convenient and helpful but not absolutely necessary. Those in the first class you must have to start with or almost at the start: those in the second you can acquire gradually as you need them or as funds allow'.*

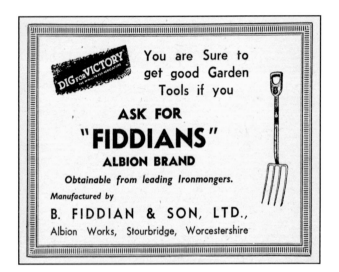

DIG FOR VICTORY
You are Sure to get good Garden Tools if you
ASK FOR
"FIDDIANS"
ALBION BRAND
Obtainable from leading Ironmongers.
Manufactured by
B. FIDDIAN & SON, LTD.,
Albion Works, Stourbridge, Worcestershire

Essential tools included spade, fork, hand fork, rake, trowel, watering can and a Dutch hoe. Additional tools included those used for lawns or paths (not needed on an allotment) such as roller, shears, lawnmower, as well as a dibber, secateurs, edge cutter, wheelbarrow, syringe (for spraying), and various carpentry tools. It was recommended that women purchase smaller versions of spades or forks, which would be lighter; some women had no choice of course and got what they were given! Mrs Pat Ashby of Bedford recalls: *'I was presented with a well-worn light spade, a fork, a trowel, a dibber for planting out, a line (two pieces of wood with a long string to use as a guide when planting up the rows), and a tin with a wire handle containing oil and a paintbrush. I was instructed to clean my tools after use and oil them to keep them from rusting. I still use these tools 60 years on.'* New allotment sites sometimes provided communal tool sheds; the **Daily Mail**'s book, **Grow it Yourself** stated that: *'In many allotments the owners of the plots build themselves more or less rude shacks in which to place their tools under lock and key for safety. The tendency of local authorities is to prevent these rough and ready erections because of their unsightliness, or to standardise them on a neat pattern. I hope that in the new allotment campaign this practice, or the building of communal tool sheds, will be followed.'* However, with pilfering rife wise gardeners took their tools home at the end of the day.

Left
Suppliers of garden tools were quick to use the Dig for Victory slogan for advertising as the number of new gardeners led to a huge rise in demand.

Below
Bastard trenching of grassland, from the RHS *Vegetable Garden Displayed*. Many of the new allotments taken on during the war were located in areas of grassland and the term 'bastard trenching' occurred in the first pages of most wartime garden books. A spade was an essential tool for these new sites.

1
2
BASTARD TRENCHING GRASSLAND
1. Preparing first trench—soil removed, breaking up second spit.
2. Placing turf from second trench upside down in first trench.
3. After chopping turf in first trench covering with soil from second trench, working from left to right across trench width.
4. Transferring " crumbs " from second to first trench.
3
4

Digging

As befitted a book aimed at the novice, the RHS **Vegetable Garden Displayed** devoted several pages to explaining the techniques of ordinary digging, spit digging, and bastard trenching on both cultivated ground and grassland. **Grow It Yourself**, the **Daily Mail**'s 'Practical Instruction Book on Food from the Garden in Wartime' went right back to basics with the following instructions on 'How to Use a Spade':

'Grasp the top of the handle with the right hand, palm outward. The grip must be firm without rigidity, so that the spade can be swung freely in any direction.

'The left hand will pass down the shaft to a point at which it is most convenient for you to grip, and the palm of the hand will be inward, over the shaft.

'The spade must be held upright on the ground to be dug. 'The left foot should be placed on the top of the blade with the boot heel close to the metal.

'With the body and leg thrust evenly balanced, the blade should be forced into the ground to its full depth.

'Then the handle should be pulled towards you.

'With the left hand passing lower down the shaft the spadeful of soil will be easily lifted and thrown this side or that by twisting the left hand.'

New gardeners were warned not to overdo the digging on the first few trips to the allotment or garden. Enthusiasm and novelty resulted in bad backs and abandoned plots. As ever, Mr Middleton was on hand with some sage advice in his book **The Wartime Allotment or Back Garden**: *'Many a man has broken his heart and his braces and nearly broken his back too, lost his enthusiasm, and finished up by calling a spade anything but a spade, because he was in too big a hurry. So take my advice*

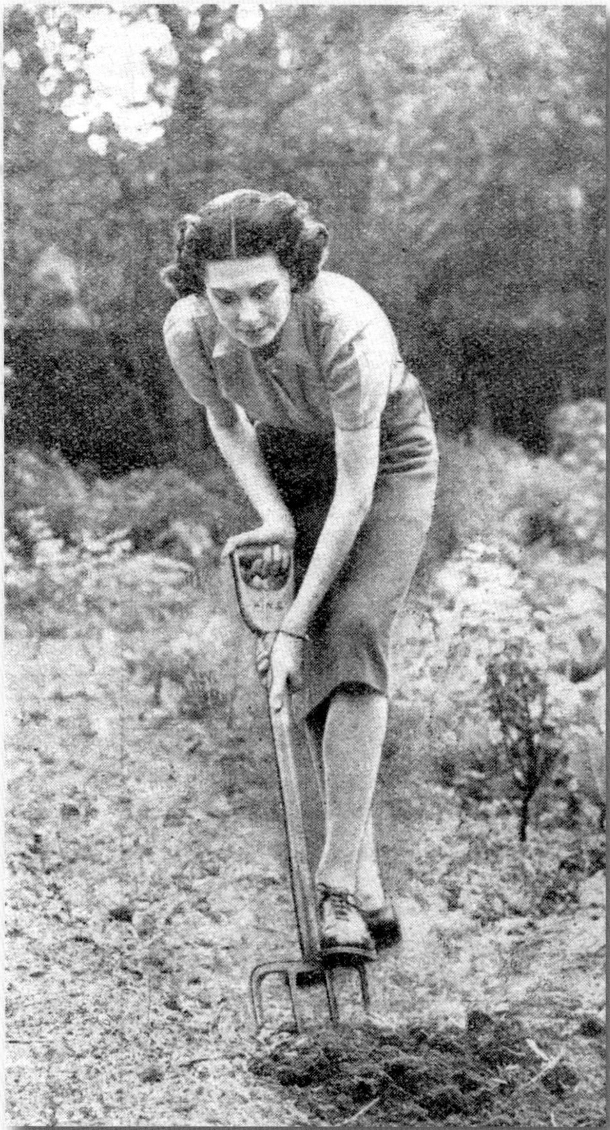

Above
The left-foot technique, as shown on the Dig for Victory leaflet, was also recommended when using a fork, as illustrated in *Woman & Home* in 1942.

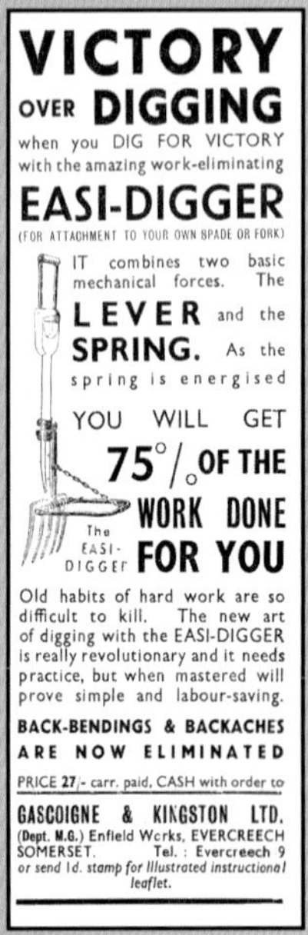
VICTORY
OVER DIGGING
when you DIG FOR VICTORY
with the amazing work-eliminating
EASI-DIGGER
(FOR ATTACHMENT TO YOUR OWN SPADE OR FORK)
IT combines two basic mechanical forces. The
LEVER and the SPRING. As the spring is energised
YOU WILL GET
75°/。OF THE WORK DONE FOR YOU
The EASI-DIGGEr
Old habits of hard work are so difficult to kill. The new art of digging with the EASI-DIGGER is really revolutionary and it needs practice, but when mastered will prove simple and labour-saving.
BACK-BENDINGS & BACKACHES ARE NOW ELIMINATED
PRICE 27/- carr. paid, CASH with order to
GASCOIGNE & KINGSTON LTD.
(Dept. M.G.) Enfield Works, EVERCREECH SOMERSET. Tel.: Evercreech 9
or send 1d. stamp for Illustrated instructional leaflet.

when you start digging and let "hasten slowly" be your motto. Do a little at a time till you get used to it; do it thoroughly and well and stop as soon as your back begins to ache. If you can get somebody else to do it for you, so much the better; if you cannot, take it easy, you will soon get to like it and it will do you the world of good.' Women were recommended to dig for only 30–40 minutes at a time at first, increasing this by increments of 10 minutes when they felt ready.

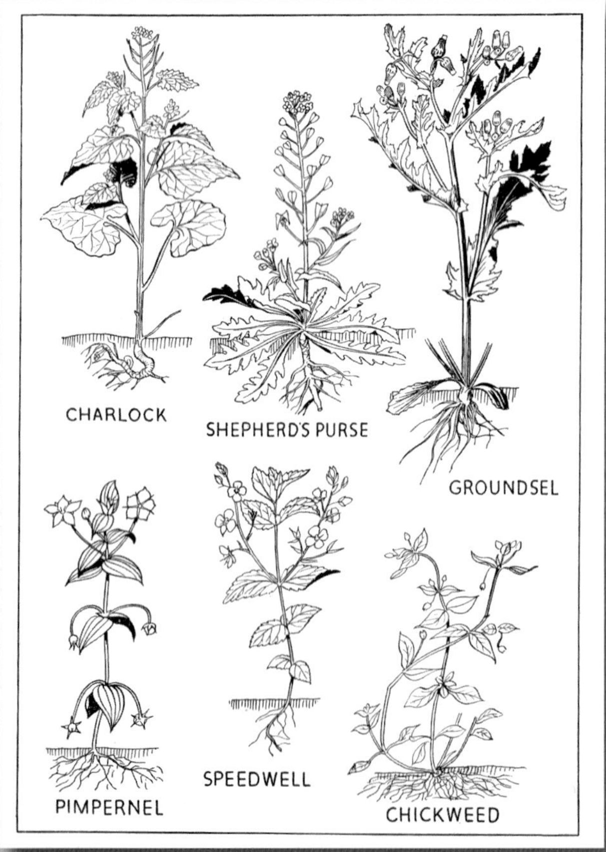
CHARLOCK
SHEPHERD'S PURSE
GROUNDSEL
PIMPERNEL
SPEEDWELL
CHICKWEED

Weeding

Although hardly a special wartime technique, the importance of keeping up the 'war on weeds' was continually stressed during the 1940s. Weeds were said to *'snatch the precious before they were plentiful'*, starving the plants of moisture and goodness and shading them from the life-giving sunshine. Timely weeding was a wartime duty for the sake of the nation. As **Gardening Made Easy** proclaimed: *'Weeds, those countless battalions, armed with their hooks, flying seeds, clinging tendrils, and persistent roots, often form the gardener's nightmare. War to the death is the only watchword.'* Richard Sudell included four pages of drawings of weeds for easy identification in his **Practical Gardening and Food Production**. Weeds could either be burnt, dug in, or fed to the hens and rabbits. Groundsel, sow thistles, dandelion and chickweed made excellent rabbit food. Dock, also used in wartime, is now known to create long-term liver damage in rabbits.

Cloches versus Hitler

Once the move to expand productive land had been largely achieved, the government (and gardeners) had to look to other methods with which to enhance production. Fertilisers and pest control were two areas of focus, but also important was extending periods of growth. Growing under cover of some

Above Top
For those that were flagging this new Easi-Digger supposedly did the work for you.

Below
Weeds were bad for the allotment, but good for the rabbit and hen-keeper (from *Practical Gardening and Food Production*).

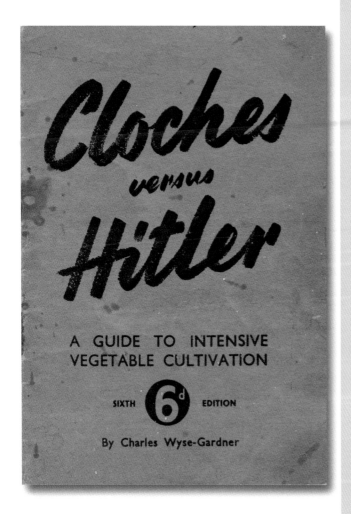

Cloches versus Hitler
A GUIDE TO INTENSIVE VEGETABLE CULTIVATION
SIXTH 6d EDITION
By Charles Wyse-Gardner

kind was a technique gardeners had used since at least the Roman period. 'Domestic' greenhouses for the amateur gardener had been available since the middle of the 19th century, and many a suburban garden had one in place from before the war. However, control of glass production meant that new recruits to the gardening army found it difficult to obtain glass or bricks, let alone fuel for a stove. By the start of 1940 no timber was available for the construction of private glasshouses, and companies such as Duncan Tucker (of London) had been 'required' to prioritise glasshouses for commercial growers alongside somewhat mysterious 'Military and Civil Defence Projects'; Boulton & Paul Ltd, another greenhouse supplier, also had to announce a 'temporary suspension of business' in January 1940, and was only able to sell a few pre-war stocks until further notice. Boulton & Paul were engaged on aircraft construction – a part of their company which had already had considerable success. If you did succeed in obtaining a glasshouse there was a real possibility that you would have to cover it with camouflage in some way. In January 1940 both French and English governments considered camouflage to disguise the light reflecting from glasshouses.

We carry on—
. . but NOT
Business
as Usual!
In War as in Peace we are carrying on — but War has brought changes and many new and pressing problems. For example, all stocks of timber have been placed under Government Control and timber is not now available for the building of Private Glasshouses. More and more sections of our business (we are, as you know, the largest Horticultural Builders in the United Kingdom) are being applied to the manufacture of war-time productions including timber structures of every kind. Quite apart from meeting Military and Civil Defence requirements, we are building Glasshouses for Commercial Growers which by increasing home crops of foodstuffs will restrict this country's imports and free ships for other vital supplies.
Duncan Tucker (Tottenham) Ltd
ESTABLISHED 1830.
TOTTENHAM, LONDON, N.15

In the absence of glasshouses, many turned to smaller-scale shelters. The most common method of encouraging extended cropping was the use of cloches, and in particular 'low barn continuous cloches'. Individual sheets of glass hinged together into long rows by complex metal hinges became a common sight on allotments all round the country. Messrs Chase were the best-known makers of these flexible systems and cornered the market with their patriotic advertising. Starting up on the eve of the First World War, 'Chase Continuous Cloches' had wartime experience behind them already. The experimental gardens at the Chase factory included not only extended cropping but also quick-catch cropping of carrots and onions under the 'low barn' system. It was, however, their slogan 'Cloches versus Hitler' that made them so well known, a slogan that also formed the title of their book of wartime garden advice,

Right
Cloches versus Hitler was one of the most famous phrases of the gardening war. As well as being used in advertisements, a booklet of the same name could be acquired from Chase.

Below
For many gardeners the choice was largely academic as they were either unobtainable in wartime or too expensive for the novice.

Far Right
Continuous Cloches had some of the most inventive advertising.

This shows two rows of lettuce comfortably housed under a "Low Barn." A catch-crop of carrots, onions, etc., is often planted down the centre.
29 YEARS' EXPERIENCE
in our experimental gardens is embodied in our fully-illustrated wartime booklet.
"CLOCHES versus HITLER"
by
Charles Wyse-Gardner
Price 5d. post free, from Chase Protected Cultivation Ltd. Dept. E.P., Chertsey, Surrey Full cloche list on request.
Chase Continuous Cloches

written by the suspiciously named 'Charles Wyse-Gardener'. Cloches came in all shapes and sizes to account for the different vegetables. Most gardeners had to make do with the 'standard' tent pattern, which was the cheapest (and easiest). The small wires and clips could be fiddly, and had a nasty habit of springing out and giving a painful tweak to cold hands. The barn pattern was also popular for taller crops. Movable cloches were also recommended by the **Gardeners' Chronicle** for early crops, including raising broad beans, French beans, peas, cauliflower, broccoli and turnips as well as production of year-round salads. Homemade cloches could also be made of old window panes joined by wooden chocks. These looked much less complicated than the real thing!

'Frames', the generic term for permanent wood and glass low structures, were also commonly available for extending the vegetable season in larger, established gardens. In January 1940, the **Gardeners' Chronicle** suggested that *'Owing to the great reduction of stocks of half-hardy-flowering plants used in summer bedding, many gardeners will find themselves in the unusual position of having several cold frames available for early vegetables.'* They

Types of Continuous Cloches
Full range of styles and sizes on page 2 of cover.
Tent Pattern
Barn Pattern
Low Barn Pattern
Tomato 'T' Cloche
Page 3
Cloches versus Hitler

NO FROST ADMITTED

FROST RAID SHELTERS

Each year thousands of pounds worth of seeds are lost through frost, heavy rain and birds. ALL THIS CAN BE PREVENTED simply, cheaply and completely, by using CHASE Cloches. And the crops mature WEEKS earlier, when vegetables are very dear to buy.

DOUBLE YOUR OUTPUT

By using CHASE Cloches, growth is so speeded up that two or three crops can be grown instead of one. The Cloches are so portable that they can be moved from one crop to another and kept in use all the year round. This is REAL economy.

MAKE YOUR OWN CLIMATE WITH

LOW Carriage Paid PRICES

Size "A", as illustrated, glass 14 in. × 9 in. 55 Cloches to cover 64 ft. row, 54/-. 28 Cloches to cover 32½ ft. row, 30/-. Trial Set of 14 Cloches to cover 16 ft. row, 17/-.

CLOCHES v. HITLER

New war booklet tells how to double your output of food crops. Learn how to fight Hitler efficiently on the FOOD FRONT by sending for booklet, 4d. in stamps.

Chase Continuous Cloches

"TRAPS TO CATCH THE SUNBEAMS!"

WRITE NOW FOR FULL FREE LIST TO

CHASE PROTECTED CULTIVATION Ltd., Dept. DP., Chertsey, Surrey

TAS/Cc. 524

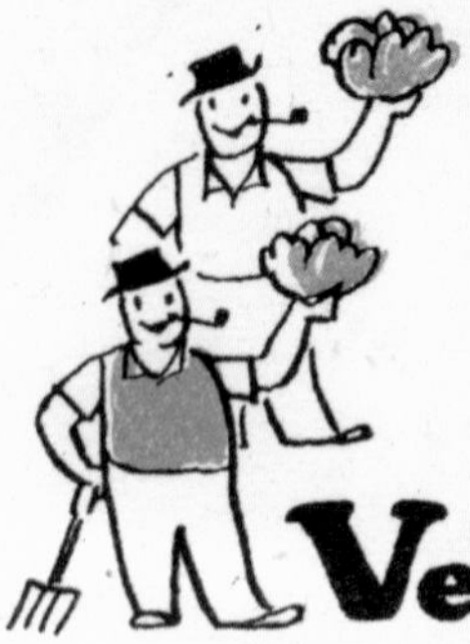

Double cropping

— *without intercropping*

Vegetable production is now called DIGGING FOR VICTORY **and deep digging is**

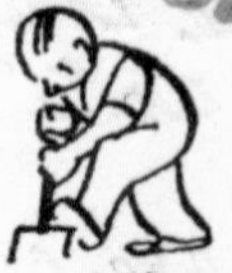

recommended.

Every pound of food produced is so much money saved

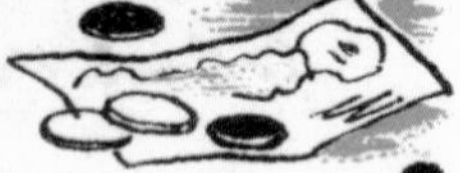

—less your out-of-pocket exs., of course. Five shillings worth of

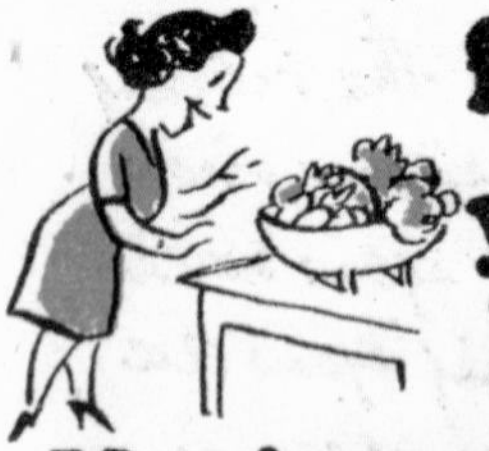

food for one shilling helps you, helps shipping and helps the National Effort —

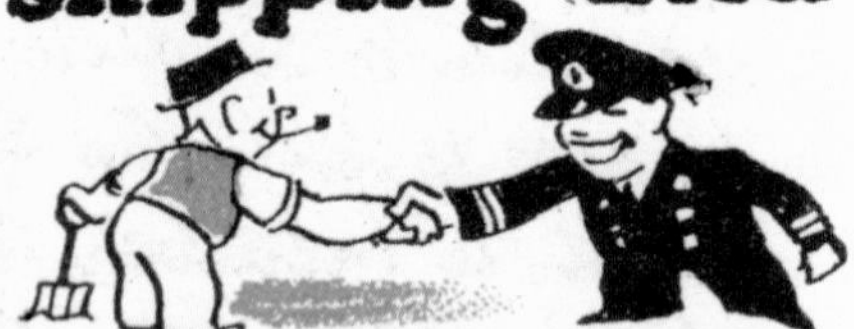

but where does the Saving go?

Put that Saving into NATIONAL SAVINGS CERTIFICATES**... and get a second crop**

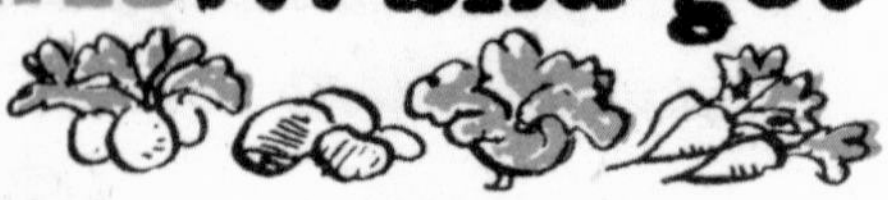

One of the few cases when you eat your Cake and keep it—and it earns Tax-free interest too

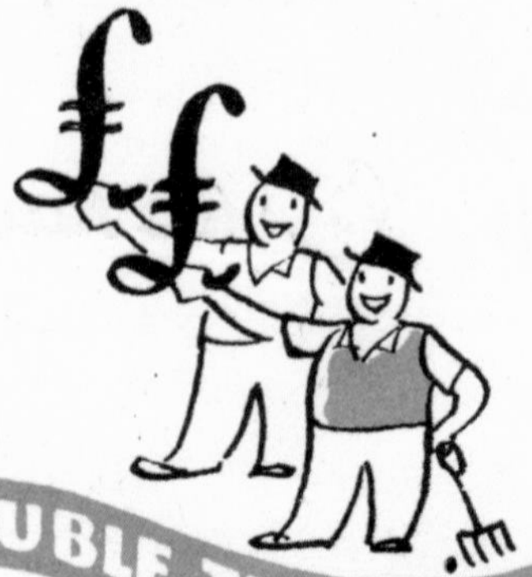

DOUBLE THE CROP

W.F.L. 83. Issued by the National Savings Committee, London. Scottish Savings Committee, Edinburgh.

went on to suggest turnips, lettuces, radishes, carrots and beetroot for these frames, and gave instructions for adding some heat to them, thus widening the range that could be grown. *'Few gardeners are blessed with heated frames suitable for vegetable growing, but quite good results may be obtained if beds of fermenting material are made up. Long stable litter mixed with twice its bulk of clean, fresh, leaves (preferably Beech or Oak) is the most suitable material but where stable litter is scarce the quantity of leaves may be increased.'*

With the combined aid of the hot bed and cold frame, cropping periods could be considerably extended. Carrots such as Amsterdam Forcing could be matured to a good crop by the middle of April, turnips by March, and cauliflowers by mid-May. Dwarf beans could be accommodated in the larger frames, and even the humble radish was put into frames. When winter vegetables were in short supply, a crop of radish could be a welcome change. For the adventurous eater, endive and chicory were also recommended as a winter salad suitable for frames, as was mustard and cress – although the easiest place to raise that was indoors on a window sill.

Hardening-off of seedlings raised in cold frames was the subject of an article in **Garden Work** in spring 1943. Detailed instructions on ventilation of the frames and gradual exposure to air and light seem to have been more suitable for a professional than the amateur gardener that the magazine was aimed at. Exhortations to water the plants in the frame 'between 10 and 11 a.m., choosing if possible a fine day' seem particularly unrealistic for most victory diggers who were juggling a full-time job with home front duties and gardening 'as and when'. For most amateurs the cold frame allowed early and reliable seedlings for planting out into the vegetable plot or allotment, and remained popular throughout the war. Sowing some early seed 'under glass' became almost a catch-phrase in gardening circles as long as glass could still be begged, bought or borrowed. As supplies of material started to dry up, however, prices rose and quality fell. By May 1944 a small 3ft by 4ft garden frame made of composition board and cedar wood and advertised as 'for Food Production' cost £3 10s.

Intercropping was also a popular method of increasing production, although some of the gardening press was concerned about overcrowding causing an increase in pests and a decrease in crop sizes. Popular intercropping crops included spring onions and lettuces.

Hydroponics was a new and unusual technique in the 1940s, so new in fact that even the advertisements had to carry an explanation of the word as a subheading. Gardening without soil, using chemical fertiliser and nutrients in a water base, had been used in market gardens in the USA and Canada but had made little headway in Britain. However, at a time when soil was in short supply and new techniques were being given more consideration, a Liverpool-based company made some progress in selling the technique to amateurs and commercial growers in 1941. Richard Sudell included 'Soilless Culture' in his book **Practical Gardening**, suggesting that a homemade wooden window box with a wire mesh

c|l
This advertisement manages to sidestep the controversy over intercropping by recommending you put the profits from your crop into National Savings!

support for the plants might be used. However, he warned that *'amateurs are not advised to try soilless culture without reference to experts, as a means of food production'.*

STRAW CHIMNEY
6" SOIL
4" STRAW
TRENCH

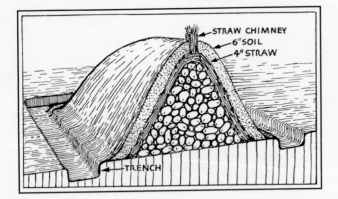

Storage

Once the victory gardener had achieved the dreamed-of crop, the problem was all too often what on earth to do with it? Although small ice-cream makers had been available from the Victorian period onwards, domestic freezers were unknown in England during the pre-war period, and refrigerators for storing vegetables and fruits an expensive rarity. All foodstuffs therefore had to be stored in larders, sheds or cellars. Sheds were unfortunately in short supply as timber was unavailable for domestic use. Some vegetables were of course suited to being left where they were growing until needed (leeks and cabbages for example), but many root vegetables, onions, and tubers needed lifting and storing. Traditionally this could be done in an earthen 'clamp', a sort of multi-layered earthen mound, or in boxes or sacks in a cool, dark, place. Few housewives or gardeners had the time available to construct clamps and then go and extract their vegetables from them as needed and most preferred to have them 'on hand' in a shed or cellar – the latter being prone to damp. Potatoes were the most common crop to be clamped, and even then only for crops of a ton or more. A clamp was supposed to keep the potatoes through to the next spring, although if located in a public place pilfering was always a problem. Fortunately many more houses were built with large larders in the pre-war period and so some boxes of cleaned vegetables could be placed there. Dig for Victory leaflet no. 3, Storing Vegetables for Winter Use, informed the hard-pressed housewife where she might best stash the vegetables and marrows brought home from the allotment. Some vegetables preferred slightly higher temperatures, and marrows were often kept in drawers in the cool spare bedroom. Tomatoes might also be ripened by laying out in spare bedrooms, with green fruit ripening well into December, if not already used for chutneys. Many must have found the demands for bedrooms, attics, larders and cellars frustrating at a time when families were in upheaval and might also be housing evacuees, bombed-out friends and relatives and billeted men in addition to the family itself.

Pruning

Fruit, even apples and pears, had been cheaply imported before the war and many orchards and old garden trees had become neglected. At the outbreak of war it was not realised how long the situation would last – 'It'll all be over by Christmas' – so general advice had been not to plant fruit bushes or trees that would take several years to start cropping. Old orchards had often been left or even dug out in the rush for land to cultivate with other crops. By the third year of war the situation had changed and people were encouraged to plant fruit bushes and renovate existing fruit trees. Throughout the country acres of neglected fruit trees were brought back into production, and gardeners rediscovered the joy of their old apple and pear trees and relearnt the skills of pruning and renovation. As ever the Ministry of Agriculture was on hand with advice and warnings: *'The prunings of all fruits may contain disease and harbour pests so it is wise to collect and burn. The ash contains potash and is a valuable dressing for fruit trees'* – Dig for Victory leaflet no. 25 (How to Prune Fruit Trees and Bushes).

Left

A section through a potato clamp; the straw chimney gave away the presence of the precious crop.

Below

The front of leaflet no. 25 on 'How to Prune Fruit Trees and Bushes'. This is one of the few Dig for Victory leaflets with an illustration on the first page. It was issued when MAF was based at the Berri Court Hotel, Lytham St Anne's (Lancs), quite late in the war when fruit started to be in short supply.

HOW TO PRUNE FRUIT TREES AND BUSHES

DIG FOR VICTORY
LEAFLET NO.25

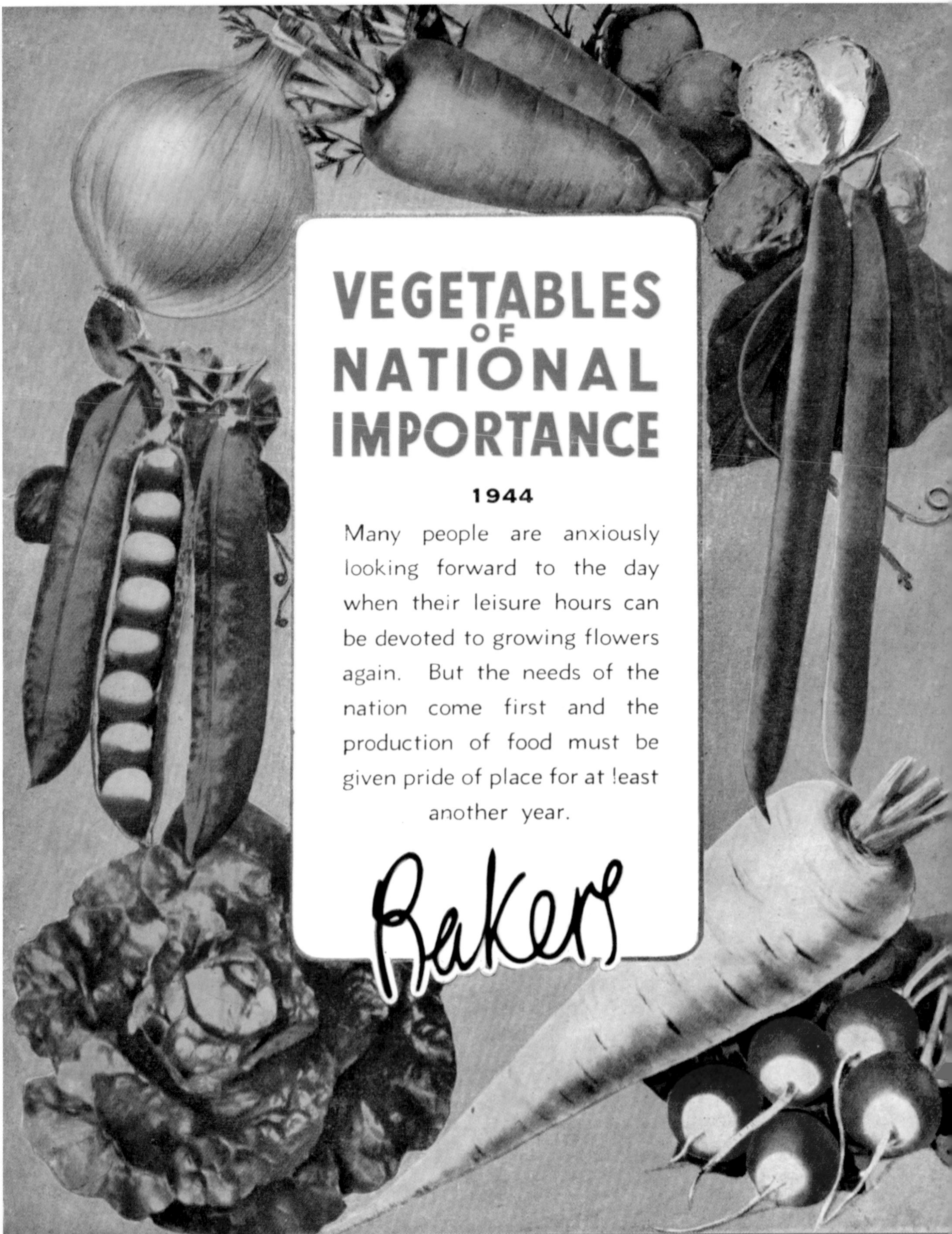
VEGETABLES OF NATIONAL IMPORTANCE
1944
Many people are anxiously looking forward to the day when their leisure hours can be devoted to growing flowers again. But the needs of the nation come first and the production of food must be given pride of place for at least another year.
Bakers

Sowing the seeds of victory: nurseries, seeds suppliers & market gardens

In the days before the garden centre, almost all gardeners bought their supplies from a nursery or seedsman. These included large companies, such as Carters or Suttons, supplying all types of seeds and bulbs, and small specialist growers providing unusual varieties of bulbs or herbaceous plants. The small suburban gardener would expect to have to send off for seeds if they wanted anything more than the basics provided by the local hardware store. The only exception to this general rule was Woolworths, which had taken on the mantle of seed supplier to the suburbs, with packets sold for a penny each and rose plants for sixpence. Cuthbert's seeds in particular were available through Woolworths and were a popular choice during wartime. Roses, fruit bushes and other large herbaceous and shrub plants, along with fruit trees, would be grown in beds at the nursery and then lifted and sold bare rooted; this meant they were available to buy and plant only in the dormant months of the year. Very few plants were sold in pots, just needing transplanting into the ground. For nurseries specialising in these bare-rooted plants the timing of the outbreak of war was particularly unfortunate as trade was at its height in the autumn and early spring months.

Most of the nurseries issued a catalogue once a year, taking the opportunity to highlight new varieties and strains. Depending on whether it was a specialist or general nursery, the catalogue usually appeared in autumn or winter in preparation for the new year, again the worst of timing in that first year of war, and things were not about to improve.

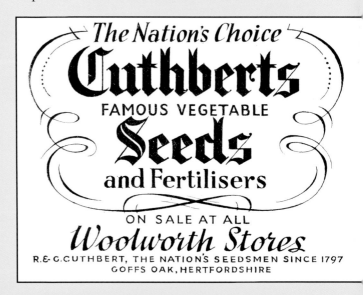

The Nation's Choice
Cuthberts
FAMOUS VEGETABLE
Seeds
and Fertilisers

ON SALE AT ALL
Woolworth Stores
R. & G. CUTHBERT, THE NATION'S SEEDSMEN SINCE 1797
GOFFS OAK, HERTFORDSHIRE

Left
Baker's seeds, 1944. When Digging for Victory vegetables truly were 'of national importance'.
(MUSEUM OF GARDEN HISTORY 2004 – 066)

Above
Cuthbert's seeds were available at Woolworths (From *Garden Work*, 20 March 1943).

Ryders'
SEEDS
FOR BEST RESULTS
1941
SOW FOR VICTORY
RYDER & SON (1920) LTD. ST ALBANS, ENGLAND
Ryders'
SEEDS
FOR BEST RESULTS
1941
SOW FOR VICTORY
RYDER & SON (1920) LTD. ST ALBANS, ENGLAND

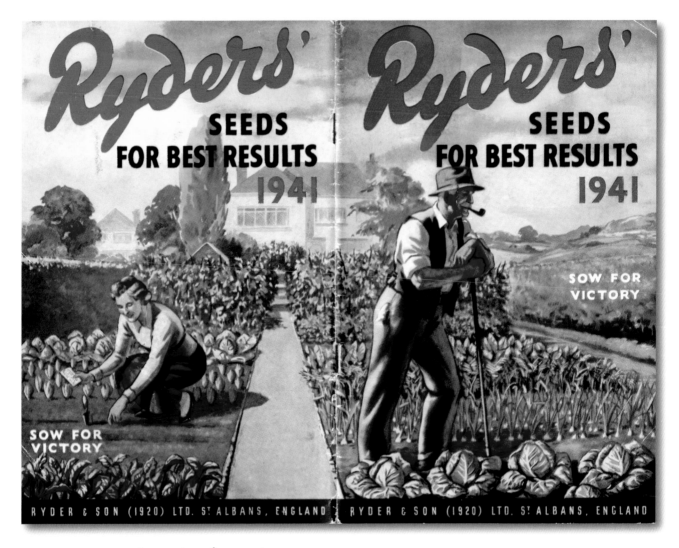

Nurseries Supplying Dig for Victory

For new victory diggers just setting out and anxious to purchase seed in this period of high demand and short supply, a complete 'Victory Pack' was perhaps the best solution. By spring 1940, Sowerbutts, seedsmen of Ashton-under-Lyne, created a mixed pack of 20 different varieties of vegetables (over 7,000 seeds in all). Perfect for the novice and including free 'cultural hints', this starter pack cost a mere 2s 6d. Dobbie & Co. of Edinburgh sold a pack of 16 different types of vegetables, enough to feed a family of five or six, for 5s – twice the price and fewer vegetables than Sowerbutts, but perhaps there were more seeds. Ryder & Son Ltd of St Albans did a V1 collection for the same price, but promised 'the best possible results' and unusually heavy cropping potential. If you felt that 5s was too much, then Alfred Dawkins of Chelsea (London) could provide a 'Utility' collection of 10 varieties of seeds including peas, beans, carrots and onions for 2s 6d. The well-known specialist seed suppliers Thomson & Morgan, however, stuck to selling its 4,000 varieties of flowers and 'unusual vegetable seeds' individually during the first year of war with no 'quick-fix' assorted packs.

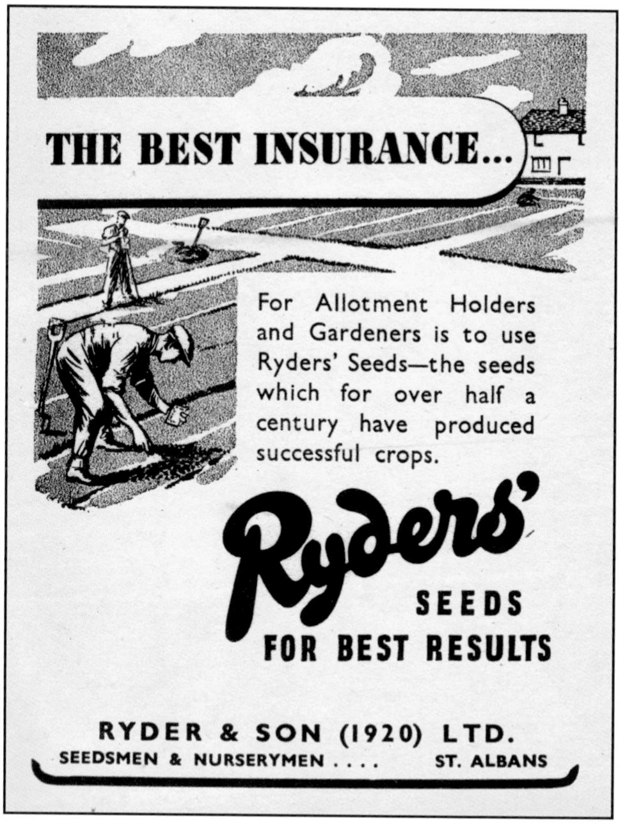
THE BEST INSURANCE...
For Allotment Holders and Gardeners is to use Ryders' Seeds—the seeds which for over half a century have produced successful crops.
Ryders'
SEEDS
FOR BEST RESULTS
RYDER & SON (1920) LTD.
SEEDSMEN & NURSERYMEN . . . . ST. ALBANS

Far Left
A splendid Dig for Victory garden created with Ryders' seeds.
Left
Ryders' seeds advertised specifically to allotment-holders.
Below
By November 1939 the list of nursery businesses for sale was lengthening.

BUSINESSES FOR SALE, &c.

A COMPACT Freehold Nursery in good-class district, Hampshire. 2½ acres with modern House, 5 rooms, bathroom, etc., all services. 8 Glasshouses (over 600 feet run), heated and in good order. Well-built Piggeries, Packing and Potting Sheds, Frames, etc. Price, complete with Stock, £1,950. Part can remain.—Apply, AUBREY & CO., 19-23, Ludgate Hill, London, E.C.4.

AN excellent Freehold Nursery in Notts., 26½ acres, with modern brick Bungalow, 4 rooms and bathroom; 7 Glasshouses (over 500 feet run), all in good order. Also large Piggery, Packing and Potting Sheds, Frames, etc. Price, complete with Stock, £2,000. Half might remain.—Apply, AUBREY & CO., above.

NURSERY, near Bournemouth, 2½ acres 2 Glasshouses, each 100 by 25 feet, heated and in first-class order; 100 feet of Dutch Lights. Rent £45 yearly. Lease 20 years. Price for Stock, Implements etc., £215.—Apply, AUBREY & CO., above.

Theoretically of course the war should have been good news to nurseries and seedsmen, who gained a sudden surge of customers, but with tight controls over what they could and couldn't grow and sell, shortages of space for deliveries by road or rail, and lack of labour, many found the war years difficult.

Going Out of Business

In his 1940 book **A Garden Goes to War**, Stephen Cheveley recorded a visit to his local nursery in the first weeks of the war in search of cabbage plants. Arriving on a Sunday afternoon, Cheveley was greeted by the sight of a glorious selection of autumn flowers and a nursery owner perplexed as to how he could keep his business going during the war. He knew that he would have to convert to food crops but the nursery set-up was not suited to these: *'the greenhouse must go for tomatoes. The land would have to carry onions, salad crops, and perhaps cauliflowers and other brassicas. But the big problem was that the place was not laid out on a sufficiently large scale to permit using horses, and the necessary implements, even if he had them. All the work was done by hand and it would not pay to produce vegetables entirely by hand labour.'*

The difficulties that Cheveley's local nurseryman anticipated in converting to food production were echoed throughout the country. Larger seed suppliers and nurseries had of course been aware of government war planning through 1939, and many were prepared for the outbreak of war and the important role they were to play. The immediate need was the provision of seeds and seedling plants for the hundreds of thousands of new gardeners – a task difficult enough in itself. However while the Grow More and Dig for Victory campaigns were being launched, the government was also bringing in new regulations concerning what the nurseries themselves could and could not grow during wartime. In counties with substantial horticultural industries the War Agricultural Executive Committees established Horticultural Sub-Committees to advise on cropping in the best national interest land previously devoted to horticultural crops – all reporting back to the Ministry of Agriculture. Needless to say, the organisation was frustratingly bureaucratic and delays and contradictions were common.

Nurseries were therefore almost continuously undergoing massive reorganisation. Beds that had been adapted to the specific needs of bulbs, flowering plants and shrubs were simply not suited for the raising of vegetables or vegetable seeds. The labour force was often ignorant of vegetable production, having trained specifically in decorative horticulture or hothouse production. To add to the difficulties facing them, many of the nurseries depended on ranges of glasshousing, either for 'forcing' early flowers and bulbs, or for raising tender plants. Even small nurseries had large runs of glasshousing. Aubrey & Co. of London who handled sales and auctions were selling a nursery of 2.5 acres in 1939, which had over 600ft of glasshousing. Even where glasshouses had not originally been heated, restrictions on glass and

timber were to make the upkeep of these almost impossible under wartime conditions. Nurseries which included orchards and fruit trees often ripped up at least part of their stock in the first months of the war to make way for more essential 'short-term' crops, before it was realised that fruit trees were going to be needed later in the war.

In the months that followed the declaration of war the government announced that nurseries would have to convert almost entirely to food production, retaining only 10% of their original stock. Tomatoes in particular were a crop that the government encouraged nurserymen to supply. In 1938 over 200,000 tons of tomatoes had been imported (mainly from Holland and the Channel Islands), dwarfing the 60,000 tons grown at home. Now every possible glasshouse space was to be turned over to tomatoes, whether or not they were ideally suited. Some nurseries were more affected by wartime restrictions and cutbacks than others. John Hill & Sons (Staffordshire), a tree nursery, were well aware from the outset of the precariousness of their business at a time when vegetables were the order of the day. Using the traditional analogy between England and the 'old oak tree', John Hill called on their clients not to let the maintaining of trees become a lost art.

Producers of specialist hothouse plants, such as the immensely popular orchids and hippeastrum, or camellias, or even collectors' outdoor plants such as alpines and rock plants, were especially vulnerable to changes in availability of heating, glass-housing and labour, in addition to the new government restrictions on the growing of non-productive foods. Even those nurseries that

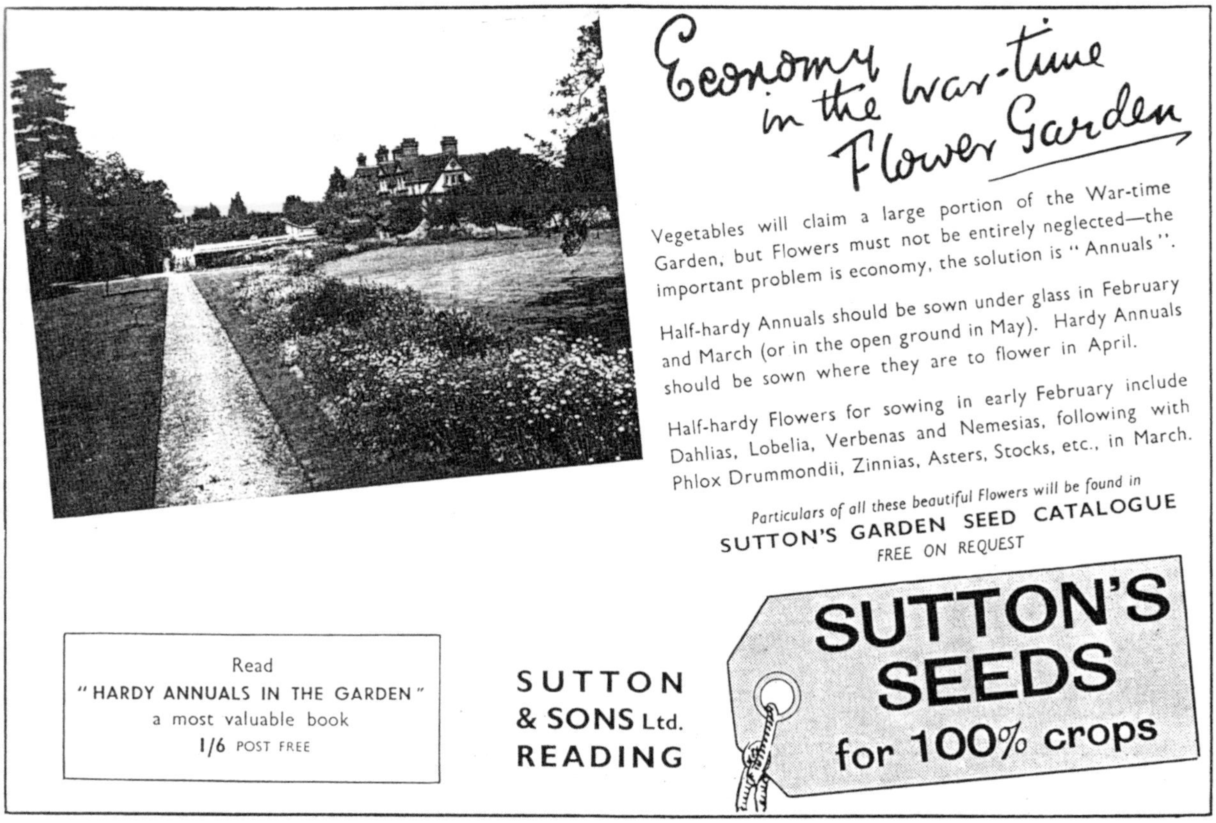
Economy in the War-time Flower Garden
Vegetables will claim a large portion of the War-time Garden, but Flowers must not be entirely neglected—the important problem is economy, the solution is " Annuals ".
Half-hardy Annuals should be sown under glass in February and March (or in the open ground in May). Hardy Annuals should be sown where they are to flower in April.
Half-hardy Flowers for sowing in early February include Dahlias, Lobelia, Verbenas and Nemesias, following with Phlox Drummondii, Zinnias, Asters, Stocks, etc., in March.
Particulars of all these beautiful Flowers will be found in
SUTTON'S GARDEN SEED CATALOGUE
FREE ON REQUEST
Read " HARDY ANNUALS IN THE GARDEN " a most valuable book 1/6 POST FREE
SUTTON & SONS Ltd. READING
SUTTON'S SEEDS for 100% crops

Above
'Economy in the War-time Flower Garden' from Sutton's Seeds(the *Gardeners' Chronicle,* 3 February 1940).

concentrated on herbaceous and border flowers found their trade dwindling, as people rooted out their chrysanthemums and dahlias to make way for vegetables. In autumn 1939 the Dahlia Society had cancelled its autumn show, and the Royal Botanical and Horticultural Society of Manchester and the Northern Counties was one of many societies that also cancelled its regional Chrysanthemum and Autumn Flower Show. With no outlets to display (and sell) their wares the specialist nurseries would have suffered even if the government had not campaigned for a concentration on food production. Due to the time of year at which war was declared those nurseries specialising in autumn plants and spring bulbs which needed to be purchased and planted in the preceding autumn were of course the first to be affected.

By November 1939 professional gardening papers such as the **Gardeners' Chronicle** were crowded with advertisements from nurseries desperate to get rid of surplus unsold stock. Plants were offered at greatly reduced prices as it was realised that that autumn might be the last chance for several years to realise capital expenditure. The collapse of business had been foreseen in the pages of the same magazine in the very first week of war. Headed 'Flowers in War-Time' the editors urged that *'We sincerely hope . . . that orders for bulbs will* *not be cancelled or even unduly curtailed as spring-time will come as certainly as summer and winter, and we may need the beauty of flowers.'*

The situation was made worse by the emergency powers, which enabled the government to dictate to the nurseries what they should grow. Although the situation changed throughout the war depending on what stock was being grown, nurseries were limited to approximately 10% of ground under non-food production or a percentage of their 1939 area. This necessitated the widespread removal and destruction of nursery stocks. R. Tucker & Sons of Faringdon (Buckinghamshire) spelled out the situation in a large advertisement addressed to their clientele in October 1939: *'In spite of severe handicaps caused by the war we are endeavouring to carry on business as usual. We have enormous stocks of all types of Nursery Stock, which are in better condition than ever before. Together with all nurserymen we have offered our entire resources to the Government and are doing everything in our power to produce more food. However, unless we can clear large quantities of our stock during the next six months we shall not be able to carry out our obligations. We therefore appeal to our customers to plant as usual. Owing to government restrictions, all nurserymen will have to increase their acreage for food production. This means that nurserymen will have to cut down their stocks and so prices are bound to rise during the next few seasons.'* Hidden within this mixed message of present over-abundance and future rising prices was a note of panic, as Tucker & Sons tried to sell their specialist plants including honeysuckle varieties, hedging plants and ornamental and avenue trees. In December 1940 St John's Nursery (Sevenoaks) had a clearance sale of stock in order to clear their land for food growing; this included 20,000 roses of all kinds and 5,000 fruit trees.

O.A.K. Nurseries Ltd. of Purley, Reading, also made a virtue out of necessity by offering to sell all its plants at *'less than normal wholesale prices. . . . We are making our contribution to the general effort – and helping you to make yours'*, they claimed. Their advertisement of April 1941 does contain some of the recommended Dig for Victory crops, such as onion plants, spring cabbage, cauliflower and Brussels sprout plants (1s for 50), but also included lupins, delphiniums, oriental poppies, copper beech trees and roses. Interestingly they included in their sale list bamboo clumps. In the

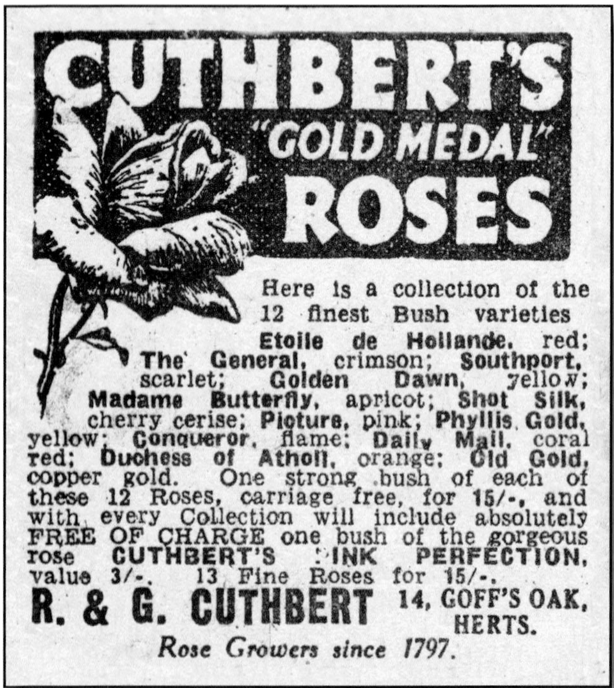
CUTHBERT'S
"GOLD MEDAL"
ROSES
Here is a collection of the 12 finest Bush varieties
Etoile de Hollande, red; The General, crimson; Southport, scarlet; Golden Dawn, yellow; Madame Butterfly, apricot; Shot Silk, cherry cerise; Picture, pink; Phyllis Gold, yellow; Conqueror, flame; Daily Mail, coral red; Duchess of Atholl, orange; Old Gold, copper gold. One strong bush of each of these 12 Roses, carriage free, for 15/-, and with every Collection will include absolutely FREE OF CHARGE one bush of the gorgeous rose CUTHBERT'S PINK PERFECTION, value 3/-. 13 Fine Roses for 15/-.
R. & G. CUTHBERT 14, GOFF'S OAK, HERTS.
Rose Growers since 1797.

Above
Cuthbert's gold medal roses advert from December 1941.

1930s bamboo was usually used in Japanese style gardens which were to become deeply unpopular when Japan entered the war.

Some specialist nurseries did continue to produce, and show, at least in the early years of the war. At the Southport Flower Show of August 1940, fifty trade exhibits were set up, including displays of orchids, carnations, sweet peas, water lilies, begonias and roses. The orchid stand was by Messrs Charlesworth & Co., while carnations were provided by both Messrs C. Engelmann Ltd, and the famous Allwood Brothers Nursery.

Rose Nurseries

Roses had become the backbone of the English suburban garden during the interwar years. Developments in breeding of the hybrid tea rose had seen a huge rise in its popularity in the early twentieth century. Available in a stunning array of colours, this long-flowering rose was the standard decoration for front gardens throughout the 1920s and '30s. Woolworths are thought to have been the first to sell hybrid tea roses over the counter. These were relatively inexpensive at sixpence each, and were popular among gardeners who were less confident in purchasing from catalogues and nurseries. Several specialist rose nurseries had grown up in the years between the wars, the most famous of which were Harry Wheatcroft & Sons and the nursery of Doug Gandy. Harry Wheatcroft had founded his nursery in the immediate aftermath of the First World War to the north-east of Nottingham. Despite the poor soils in the area, the smoke from the city helped the Wheatcroft brothers to establish

a successful business, by preventing the outbreak of the dreaded rose 'black spot'. By the 1920s Harry and Alfred were able to purchase 10,000 rose stocks, and by 1930 had shown their new varieties at the Chelsea Show. On the eve of war the company had over 600,000 rose trees on a much-enlarged site, many of them unique hybrids. The estimated value of their stock was over £100,000 and under government regulations they were eventually required to uproot and burn all but 10%, converting the rest of the land to food production.

The Wheatcrofts' nearest rival, Doug Gandy, had started his business on an allotment site in South Kilworth in Leicestershire. Eventually taking over the whole allotment field (unused since the First World War), he built up a substantial stock of some 30,000–40,000 roses. In 1939 he moved to a new site of 60 acres in North Kilworth, but on the outbreak of war was told by the government to convert to market gardening. Found growing strawberries, a crop considered of little use by the government, Gandy was told to replace these with cabbages within a fortnight or face imprisonment. He was not the only market gardener who tried to get round the regulations. A grower in Somerset was fined £10 plus costs in February 1941 for growing strawberries instead of cabbages on a quarter-acre of land. By 1943 the restrictions on what could be done were considerably tightened and punishments increased. A nurseryman in Devon was fined £15 for growing tulips, a crop which the judge described as 'very profitable', as people were prepared to go to any lengths to obtain flowers for weddings and funerals.

R. Tucker & Sons of Berkshire, another famous

rose nursery, converted their rosebeds to grow onions to produce seed for victory diggers. Their nurseries were home to a specially selected stock of the onion variety 'Sandy Prize', and despite the poor weather in 1941 they were able to provide large quantities of seed for the following year. Carters' seeds also grew roses and sold both individual varieties and their special 'collections' of 12 mixed flowering roses. In an advertisement in November 1939, Carters rather mysteriously announced that one or more of these mixed-rose collections might 'solve the problem in bedding for the difficult period'.

By the end of September 1939 the situation was so serious that most of the gardening periodicals carried editorials extolling the virtues of flowers. Although most of the argument dwelt on the bright and gay nature of the flowerbed, lifting wartime spirits, the **Gardeners' Chronicle** made the point that *Nurserymen and seedsmen . . . need all the custom they can get. They have served us well in peacetime and so far as is possible we must try to help them to keep their businesses going during the war.'* The one bright spot for flower producers was the increase in weddings, and demand for bouquets was high. But the closure of theatres and the blackout meant that generally demand was, in the words of the trade magazines, 'microscopic'. Prices were also higher than before the war as costs of labour, packaging materials and fertilisers rose.

By the end of the first month of the war it was obvious to all that nurserymen were already suffering. The Royal Horticultural Society put out a special plea on their behalf: *The Council of the Royal Horticultural Society . . . draws the attention of fellows of the Society and of the public to the desirability of continuing to place orders with nurserymen. If orders are absent very much of the work that nurserymen have done during the past few years will be wasted. Moreover, it would be a calamity if, owing to the scarcity of orders, many of them were compelled to close their businesses entirely, for unless some stock is retained during the war it will be many years after the cessation of hostilities before they will be again in a position to play their essential part in the horticultural life of the country. It is hoped that these points will be kept in mind by all amateur gardeners and that orders for trees, shrubs and other plants will not be discontinued unless this is found to be absolutely necessary.'*

Despite this plea by the RHS, the 'businesses for sale' section of garden magazines soon saw a dramatic increase in size. Many nursery owners decided that the adaptation to wartime production, combined with loss of valuable stock (often built up over many years if not generations) made the future impossible. Loss of qualified labour was the final straw as men skilled in specialisms such as orchid propagation or hybridisation were called up to the front. Nursery sales often included all stock as well as glasshousing, cold frames, piggeries (used for production of manure) and housing for employees.

Nurseries Carrying On Under War Regulations

Those nurseries that did carry on during the war did so by adapting and complying with government regulations, which included an agreed commitment to food production, overseen by a county representative of the War Agricultural Committees. The majority of nursery glasshousing was cleared of flowers and used to grow tomatoes, which many amateur gardeners found difficult to grow but which added variety and nutrition to the diet. Outdoor beds and fields were used for vegetables, including the production of baby plants such as cabbage for growing on by amateur gardeners. At Woods Nursery in Woodbridge (Suffolk), later to become the famous Notcutts, five of the seven glasshouses were given over to tomatoes, with only two retained for propagation of decorative stock, and the cold frames reserved for cucumbers. Many unique varieties originally created by Roger Crompton Notcutts were lost, including rare chrysanthemums. By 1947 the number of varieties of plants grown had dropped from its pre-war level of thousands to just 989.

Initially the regulations for the proportion of areas allowed for flowers and other crops was quite generous. Up to 75% of the acreage grown in 1939 for non-bulb flowers under glass, 50% in the open air; but with no fresh planting of perennials, asparagus or nursery stocks. Nursery stock (rather than plants for that season) was not to occupy more than 10% of the area of any firm. However, as with everything else, restrictions tightened as the war went on. Some specialised nurseries did manage to adapt and continue to offer a combination of vegetables and flowers. Allwood Brothers of Haywards Heath (Sussex) were famous for their pinks, dianthus and carnations. Originally founded by Montagu Allwood the nurseries had created the scented *Dianthus Alwoodii*, which was the basis for many other varieties from c.1915 onwards. During the war the Allwood nurseries complied with government regulations, but somehow combined this with continuing to breed and sell all types of pinks, dianthus and so on. A favourite of the amateur gardener, *Allwoodii* carnations were recommended in the columns of **Garden Work** throughout the war. Their advertisement in **Garden Work** of May 1943 highlighted their dianthus seedlings ('Four Varieties of Rainbow Loveli-

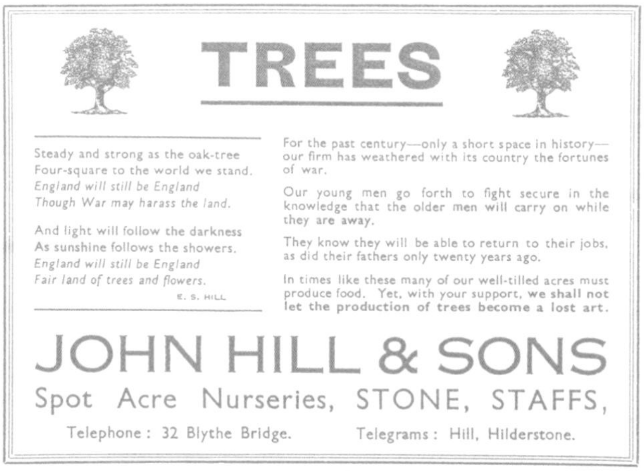

TREES
Steady and strong as the oak-tree
Four-square to the world we stand.
England will still be England
Though War may harass the land.
And light will follow the darkness
As sunshine follows the showers.
England will still be England
Fair land of trees and flowers.
E. S. HILL
For the past century—only a short space in history—our firm has weathered with its country the fortunes of war.
Our young men go forth to fight secure in the knowledge that the older men will carry on while they are away.
They know they will be able to return to their jobs, as did their fathers only twenty years ago.
In times like these many of our well-tilled acres must produce food. Yet, with your support, we shall not let the production of trees become a lost art.
JOHN HILL & SONS
Spot Acre Nurseries, STONE, STAFFS,
Telephone : 32 Blythe Bridge.
Telegrams : Hill, Hilderstone.

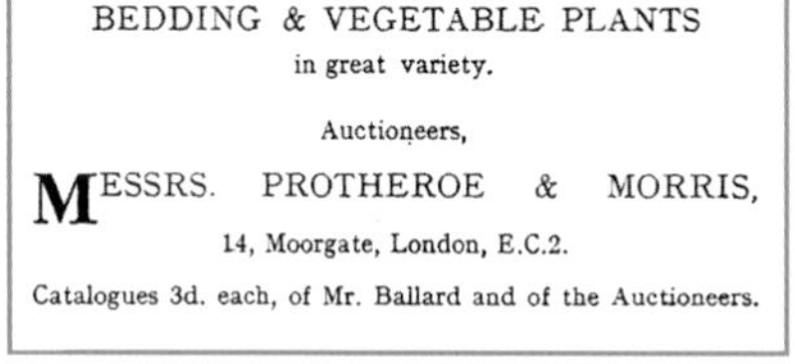

SALES BY AUCTION, &c.
THE OLD COURT NURSERIES,
COLWALL, Near MALVERN.
AUCTION SALE
by Order of Mr. Ernest Ballard, the well-known specialist in Michaelmas Daisies and Alpine Plants.
SATURDAY, MAY 13th,
At 11 a.m., at the Nurseries, as above.
RARE ALPINES,
BEDDING & VEGETABLE PLANTS
in great variety.
Auctioneers,
MESSRS. PROTHEROE & MORRIS,
14, Moorgate, London, E.C.2.
Catalogues 3d. each, of Mr. Ballard and of the Auctioneers.

Above
John Hill & Sons nursery were optimistic in their outlook in November 1939, looking forward already to the return of the young men who had only just left to fight. When the war did eventually end few estates were able to afford to take on the levels of staff they had once employed.

Right
Even by May 1944 some nurseries had sufficient stock of specialist plants to hold their annual auctions. Here Old Court Nurseries, Malvern, are auctioning their alpine plants, as well as bedding and vegetable plants.

ness') including the locally named 'Sweet Wivelsfield' and perpetual flowering *Allwoodii* carnations. But the same advertisement also devoted space to runner beans, culinary peas, and even buckwheat for growing as chicken feed. An advertisement earlier in the same year had offered onion plants, garden peas and cauliflower plants, as well as chive, leek and onion seed. The advertisements included the 'signature' 'Allwood Brothers, Food Growers'. Allwood nurseries survived the long years of the war, branching out to breed vegetable seeds including Allwood's Prolific garden pea, selected onion plants and runner beans, although in the spring of 1943 there was only a limited stock of runner beans (1s 9d a half pint for a 'market variety').

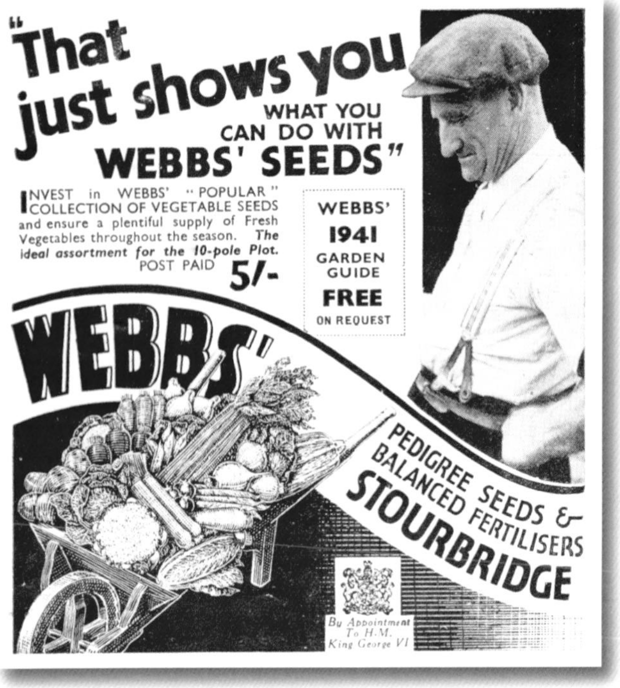
"That just shows you
WHAT YOU CAN DO WITH
WEBBS' SEEDS"
INVEST in WEBBS' "POPULAR" COLLECTION OF VEGETABLE SEEDS and ensure a plentiful supply of Fresh Vegetables throughout the season. The ideal assortment for the 10-pole Plot.
POST PAID 5/-
WEBBS' 1941 GARDEN GUIDE FREE ON REQUEST
WEBBS'
PEDIGREE SEEDS & BALANCED FERTILISERS
STOURBRIDGE
By Appointment To H.M. King George VI

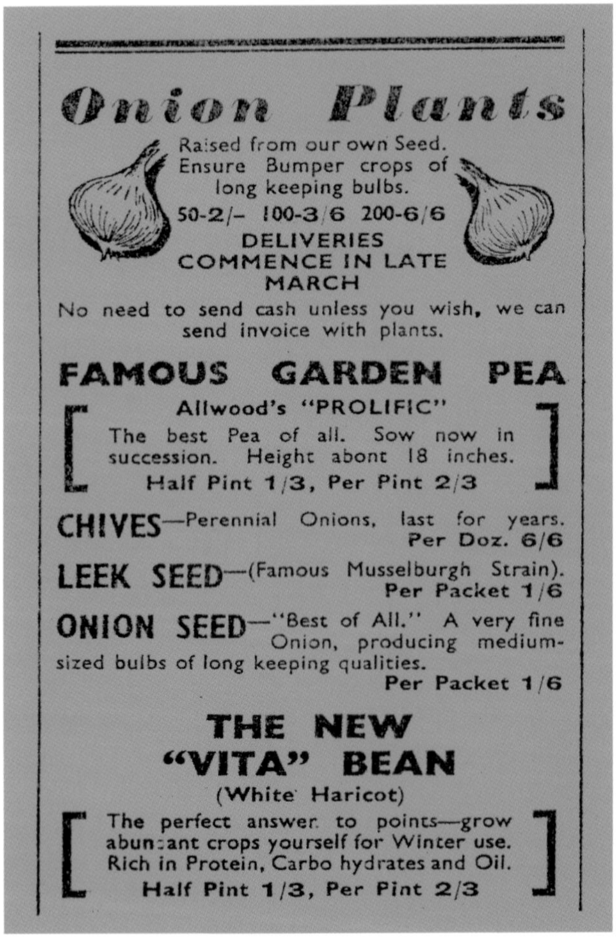
Onion Plants
Raised from our own Seed. Ensure Bumper crops of long keeping bulbs.
50-2/- 100-3/6 200-6/6
DELIVERIES COMMENCE IN LATE MARCH
No need to send cash unless you wish, we can send invoice with plants.
FAMOUS GARDEN PEA
Allwood's "PROLIFIC"
The best Pea of all. Sow now in succession. Height abont 18 inches.
Half Pint 1/3, Per Pint 2/3
CHIVES—Perennial Onions, last for years. Per Doz. 6/6
LEEK SEED—(Famous Musselburgh Strain). Per Packet 1/6
ONION SEED—"Best of All." A very fine Onion, producing medium-sized bulbs of long keeping qualities. Per Packet 1/6
THE NEW "VITA" BEAN
(White Haricot)
The perfect answer to points—grow abundant crops yourself for Winter use. Rich in Protein, Carbo hydrates and Oil.
Half Pint 1/3, Per Pint 2/3

Allwoods continued in the family until 1991, when the name and stock was bought out.

Mr S.J. Miles, a commercial carnation grower from Bayham Abbey Gardens, was also forced to adapt rapidly, and turned his carnation nurseries to tomato growing. Mr Miles even wrote an article in the **Gardeners' Chronicle** about his success at adaptation under the rather misleading title of '*The war-time cultivation of carnations*'. **The British Carnation Yearbook** was still published in 1941 but was described as '*for obvious reasons less bulky than in peacetime*'. Mr F. Hanger of Exbury contributed a '*feeling and convincing*' piece on coping with carnation growing in unheated glasshousing, although sympathies must have been more forthcoming for the secretary and editor of the Carnation Society whose carnation-growing area in East Sheen was actually bombed. Despite the restrictions on glasshousing and heating, some specialist nurseries continued to function. Charlesworth & Co.

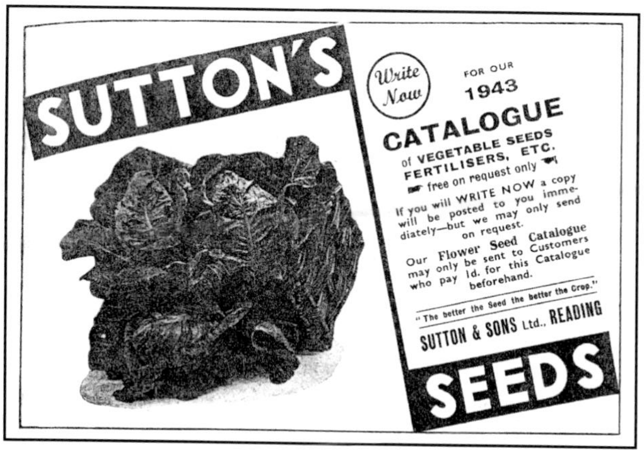
SUTTON'S
Write Now
FOR OUR
1943
CATALOGUE
of VEGETABLE SEEDS
FERTILISERS, ETC.
free on request only
If you will WRITE NOW a copy will be posted to you immediately—but we may only send on request.
Our Flower Seed Catalogue may only be sent to Customers who pay 1d. for this Catalogue beforehand.
"The better the Seed the better the Crop."
SUTTON & SONS Ltd., READING
SEEDS

Far Left
By March 1943 Allwood Bros were advertising as 'Food Growers', a change from their peacetime business of carnations.

Left
A typical advertisement for the wonders of Webbs' seeds. Advertisements for all sorts of gardening products in this period showed wheelbarrows full of vegetables.

Above
By 1943 catalogues for seeds could only be sent on request.

of Haywards Heath (Sussex) were still advertising as 'The Largest Raisers, Growers & Exporters' of orchids in the country in 1942.

The larger seed companies such as Webbs, Carters and Suttons were well placed to survive the war years, and in fact expanded as demand for vegetable seeds grew. In spring 1941 Webbs were offering their 'popular collection' of vegetable seeds packaged as an 'ideal assortment for the 10-pole plot'. At only 5s these were guaranteed to ensure a plentiful supply of fresh vegetables through the season. In their advertisement a rather self-satisfied 'belt and braces' man looks admiringly at a drawing of a wheelbarrow full of the delights of the year's toil. Other nurseries also made a virtue out of necessity and advertised productive garden plants for sale. Hayland Nursery, in Kingsbury (Middlesex), sold a wide variety of tomato plants mail order. Packed in special cardboard pots and placed in trays these were ideal for the novice gardener, although at 7s a dozen they were a lot more expensive than producing from seed. Varieties available in 1943 included Market King, Ailsa Craig, Essex Wonder, Carter's Sunrise, and Sutton's Open Air. For those not prepared to pay for plants the seeds themselves were available via the Carter's and Sutton's catalogues. Any sales and profits for nurseries had to be made within the country, as by autumn 1940 the export of seeds of all types of vegetables was forbidden. Peas, broad beans, runner beans, leeks, broccoli, carrots, lettuces, spinach – were banned from leaving the country.

The seedsmen suffered a further blow in 1943 when sending out catalogues was restricted. Rather than targeting those that had purchased before, seedsmen could only send to those who specifically wrote in and requested catalogues. In addition. although vegetable seed catalogues were free, flower seed catalogues often had to be paid for, a further small but significant discouragement to the flower gardener.

Market Gardens and Fruit Farms

Although most market gardens (rather than nurseries) were, by their very nature, well suited for the wartime effort, there were still adaptations to be made and regulations to obey. The county-based War Agricultural Committees oversaw what could be produced and by what means. They also advised on labour and volunteer or Land Army replacements for staff who had been called up or volunteered despite being in agricultural posts. Certain crops were disallowed and market gardens which specialised in them had to root up crops and replant. Strawberries, for example, were discouraged, and acres of plants were destroyed in the county of Kent. In September 1939 the Minister of Agriculture advised that: *'Strawberries present a special case because of the number of poor and unproductive stocks in the country and the luxury character of the crop. Unthrifty beds and beds of three years of age and over should be grubbed and the land freed for potatoes or cereals. The occupier should be given permission to replant an area of land not exceeding seventy-five percent of that grubbed providing the Committee approve the strain worthy of planting.'* In July 1940 it was prohibited for market gardeners to grow any strawberries under glass for 'trade', and mushrooms grown in glasshousing could only occupy up to 50% of pre-war space. Raspberries, gooseberries, loganberries and currants were to be maintained but not increased without special consent despite the fact that these crops were not easy to obtain elsewhere and did not travel well.

The government's attitude towards fruit trees and fruit farms seems at first sight rather at odds with its general campaign to grow more food. At the outbreak of war it was announced by the Ministry of Agriculture that all derelict and badly neglected orchards should be grubbed up and the land made available for potatoes, which would be more productive. In addition, no new fruit trees were to be planted by market growers, except with the explicit permission of the War Agricultural Executive Committee (which would only be given in very

exceptional circumstances). Although it was understood that fruit would be in limited supply during the war, it was not at first realised how restricted this would become. In addition it was noted that fruit trees took several years to reach fruiting maturity and thus it was thought planting or renovation would not pay off until the war was over. Fruit farms and fruit tree nurseries also necessitated substantial labour at certain seasons, in particular for skilled hand-pruning, and as conscription widened most of the labour force was taken away. The government urged established growers to produce maximum crops from existing trees, using insecticides and fertilisers to achieve an increase in productivity. Working on fruit farms was to become one of the many ways to 'Lend a Hand on the Land'. As well as Land Girls, children were 'employed' either in school groups or as scout packs, and the dense fruit farms of Kent and the jam producers around the villages north of Cambridge took in children for periods of a week or two.

Development of Varieties

With the urgent need for high production rates, seedsmen and nurseries were anxious to develop varieties with high yields or good disease resistance. Each seed supplier claimed to have better seeds than the others. Webb's seeds of Stourbridge was typical in its claim that *'It is of paramount importance to obtain maximum return from the soil. This can only be done by using [Webb's] Pedigree Seeds.'* New varieties were patriotically named, to give extra appeal to victory diggers. 'Home Guard' potatoes for example were introduced in 1942 as a 'first early'. With its creamy white flesh and firm texture 'Home Guard' was advertised as a good 'cooker' for the start of the season. Good for boiling it was described as a 'general purpose potato'; its only problem was a susceptibility to potato blight. Blight was the dreaded scourge of the allotment-holder as once it appeared on one plot it could devastate everyone's crop across the whole area. Potatoes became the subject of intense interest, and in particular ways in which one might overcome the dreaded potato blight. Many nurseries claimed to source their potatoes only from Scotland, where blight was less of a problem. 'Highland grown seed potatoes' were the boast of Alexander & Brown of Perth, who also offered a free copy of **My Garden Book.**

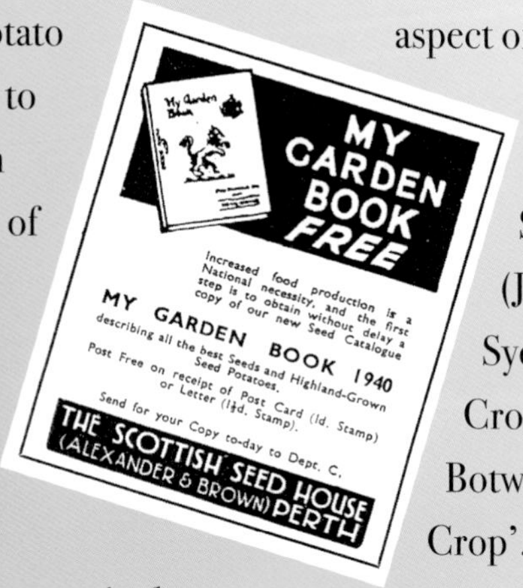
MY GARDEN BOOK FREE
Increased food production is a National necessity, and the first step is to obtain without delay a copy of our new Seed Catalogue
MY GARDEN BOOK 1940
describing all the best Seeds and Highland-Grown Seed Potatoes.
Post Free on receipt of Post Card (1d. Stamp) or Letter (1½d. Stamp).
Send for your Copy to-day to Dept. C.
THE SCOTTISH SEED HOUSE
(ALEXANDER & BROWN) PERTH

In spring 1941 seed potatoes were in desperately short supply, and particularly Scottish seed potato. Severe weather in January and February that year made it impossible to dispatch any seed potatoes from Scotland. The following month restrictions on transport generally, including a specific ban on seed potatoes being carried to certain counties, exacerbated the situation. Seed potatoes were fighting with evacuees for space on the railways. Ironically some seed potatoes had to be shipped from Scottish ports to ports in the east and south of England. Messrs Dobbie and Co., seedsmen of Edinburgh, had made representations to the government on behalf of the Scottish seed potato trade but allotment-holders were beginning to panic as Easter loomed and no seed potatoes were available. Marching side by side with the variety Home Guard (although not planted in proximity for fear of blight transference) was Clibrans' 'Victory' tomato, supposedly averaging nearly 13lb of tomatoes per plant. Clibrans (of Altrincham) also claimed its colour and quality were of the highest quality, making 'Clibrans' Victory' the 'world's best tomato'.

After disease resistance, maximum yields were a constant concern of all growers, amateur and professional, and seed suppliers focused on this aspect of their varieties. Endless advertisements claimed 'maximum yield' (Ryder & Son Seeds of St Albans and Webb's Pedigree Seeds, Stourbridge), 'Bumper Crops' (John Peed & Son, West Norwood and Sydenham's Seeds of Birmingham), or 'Prize Crops' (Hawker & Botwood Co.). Hawker & Botwood even sold a product called 'Prize Crop'. Even where new varieties were not created, long-established varieties might be given heightened attention due to their dependability. The Rivers' fruit nurseries, originally set up in Hertfordshire in 1725, used their long-established pedigree as a marketing strength during the war. Sales of soft and tree fruit stock expanded as imported fruit became scarce and, as Rivers carefully pointed out, planting your own trees and bushes would be invaluable: *'Make sure of supplies by planting now from Rivers' dependable fruiting stock grown in the famous fruit tree nurseries established by Rivers 216 years ago. Every variety and shape available suitable for planting on walls, fences, etc., and to make every corner productive.'*

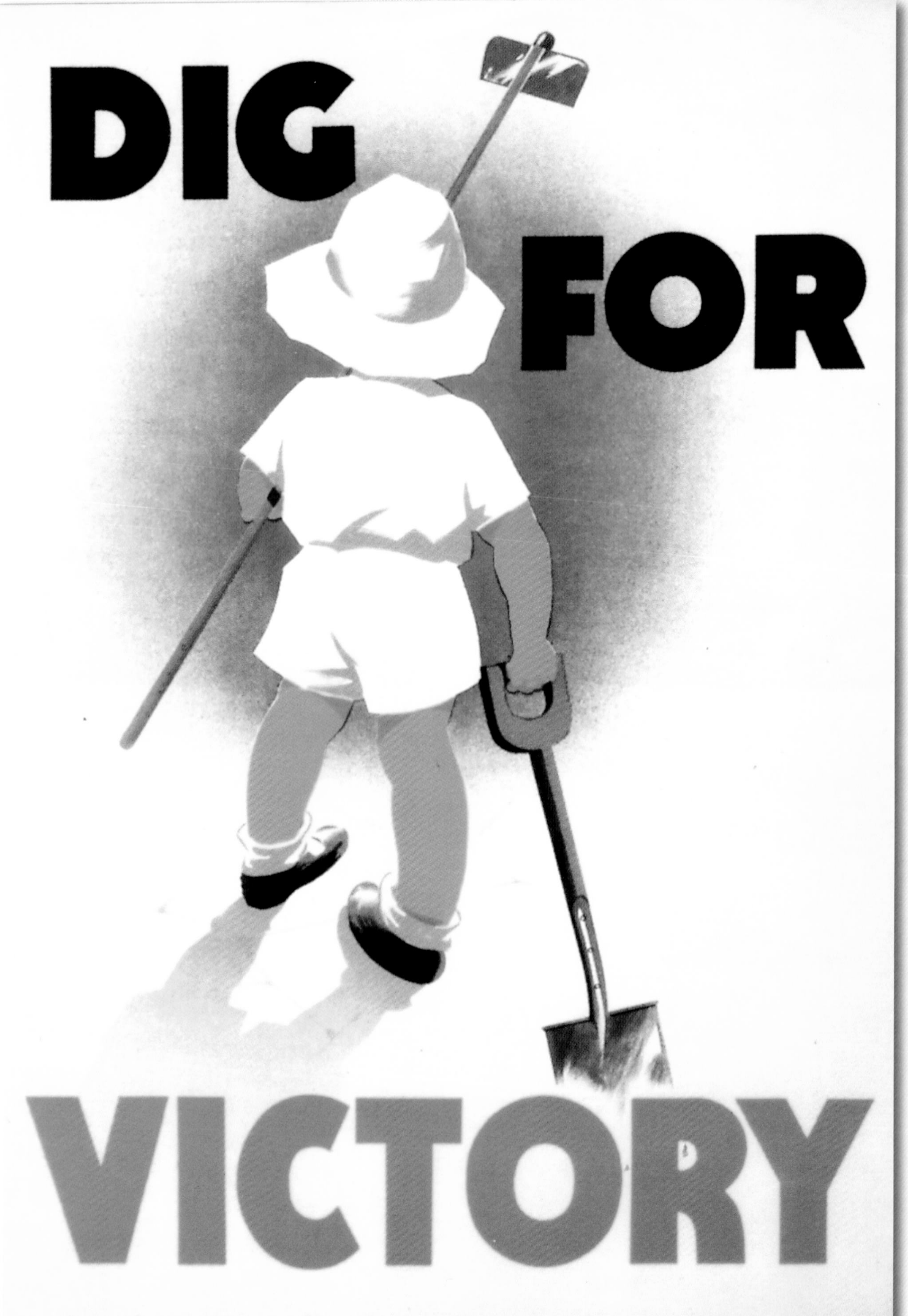
DIG
FOR
VICTORY

Children & gardening

During the First World War keeping school gardens became a patriotic duty and most schoolchildren (and their teachers) jumped at the chance of outdoor time away from the rather rigid timetables and rote learning. High profile schools were encouraged to set an example. At Eton vegetable cultivation was included in the curriculum, and parts of the school playing fields were dug up to make 'allotments' for the boys.

The War Gardens Commission in America had also specifically targeted schools in the First World War. Calling on the *'mighty army of boys and girls,*

Left
This popular Dig for Victory poster was the result of a competition organised by the *Smallholder* magazine. The competition attracted over 2,000 entries and was won by Miss Mary Tumbridge, from Nottingham. The *Gardeners' Chronicle* commented that it was particularly appropriate that the winner was a woman, as they were becoming essential to the Dig for Victory campaign.

Below
Teachers were renowned for 'overseeing' their pupils' efforts rather than joining in!
HMSO

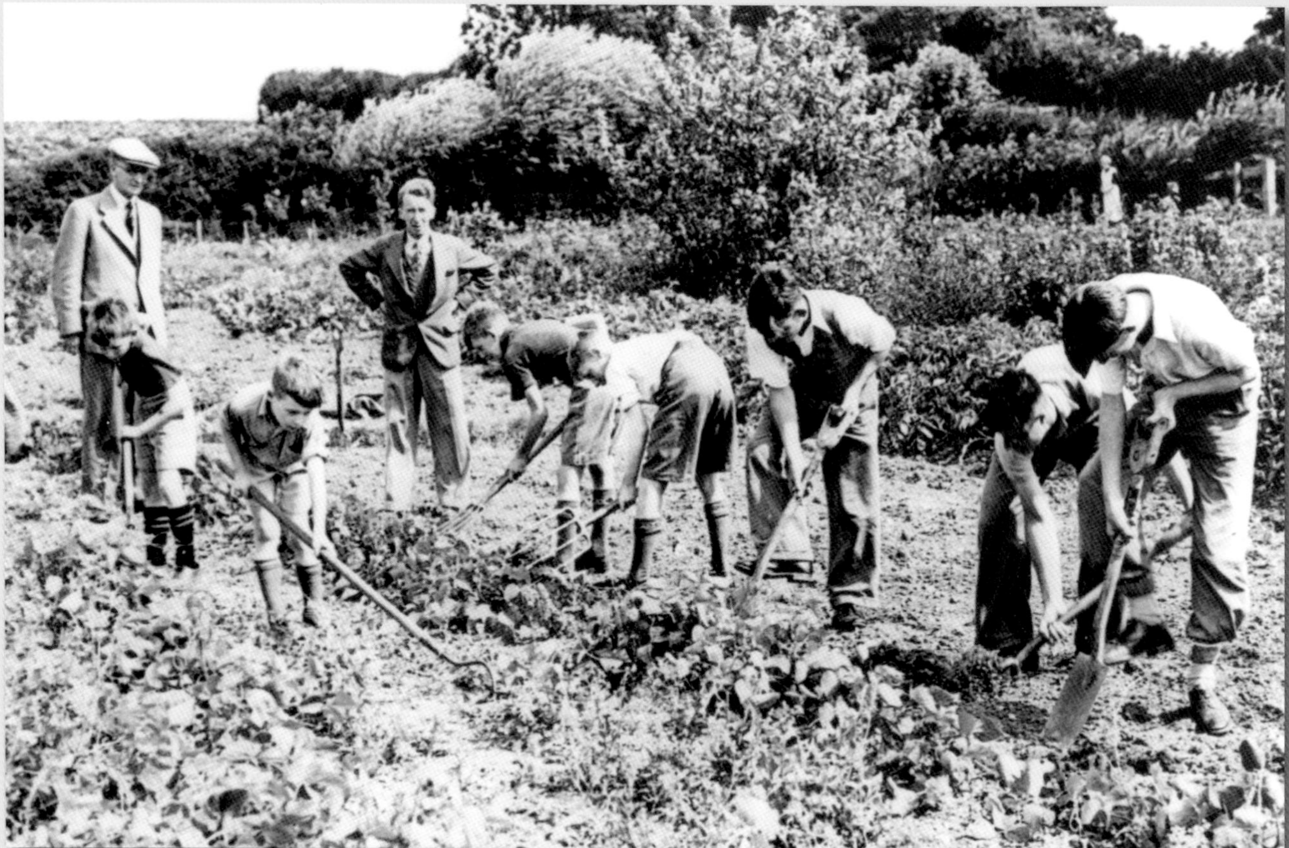

Boys from Eton College coming back from working on their vegetable plots.

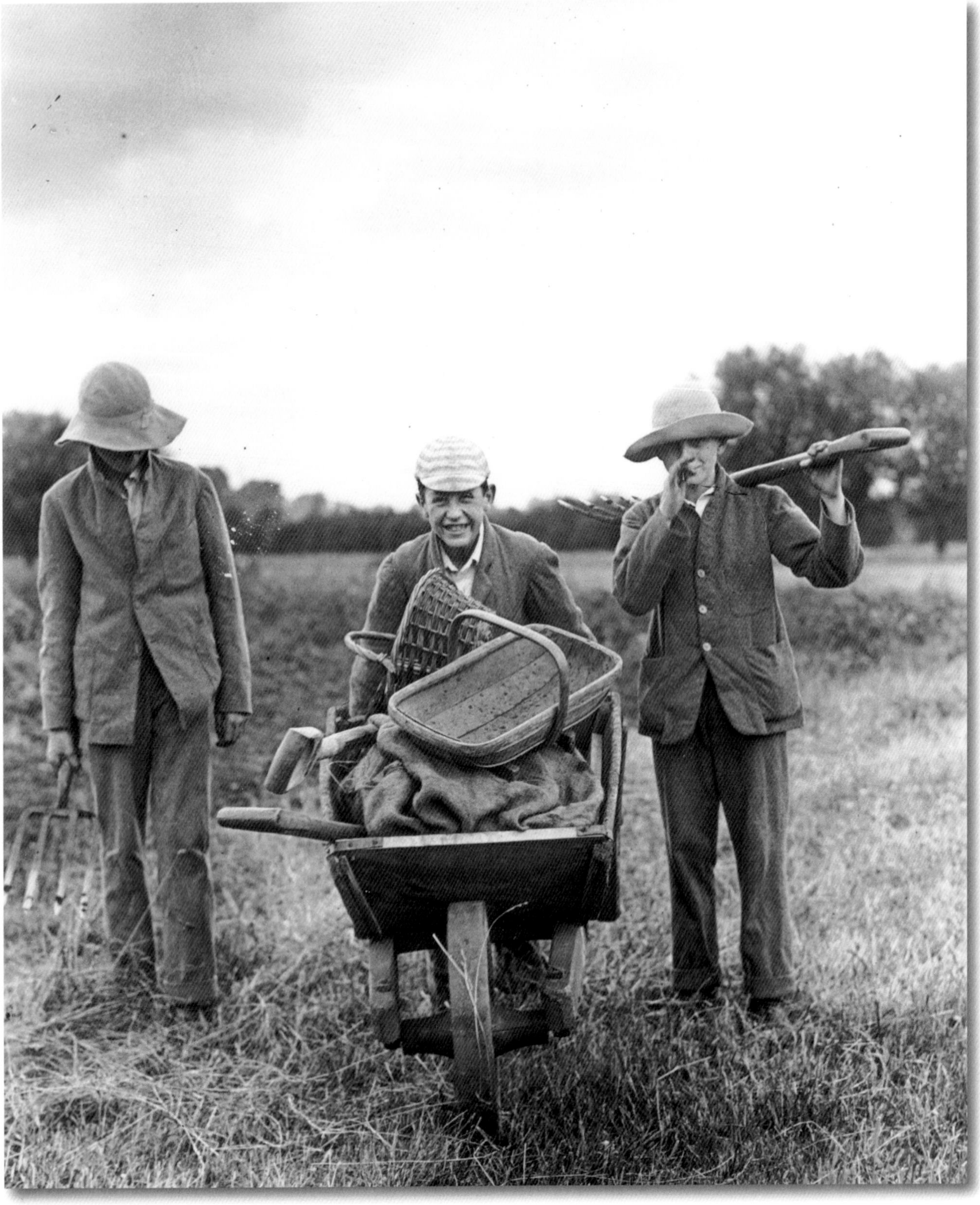

thirty to fifty million strong, who have heads, hearts and hands, leisure time and patriotism to spare'. The US government urged them to create gardens in their schoolyards and any uncultivated land. Many schools both in England and the USA retained their horticultural lessons during the postwar period, often combined with nature, or outdoor 'science' studies. The Midhurst Grammar School, Sussex, was fortunate in having a large walled kitchen garden area where the boys learnt sowing and cropping.

With the outbreak of the Second World War, school gardens were again to play a vital role, and any school that had land attached to it became the proud possessor of a 'Victory' garden. Pupils would usually have two or more lessons a week in the gardens, as well as some after-school training for those who were enthusiastic. Some schools lost all their flowerbeds in an effort to produce more food. Children at the Merchant Taylor's school at Ashwell (Hertfordshire), for instance, dug up the flowerbeds and replanted them with vegetables, planting an additional 3 acres outside the school grounds.

Schools Cultivate Victory

Not all schools had enough ground, or suitable ground, for productive gardens but with the emphasis on all-out production they were encouraged to approach local householders and landowners to provide space for a 'school garden'. At Oving (West Sussex) the Parochial School was given permission to cultivate plots in the vicarage across the road. Fred Shopland, a pupil at the time, recalls there being 12 plots, with a boy and a girl in charge

of each. Competition between the plots was intense, and there was a clear understanding that the plots were helping the war effort. For Fred it was the start of a life to be spent in agriculture and at the allotment. As the war progressed, every school was expected to have a garden producing both school dinners and 'extras' for the children's families.

Any produce was usually destined for the school kitchens, although some might go to a communal village store, or even be divided up among parents and teachers. At least that was the theory; with many headteachers living 'on the spot' the gardens may also have served as a supplement to their own endeavours. Certainly Norman Owen from Lancashire recalls that the produce from their village school plot never seemed to get shared around. The gardens in his school included a greenhouse, strawberry beds, vegetable plots and three apple trees. Local farmers supplied the school with manure and there was a well for water. What happened to the produce was a mystery to the children until one evening, Norman claims, he saw the headmaster coming from the garden *'staggering under the weight of two large baskets crammed full of garden produce'*. At Luton (Bedfordshire) some at least of the school garden produce was sold in aid of school funds. The school gardens at Luton continued long after the war was over, supplementing the seemingly never-ending rationing, at least for some!

At Moulsecoomb school, Brighton, the senior school pupils took turns to work on their school allotments across the road, next to the mortuary chapel. Each class had its own allotment and competition was stiff. Although it was supposedly an

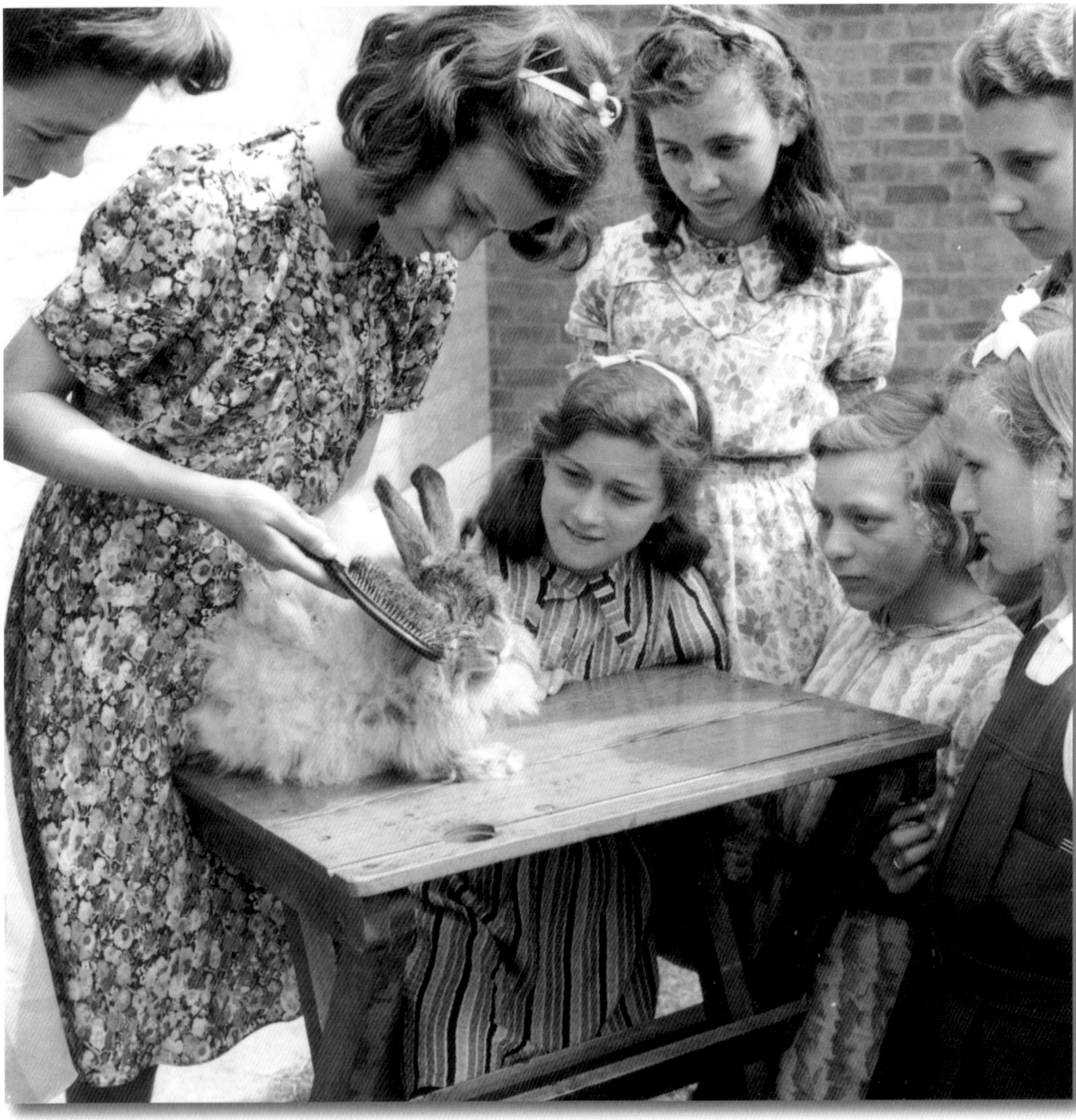

opportunity for the teachers to teach the pupils how to Dig for Victory, many of the pupils came from the surrounding rural villages and knew far more about digging and planting than the teachers. At Rayleigh, Essex, a local gardener was employed to teach the willing pupils and all went well in the first year. Starting with seed packets costing 1d each, crops flourished and each of the pupils took home their rewards for the hard work done. The second year was unfortunately not as successful as a land mine came down close to the school allotment fields, creating havoc, mud and metal all over the garden produce.

The boys at the BMC and Bedford School had

their work cut out when their headmaster decided to extend the school fields and form a series of allotments. The newly purchased land had been home to allotments in the First World War, but had become rough pasture and scrubland by the time the boys took it on. Mr H.W. Liddle, the headmaster, announced that: *'Each form will have a spade or fork for uplifting buried iron posts, iron sheeting, bedsteads, wire and wire netting...'*. To encourage competition the field was divided into smaller areas with each form having a specific area. A School Agricultural Committee was established to oversee the allotments, and by spring 1940 the area was ready to be planted out. Volunteers were called for to plant the potatoes. Setting an example the masters started at 6am, and worked alongside the pupils until the work finished at 9pm. Soon a Land Service Corps was established for boys over the age of 14, under the direction of the enthusiastic Mr Liddle, and work went on apace. When the crop was eventually sold a profit of £40 had been made but the effort had put a strain on other areas of school life. For the rest of the war part of the large field was let to a tenant, while smaller plots were tended by small parties, each consisting of a master and three boys. During their holidays some of the pupils from the Bedford Modern School also chose to work at Rawlins' Farm in Biddenham (Beds), earning pocket money and helping the war effort.

Some schools had specific gardening teachers, although others 'got by' with teachers who had more or less experience. At Sunny Hill School, Bruton (Somerset), Viola Williams was originally the school gardener, and during wartime became the gardening teacher. The newly dug fields fed

Left
In addition to raising vegetables some schools encouraged keeping livestock. This angora rabbit would provide wool, but would need constant care and attention.
HMSO

Above
In Bedford the headmaster H.W. Liddle encouraged the boys to Dig for Victory in the new school field in Clapham Road, Bedford. The headmaster also established a Land Service Corps for boys over 14.

240 pupils, although it was difficult to ensure crops were at their best during term time only. Viola Wiliams had previously been head gardener at Cheltenham Ladies' College, where she had tried to convert the playing fields to potatoes. In the same way that female professional gardeners were rare before the war, in many schools working on the vegetable plot or allotment was a task for the boys, while the girls stayed in school to do cooking or sewing. At Quinton Church of England School the girls learned dancing while the boys tended the vegetables on land provided by the parish. At Littleworth Senior School in Hednesforth, Staffordshire, all the senior boys spent one whole morning or afternoon every week in the school gardens. Five acres of vegetable gardens, including pigs, poultry, rabbits and bees were kept. Cold frames

and livestock runs were made during woodwork classes, and the boys even took practical 'homework', by encouraging their parents to start growing vegetables at home. A model allotment, based on the government's leaflets, was also created to encourage parents to join in. Schools were sometimes given allotments which had originally been set aside for townspeople. In Newcastle upon Tyne, 700 extra allotment plots made available in 1941 remained vacant despite the best efforts of the reinvigorated Dig for Victory campaign. The plots were offered to the senior classes of all the Newcastle schools, putting their parents to shame. Across in Sunderland, the **Gardeners' Chronicle** of December 1941 reported that: *'The suspension of its school building programme left the Sunderland Education Committee with a good deal of unoccupied land; consequently arrangements were made there for five acres to be cultivated by the scholars and about ten acres by the Works Department. . . . A tool shed was erected on each of the four sites and tools provided to permit two parties (forty pupils) to work at the same time.'*

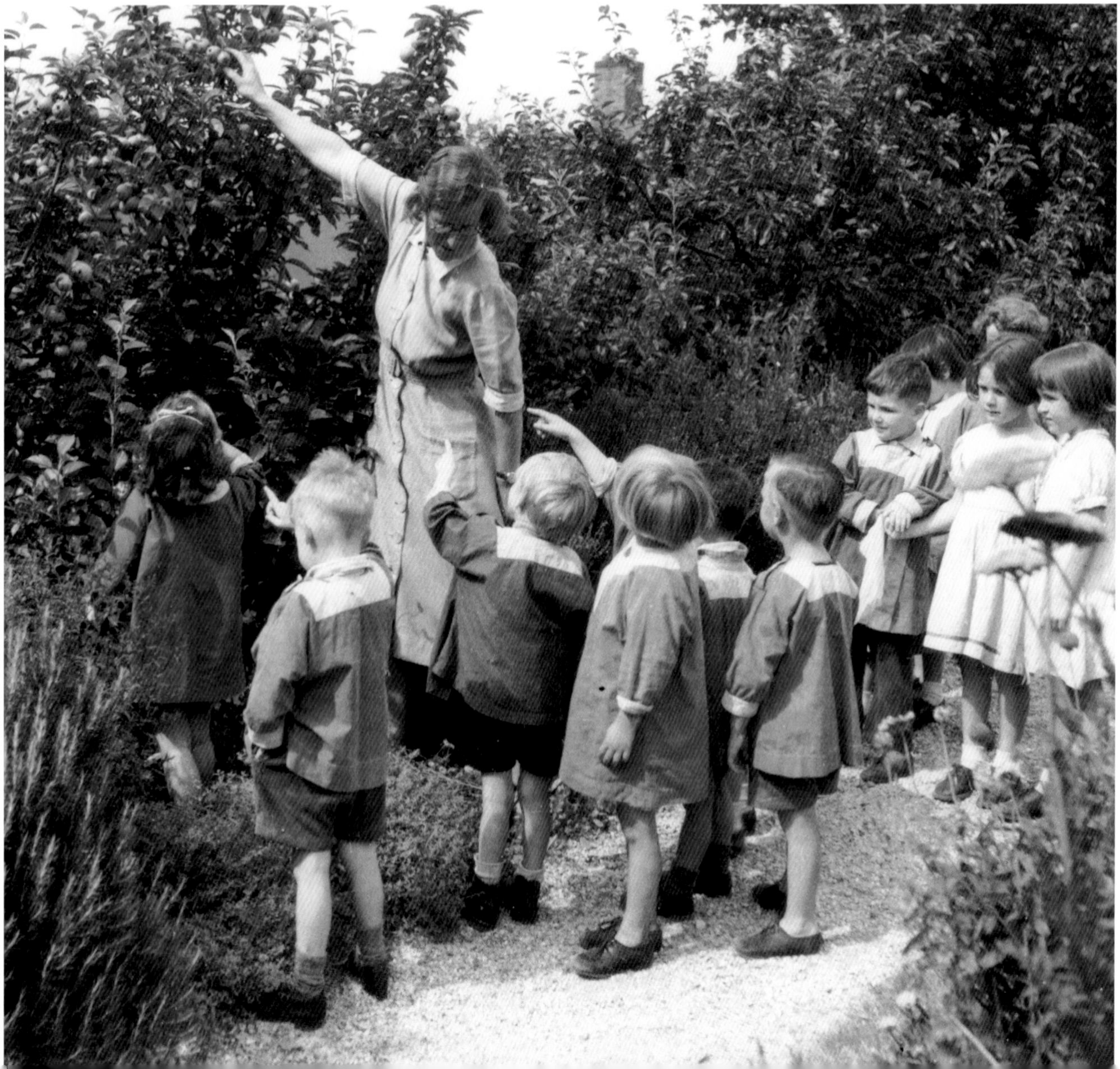

In May 1942 the **Gardeners' Chronicle** reported that: *'Twenty thousand children in the West Riding of Yorkshire are producing food and making sure of their canteen dinners next winter. Before the war about 90 acres were cultivated by elementary school children, to-day the area is over four hundred acres. Greenhouses and garden frames, rabbit hutches and pig-styes have been made by the boys out of antiquated school desks, old bricks and second-hand materials.'*

Few photographs survive of these proud school gardens, and even more rare is film footage of schoolchildren in action among the vegetables. Arthur Hulme, the headmaster at Elworth Primary School in Sandbach, Cheshire, was however something of an amateur documentary maker. Equipped with the latest Kodachrome 16mm films, he recorded the lives of his pupils in the years 1942–3. Among the detail of daily gas mask and first aid exercises are live action shots of the children hard at work in the school gardens and coaxing cucumbers into growth under cold frames. The government had banned cucumbers as a crop in the hothouses of large country house gardens, as they were thought to have little nutritional value, but the children were outside government control and able to liven their salads with the crunchy crop. Another keen amateur film-maker captured the pupils at Hepworth School in Holmfirth, Yorkshire, tending their victory garden in 1943.

Left
Tarner Land Nursery School, Brighton, was unusual in the pre-war period for its close links with nature. Here pupils choose their own lunchtime apples. On the outbreak of war it had a head start on its horticultural rivals. HMSO

What was successful in the school garden became a staple of school dinners, and easily grown crops such as carrots, potatoes and spinach became mainstays, although erratic electricity or fuel supplies often made these home-grown dinners less attractive than might be hoped. At Tarner Land Nursery School in Brighton, the link between garden and plate was even more pronounced, with these nursery-age children choosing the apple they wanted while it was still on the tree. Originally established in the 1930s as a school that stressed the importance of outdoor activities for younger children from poor backgrounds, the school came into its own during the war years with its gardening ethos. A more unusual scheme was that at Sidcup Senior School in Kent, where each boy was made responsible for a single apple tree. While at school he budded and trained the tree and fruit, and was apparently allowed to take the apple tree with him when he left.

In any story there are exceptions, and at Bridport School, an ex-pupil recalls having to destroy their school gardens to install air-raid trenches for the children. The gardens had won prizes in previous years, and seeing their hard work and prize vegetables and flowers destroyed must have been hard for the children, especially when the push for air-raid shelters was followed promptly by exhortations to Dig for Victory! Belmont School in Falmouth also dug trenches through their gardens, this time in zig-zag patterns. For Jim Wilcox, a teenager during the war, school memories include *'helping to dig a "Victory" garden and eating the pretty awful produce'.* For others the school garden was more idyllic, complete with lawns, maypoles, free food, fresh fruit, and happy lessons on gardening.

Evacuees Support Themselves

Evacuees from Southwark gardening in Devon.

Evacuation of children from London and the large urban centres such as Liverpool and Birmingham began early, and led to further pressures on fresh food in the rural districts in which they were billeted. In many instances the newly arrived children were encouraged to help with food production either in the school garden, on nearby allotments or in local gardens which provided extra produce for school dinners. For many of the urban children this was their first experience of gardening, especially for those evacuated early on when the urban allotments had not been fully established.   Village Produce

Associations also clubbed together to feed extra schoolchildren, in return for helping hands in the gardens and on allotments. In an effort to encourage more home production of school meals, the government highlighted the village of Knighton-on-Teme in Worcestershire, where 130 meals a day were produced for the children using vegetables from local gardens tended by the schoolchildren themselves. The villagers were paid for their produce either in cash or in kind, and the school was able to feed all its extra mouths. Raising money by selling vegetables was a constant theme of school life as

pupils were encouraged to feel part of the war effort.

Boarding and even day schools based in urban or 'at risk' areas were commonly evacuated *en masse* to country houses where the grounds would already include a large kitchen garden or lawns ready to be ploughed up. At Cally House in Castle Douglas, Kircudbrightshire, Glasgow schoolchildren worked in the one hectare walled gardens originally built in the 18th century, and until the First World War immaculately tended by a large workforce. Taken over by the Forestry Commission in 1939, the walled garden was ideal as a 'Victory' garden. Wielding full-size forks, spades and hoes, they took advantage of the rich soil, glasshousing and 'hot' walls (although no coal was available to maintain the heat).

The boys of Westcliffe High School in Essex were destined to be disappointed twice with their crops. On the outbreak of war in 1939 they pre-empted the Dig for Victory campaign by double-digging some of the sports ground area after school hours. By the first week of June 1940 they had looked admiringly at the acre of ground thus created, full of spring cabbage, 180 new tomato plants, and rows and rows of young seedlings. Alas, one week later the boys were evacuated to a small north-Midland town, and the army moved in on both the school buildings and the crops. Undaunted, the boys started again in their new accommodation and by spring 1941 two large plots, previously fit only for pasture, were dug and sown. Two hundred-weight each of carrots, parsnips, beetroot and runner beans were grown and shared with their hosts and foster families. By the autumn of 1941 another plot was acquired and in May 1942 yet another. Twelve hundred savoy plants were sitting snugly in this last plot, courtesy of only eight 'stalwart boys', when it was suddenly announced that conditions of war had improved so much that it was safe for the school to return to its original home, leaving its savoys behind. They did however take with them £20 earned from the 'seeds fund', which they then used to purchase manure and seeds to start again in the old allotments dug before evacuation!

Above Left
At Knighton-on-Teme, Worcestershire, pupils were allowed to work in village gardens in return for crops for the school's kitchens. Knighton had a large number of evacuee children to feed. HMSO
Above Right
Glasgow schoolchildren ready to work in the gardens of Cally, Kircudbrightshire.

Weeding the Home Plot

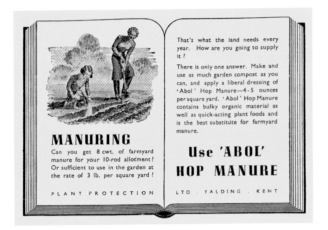

MANURING
Can you get 8 cwt. of farmyard manure for your 10-rod allotment? Or sufficient to use in the garden at the rate of 3 lb. per square yard?
That's what the land needs every year. How are you going to supply it?
There is only one answer. Make and use as much garden compost as you can, and apply a liberal dressing of 'Abol' Hop Manure—4-5 ounces per square yard. 'Abol' Hop Manure contains bulky organic material as well as quick-acting plant foods and is the best substitute for farmyard manure.
Use 'ABOL' HOP MANURE
PLANT PROTECTION LTD . YALDING . KENT

Children also helped out in gardens and allotments at home, in some instances sparking a lifetime's love of gardening, in others the reverse! As the war continued the government became anxious to encourage children and women to play a larger part in the productive garden, replacing men who had been conscripted or were carrying out other duties in the ARP or Home Guard. Children often worked by their parents' side, carrying out such hated tasks as weeding in the wet and cold ground or watering through the drier summer, but some were allowed more 'responsible' tasks including sowing seeds and feeding the livestock. Older children could be put to work digging. Boys especially were expected to be able to use adult sized spades and forks in the less health and safety conscious '40s! 'Caterpillar picking' was a child's somewhat safer duty. Armed with a jam jar of water (to drown the offending pests) even the youngest sibling could contribute to the success of the garden plot. Frances Dawson recalls that: *'My gardening memories are of the embankment of the Drayton Park Underground being dug up, and going over there. My uncle would look after the plot and we three children would each have a jam jar of water. We would have to pick off all the caterpillars from the cauliflowers and drown them in the water. We were told never to go near the rail track. I am sure there was a fence but I don't remember one. I do remember lovely black fine soil, but maybe this was soot.'*

Concerning Allotments in the **Gardeners' Chronicle**, July 1943, reported on a disaster – *' "There are some chives in the allotment" said ten-year-old David, when his mother had no onions for seasoning the stuffing for Sunday dinner. He was told to get them. Mother had not used "chives" before, but she trimmed the roots and put them into the stuffing. The general opinion was that the stuffing was a bit strong. "We had no onions so we got some chives out of the allotment", father was told on his return. "Chives?" he gasped, "I've no chives there". He fled to the allotment – only to find that his best Spanish Irises had gone!'*

For children with 'backyarder' parents, learning to keep livestock also became part of the wartime duties. Michael Neal of Luton earned 1s 6d weekly pocket money throughout the war years, mucking out the hens, ducks, rabbits and goat as well as fetching and carrying from the corn merchants and weeding and digging the adjoining allotment.

In 1942 the government started to emphasise the contribution children could make on home and family allotments (as well as school allotments), with a series of official photographs and newsreels showing children taking responsibility for their own allotments. Jimmy West represented not only the vital role of children in gardening but also the 'special relationship' between England and the USA at this time, and the bravery of Londoners in the Blitz. The caption on the Ministry of Information photograph read *Jimmy West (11) plants bean seeds on a makeshift allotment cultivated from a London bombsite. The seeds he is sowing were donated by*

Left Below
Jimmy and his allotmenting friends became one of the Dig for Victory 'mascots'. HMSO

Below
Using a hazardous assortment of tools (in reality not easily available) these boys are supposedly creating new allotment sites. HMSO

America. Jimmy had once been evacuated to Ware in Hertfordshire, but had apparently "returned to London to put London right". He and his friends, helped by the Bethnal Green Bombed Sites Associa- tion, were creating allotments on patches of waste- land where once houses had stood. They, and others like them, were trained in basic gardening by the Webbe Boys Club, who also helped with the tools.' John Gifford (aged 10) and Alfred Gifford (aged 13) of Broadstairs were featured in the gardening press for keeping the family allotment going.

Children and The Onion Club

As well as helping in the garden and on the allotments, children were sometimes specifically targeted for smaller campaigns and efforts. One of these was 'The Onion Club'. Set up by the Red Cross Agri- cultural Fund, this scheme was designed to ensure that men and women in the forces received sufficient onions. By 1943 there simply weren't enough onions on sale through normal commercial growers and quality and variety in mess halls was suffering. The Red Cross issued a series of appeals asking groups of young people to club together and grow onions which could then be sold at a controlled price to the NAAFI. Onion plots in the garden or school were ideal, and young children were especially targeted, as careful and fiddly weeding was essential to good onion crops. Groups could also 'compete' for the largest harvest and their school's contribution to the Red Cross Fund. It was hoped that a thousand clubs would be formed, each growing 2–3 tons, with the majority being attached to schools or youth clubs.

An advertisement placed in gardening maga- zines in March 1943 explained how the scheme worked: *'Twenty or more young people form an onion club, seek the advice and co-operation of an experienced gardener and obtain the use of, say, a quarter of an acre of good land – possibly un- tenanted allotments or portions of school gardens. On this they plant their onions and give the required attention to them throughout the season. Then, if particulars of the club have been sent to the Red Cross Onion Club Committee, arrangements will be made for the NAAFI or the contractors to the Admiralty to collect the onions. Payment will be made at the controlled price (now £25 a ton) to the club, which will remit the proceeds to the Red Cross Agricultural Fund.'*

The scheme was surprisingly successful, with many schools adding a few extra rows of onions to their plots, and some planting large areas. At Walpole Highway, Wisbech, schoolchildren raised nearly 200lb of onions for the local Red Cross Onion Club. By the summer of 1944 'Onion Days' and even 'Onion Weeks' had sprung up to advance the Red Cross campaign, with targets for tonnages of onions, and specific onion shows. Adults of course muscled in on these, and prizes for the largest onion reappeared. These had been largely suppressed during the height of the wartime Victory campaign as being 'wasteful', as giant onions rarely tasted as good as they looked.

Children Helping Harvests and Fruit Farms

In rural areas evacuees and local children also helped in the fields or orchards at harvest time. At Garth School in Llangurig (Powys), the evacuees went out collecting wool from the fences and hedges for bandages, as well as sphagnum moss and foxglove seeds for their medicinal value. Boarding school children in rural areas might also be asked to 'lend a hand' in the fields. The potato harvest had always called on village children, usually to the chagrin of the school authorities, but now the schools sent their children willingly. Older children might be paid for the work but younger ones were more often rewarded in kind with the small potatoes missed by the diggers. Gleaning the cornfields also provided food for school hens. In 1942 a specific scheme was set up to encourage schools to send children to help with the harvest. For many children working and camping on the farm was reminiscent of Boy Scouts or Girl Guides camps. These 'harvest camps' became very popular, and in the first year of operation 650 camps were set up with public and secondary schools sending over 31,000 children. In 1943 the aim was to almost double that number. Financial assistance was available, with food and travel arrangements being met and schools were even encouraged to send children during term time as well as in the holidays. In Cambridgeshire and Essex the extensive Tiptree and Histon fruit farms were sustained by large groups of schoolchildren and holiday camps, hopefully picking more than they ate!

Left
One of a series of photographs taken to celebrate the home harvest during wartime.
Right
School parties or children's clubs and organisations were used to help bring in the fruit harvest.
HMSO

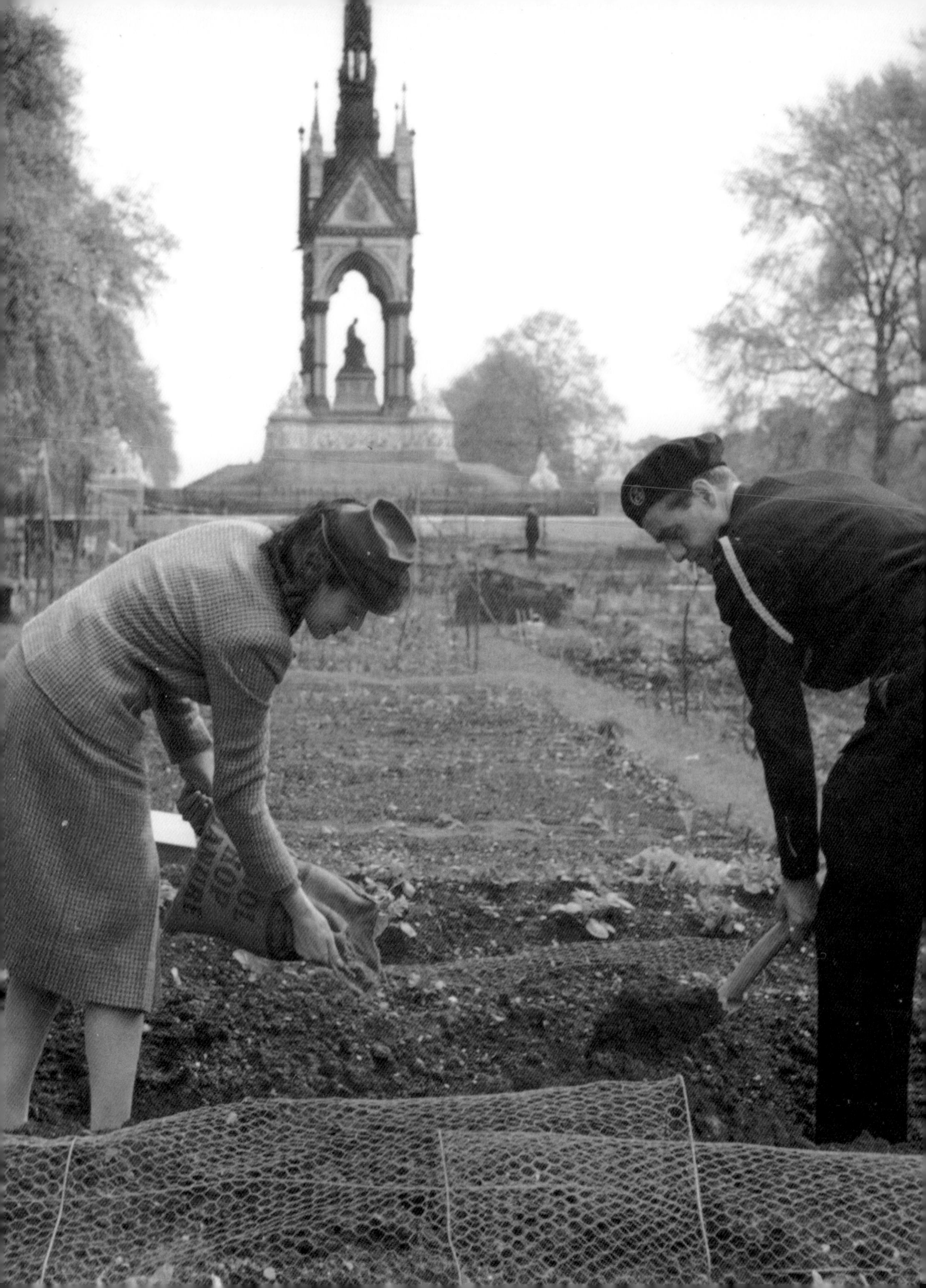

The role of women

Although women had formed a vital part of the effort on the home front in 1914–18, their achievements in the fields and farms had been largely forgotten by 1939, and they were once more firmly relegated to the flowerbeds. In the 1930s there was a general bias against women working in gardens, either as professional gardeners or as amateurs in the vegetable plot or on the allotment. While housewives often tended the flower garden, or even occasionally mowed the lawn, vegetables were seen as man's work and the allotment a male bastion. At the start of the war nothing really changed, until conscription started to bite there were still sufficient men at home to enable many families to have an allotment or victory garden without calling on the housewife. Men in reserved occupations, or too young or old for conscription, were the foot soldiers of the Dig for Victory campaign. In the winter of 1939 the idea of women working in gardens was still regarded by some as humorous: a letter in the **Gardeners' Chronicle** dated 30 December 1939 ran, '*A photograph of … nurses digging up Tavistock Square must have caused some amusement to practical men. What a picture! Dutch hoes were being used, and the nurses wore low shoes. Another picture I saw was of a girl demonstrating Spring Cabbage planting, also in low shoes, not to mention silk stockings.*'

However as conscription widened and home front duties multiplied (there were 1.4 million ARP workers needed, plus AFS and Home Guard among others) men had less and less time available to grow food for the family. In 1941, as the shortage of male labour became acute, the government started a concerted campaign to encourage women and children into the vegetable garden and on to the allotment. Of course women also had many more demands on their time than before the war, with many balancing a daytime job with traditional housewife duties and child care. But many responded to the government's campaign and broke down the social and cultural barriers to make it on to the

Left
An early propaganda photograph depicting what was seen by many as a woman's role in the garden; the man is doing all the heavy work while she, totally unsuitably dressed, is helping him with light work. HMSO

Below
Even towards the end of the war, women were not often shown actively gardening in the pages of *Garden Work*. This rare picture is in response to a female correspondent writing for information on when to cut down daffodil leaves. Generally women only wrote in in connection with flowers and houseplants.

YOU CAN GATHER ALL THE FLOWERS BUT DON'T TAKE MUCH OF THE FOLIAGE.

allotment. Once there they often had considerable prejudice to overcome, but many persevered and women played a major role in providing fresh food for their own families and the nation during the war, both in the garden and on the land.

As the war progressed this became harder. In 1941 war work became compulsory for all women aged 20 and 21, and the following year this went up to 30. In May 1943 part-time work (up to 30 hours a week) became compulsory for women aged between 18 and 45; ten million women were registered for work by the summer of 1943. In addition hundreds of thousands worked in the Women's Voluntary Service, joined the ATS, WAAF or WRNS and 80,000 joined the Women's Land Army. By the summer of 1943 90% of single women and 80% of married women were doing war work of some kind. Keeping up the allotment now became a challenge not because of the physical nature of the work, but just fitting it in to a full working day.

You help the Nation **when you help your neighbour —**

IN THE

DIG FOR VICTORY

CAMPAIGN

● The nation looks to you — the experienced gardener — for leadership in the Dig for Victory campaign. Make your peacetime hobby your wartime duty.

● Remember that many 'Victory Diggers' have had little experience and that many more must now be women. They will be glad of your tips and help.

All gardeners should post this coupon NOW

To MINISTRY OF AGRICULTURE, HOTEL LINDUM, ST. ANNES-ON-SEA

Please send me copies of free pictorial leaflets.

NAME ....

ADDRESS ....

H.111.

ISSUED BY THE MINISTRY OF AGRICULTURE

See that the beginners *Start* right

You know the importance of good digging and wise planning. But there are many newcomers to vegetable growing that don't. So keep an eye on them and help with advice when you think they need it. Chat about the crops they plan to grow. Warn them against growing too much for summer at the expense of winter vegetables. Don't let them grow too many potatoes.

* Urge them to send for the free Ministry of Agriculture leaflets — particularly No. 1 (Cropping Plan), No. 21 (How to Dig) and No. 19 (How to Sow Seeds).

Play your part in the

DIG FOR VICTORY campaign

Women at Home and on the Allotment

In 1941 it became evident that women were going to have to play an increasingly important role in the Dig for Victory campaign. Official propaganda sprang into action with a range of photographs and posters, which encouraged women to feel that they too should be venturing on to the vegetable plot. Aimed at the 'New Victory Diggers' the campaign depicted young women dressed in skirts and sensible shoes, being overseen and directed by men. The accompanying text didn't actually mention 'women', just the *'thousands who will be growing their own vegetables for the first time'*, but the message was clear: women should dig, and men should tell them how.

To try to avoid a repeat of the ridicule women gardeners had suffered in the first months of the war, some garden writers offered clothing advice for women intending to work on the allotment. **Gardening Made Easy** said: *'Don't mind too much how you look when going to and from your allotment, for gardening is hard on clothes and really presentable ones should never be worn for it. In your own garden of course appearances don't matter in the least and all you need consider are comfort and economy. A* *short knee-length skirt, breeches or shorts are most suitable. Trousers, so popular nowadays, are not so convenient because they come down too near the ground and get muddy in winter and dusty in summer. Also the necessary kneeling and crouching soon bags them at the knees. So leave this garment to the unfortunate men who have nothing else!'*

Garden Work in April 1941 reported: *'Fashion designers are keeping in close touch with the Dig for Victory campaign. They have brought out already button holes in the shape of a bunch of carrots, potatoes and swedes; an artificial stick of celery as a wartime substitute for a jewelled hat ornament, and a string of runner beans to attach to the lapel of a coat.'* Two pieces from the same magazine, written only a month apart, show the rapidly changing role of women in wartime gardens. The first, from February 1940, runs, *'Reports from various sources indicate that women gardeners are making a splendid response to the Minister of Agriculture's "Dig for Victory" Appeal. Local authorities have already received numerous applications from women for allotments. Provided that the initial digging and trenching is carried out by a member of the sterner sex, I can see no reason at all why a woman cannot run an allotment with the greatest success.'* The second takes a far less cautious line: *'The national federation of Women's Institutes plans to make a survey of all available village allotments and derelict gardens with a view to putting them to the best possible use in growing foodstuffs and feeding material for pigs and poultry. A scheme has also been evolved where Institute members will, where necessary, carry on all the work of cultivation of plots owned by men called to the services.'*

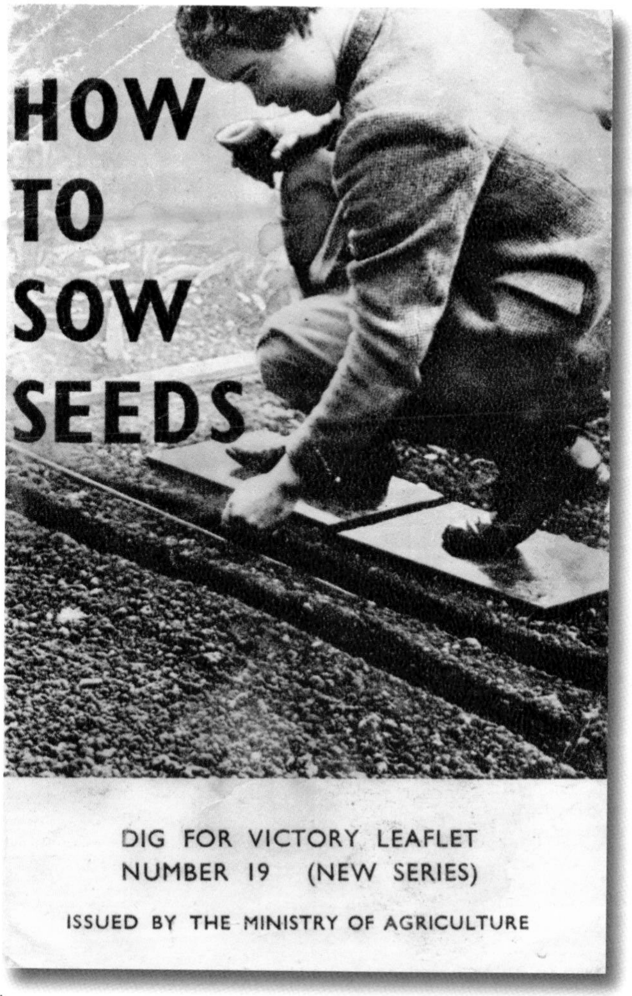
HOW
TO
SOW
SEEDS
DIG FOR VICTORY LEAFLET
NUMBER 19 (NEW SERIES)
ISSUED BY THE MINISTRY OF AGRICULTURE

Left
These official propaganda advertisements are from a series that show a woman working in the vegetable plot, albeit under supervision!
Above
This government leaflet on 'How to Sow Seeds' was the first to have a woman on the front. Sensible skirt and shoes are to the fore!

Digging as Represented in Women's Magazines

As ever, the new government campaign to grow more food was reflected in popular magazines and newspapers. One of the most popular periodicals during the war years was **Woman** magazine. With

HOW DOES YOUR GARDEN GROW?
Digging is good for the figure and good for the garden, too. Keep calm, advises Muriel Thomson, our Gardening Expert, and dig!

its mix of practical family advice and improbable love-stories it catered for housewives and young women with romance in their hearts if not actually in their lives. On the outbreak of war **Woman** immediately started to run 'Your Garden at War', an advice page written by their 'gardening expert' Muriel Thomson. Readers were obviously still unsure about their role in the actual production of vegetables, as by week two the gardening expert was writing on food storage rather than food production, and after returning to peas and greens for a couple of weeks, by week five she was back to planting wallflowers and cooking jams and preserves. In a desperate attempt to stir up more interest, the following week was headlined 'Digging is Good for the Figure', but after another week on the less attractive subject of compost, the series was shelved and the vegetable garden handed back to the man of the house. Occasionally the letters page suggests that some readers of **Woman** were taking their patriotic duties in the garden more seriously, albeit with ensuing problems. In October 1939 the popular 'expert legal counsels' page included advice on whether keeping hens in the garden could be legally construed as a 'nuisance to neighbours' (the answer was no, 'as hens are such quiet birds'!). Another writer asked for general advice on keeping rabbits, while 'Mrs L.L. of Banstead' needed to ensure her tomato crop did not fail.

The war also slowly crept into advertisements aimed at women. Unlikely though it may seem, nail polish adverts began to feature women who were working in their garden or in the fields, always wearing their Cutex nail varnish. Zixt soap made a point of emphasising the special needs of the gardening woman. A Zixt advert, from October

Left
'Digging is Good for the Figure' declared *Woman* magazine, although the accompanying illustration seems to suggest it was very bad for the back!

Below
Knight's Castile was among many soap companies that cashed in on the more active role that women were playing in the garden.

NORMA KNIGHT wants you to meet...
Mrs. Brown who has organized a gardening corps
All my neighbours have gardens and . . .
1 .. as our menfolk have joined up we women decided to carry on with the gardening and produce lots of vegetables.
2 We found that digging wasn't hard work if we were all doing it together, so now we have what we call "digging parties."
3 Then we go home to tea and a good wash with Knight's Castile. We all use Knight's Castile because it's marvellously soothing after a hard day's work.
The kindly luxurious lather of Knight's Castile soothes away that feeling of exhaustion after hard work, tones up the skin and keeps the complexion youthfully clear.
Knight's Castile
PREVENTS 'TIRED SKIN'
KC 285-96-80
JOHN KNIGHT LIMITED—SOAP MAKERS SINCE 1810

1940, ran; *'You ought to see Alice – late of Mayfair – among the cabbages and cauliflowers doing her bit in growing the nation's food. And you ought to see what her hands look like covered with the soil of Hampshire after a day's work. But ten minutes after she's come in from work they're white and ladylike again. You see Alice knows about Zixt, the wonderful soap tablet that gets dirt off the hands in a jiffy and leaves them soft and smooth.'* Should a home-coming husband discover his wife had developed 'gardener's hands' romantic disappointment was bound to follow. Hands seem to have obsessed the readers of **Woman**, or at least the advertisers, and one wonders whether a free pair of gardening gloves for every reader might have been of more use to the Dig for Victory campaign than any number of pamphlets and posters.

In July 1940 the gardening expert of **Woman** reappeared after her long break, this time with a new format designed to interest every reader. The 'Kitchen Garden Calendar' was produced in the form of a weekly table, usually split into three or four different crops, each with three columns. One column told you what should be done with the specific crop in the garden that week (planting, harvesting, pruning, etc), another told you how to preserve the crop, while the third gave helpful cooking hints. Trying to integrate the three topics produced some oddities, with instructions on sowing or planting being accompanied by cooking instructions, which would not be of use for several months. The idea was presumably to cut out and keep the kitchen garden calendars for future reference. Choice of the three vegetables or fruits seemed eclectic, and not necessarily linked to the season

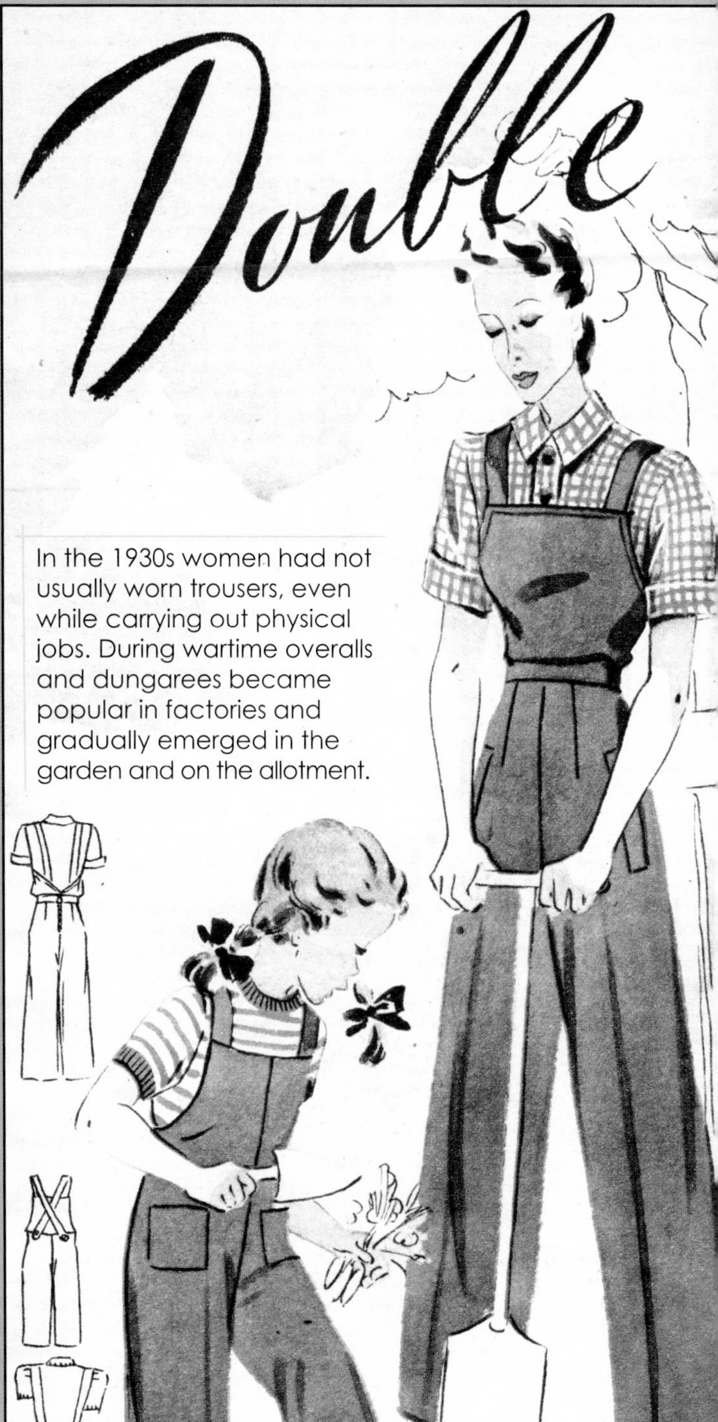
Double

In the 1930s women had not usually worn trousers, even while carrying out physical jobs. During wartime overalls and dungarees became popular in factories and gradually emerged in the garden and on the allotment.

the columns came out. Early August saw marrows, quinces, and turnips, while the end of September had a mix of strawberries, red cabbage and the more seasonal plums. Instructions on how to tend and preserve peas and broad beans must have seemed unnecessary in October when they appeared in the column, accompanied by cape gooseberries (Physalis), which was not a commonly grown plant at all.

As the government started to intensify its campaign to get women out into the garden with a spade a series of letters and yet more recipes reminded the readers of **Woman** that food production was their duty, regardless of its impact on their hands. One woman was instructed on what to put into her allotment once it was fully dug and manured, while in the same edition a whole page was given over to 'meals from the allotment', featuring recipes for celery soup, potato pie, and stuffed onions, the latter probably pointless for most of its readers for whom onions were becoming as scarce as silk stockings. This letter from Miss J.W. of Horsham to **Woman** suggests that many women were relishing the opportunity to flex their muscles for a change: *'We live in the country and have a large rambling garden and orchard, but nobody but my mother ever took much interest in either. Consequently, for years, it looked wild and desolate. You should see it now though! We have all gone back to the land and are now digging for victory with a vengeance. The boys have taken a nice slice off the coal bill by chopping down some old half-dead trees, and we have all dug and weeded and pruned and planted till our backs felt like breaking. But the results have been worth it. Mother laughs and says it takes Hitler to do in a few months what she's been trying to do for years.'*

However, not all women were happy at their gardening work. *'In the kitchen gardens, allotments and fields of our countryside, you will see women playing their part in growing food. Sometimes they are fighting a lone battle in their gardens and plots against insect pests and weather. They are often disappointed and very tired, but they stick to it and see it through'*, said Mrs R.S. Hudson, wife of the Minister of Agriculture, writing in 1943.

Getting women to grow vegetables in their own back gardens was one thing, but getting them down to the allotment was another. Before the outbreak of war allotments had been seen as a 'man's place', with the emphasis on hard digging, 'providing for the family', and of course 'men and sheds'. Women simply weren't welcome on allotment sites. However it was soon apparent that this was going to have to change. With the increased number of allotments and the decreasing number of men available, some districts started to run 'Women's Allotment Week Campaigns' to recruit women plot-holders. At Yiewsley and West Drayton (Middlesex) one such week in late 1941 resulted in a remarkable 132 women enrolling for new allotments, suggesting that perhaps there was already a suppressed interest. The Yiewsley District Council expected this number to almost double by the springtime, although it was not made clear why. A more practical approach was that of Swindon Allotments Association, which reduced the membership fee for women, to a mere 9d a week. This started a trend and soon other allotment associations were offering special rates to women, and to 'juvenile' groups.

The low number of women taking on allotments in the first two years of war was evidenced by the

kitchen garden calendar

SOWING   GROWING   PROTECTING

BRUSSELS SPROUTS

SOW IN DRILLS

Brussels sprouts are quite indispensable as a winter vegetable. With proper care, it should be possible to pick from a bed of them continuously for about twenty weeks. By now they should be in full swing, and should remain so until March.

For very early crops the seed should be sown under cover early in March, but the main crop should be sown in the open towards the end of March or early in April. A quarter of an ounce of seed would sow a row fifty feet long —or, roughly—two thousand plants. Sow in drills an inch deep and six inches apart.

PICK OUT SEEDLINGS

Seedling Brussels sprouts that have been sown in the open should be left until they form their third leaf, then they should be pricked out six inches apart both ways. By June they will be ready to be transplanted to their permanent bed, where they should be allowed plenty of room. The rows should be three feet apart and the plants two feet apart, except in the case of dwarf varieties, which can be put a little closer together. This double transplanting is justified by the good roots and sturdy plants it produces. The first sprouts will be ready to pick about six months after sowing.

CLUB ROOT DISEASE

A successful crop of Brussels sprouts depends on a sunny bed of rich, well manured soil. They are seldom any good when grown in light or shallow soil.

One of the diseases that frequently attacks Brussels sprouts in gardens and allotments is club root. The diseased plants appear stunted and sickly, and the roots show abnormal swellings and contortions which eventually rot. This disease is often encouraged by using the same piece of land repeatedly for crops of the cabbage family. One of the best preventives is very thorough liming of the soil. The lime should be finely powdered.

PARSNIPS

VALUABLE WINTER FOOD

Parsnips are not universal favourites —often because they are carelessly cooked. But their sweetness makes them a very valuable winter food, particularly now that we have not an unlimited sugar ration.

Parsnips can be sown very early in the year—by the end of February, or early in March. The best plan is to sow them direct in their permanent bed, which should first be dug very deeply and well limed. Draw your drills fifteen inches apart and an inch deep, and sow three seeds together at intervals of a foot. Half an ounce should produce fifteen hundred plants.

ROOTS NEED DEPTH

It is far more economical to have sown your parsnip seeds in groups of three at intervals of a foot. One of the three seeds is pretty certain to have produced a good seedling, and the other two should be removed. Unlike carrot thinnings, the thinnings of parsnips are very little use, so it is better to avoid wastage.

It takes about six months from sowing for parsnips to arrive at maturity. They are good-natured vegetables to grow, as they thrive in almost any soil. But it must be deeply dug.

Constant hoeing is the only culture necessary during their growth.

LEAVE IN THE GROUND

No stable manure should be applied to your parsnip bed, or the roots will tend to fork and be deformed. After you have thinned out your seedlings, you would do well to apply an ounce of nitrate of soda per square yard.

If possible you should let the parsnips remain in the ground all winter, and just lift them as required. The roots are in much better condition if this is done, and the flesh is more juicy. But if you cannot spare the space, the roots can be lifted and made into a compact pile.

Three inches of soil should be heaped on the pile.

KALE

THRIVES IN FROST

This is one of the very hardiest of winter vegetables. In fact, the greater the frost the more delicate is the flavour. There are a great many different kinds of kale, some grown for their asparagus-like shoots in spring, others having variegated and beautifully tinted leaves. But the majority have very curly green leaves for use now, which are followed in the spring by a profusion of sprouts.

The best time to sow kale is in early April. The seed should be sown in drills half an inch deep and six inches apart. An ounce of seed would produce about two thousand plants.

LIME PERMANENT BED

Kale seedlings take about a week to a fortnight to appear above ground after sowing. In the seedling stage they require very much the same treatment that you would give to Brussels sprouts. Prick out the seedlings when they have formed their third or fourth leaf, and transplant to their permanent quarters in June. The plants should be two feet apart in the rows, and there should be at least thirty inches between the rows. This permanent bed ought to be limed before the plants are moved into it. You should be able to begin using your kale four months after sowing.

CATERPILLAR PEST

When your young kale plants have been in their permanent bed about a month, nitrate of soda should be applied at the rate of two ounces per square yard.

But no treatment of the ground will help you to control the caterpillar pest. There is no easy way of keeping caterpillars down. Removing and crushing the eggs—which are generally found in clusters on the undersides of the leaves —is the best plan. Dusting with derris powder and spraying with insecticides are the only other good methods of control.

CAPE GOOSEBERRIES

GROWN FOR JAM

There is so much competition nowadays amongst gardeners to make every corner produce food, that this new Cape gooseberry, which produces fruit that makes delicious jam, has been deservedly popular. Formerly, Cape gooseberries have chiefly been grown for the pretty lantern-like effect of their ripened seed pods, which make a substitute for flowers during the winter. But there is now a variety on the market which ripens its fruits in the open. The plants are amazingly prolific, and continue ripening their fruits until cut by the frost. Sow some seed under glass early in the spring.

GROWN LIKE TOMATOES

The Cape gooseberry, or *Physalis*, as it is properly called, wants the same sort of treatment as tomatoes. *Physalis edulis* should be treated as a greenhouse tomato, but *Physalis ixiocarpa* should be treated as an outdoor tomato. For once the fear of spring frosts is over, it is perfectly hardy.

Choose an open sunny spot for your bed, and put the young plants in rows three or four feet apart each way. It is important to allow plenty of room, as the plants have a low spreading habit. The fruit ripens in the autumn, and is ready for use when the berries turn from green to pale yellow.

GUARD AGAINST FROST

Cape gooseberries are perennials, but the species producing edible berries would find our winter too much for them. So they should either be taken up before any severe frosts set in, and wintered in a greenhouse or they should be treated as annuals.

It will help the fruits to develop if, from mid-summer, you apply weak liquid manure to the roots. Pick the berries as soon as they are ripe, so that the plant's energy can go into producing more. The green ones still on the branches when frost sets in should be used for jam too. They make quite good jam.

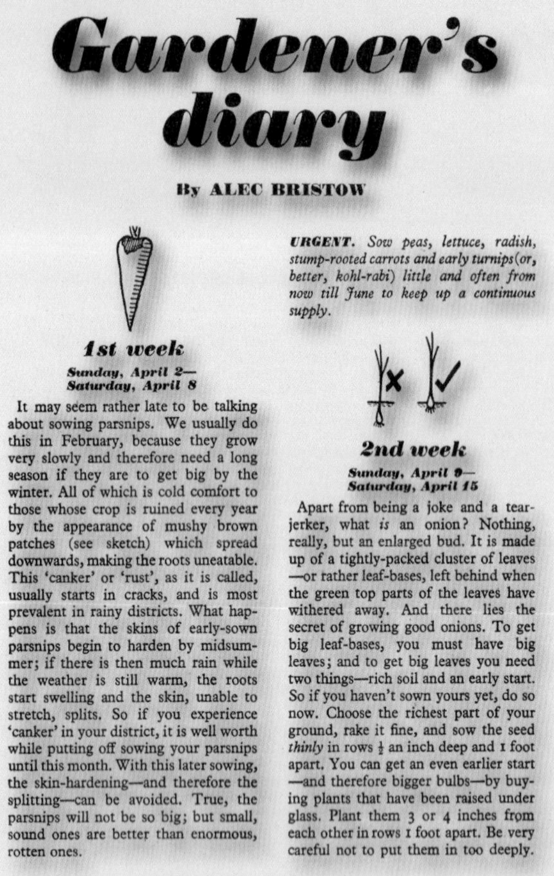

Gardener's diary

By ALEC BRISTOW

URGENT. *Sow peas, lettuce, radish, stump-rooted carrots and early turnips (or, better, kohl-rabi) little and often from now till June to keep up a continuous supply.*

1st week

Sunday, April 2—Saturday, April 8

It may seem rather late to be talking about sowing parsnips. We usually do this in February, because they grow very slowly and therefore need a long season if they are to get big by the winter. All of which is cold comfort to those whose crop is ruined every year by the appearance of mushy brown patches (see sketch) which spread downwards, making the roots uneatable. This 'canker' or 'rust', as it is called, usually starts in cracks, and is most prevalent in rainy districts. What happens is that the skins of early-sown parsnips begin to harden by midsummer; if there is then much rain while the weather is still warm, the roots start swelling and the skin, unable to stretch, splits. So if you experience 'canker' in your district, it is well worth while putting off sowing your parsnips until this month. With this later sowing, the skin-hardening—and therefore the splitting—can be avoided. True, the parsnips will not be so big; but small, sound ones are better than enormous, rotten ones.

2nd week

Sunday, April 9—Saturday, April 15

Apart from being a joke and a tear-jerker, what *is* an onion? Nothing, really, but an enlarged bud. It is made up of a tightly-packed cluster of leaves —or rather leaf-bases, left behind when the green top parts of the leaves have withered away. And there lies the secret of growing good onions. To get big leaf-bases, you must have big leaves; and to get big leaves you need two things—rich soil and an early start. So if you haven't sown yours yet, do so now. Choose the richest part of your ground, rake it fine, and sow the seed *thinly* in rows ½ an inch deep and 1 foot apart. You can get an even earlier start —and therefore bigger bulbs—by buying plants that have been raised under glass. Plant them 3 or 4 inches from each other in rows 1 foot apart. Be very careful not to put them in too deeply.

numbers recorded by the Ministry of Agriculture in their award scheme. Of 791 entries for the Certificate of Merit scheme for allotment-holders in Bridgwater, for example, only seven entrants were women (of whom three were given certificates). In fact across the entire 37 counties that sent in entries, only 108 entrants were women. Of course this may just indicate that women were too busy digging and cropping to bother with certificates! In some areas women obviously felt they could do without the advice often all too frequently available from neighbouring male allotment-holders, and Women's Allotment Associations were formed. Others were only too grateful for the help and encouragement.

Pat Ashby of Bedfordshire remembers: *'On my first visit to my plot I was dubiously accepted by my neighbours, Mr Carr on one side and Mr Day on the adjacent six plots which he used as a smallholding. Both were men of the soil, wore ancient suits and cloth caps and were of indeterminate age. My two friends spent every day on their allotments – it was their life, and looked after my plot if I was not there. One day I found a load of leaves behind my shed on top of my rhubarb crowns, which the council had delivered at no charge to all allotments. They had made sure that I had a load. The rhubarb next spring was delicious. I have many happy memories of my two old boys who sceptically accepted a young woman as their neighbour and who taught me more about gardening than I could ever learn from books. I still keep in touch with Mr Day's only surviving daughter who is now 96; she spent many years in the Land Army.'* In 2008 Pat Ashby still owned the fork that she had been given by her 'neighbour' on the day she started her allotment.

Below
Although these potatoes seem small the women gardeners appear pleased with them.

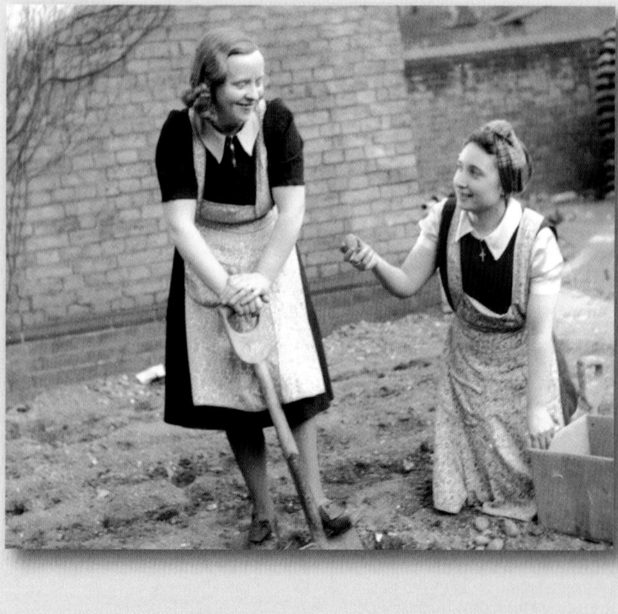

In autumn 1941 the gardening press started to carry 'encouraging' news of women who ran allotments. The story of Miss M.E. Ibberson of Sheffield, who cultivated two plots and won a smallholder's medal (despite being over 70) would, it was hoped, 'inspire many other women'. Mrs C. Sayer of Ipswich was reported as having won first prize in that town's competition for the best allotment – although looked at in another way, it was worrying that the fact a woman had won was still thought so notable as to be national news. At Port Sunlight women were reported to have taken over 400 allotments on behalf of men called up for National Service, while at Coton Field Allotments in Stafford the Duke of Kent specifically targeted female allotment-holders for praise during his visit in November 1941, no doubt following government instructions!

From 1942 onwards women were increasingly pressurised to take on allotments in their own right, or at the very least cultivate a plot which was taken in their husband's name. By October of that year the government believed that over 10,000 women had officially taken up wartime allotments in England and Wales. Middlesex alone had 1,650 female allotment-holders, Yorkshire 1,200, while Finchley had more than any other borough in the country (550). Some cities that had suffered badly from the blitz also had a high percentage of women plot-holders, often utilising bombsites. Bath had 160 female allotment-holders and Sheffield 200. In Hull 50 women were said to be cultivating allotments on a peacetime football pitch.

These 1942 numbers were regarded by the government as 'just a start' to the main campaign to involve women in the victory campaign. After all, although 10,000 was an encouraging figure it was a small percentage of the total of 3 million allotments that the government was aiming for. By February 1942 Preston had its own women gardeners' association. Members not only grew their own produce but also cooked and served it – something few male allotment-holders claimed to do! For many women the time on the allotment must have come as light relief from their other 'duties'. An (unnamed) Cornishwoman, whose husband was on service, was reported in November 1942 as *'harvesting from her ten rod plot nearly 100lb of onions and over 7cwt of potatoes as well as other vegetables and raised fifteen hundred leeks. She works eight hours a day in a factory, runs a home and two children, as well as a brood of chickens.'* Mrs Somers in Bristol was running two allotments simultaneously in 1943, as well as her own garden, and acting as secretary to the Townswomen's Guild. As well as a contribution to the family food store, many women experienced a real sense of achievement as a reward for their hard work. Pat Ashby recalls that *'I was so proud of my achievement when I cycled home with baskets of fresh vegetables and fruit and occasional bunches of flowers'.*

In spite of all this the view that women were the weaker sex persisted. The **Gardeners' Chronicle** of January 1942 reported that: *'An Essex Rural District Council referring to the call-up of men allotment-holders, expressed the view that although women should be able to do the lighter tasks on allotments, such as planting, the heavy work of digging for which few women were suited, had to be done first.'*

Less Time for Housework
-more need for
FOR LINOLEUM WOOD FLOORS AND FURNITURE
MANSION
ANTISEPTIC WAX
POLISH
Housewives engaged in part time war work find Mansion Polish a real help in keeping the home bright, clean and healthy.
USE SPARINGLY—SUPPLY IS RESTRICTED.
FOR FLOORS, FURNITURE & LINOLEUM

For some married women taking on an allotment was just not feasible, even if they had accepted the shift in social and cultural attitudes. Juggling housework, cooking, endless queuing in the shops, and child care with new jobs in factories, on buses, etc., many also carried out voluntary duties and had little time to spare for digging vegetables. So the government turned its attention to younger women and unmarried girls. Office girls, more used to the typing pool than the compost heap, were encouraged to get down to the local allotments. At Newcastle-under-Lyme a girls' club took on a series of Dig for Victory plots. Open to girls over fourteen years of age, they were encouraged in their endeavours by the mayor who cut the first sod, notably leaving them to cut the rest.

Despite the government's campaign, in 1943 women were still more usually associated with cooking vegetables than growing them. 'Concerning Allotments' in the **Gardeners' Chronicle** of 27 March 1943 noted that *'It is interesting to enquire to what extent the housewife is consulted about the cropping of the garden or allotment. Extensive enquiries last year revealed that only about half the gardeners approached consulted their womenfolk, but the proportion varied considerably in the different areas. Victory diggers in the north, east and south-east seem to ask their wives what they shall sow or plant much more than those in the Midlands, south, south-west and Wales.'*

In September 1944 a survey revealed that the number of women cultivating allotments in their own name was still about 10,000, a disappointment given all the government propaganda. Many more tended plots originally taken out in the name of husbands now away in the forces, or busy on other war duties. In addition thousands more worked in their own gardens, an easier option with less time spent travelling to and from busy household duties, and fewer men telling them what to do. Incredibly, there were still some reservations in more traditional areas of the country about the role of women in the vegetable plot. Lord Raglan, Lord Lieutenant of Monmouthshire, declared in September 1944 that *'I have never yet seen a woman in a cottage garden'.*

Lord Raglan might have benefited from visiting Marjorie Williams, who described working in her kitchen garden at Lamledra, Cornwall. *'One evening in the dusk, John Vercoe came thundering up with a lorry load of manure from Trevague. He tipped it all out in the field by the top garage, remarking cheerfully, "Now you've got something to get on with. Fine dung this . . . pig! Can't think how you'll manage all of it", and drove away with a wave of his hand. It took me four successive evenings to cart it away in 42 barrow loads and pile it in different spots in the kitchen garden I had already planned for it. I did it all in the dusk and by moonlight, as I did not want to be seen by the coastguards or anyone coming up to the house wheeling manure lest they should be shocked. I dug it all into trenches for peas and beans and for the leek and potato crop.'*

Women's Gardening Schools, WFGA, Professional Gardeners and Land Girls

THE WOMEN'S FARM AND GARDEN ASSOCIATION (Inc.)
Established 1899
Courtauld House, Byng Place, W.C.1

Advisory and Employment Departments for trained and experienced women gardeners, dairy maids and farm workers. Also war Garden Apprenticeship Scheme for unskilled women (16–40), approved by the Ministry of Agriculture.

For all particulars, apply to the Secretary,
EUSton 3651

In addition to the 'ordinary housewife', fitting in spare moments in the garden and allotment, organisations such as the Women's Farm & Garden Association (WFGA), and the Girls' Training Corps helped the more committed women in the intricacies of food production. The WFGA had originally been founded in 1899 (under a slightly different title), to encourage employment opportunities for women in horticulture and agriculture. It ran courses, examinations and training as well as coordinating the Women's Land Corps during the

First World War, until this was absorbed into the Women's Land Army. The WFGA also provided vital training for those who chose to work full time on farms and market gardens during the war. In summer 1940 the WFGA started an apprenticeship scheme for women wanting to work professionally in horticulture to try and replace the newly called up professional male gardeners. This followed on the heels of changing call-up regulations, which meant that many professional gardeners were no longer in reserved occupations. Advertisements in the gardening and popular press increasingly sought a 'Lady Gardener', or 'Lady Gardener of good character'. In January 1941, the famous Tresco estate in the Isles of Scilly just advertised for 'Women' to keep the estate going.

As the war progressed there were increasing opportunities for trained women gardeners to take on positions in public parks, in training colleges and in training members of the Women's Land Army. Women were still not paid the same amount as men for their work, although the Parks Department of Sutton in Surrey was apparently so delighted with the work of its female members of staff that it generously decided to pay them the same as the men they had replaced. This attitude was rare however, and women trying to make

Left
Mansion Polish realised the difficulties many women were having in juggling the many home front duties. Note the gloves to protect her hands and also her firmly tied-up hair.

Above
Advertisement for the services of the Women's Farm & Garden Association. The WFGA were to prove essential in placing and training women in farming, horticulture and market gardens around the country.

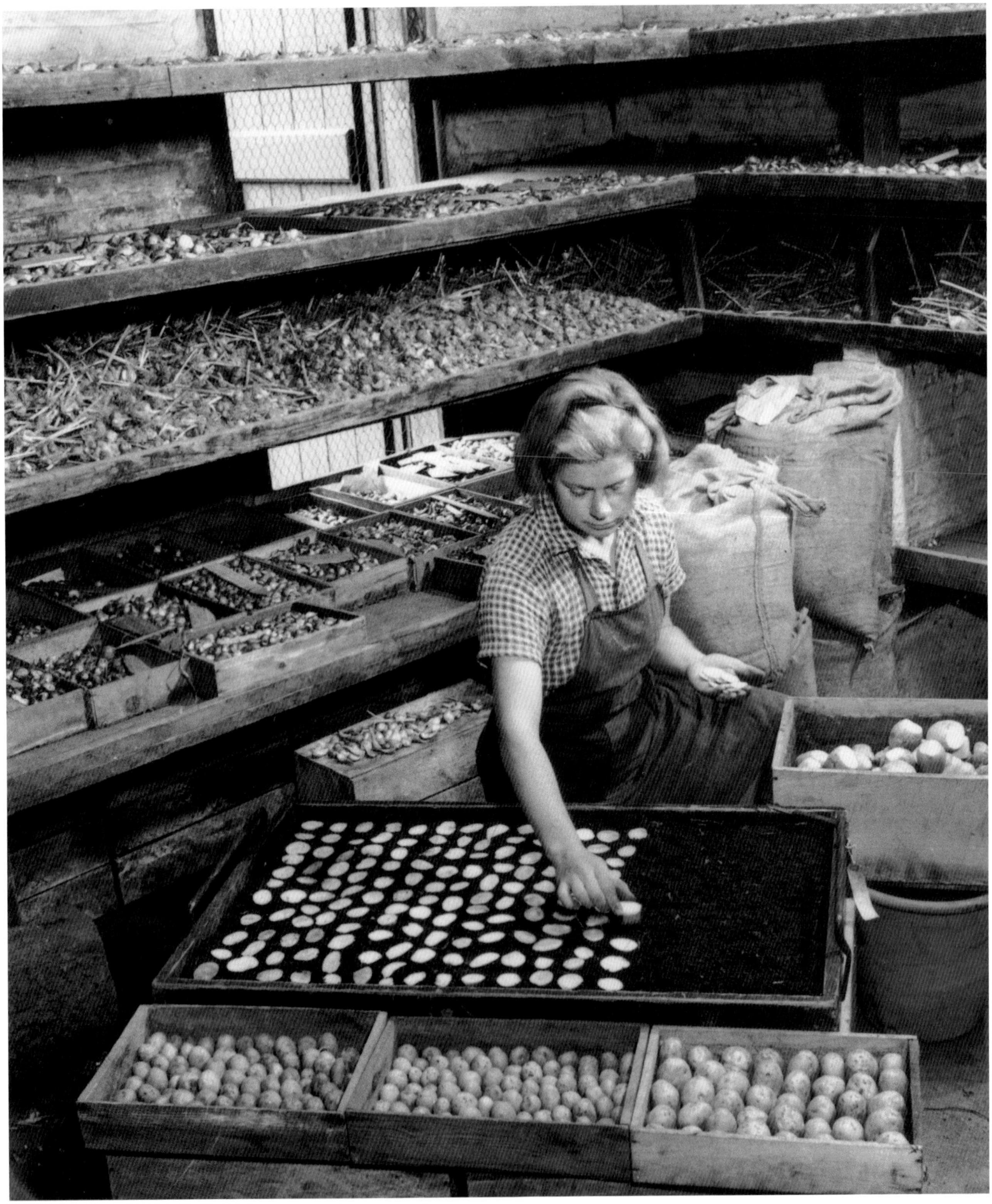

Above

A female worker at Kew Gardens undertaking experimental work on the planting of pieces of potato rather than whole potatoes, as seed potatoes became scarce. HMSO headway in a career in gardening were usually discriminated against. Before the war the famous botanical gardens at Kew and Wisley had refused to accept women for studentships, putting women at a serious disadvantage for passing the National Diploma in Horticulture. During the war both gardens were forced to employ large numbers of women in the gardens and laboratories. The ban on female studentships became untenable, although in December 1943 the gardening press intoned that *'there may be posts for which, for reasons other than intellectual [women gardeners] can never satisfactorily fill'.* Despite the hard work put in by the government and the WFGA, women were often still seen as the 'last option' by employers. Advertisements such as this were common: *'Young Man under military age or Older Man, or Land Girl, to replace employee called up, as Undergardener, Handy Man. To drive car occasionally. Accommodation can be arranged: Mrs Roscoe, Hornhill Court, St Peter, Bucks.'*

Also vital in the training of women gardeners were the specialist horticultural schools. Schools for 'lady gardeners' had been a minor success in the early decades of the twentieth century, but by the outbreak of the Second World War only two of these gardening schools for women were still in existence: the Women's Horticultural College Waterperry, under its famous principal, Beatrix Havergal, and the Swanley Horticultural College for Women. By March 1940 Swanley College was giving a scholarship for a year to a member of the Women's Land Army (worth £25). Swanley was one of the larger gardens to make use of 'London dung', literally the sweepings from the London streets, often mixed with refuse from shops and hairdressers. A high point was the discovery of an occasional lost coin.

Anne Kendrick, an ex-Swanley student, spent the war years working at Winchester College public school as head gardener. She later recalled them as difficult years spent taking on all the work for little reward. The supply of trained women gardeners was also kept up by Waterperry. At the outbreak of war in 1939 there were still relatively few full-time staff and students at Waterperry but between then and 1945 there was a constant influx of Land Army and other women on short courses. By 1945 there were at least six senior staff covering productive and decorative gardening. Waterperry also took on an extra 25 acres of land, ploughed up under the watchful eye of the 'War Ag'. Potatoes, corn, and cabbages took up an increasing amount of the students' days. Acres of strawberries joined pigs, hens and carthorses as part of the war effort. Cropping was assisted by locally billeted men. The students and their Land Girl trainees learned all aspects of vegetable and fruit production, as well as the wider realms of horticulture that it was hoped they would again need after the war was over.

By February 1941, the **Gardeners' Chronicle** was reporting *'We are informed that the demand for trained women gardeners, to replace men called up for the Services, already greatly exceeds supply. Therefore in order to maintain and increase the yield of home grown produce, the Women's Farm and Garden Association is organising a training scheme (The Wilts and Dorset Apprenticeship Scheme) which should provide immediate help in gardens where there is a shortage of skilled labour.'*

In 1943 Cecil Beaton, then an official government photographer, was sent to Waterperry to record the work of the women there. At the outbreak of war the college had planted acres of new orchards at the college where the girls could learn fruit production, and Beaton recorded the Head of Fruit Growing, Miss Cockin, demonstrating the latest chemical techniques for disease prevention, using Nico dust.

Although the Land Army girls became famous for their gritty and determined work on farms, often in freezing conditions, many of them were assigned to large private house gardens in use as hospitals, military bases, and so on. Others were sent to market gardens, which were also desperately short of workers. Renee Katz from the East End of London joined many other land girls in the area around Cambridgeshire, where fruit farms abounded. She was billeted to Willingham, a fen-edge village, and cycled to whichever farm she was to work on along with the other girls. Audrey Manning worked in a market garden at Offham (Kent) with another Land Girl, Peggy. Along with the local women, they packed lettuces twenty-four to a box, pulled radishes and washed and tied them into bundles, packed rhubarb into boxes and spent days at a time picking peas off the bines, which had previously been pulled and left in huge piles. But what she recalls with fondness was the strawberry picking: '*One especially nice job was picking strawberries early in the morning before the sun was hot. We were paid piecework rates for this, so there was only time to eat an occasional strawberry.*' There was also an onion field, where she spent weeks crawling along the rows hand-hoeing, with sacking round her knees.

Originally from Barrow-in-Furness, Mabel Thomas was one of the 'lucky' Land Army girls who spent their time in the relatively luxurious setting of an old kitchen garden rather than in the fields. '*I was employed in the horticultural section of the WLA, my work being mainly in the greenhouses, thinning the grapes on the vines, pollinating the peaches and nectarines with a rabbit's foot and making sure that everything was well watered. I also picked the soft fruit, climbed the apple trees in the orchard, packing the surplus fruit ready to take to the shops in Cardigan for sale. The head gardener, together with four other gardeners, was involved in keeping the estate in good order with the digging of the gardens, mowing the lawns, etc, although I did a lot of the planting out. During the war, Pentre Mansion, owned by the Saunders-Davies family, was commandeered by the Military Authorities to be used as an Auxiliary Hospital and Convalescence Home for sick and wounded servicemen. They occupied one half whilst the family lived in the other.*'

The war revolutionised, at least for a while, the role of professional and amateur women gardeners, but within a few years many of the old attitudes had returned. In his 1951 book **Allotment Gardening**, Martyn Hall declared that: '*There are some women who manage an allotment of their own and most of them make quite a good job of it. Many more give valuable help to their husbands in the lighter tasks of hoeing and weeding and gathering crops.*' Clearly Martyn Hall had conveniently forgotten the capabilities of the 90,000-strong Land Army, which had staffed the gardens, market gardens and farms of wartime England.

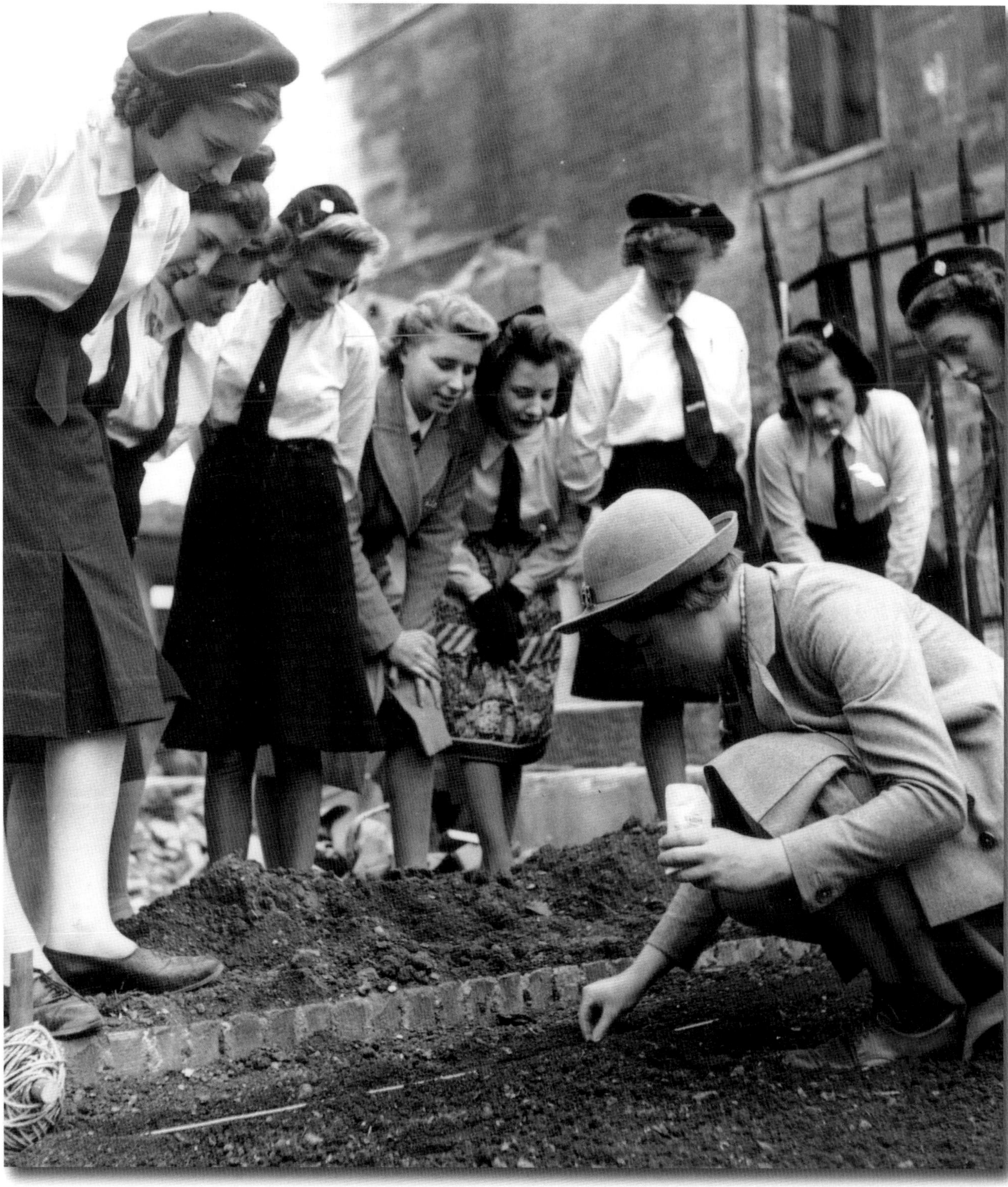

Members of the Girls' Training Corps prepare the ground for an allotment in what was once the garden of 145 Piccadilly, the former home of George V1. HMSO

RABBITS for FOOD FUR & PROFIT

BY C·H·WILLIAMS

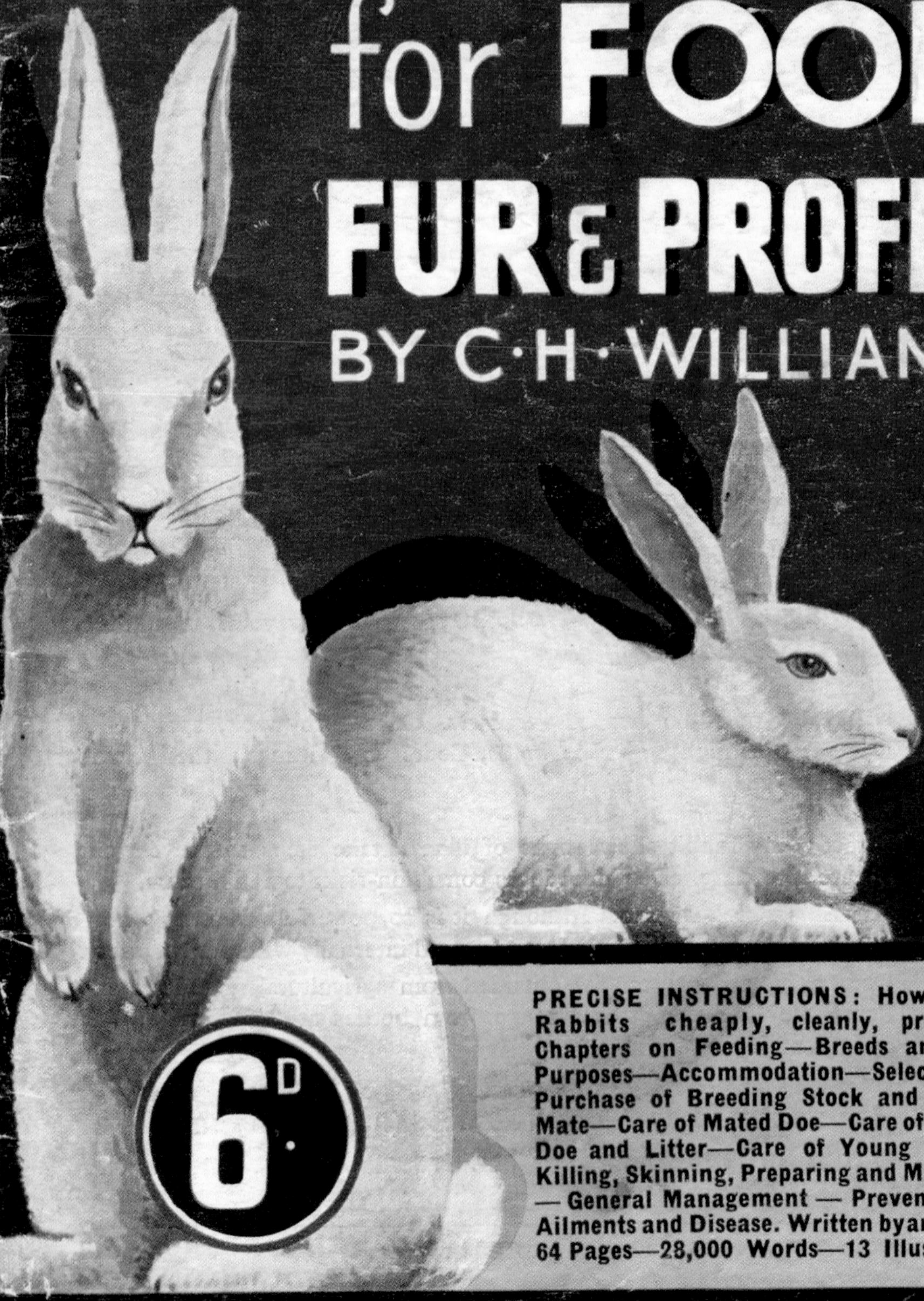

6D·

PRECISE INSTRUCTIONS: How to keep Rabbits cheaply, cleanly, profitably. Chapters on Feeding—Breeds and their Purposes—Accommodation—Selection and Purchase of Breeding Stock and How to Mate—Care of Mated Doe—Care of Nursing Doe and Litter—Care of Young Stock—Killing, Skinning, Preparing and Marketing — General Management — Prevention of Ailments and Disease. Written by an Expert. 64 Pages—28,000 Words—13 Illustrations

Livestock on the lawn

Having urged the patriotic gardener to dig up their flowers, trench their lawns and convert their annual bedding to outdoor tomatoes, the government decided that keeping hens, rabbits and pigs also came under the heading of 'Dig for Victory'. Learning again from the experience of the First World War it was recognised that meat and other forms of protein such as eggs and cheese would soon be in short supply, and that households should be encouraged to try and supplement the quantities available on ration. The gardening press soon took up the call, and in December 1939 the **Gardeners' Chronicle** ran an article on keeping livestock in the garden. Hens, ducks, runner ducks (for gardens without ponds), geese, rabbits, goats and pigs were all commended to the amateur gardener. With remarkable pre-science the **Gardeners' Chronicle** declared that *'purchased food for livestock will be increasingly costly and hard to come by'.* Where there was room gardeners could even grow their own feed for the chosen animals, ranging from grass for rabbits to buckwheat, sunflowers and maize for hens. *'In communities of neighbourly people it should not be difficult to arrange . . . co-operative schemes to be put into practice on a barter basis. "You grow Buckwheat or Maize or Mustard for my fowls and I will repay you with the equivalent in eggs". Those who have the knowledge and the facilities to grow the food for live-stock will have a double satisfaction; the knowledge that they are doing the best for their country and for themselves.'*

Local councils were told to rescind regulations against keeping livestock in back gardens and on allotments, and instructions were issued for building hen runs and rabbit hutches. Hens were the first to receive attention as early as 1940, but by 1942 it was proclaimed that it was the 'wartime patriotic duty' of all to keep hens, 'table rabbits' and if

Left
Despite its attractive cover, this book was as ruthless about rabbits as its title suggests.

Below
Backs to the Land was a radio programme giving advice on the many problems encountered by those who tried to convert their urban backyard into a farm. COURTESY OF RADIO TIMES

'BACKS TO THE LAND' today at 1.15 brings you more expert advice on how to turn that backyard to the best account.

possible bees or a even a pig. Beyond patriotic duty there was also the cherished hope that a few rabbits or hens might actually make a considerable profit by sales of surplus eggs and meat. Few would have believed the rather optimistic claim made by G. Ryley-Scott, that hens would turn into 'Gold from Your Backyard' (a claim he actually defined as 15s to £1 per bird), but even a few extra shillings would make a difference to the household budget. Soon suburban back gardens were alive with the sights, sounds and of course smells, of the countryside. There was even a new term for these small-scale farmers; suburban 'backyarders'.

Hens

In 1939 there had been approximately 5 million hens being kept in gardens and backyards; by the end of the war it was estimated that one and a quarter million people between them kept 11.5 million birds and produced 25% of Britain's eggs. This figure is likely to have been a gross underestimate, as it was based on official returns. Before the outbreak of war, over a third of eggs coming into Great Britain were imported from Denmark. Following the German occupation of Denmark in April 1940, the **Daily Telegraph** commented that *'Although home produced eggs are plentiful at the moment they are likely to be scarce in the autumn and winter'*. Eggs also became more important in the diet as meat rationing was introduced in March 1940, followed by cheese rationing in May 1941. Eggs themselves were not rationed until June 1941, by which time it had become obvious that so far home producers were failing to make up for the loss of the Danish

imports. The **Yorkshire Evening Post** noted that *'Those who wish to have eggs next autumn had better buy and pickle them now, or else keep backyard poultry'.* Housewives obviously felt that eggs were indeed essential. As G. Ryley-Scott declared in his **Produce Your Own Eggs**, *'The householder . . . who supplies his own family, and other families in the vicinity as well, with eggs, and thus cuts down the consumption of meat and fish, is performing a wartime service of no small magnitude.'*

To assist in this increase of hen keepers, the government issued an Order in Council that allowed anyone to keep hens in his backyard or allotment without reference to the landlord and to erect such houses or equipment as necessary. The same patriotic duty that called for more hen keepers also called on their neighbours to turn a blind eye (or ear) to the early morning cock-crow, the unsightly henhouse and the occasional break-in; although as Ryley-Scott noted, *'Poultry and Plants will not flourish on the same ground. Therefore if your hens make a habit of seeking enjoyment in your neighbour's garden you can expect black looks and possibly heated words.'* The solution was properly constructed fencing and *'the selection of fowls which are not addicted to high flying'.* Hen housing, along with rabbit hutches, became increasingly difficult to get as the war went on, and although the numerous pamphlets available gave instructions for ideal henhouses and runs, shortages of timber frequently resulted in far more 'picturesque' constructions. These often made use of old packing cases, doors, tea chests, and sacking, while old tennis and football nets were recommended as an alternative to chicken wire, which became impossible to obtain

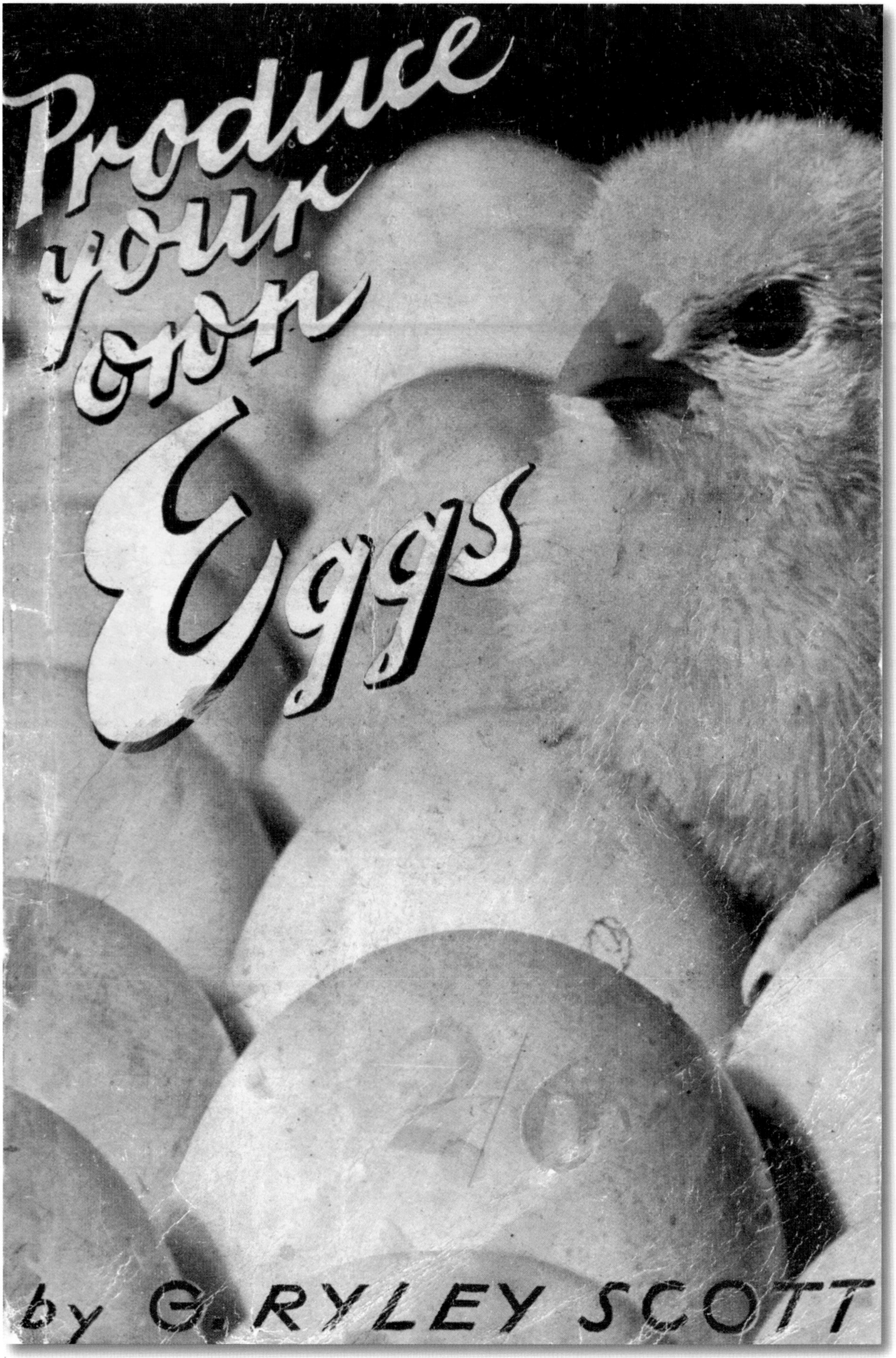
Produce your own Eggs
2/6
by G. RYLEY SCOTT
One of the many books printed at the time showing first-timers how to produce eggs.

except through Domestic Poultry Clubs or with a permit from the War Agricultural Committee.

By 1941 demand for hens meant that stocks of birds had become restricted. Most people started with three of four hens (bought young as pullets) and an optional cockerel. A beginner was only allowed to purchase food for up to twelve birds through their Domestic Poultry Keepers Club. The government warned people against buying their birds from 'backstreet traders' and instead to join Domestic Poultry Keepers Clubs and to get reliable stock either through these or by sending away to established hatcheries. These in turn took to advertising in the gardening press.

LYDDITE CHICKS are filled with ENERGY
THEY BURST FROM THEIR SHELLS WITH THE ENERGY OF HIGH EXPLOSIVE AND GO AHEAD IN THE SAME DIRECT WAY
Chicks (sexed, sex-linked or guaranteed not sexed) supplied in any quantity from 12 upwards
W. C. BLACKLOCKS BAYS, LYDD, KENT
and Lyddite Chicks (Somerset), Ltd., Winford Manor, Bristol.

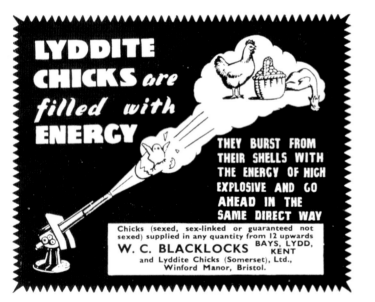

The **Gardeners' Chronicle** of August 1940 recommended that *'Crops which could be used [to feed] poultry are Mustard, and particularly Brassicas such as Savoys. There is also the Jerusalem Artichoke, of which wise gardeners – who in ordinary times have something better to grow – having planted wide breadths during the present year, have far more than they are likely to need.'* Jerusalem artichokes were recommended as a human foodstuff by the government, but widely disliked both because of taste and their notorious side-effect of 'wind'. Whether they had a similar effect on poultry is not recorded.

The government food issue for hens was called 'balancer meal'. This consisted of ground cereals which were designed to be mixed with 'the usual' household scraps that all domestic livestock were given. The advice on food scraps given in the 1941 edition of **Produce Your Own Eggs** hints at luxuries not available later in the war, in its advice that *'banana peel must not be given to hens'*. During the war it was technically forbidden to feed the hens any food that was fit for human consumption but it was a fine line, and many a household peeled their vegetables rather more generously than Lord Woolton urged, so that there would be scraps enough for the hens and rabbits. If food waste was found in rubbish bins households could be, and were, prosecuted under the strict regulations; in fact some households may have got hens just to get around this compulsion to eat unappetising scraps.

After 1941 the ration allowance of chicken feed was only obtained by giving up the shell egg ration of the family. This acted as a further limiter on the numbers of hens that could be kept. However by taking the neighbours' shell egg coupons and also their food waste, quite a large flock could be kept, usually providing many more eggs (not to mention feathers and meat) than would have been obtained via the ration. Even after giving eggs to the neighbours, there would still be a surplus that could be sold or bartered for other items in short supply. In

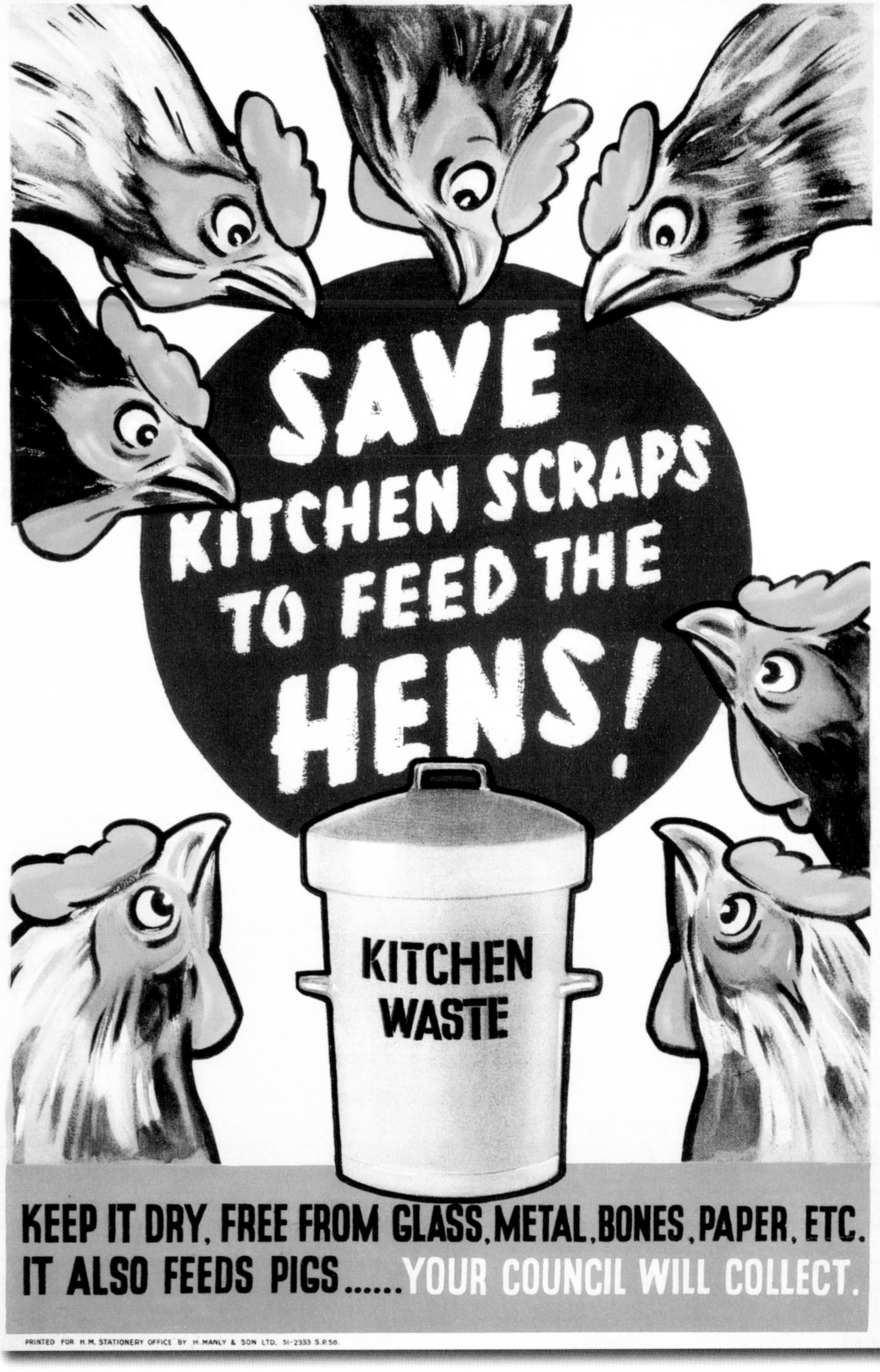
SAVE
KITCHEN SCRAPS
TO FEED THE
HENS!
KITCHEN
WASTE
KEEP IT DRY, FREE FROM GLASS, METAL, BONES, PAPER, ETC.
IT ALSO FEEDS PIGS...... YOUR COUNCIL WILL COLLECT.
PRINTED FOR H.M. STATIONERY OFFICE BY H.MANLY & SON LTD. 51-2333 S.P.56.

1942 one person's shell egg ration allowed you 4lb of balancer meal, which was supposed to be mixed with 8lb of household waste, preferably with some cod liver oil added for vitamin D.

The balancer meal was designed only to supplement rather than replace household scraps and allotment waste as poultry food, but there were concerns that the low levels had resulted in some keepers feeding their hens food fit for human consumption. Many hens obviously did not get enough food, or were in poor condition or too old, as although numbers of hens being kept more than doubled from 1939 to 1945, egg production did not double – although again, statistics may not reflect the reality of home production. In June 1943 the ration for balancer meal for hens was increased from 4lb to 5lb per month per hen for those who were registered as domestic poultry keepers, in an attempt to increase egg production. **Garden Work** urged its readers to use the extra ration to improve the feeding of their existing hens and not to make it a reason for attempting to keep more hens. To encourage good layers there were egg-laying trials and competitions. The Domestic Poultry Keepers Clubs gave advice and encouragement, but some birds were just not given enough food to provide for good laying. Calcium is also essential for egg production and scraps often did not provide enough. Where eggs were sold or given away the essential shells may not have made their way back to the hen keeper – who would otherwise have used them as a calcium supplement.

Some gardeners tried to 'grow their own' meal of oats or corn. Maize merited a whole page discussion in the **Gardeners' Chronicle** of March 1940,

EGGS NOT SCARCE IN THIS HOME

MRS. H. V. L., of East Wittering, writes :— "As it was impossible to get eggs, I bought 3 hens and 2 pullets. I put Karswood Poultry Spice in their mash and, one after another, they started to lay and they are averaging 5 eggs each every 8 days. What's more, they are keeping it up! The 2 pullets were due to lay at the end of February, but, believe me, the Karswood mash brought them on and they started laying the last week in January. In the last 7 days, the pair of them have laid 6 eggs each. You don't know what a blessing the eggs have been to my 4 children during the meat shortage, and I feel sure it was Karswood Spice which got the birds going like steam engines." By giving YOUR birds Karswood Spice (wonder egg-producer, containing ground insects) you, too, can get eggs aplenty. Prove this to your profit. Packets 2½d., 7½d., 1/3d., from Corn Dealers.

Above
As eggs became scarcer hens became more popular.

Right
A ration book for a domestic poultry keeper. Although supposedly compulsory many people who kept a few hens during the war seem never to have heard of these ration books!

when it was declared to be *'the best of all crops for poultry'*, with large crops predicted in warm years, plus a lot of waste that was ideal for the compost heap. Oddly some of the varieties recommended were grown for human consumption in America, but 'corn on the cob' was not part of the diet in the UK and so the hens got all the benefit.

ON HIS MAJESTY'S SERVICE

OFFICIAL PAID

DOMESTIC POULTRY KEEPER'S RATION BOOK

POULTRY FOOD (BALANCER MEAL)

Period 1st October, 1942,—31st March, 1943.

F.S.R. 1
6

Holder's Name Mrs A. Burnell

Address Heathgate, Bleadon Hill, Weston S. Mare, Somerset.

Date of Issue
(See Note 1 on page 2)

153A

If undelivered, to be returned to Ministry of Agriculture and Fisheries, Glendower, North Promenade, St. Annes, Lytham St. Annes, Lancs.

Serial Number of Book
This number to be quoted in all correspondence. 4/ A 538530

153A.

READ CAREFULLY THE INSTRUCTIONS ON PAGES 2 AND 4.

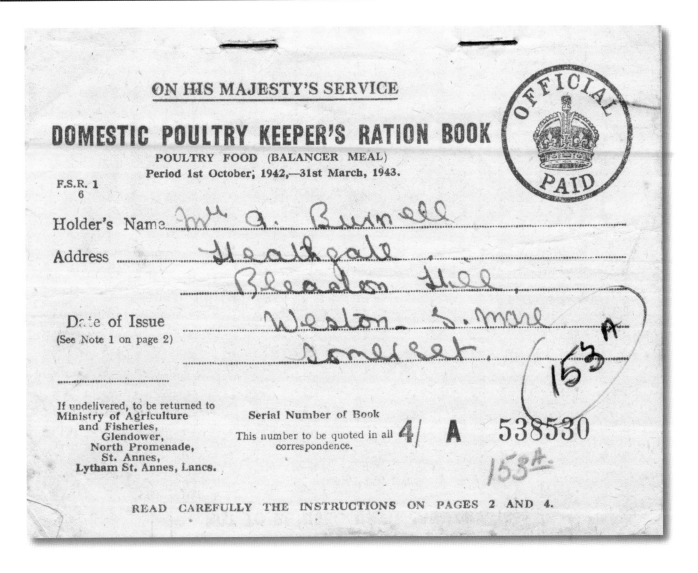

Hens were frequently kept on allotment land, often necessitating either a change of the original rules, or the turning of a 'blind eye'. In Luton the council gave permission for people to use areas of land that backed on to their gardens as unofficial 'allotments', in addition to the official allotment sites. Here one man kept chickens, ducks, rabbits, bees and even a goat, later successfully claiming squatter's rights to the land, which he had fenced off some 30 years earlier. Ironically many of the larger poultry farmers found it difficult to keep going during the early years of the war, as costs rose and foodstuffs were in limited availability, and so were sometimes willing to rent out or sell old housing to small-scale domestic keepers – who also used these old poultry houses for rabbits. Commercial poultry farming declined by 30% during the war years, again putting the onus on the backyarders.

Peter Blackburn of York recalls helping his father construct extra housing for hens and rabbits in their garden: *'He and I built extra rabbit hutches behind the garage and a chicken run in the right-hand corner of the garden plot, facing down the garden from the back of the house, which utilised the*

FEATHERS

They provide a stock of necessary comforts for you and your family

Above

Hens produced feathers for pillows, eiderdowns and cushions.

corner fencing, which housed at least a dozen chickens. Our next door neighbour's garden (on the right of ours) backed onto a plot of land that had been too small to build on. This was gradually cleared and used as an extended garden and chicken run for both families.' After his father was called up in 1942, when the age parameters were widened, Peter and his mother took on the care of the rabbits, chickens and garden.

Rabbits

With their reputation for breeding and rapid growth the rabbit became the unfortunate target of the government's campaign to 'raise your own meat and protein'. The book, **Meat from Your Garden: A Handy Guide to Table Rabbit Keeping**, calculated that with constant breeding a buck and three does would produce at least 55 young rabbits a year, *'enough for at least one extra meat meal a week'* for the family. In a culture where meat was still the most important element of the meal this was an attractive proposition. At the outbreak of war butchers had also traded in wild rabbits, and doubtless many country butchers continued to do this 'under the counter', but in urban areas supply and demand meant that prices rocketed until the government intervened and a fixed price was set, putting rabbit meat out of the reach of many families. Keeping a few rabbits at home was promoted by the government as an ideal solution. **Rabbits for Profit (Food and Fur)** by W. King Wilson went further, claiming that *'To keep a few rabbits on a small scale is a patriotic thing to do'*. Numerous small booklets on rabbit keeping were printed, especially once meat rationing hit home, and by the end of the war it was estimated that over a million rabbits were being kept – although one presumes that the figure was a very fluctuating one! By 1942 H. Dyson was urging the government to aim for 25,000 rabbit keepers, each with four does, from which he calculated nine million pounds of meat a year could be produced. Many keepers had much higher numbers of stock, with allotment and back-yard sheds being fitted out with stacked hutches to accommodate 20 or more breeding does.

Most rabbits kept in small domestic gardens were kept in small hutches, with sizes of 4ft by 2ft recommended, although the larger breeders used indoor stacking hutches as small as 3ft 6in by 18in, well below the size indicated by welfare regulations today. Morant hutches, typically a movable 'A' frame construction with an indoor and outdoor section, allowed the rabbits to gain air and light and some natural grazing but needed larger supplies of chicken wire and lawn grass than many people could obtain. Whether many keepers let the rabbits graze naturally

THE COUNTRY LIFE
HOME FRONT
SERIES FOR INTENSIVE CULTIVATION

RABBIT KEEPING FOR FOOD

Price: **SIXPENCE NET**

on the lawn, as the rather idyllic picture on p.185 indicates, is questionable.

As with hens, domestic rabbit clubs were set up to coordinate both supplies of rabbits and distribution of feeding bran. The scheme distinguished between 'large breeders' (with eight or more breeding does), and domestic producers, with fewer than eight. Unlike hens, no other rations had to be given up for the rabbit food, but it was made a condition of supply that *'not less than ten percent of the progeny of does [female rabbits] be made available to the general public for sale through an approved buyer'*. Buyers included canteens, schools and butchers.

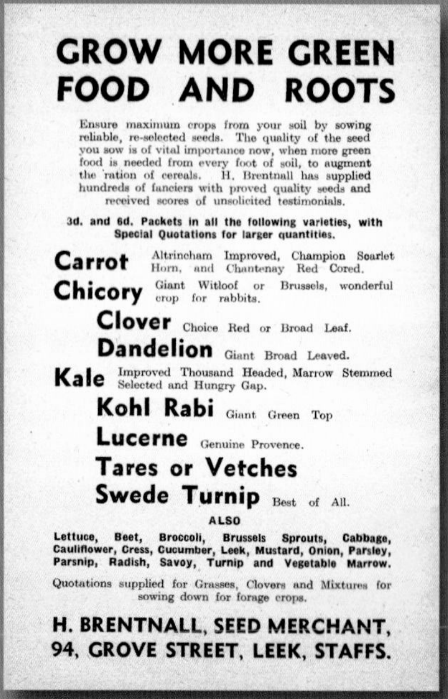
GROW MORE GREEN FOOD AND ROOTS
Ensure maximum crops from your soil by sowing reliable, re-selected seeds. The quality of the seed you sow is of vital importance now, when more green food is needed from every foot of soil, to augment the ration of cereals. H. Brentnall has supplied hundreds of fanciers with proved quality seeds and received scores of unsolicited testimonials.
3d. and 6d. Packets in all the following varieties, with Special Quotations for larger quantities.
Carrot Altrincham Improved, Champion Scarlet Horn, and Chantenay Red Cored.
Chicory Giant Witloof or Brussels, wonderful crop for rabbits.
Clover Choice Red or Broad Leaf.
Dandelion Giant Broad Leaved.
Kale Improved Thousand Headed, Marrow Stemmed Selected and Hungry Gap.
Kohl Rabi Giant Green Top
Lucerne Genuine Provence.
Tares or Vetches
Swede Turnip Best of All.
ALSO
Lettuce, Beet, Broccoli, Brussels Sprouts, Cabbage, Cauliflower, Cress, Cucumber, Leek, Mustard, Onion, Parsley, Parsnip, Radish, Savoy, Turnip and Vegetable Marrow.
Quotations supplied for Grasses, Clovers and Mixtures for sowing down for forage crops.
H. BRENTNALL, SEED MERCHANT, 94, GROVE STREET, LEEK, STAFFS.

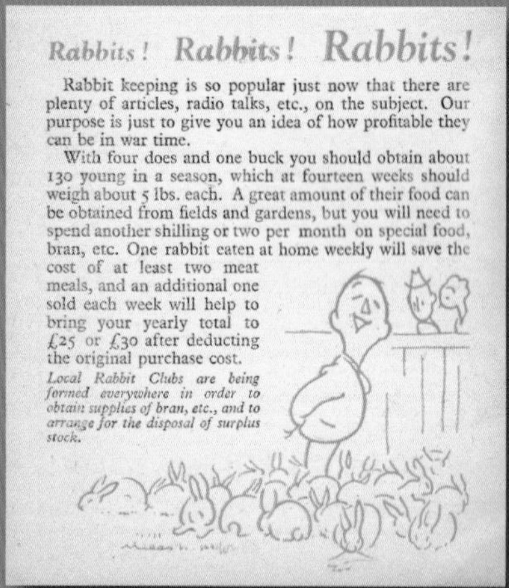
Rabbits! Rabbits! Rabbits!
Rabbit keeping is so popular just now that there are plenty of articles, radio talks, etc., on the subject. Our purpose is just to give you an idea of how profitable they can be in war time.
With four does and one buck you should obtain about 130 young in a season, which at fourteen weeks should weigh about 5 lbs. each. A great amount of their food can be obtained from fields and gardens, but you will need to spend another shilling or two per month on special food, bran, etc. One rabbit eaten at home weekly will save the cost of at least two meat meals, and an additional one sold each week will help to bring your yearly total to £25 or £30 after deducting the original purchase cost.
Local Rabbit Clubs are being formed everywhere in order to obtain supplies of bran, etc., and to arrange for the disposal of surplus stock.

When discussing feed, these booklets recommended balancing the standard bran or oat feed with weeds from the allotment or vegetable gardens, while many rabbits were also fed left-over kitchen scraps. Weight for age ratio was a constant concern for the larger or more ambitious domestic breeder, and specially fattening foods could be obtained, usually containing oats or molasses. In addition some vegetable seed suppliers provided seeds for rabbit greens, although many an allotment-holder must have wondered at the wisdom of purposely seeding dandelions and clover on his plot! Finding food for the rabbits became a constant challenge and the government had to issue specific guidance that rabbit food might be cut from roadside verges, subject to permission from local authorities.

In August 1943 the **Gardeners' Chronicle** reported that *'At the Reading "Victory Garden Show" school children could compete in over a dozen classes including one interesting class for a collection of pressed, named and mounted wild leaves and flowers suitable for rabbit food. Classes are also provided for flowers, honey and rabbits.'* A month later, the periodical reported that: *'The parents of three Bridgwater schoolboys aged eleven, twelve and thirteen, recently had to pay costs when the boys, who were looking for rabbit food, were summoned for trespassing on allotments. The magistrates told the boys that they were liable to heavy fines, and could have been sent to prison if they had been older.'*

Rabbit clubs sprang up everywhere to share tips, share out essential hutch and chicken wire materials, and also to swap rabbits, to prevent in-breeding. Which breed of rabbit to keep was not just of interest to the traditional 'rabbit

Top
Every type of rabbit food was available as seed, even weeds.
Above
Rabbits could get out of hand, especially if you achieved the estimated 130 young a year from one doe that this advertisement boasts of.
Right
The government's estimate was a slightly more conservative twelve rabbits a year from one doe. This is the official advertisement offering guidance for prospective rabbit breeders.

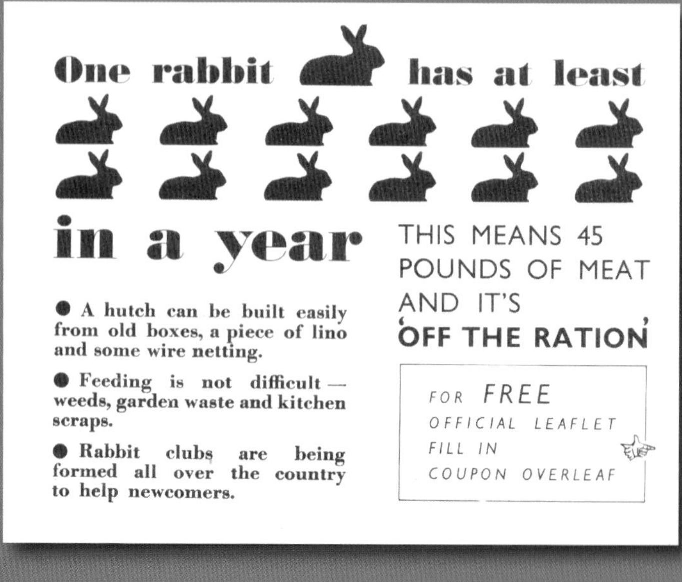
One rabbit has at least
in a year
THIS MEANS 45 POUNDS OF MEAT AND IT'S 'OFF THE RATION'
● A hutch can be built easily from old boxes, a piece of lino and some wire netting.
● Feeding is not difficult — weeds, garden waste and kitchen scraps.
● Rabbit clubs are being formed all over the country to help newcomers.
FOR FREE OFFICIAL LEAFLET FILL IN COUPON OVERLEAF

HOW TO KEEP RABBITS

1/-

THIS BOOK TELLS YOU HOW YOU CAN JOIN
IN THE GOVERNMENT SCHEME TO PRODUCE
MORE DOMESTIC RABBIT MEAT, FURS AND
WOOL FOR YOURSELF AND FOR THE NATION

PUBLISHED BY "FUR & FEATHER, IDLE, BRADFORD, YORKS.

fanciers' but also to those interested in the colour of fur for mittens and hats, or eventual 'table weight'. However keeping a rabbit pure bred was not always easy, and many must have evolved over time into what **The Country Life Home Front** book on rabbits refers to as the 'Cottage Rabbit'. Disease among the backyard rabbits was given short shrift, as with laying hens, and the sickly rabbit was dispatched with the admonition that *'specifics [of medicines] take so long that the trouble and expense are more than most rabbits are worth'.*

Pelts (rabbit skins) were also sold, and gloves, hats, collars and even entire coats were available. If you wanted to make clothes from your own rabbits but did not have the skills, you could send away the pelts and have them made up for you by a company such as M. Gordon at High Wycombe who charged 10s to make up a pair of gloves, or 84s for a coat of 25 pelts. The hair from angora rabbits was also spun into wool, and a high price was paid for good quality wool, although a lot of rabbit wool was needed for a jumper.

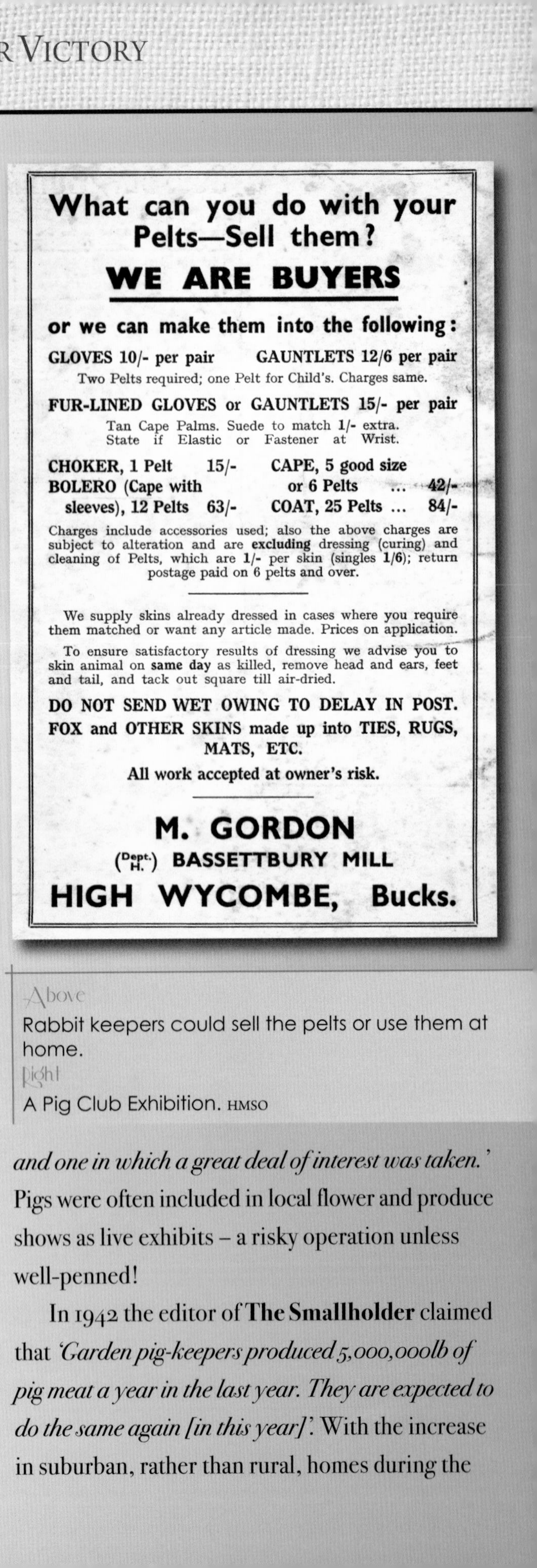

What can you do with your Pelts—Sell them?

WE ARE BUYERS

or we can make them into the following:

GLOVES 10/- per pair **GAUNTLETS 12/6 per pair**
Two Pelts required; one Pelt for Child's. Charges same.

FUR-LINED GLOVES or GAUNTLETS 15/- per pair
Tan Cape Palms. Suede to match 1/- extra.
State if Elastic or Fastener at Wrist.

CHOKER, 1 Pelt 15/-
BOLERO (Cape with sleeves), 12 Pelts 63/-
CAPE, 5 good size or 6 Pelts ... 42/-
COAT, 25 Pelts ... 84/-

Charges include accessories used; also the above charges are subject to alteration and are **excluding** dressing (curing) and cleaning of Pelts, which are 1/- per skin (singles 1/6); return postage paid on 6 pelts and over.

We supply skins already dressed in cases where you require them matched or want any article made. Prices on application.

To ensure satisfactory results of dressing we advise you to skin animal on **same day** as killed, remove head and ears, feet and tail, and tack out square till air-dried.

DO NOT SEND WET OWING TO DELAY IN POST.
FOX and OTHER SKINS made up into TIES, RUGS, MATS, ETC.
All work accepted at owner's risk.

M. GORDON
(Dept. H.) BASSETTBURY MILL
HIGH WYCOMBE, Bucks.

Above
Rabbit keepers could sell the pelts or use them at home.

Right
A Pig Club Exhibition. HMSO

Pigs

Pre-war most bacon was imported, and bacon and ham were among the first items to be rationed in January 1940 at the rate of 4oz a week. Keeping a pig at home was one way round the problem of reduced supplies. The report of the Southport Flower Show in September 1940 noted: *'Instead of horse-leaping competitions there were pigs housed in an improvised sty of a kind that anyone could build from scrap wood and sheets of galvanised iron – a homely example of the possibilities of pig-keeping and one in which a great deal of interest was taken.'* Pigs were often included in local flower and produce shows as live exhibits – a risky operation unless well-penned!

In 1942 the editor of **The Smallholder** claimed that *'Garden pig-keepers produced 5,000,000lb of pig meat a year in the last year. They are expected to do the same again [in this year]'.* With the increase in suburban, rather than rural, homes during the

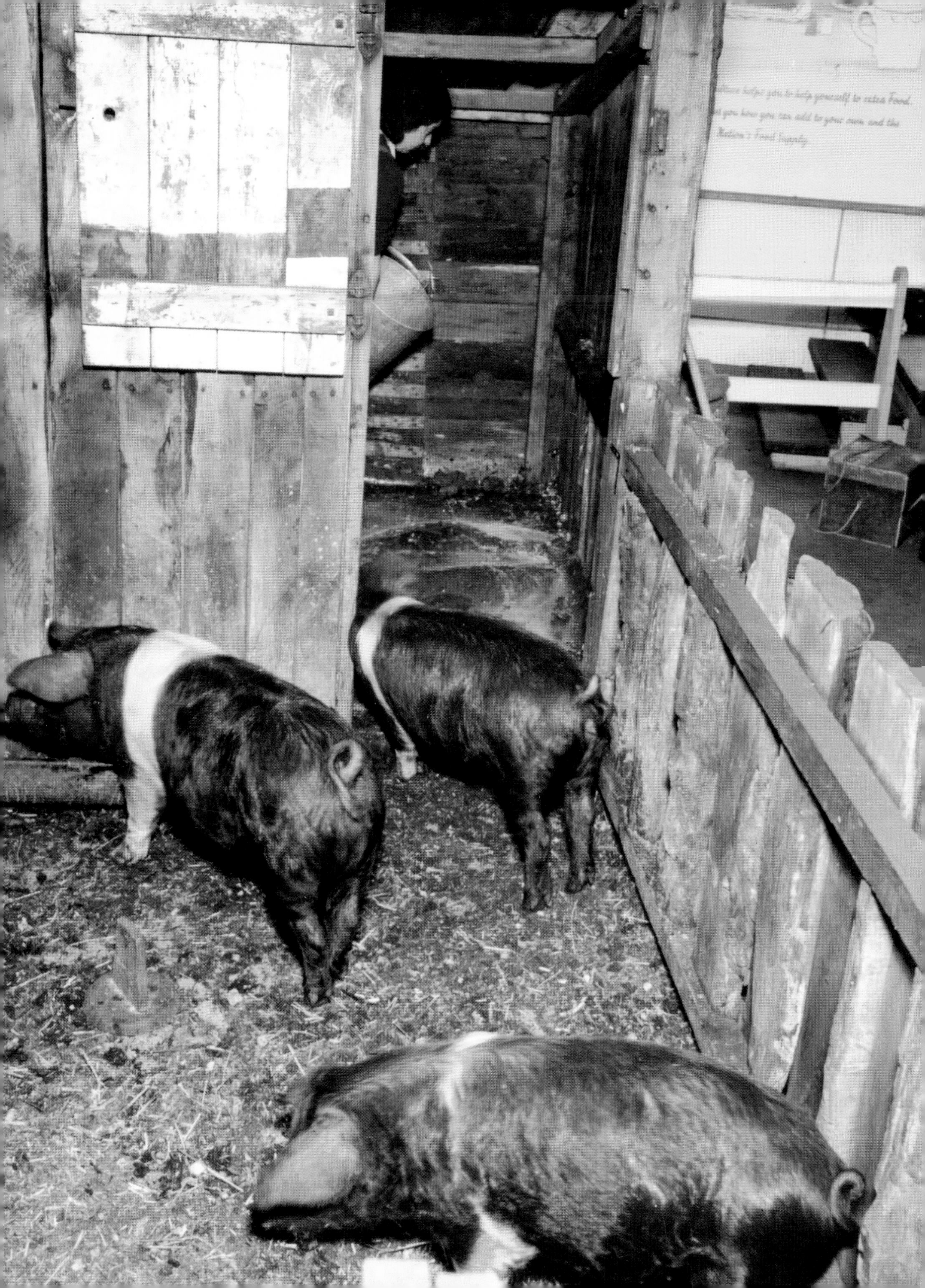
helps you to help yourself to extra Food.
you how you can add to your own and the
Nation's Food Supply.

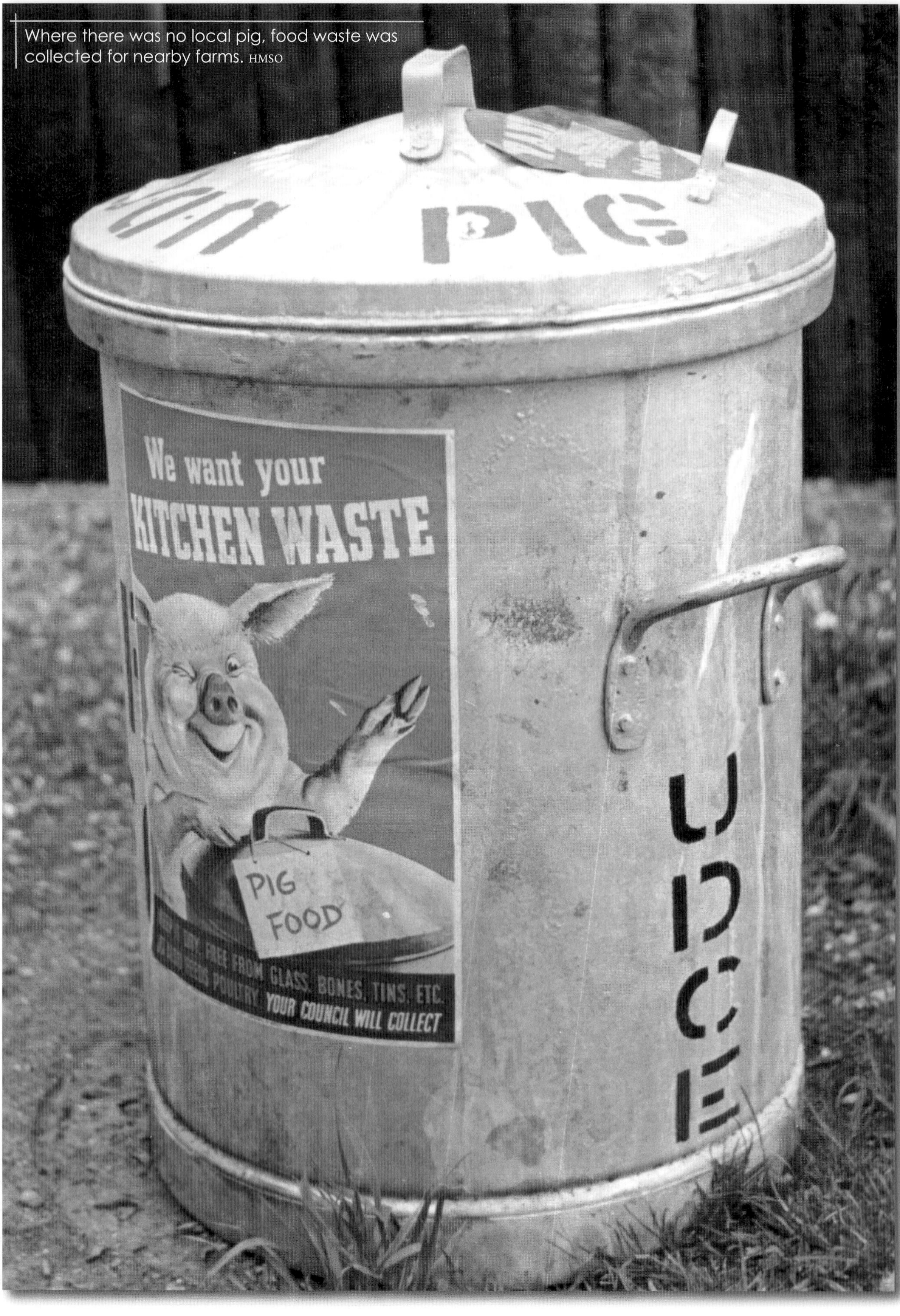
PIG
We want your
KITCHEN WASTE
PIG FOOD
FREE FROM GLASS, BONES, TINS, ETC.
YOUR COUNCIL WILL COLLECT

Where there was no local pig, food waste was collected for nearby farms. HMSO interwar years, he might have been being optimistic: however some householders did take to pig keeping, supplementing the official piggeries and workplace 'pig clubs'. A Small Pig Keepers Council (SPKC) was set up to provide advice and guidance for these newcomers, and approximately 7,000 local societies and pig clubs were eventually established.

The large, friendly (and mucky!) pig also appealed to children, who often had responsibility for feeding them. Many a pig was honoured with a name, and frequent visitors. Margaret Brown recalls the family garden being full of neighbours' children who had come to see Billy the pig, bringing with them kitchen slops and potato peelings to be boiled into a pig mash. In common with much of the other livestock pigs became pets, and it came as a shock to Margaret and her brother Eddie when Billy was sent to the slaughterhouse (the local pub). Heartbreak did not stop the family having a second pig to supplement the rations again. Children could also run the frequent 'errands', which could be used as cover for taking food supplies for what was known as a 'secret pig'. Norman Owen of Withnell in Lancashire recalls matter-of-factly that one of his 'jobs' was the feeding of the secret pig.

This secrecy was due to a government crackdown on private pig keeping after the first years of the war. Pigs were issued with a ration of imported meal, but so much of this was going to privately owned pigs that commercial farmers were suffering shortages. Consequently little meat went to butchers, and most people had to do without. The Ministry of Food was spurred to action; the meal ration was halved, and private pig keepers had either to give up their own bacon and ham coupons, or hand over half the pig to the Ministry when it was slaughtered. Rather than do this some keepers went 'underground'. These stricter regulations on keeping pigs meant that in some rural areas pigs became scarcer than they had been in the pre-war period, or were only available by word of mouth.

Home slaughter of the pig had its own difficulties, with a large container such as a bath or hip-bath usually needed. In most cases the local butcher could be hired to come in, but schemes were also run to teach housewives at least to dismember the carcass even if they did not do the actual slaughter.

> It is cheap, easy and profitable if you
> ## KEEP A GOAT

Goats

If 'poultry and plants' did not go together, then goats were even more of a danger in the back garden or allotment. Even during the war most goat keepers had smallholdings rather than suburban gardens. However, as **Goats** (the rather unimaginatively titled monthly magazine of the Dairy Goat Industry) noted, *'goat keeping is perfectly possible for the ordinary family'*. Exhortations to 'Laugh at Rations! Make Your Own [Goat's] Butter', and 'Grow Goat Food: Dig for Victory' make it clear that goat keeping was seen as yet another 'duty' to be fitted into the busy wartime schedule. Even more than with other livestock, keeping goats necessitated liaison with county-based War Agricultural representatives ('War Ags'), who were responsible for ensuring all livestock were declared, and that welfare and other regulations were being upheld.

Bees

Once sugar rationing was announced in January 1940 it was obvious that all things sweet would soon be in short supply. The sugar ration was 8oz a week for the duration of the war (it continued to be rationed until 1953) and for most people that had to include sugar for making cakes and biscuits, which were much more frequently made at home in those days. Although the government helpfully suggested carrots, swede, and fruit as alternatives, honey was the obvious substitute for those that could get it.

Bee keeping is a skilled business if disaster is not to follow any attempt to remove the honey, but that did not prevent many people trying to set up hives on allotments and garden plots. The government gave encouragement again by providing an extra sugar ration for bee-keepers; necessary for over-wintering bees if a good honey crop is to be taken. In fact many people bypassed the bees and used the sugar themselves, being content with a smaller honey crop. Bee Keepers Associations gave advice to members and also helped access supplies, including hives and frames.

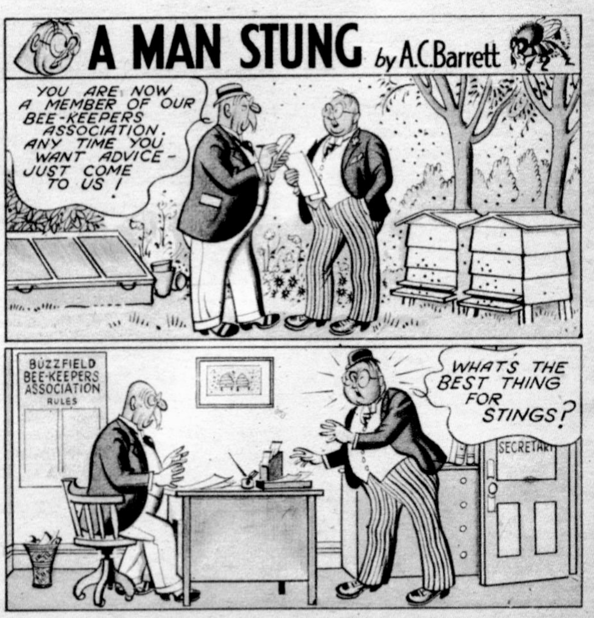
A MAN STUNG by A.C.Barrett
YOU ARE NOW A MEMBER OF OUR BEE-KEEPERS ASSOCIATION. ANY TIME YOU WANT ADVICE - JUST COME TO US!
BUZZFIELD BEE-KEEPERS ASSOCIATION RULES
WHATS THE BEST THING FOR STINGS?
SECRETAR

Above
Many novice bee-keepers must have encountered the same problems as that envisaged by A.C.Barrett in his cartoon in *Illustrated magazine*.

Death (!)

For many suburban families hens, rabbits and pigs were a novel addition to the family circle, and predictably the eventual purpose of the animal was often conveniently 'forgotten' until the inevitable time came when the dinner plate beckoned. Rabbits especially, with their long ears and twitching noses, became beloved furry friends. A traditional children's pet in times of peace the breeding of tame rabbits for meat had not been common before the war, except in rural areas. Childhood memories often describe the moment of horror on discovering that Thumper or Peter were due for the pot, or even worse, had just been served up and eaten. Looking back almost 65 years, Peter Blackburn recalled that: *'My partially sighted older sister made valiant efforts to prevent a favourite Dutch Blue rabbit from the pot, and I was somewhat reluctant to take part [in preparing the rabbit for the table], a very tearful and traumatic experience at first.'* The chickens in the Blackburn household appear to have made their own bid for life, causing even more emotional trauma. *'We went to the chicken run and tried to catch a chicken; this was not as easy as it first seemed and was somewhat funny, amusing and frustrating but eventually achieved. After some discussion and attempts to wring the chicken's neck we, rather I, suggested we chop its head off and went to find a log and axe, again with some laughs and frustration this was managed. My mother immediately let go of the dead chicken which proceeded to run headless around the run which caused great consternation for a while. The gutting and plucking was also a major event with lots of argument, shouting and laughs.'*

Even quite dedicated backyarders could find the eating of these 'familiar friends' traumatic. Mr Imms, who became an enthusiastic and organised domestic poultry keeper during the war, drew the line at eating Brownie, Spotty, Hoppity or Blackie after their sterling work producing so many eggs. Instead the milkman, then often a 'jack of all trades', stepped in to wring their necks and the dead birds were sold to boost family finances, rather than eaten by the family. Goats were also seen as delightful companions and family pets by those that embarked on backyarding during the war and one doubts if the 'two evacuee children enraptured by the goats' on Perry Pollard's smallholding in Truro were aware that the 'Glory Pie' was so called because it was actually made of 'Glory', the kid goat.

For every gardener and householder that embarked on livestock keeping during the war there were many others that either shied away from the complications (or the messy deaths), or failed in their attempts. Aiming at those who felt that rabbit keeping was perhaps not for them after all, the last page of **Meat from Your Garden: A Handy Guide to Table Rabbit Keeping** carried a full-page advertisement from C. Arthur Pearson's book department. Among their advertised list of publications are **25 Ways of Serving Potatoes**, **25 Ways of Serving Carrots**, **25 Ways of Serving Eggless Dishes**, and a whole range of other books full of meatless and eggless recipes!

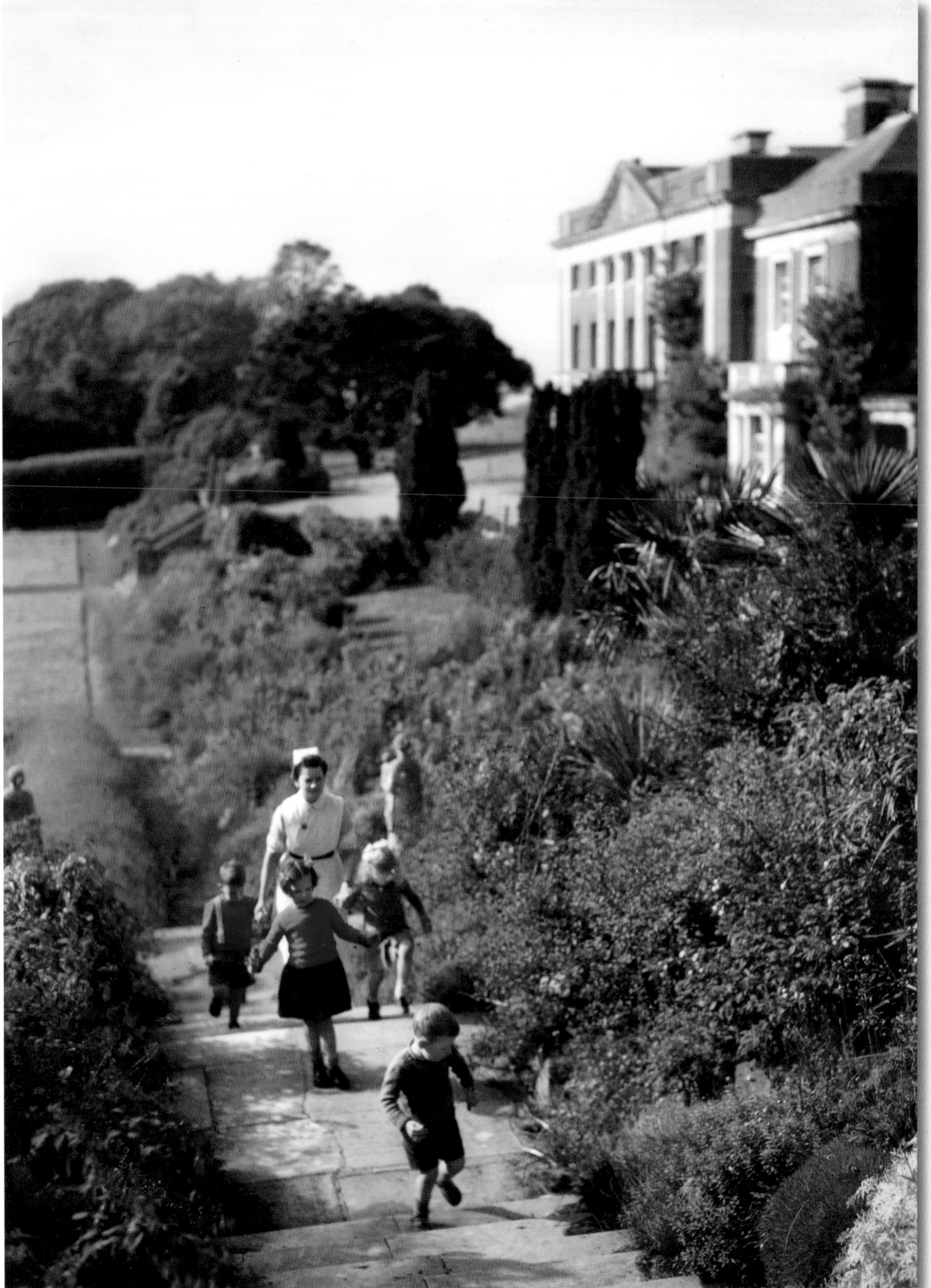

The country house battleground

'To the owner and occupier of the land and buildings described in the schedule hereto annexed. I Colonel John Doe, being one of a class of persons to whom the Secretary of State as a competent authority for the purpose of Part IV of the Defence of the Realm Regulations, 1939, has in exercise of the powers contained in That Part of the said Defence Regulations delegated the necessary authority, give notice that I, on behalf of the Secretary of Sate, take possession of the land and buildings described in the schedule hereby annexed.'

A typical Requisition Order used at the outbreak of the Second World War for country houses and other properties.

Positioned incongruously alongside allotments and suburban backyards, upper-class country houses were also on the front line of the Home Front. Pressed into service to feed the people in nearby villages, evacuee schoolchildren, or billeted forces, the gardens of country houses proved invaluable in the Dig for Victory effort. In many places the garden effort expanded beyond the traditional walled gardens and pleasure grounds. Tennis courts, bowling greens and drying grounds were dug up and planted with potatoes, cabbages and lettuce. Croquet lawns more used to the quiet clunk of wooden mallet on ball were ruthlessly sacrificed, with larger parkland areas actually going under the plough.

Even before the outbreak of war lists had been drawn up of possible uses for each house, with government departments, schools, hospitals and army billets being allocated according to suitability. Over 3,000 houses were taken over by the Ministry of Health both for convalescing soldiers and for civilian patients evacuated from cities. Fearing the imminent arrival of army convoys, some country house owners had made private arrangements in advance to receive school evacuees *en masse*, while others gritted their teeth and 'did their bit', sacrificing heirlooms and works of art in aid of national defence. Catholic families often took in convent schools, while other owners had established links with private schools. Blenheim for example took 400 boys from Malvern College, and then added a similar number from Harrow when Harrow School

Left
Young evacuees and a nurse in the grounds of a country house. Many such houses were used as evacuation hostels, especially for nursery schools. HMSO

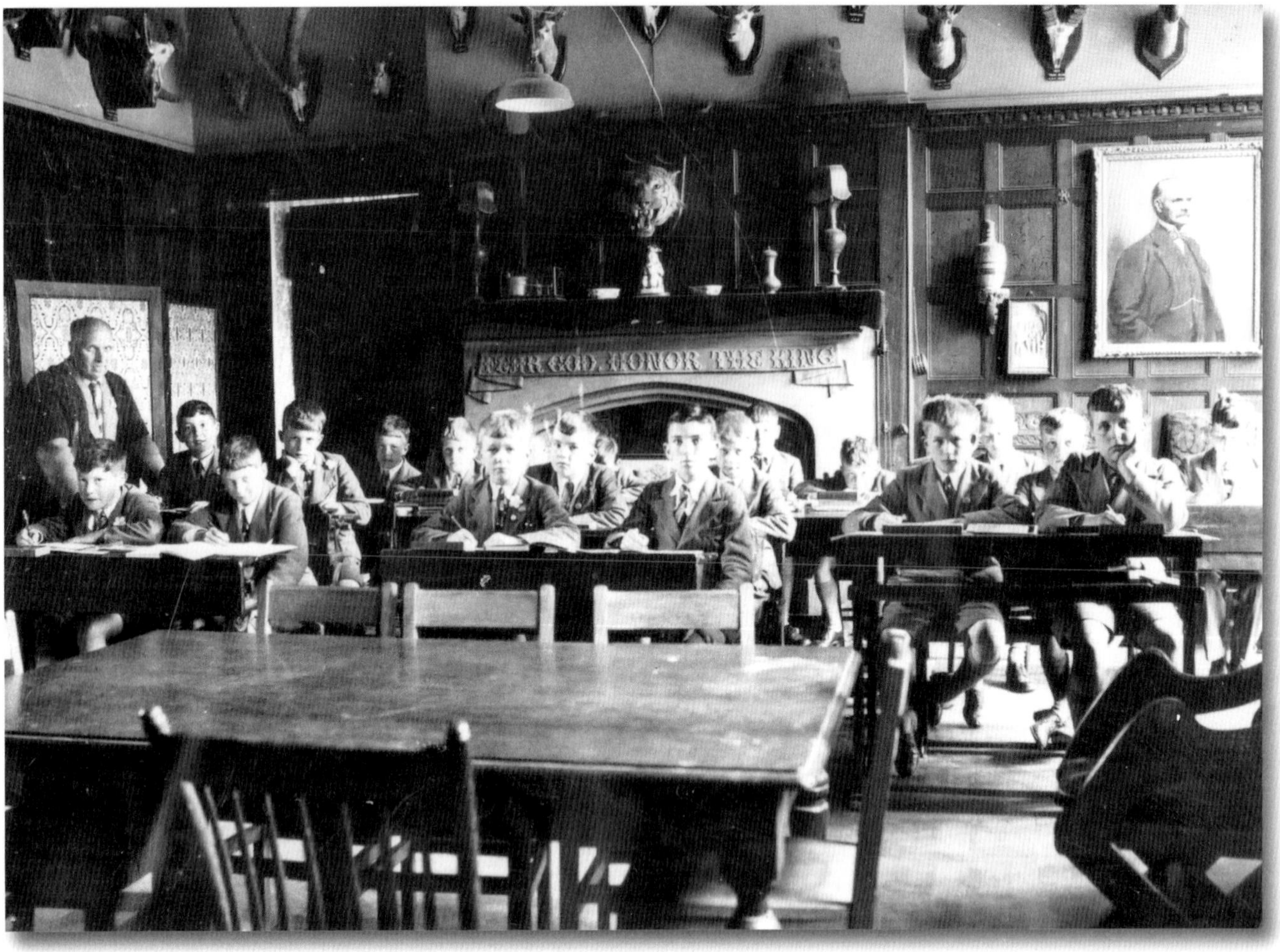
FEAR GOD. HONOR THE KING

was taken over by intelligence officers. Not all schools were as welcome; at Hinton Ampner (in Hampshire) the then owner was said to be 'apoplectic' about the unannounced arrival of 40 girls from Portsmouth.

Everywhere country houses were suddenly expected to rise to the occasion. A Welsh public school took over Chatsworth (Derbyshire), Waddesdon Manor (Bucks) became a residential nursery for 100 London children, Harewood House (Yorks), Cliveden (Bucks) and Somerleyton (Suffolk) all became military hospitals, while at Wilton (Wilts) Southern Command planned D-Day under the watchful eyes of the Van Dyke portraits.

Not all of the visitors reacted with due regard for the historic gardens in which they found themselves. At Alton Towers (then a distinguished country house) the conservatories were machine - gunned by American troops, while Canadian soldiers cut off the heads of the statues at Dunorlan Park (Kent). Rather less wantonly RAF 323 Squadron parked and maintained their aircraft under the shelter of the immense elm avenues at Wimpole Hall (Cambridgeshire). Ted Humphris, a gardener at Aynhoe Park, Northamptonshire, wrote in his autobiography, *'The military were constantly erecting new buildings, and expanding their installations. Fruit trees were felled to make* way for Nissen huts, flower borders and box hedges were swept away, and cookhouses and petrol dumps took their place. The outer kitchen garden was commandeered by the army and was staffed by military gardeners to provide vegetables for their own cookhouses. . . . It was two years after the war that the army finally left Aynhoe Park, the surrounding parkland pock-marked with abandoned concrete emplacements, empty Nissen huts, petrol stores and mourning still the many proud trees and rose gardens which had been sacrificed.'

'F.B.' wrote in the **Gardeners' Chronicle** of July 1941, *'When one sees numbers of tents pitched and occupied by our troops, stretching almost throughout the whole length of some of our cherished herbaceous borders, one wishes that a larger number* of our fighting men were plant lovers. Although the area in which these tents were pitched had been requisitioned, no intimation had been given that soldier-men were actually to live and sleep on masses of herbaceous and other plants. Nevertheless, one has to be philosophic and realize that this site was chosen because of the camouflage effect of the many shrubs and climbing roses that form the background of the borders.'

Left

Boys from King's School, Rochester, in a temporary classroom in Scotney Castle, Lamberhurst, in June 1940. HMSO

Below

Business billet: Eyhurst Court, the new home of the evacuated Atlas Insurance Company. Many evacuated businesses leased country manors. On the right is the staff canteen. It was typical for temporary buildings to litter the grounds of country houses.

By June 1940 it was estimated that 2 million acres of gardens, parks, and pastures had been ploughed up under national orders to raise edible crops, or otherwise destroyed for encampments, airfields, tank training or artillery practice. Herbaceous borders were uprooted, statues and garden buildings used for artillery practice, and driveways disappeared under trucks and tanks. At Wrest Park, Bedfordshire, employees of the Sun Insurance Company there for the duration of the war, cultivated some of the flowerbeds although the lawns were ploughed up for potatoes by Land Girls, and thousands of trees in the woodland gardens were cut down by 'lumberjills' of the Timber Corps. Everywhere parks sprouted Nissen huts and trenches, tank ranges and hospital dormitories. Nissen huts in the park at Longleat inspired a schoolgirl evacuee there to write:

'The mystery of a Nissen hut, (So elusive, so appealing),
How much of the thing is side? Or is the whole thing ceiling?'

Easton Lodge (Essex) housed the 386th Medium Bomb group of the 9th US Army Air Force. Their combat photographer recalls his Nissen hut accommodation in the grounds *'in a grove of very tall trees . . . which were the home of hundreds of ravens. We enjoyed a magnificent frontal view of the Great House*

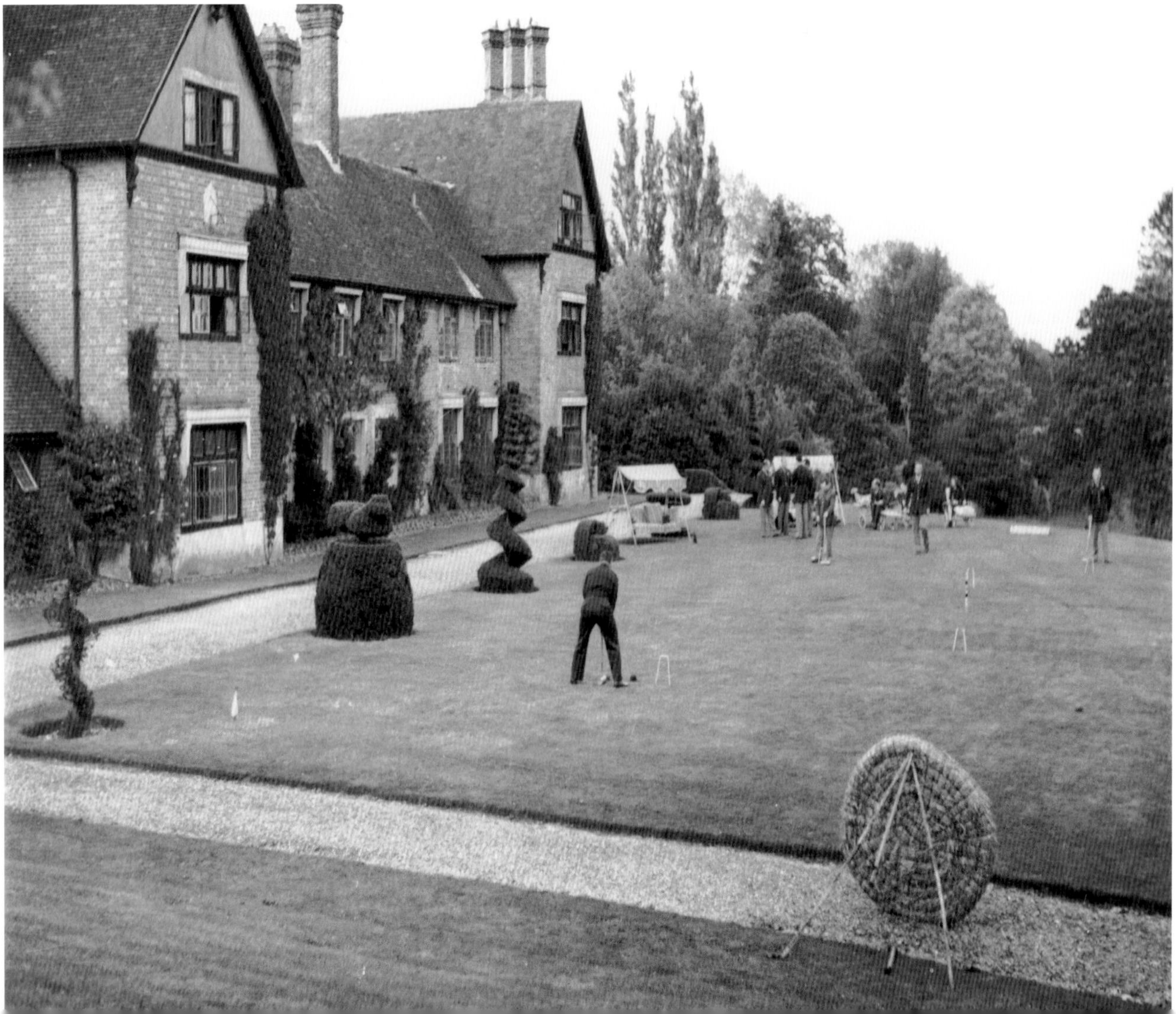

with its ivied façade.' **Country Life** magazine offered its readers the 'Country Life Emergency Hut', a sort of glorified tool-hut which could be used as offices for government officials, or similar, rather than having them in the house, *'a modest little building that would not be unsightly in any situation, and its particular merit is that after it has served its wartime purpose it can be used as a garden house, storeroom, estate office, and so forth'.*

For most country house parks and gardens the war was to mean more than simply the imposition of an aesthetically unappealing Nissen hut, or the temporary loss of gardeners to the call-up. A whole way of life was under threat, and whether the owners responded with enthusiasm to their country's call to turn orchid houses and parkland over to tomatoes and potatoes, or desperately tried to hang on to their herbaceous borders, life was never to be the same again. In some cases, where the owners had already seen the social and financial effects of the First World War, or were already in government circles, this premonition of absolute change was tangible. Writing from Knole (Kent), James Pope-Hennessy told Clarissa Churchill that *'the great dank gardens in the evening light with wide turf alleys and rhododendron flowers, and urns on pedestals; and the house and elms . . . [were] only an illusion of peace and the previous tranquil world, and the whole ordered landscape seemed quivering with imminent destruction'.*

Below
Not all country house parks and gardens were unfortunate enough to house tanks and trenches: Stanbridge Earls (Hants) became a rest and recuperation centre for US airmen. The owner, Walter Hutchinson, lived in a caravan in the park while the airmen inhabited the house and gardens. HMSO

Adaptation and Change in the Country House Garden

Regardless of whether the new residents were army, air force, intelligence or evacuees, all had to be fed, and the walled kitchen gardens and parklands of the English country house came under more pressure than ever before to produce. In many cases head gardeners who remained in their posts were forced to dig up or un-house precious plants nurtured for years and replace them with vegetables to feed the incoming hordes. Life became very different, with no fuel for boilers, a much-reduced workforce, and no replacement tools or glass available. To be overseen by county horticultural advisors who intructed them on what to plant and sometimes how to plant it often proved hard to bear for skilled horticulturalists, as these men were. It is a tribute to their sense of duty that so many of them uprooted precious and rare plants and buckled down under the new regime of productivity.

As early as September 1939 the **Gardeners' Chronicle** reported that *'All so-called luxury gardening will have to be curtailed for various reasons, such as lack of labour, fuel for glasshouses, taxation, and probably petrol for motor-mowers etc., so economy will have to be practised and this can be accomplished in many ways. Of first importance is the handling of a small staff so as to concentrate on work which is pressing at any moment. . . . Pleasure garden work, such as the mowing of lawns, will proceed normally this year, but next year it may have to be curtailed and probably only the lawns surrounding the house will be kept in order; there-*

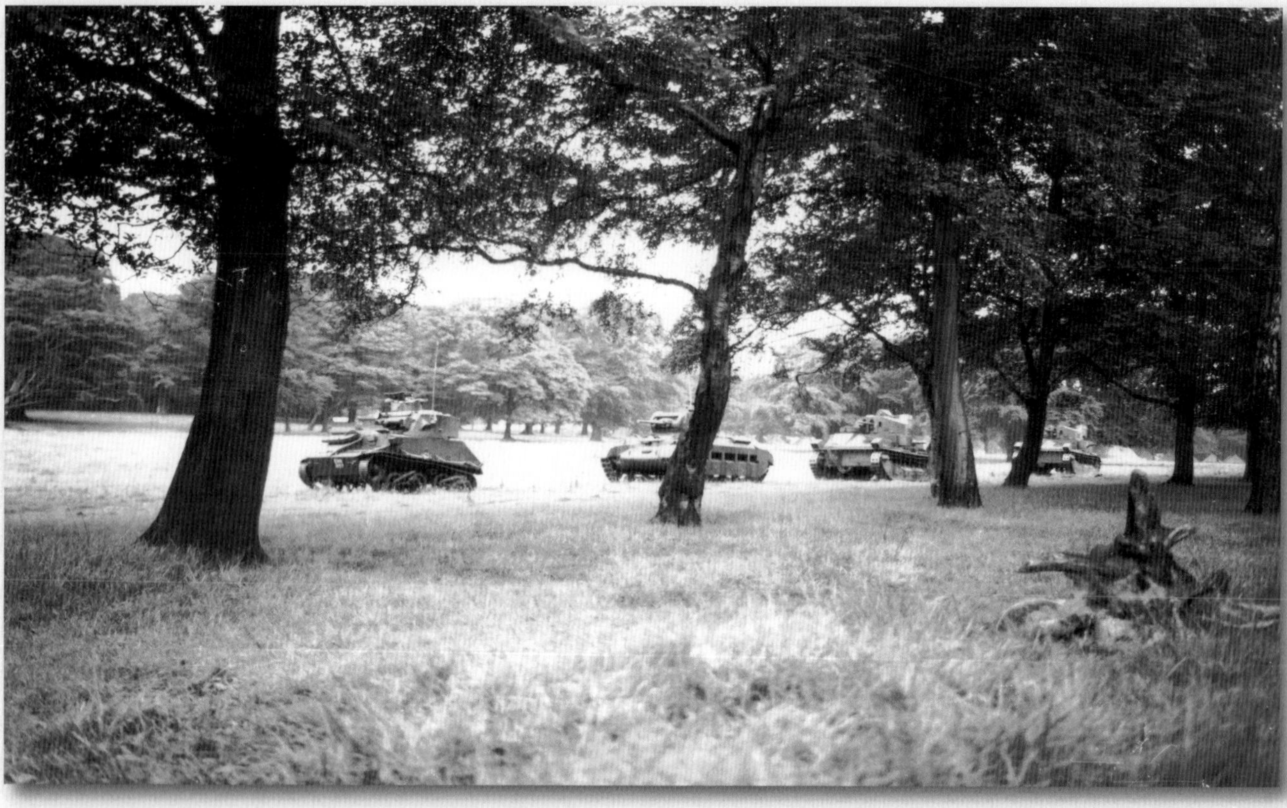

Above
This avenue of oaks in the park at Knowsley Park, Prescot, must have been taken aback to see a convoy of tanks on manoeuvres in the ancient parkland. HMSO

fore large extensive lawns that cannot be machine mowed may be fenced off and sheep allowed to feed the grass down'.

Country houses which, for whatever reason, were deemed unsuitable for use as schools, hospitals or billets, could still have their parks and pleasure grounds requisitioned. If there was a nearby village then parts of the lawns and park might be dug up for allotments, as well as having their kitchen gardens taken over for wartime produce. At Cannizaro House, Wimbledon, the proximity to the suburbs made the grounds ideal for allotments and between 40 and 80 were cultivated in the grounds at any one time during the war. In addition its sunken garden was used for growing buckwheat and small haricot beans to feed the increased numbers of hens on the estate. The **Gardeners' Chronicle** of September 1942 reported that *'Cabbages and Brussels sprouts are now growing in centuries-old lawns and extensive herbaceous borders at Longford Castle, the Earl of Radnor's seat. Five or six tons is the estimated yield of onions planted in the famous sunken Italian garden near the Avon.'*

Although immune from requisitioning for reasons of security, royal estates were turned over to food production during the war. By late summer 1943, Sandringham was producing heavy yields of potatoes, parsnips, beetroot, oats and rye, among other crops. The estate golf course had been ploughed up, along with the lawns in front of the house and the

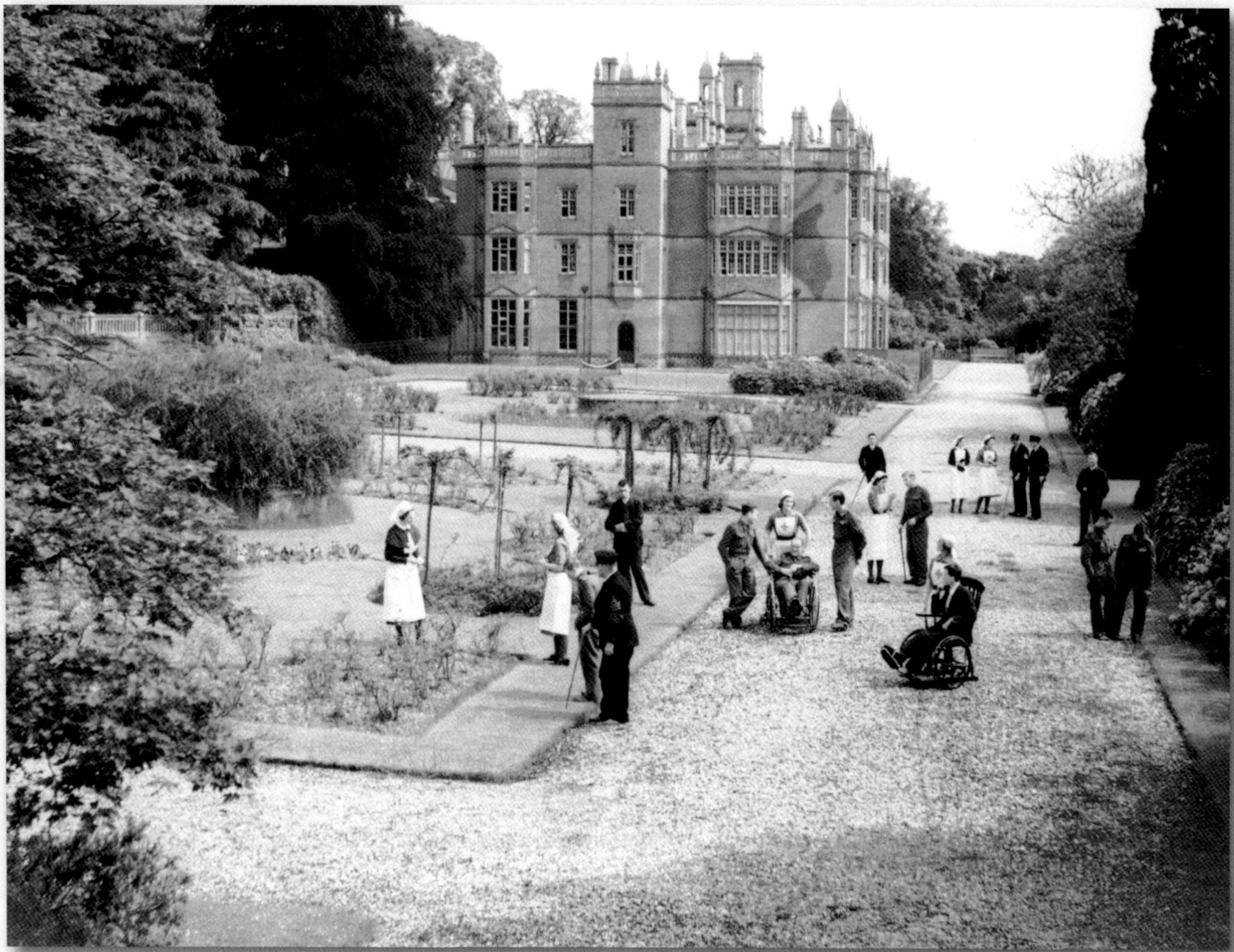

Above
This (unnamed) country house in Berkshire in the care of the Red Cross and St John kept up some of its decorative gardens, to the delight of the wounded recovering there in 1941. Many gardens incorporated vegetables and fruits into the immaculately cut beds and borders. HMSO

area next to the church. Beetroot and parsnips filled the beds in the ornamental flower garden, and rye flourished on the lawns. Fourteen Land Army girls worked on the estate and the royal 'example' was said to have created considerable interest. Only slightly less prestigious and productive was Blenheim, the home of the Duke and Duchess of Marlborough. Here beet, carrots and other vegetables with decorative foliage were planted in the flower garden for ornamental effect.

Professional gardeners of appropriate age could be conscripted even when actively employed on home food production. As the war progressed and conscription widened this caused intense strain on larger gardens, which had been accustomed to operate with large labour forces. Even those that had put all their efforts into food production for the war effort found themselves lacking the staff to keep up the contribution, let alone maintain any hothouses, bedding, or specialist collections.

Economy and labour-saving tips in the garden press included suggestions that were common enough in suburban gardens and allotments even in peacetime, but would not normally have passed the rigorous standards of the country house garden. Burning garden rubbish and spreading it on the vegetable garden; mowing lawns only once every two weeks or less; saving pea and bean sticks from one year to the next; discontinuing early forcing of vegetables and fruits; stopping all watering. Large flowerbeds were to be turfed over or sown with grass seed, leaving cultivation of tall annuals such as larkspur and scabious for decorating the house rather than beds of cutting flowers. Often the head gardener was left to make his own decisions as to what in the garden should be kept up and what allowed to lapse, as owners retreated to their other smaller properties, to avoid the influx of new residents.

The **Gardeners' Chronicle** in October 1940 told its readers that *'There must be many gardeners who find themselves in difficult positions because their employers have moved elsewhere for the duration of the war, and the evacuated home has been occupied by either private, business or official evacuees. In such cases the gardener remains and his duty to his employer may also remain, in as much as it may be his business to cultivate all the fruits and vegetables possible, and send them on to his employer's new residence, or to market to sell them locally. In other instances it may be his duty to supply the evacuees with fruits, flowers and vegetables.'*

Registering to go into official food production had considerable benefits for country house owner and gardener. Fuel became available for glass-housing, and heating pipes could be maintained and mended, along with damaged glass. Although crops were largely dictated by the ministry inspectors, there was always the opportunity for catch-crops of flowers, or for maintaining established vines and peaches on the back wall of the glasshouses. At Nuneham Park, near Oxford, peaches shared a glasshouse with lettuce, carrots and tomatoes. At Chilton the ornamental rose house was sacrificed for cauliflowers, while at Lulworth Castle (Dorset) the vines had to share their glasshouse with tomatoes, although the tomatoes fared rather badly.

In June 1940 new regulations were passed which permitted the sale of produce from private gardens, including country house kitchen gardens, without the special licence normally required during peacetime. This encouraged those with large areas of garden to consider putting down more vegetables than they needed for their own use. Queues formed on 'sale days' at many country houses that were close to urban areas, but for more distant and secluded houses a lorry scheme was introduced. At Chilton (Bucks) produce was collected and taken to Newbury where it was collected into a 'pool' from where it was distributed to shops at controlled prices. Schemes to collect and sell on vegetables were also managed by the Women's Institute and the Rural Community Councils, as well as the National Allotment Society. Wayside stalls sprang up all over the countryside as it was realised that a glut of perishable produce could, after all, bring some benefit, although it was largely the towns that stood in need of extra produce.

Women also played a conspicuous role in the country house park and garden, as Land Army girls were used to replace conscripted gardeners. Many head gardeners found this influx of women difficult to adapt to after a lifetime of a 'male only' culture. The traditional gardeners' 'bothy', used in peace-time to house the army of trainee and under-gardeners, was hastily converted to use by the Land Army. Unlike the sad fate of many a country house interior, this often resulted in an improvement in the décor and condition of the bothy.

Conscription of Gardeners

Country house gardens in the early part of the twentieth century were traditionally labour intensive, and hierarchical. A bevy of pot-boys and journeyman gardeners (so named as they journeyed around the country to progress their career experience) were overseen by under-gardeners and foreman gardeners. At the top of the pyramid was the head gardener, often a man of fearsome reputation and appearance, and immense knowledge. Requiring on average 'a man and a boy' for every acre of garden, the country house kitchen garden had evolved in a period when labour was cheap and plentiful. It had taken a knock during the First World War (when so many men never returned), but had survived to recover in the interwar period. By 1939 there were tens of thousands of country house kitchen gardens, all with their full complement of staff, almost all of whom were male.

Contrary to popular belief, being a gardener did not necessarily exempt you from call-up, although the exact conditions, ages liable, and so on, varied during the course of the war. Many young gardeners were already members of the popular Territorial Army and these were called up in the first weeks of the conflict, leaving foremen wondering how they would fill their places. Men whose garden work was in the decorative gardens, producing flowers or working in the hothouses, mowing the lawns, or general duties, were next in line if they were of appropriate age.

Harry Dodd, who was an under-gardener in private service at Ashburnham, was conscripted into the Royal Sussex Regiment. Here he found he was among '*no end of gardeners, grooms, chauffeurs and footmen, and apart from two young school-masters, we'd all come from the same sort of estate life*'. By the time that Harry left Ashburnham for the army a couple of weeks after war was declared, four or five other gardeners on the estate had already been called up. The age and conditions for con-scription changed as the war progressed; in March 1940 men of 25 years of age or over who were registered as gardeners were placed on a reserved category and not liable for military service at that time. Then, on 27 April 1940, men were required to register if they had been born between 1 January 1913 and 27 April 1920. If they were engaged on food production they would be put on the reserved occupation list, but further applications for post-ponement might have to be made. If employed in decorative horticulture they were not held to be in a reserved occupation. By June 1940 the needs of food production were even more pressing and the age for reservation fell to twenty-one for those primarily involved in food production or market gardening, and eighteen for those in agriculture. However at the same time general gardeners, bulb-growers, flower growers and even poultrymen had their reserved status withdrawn. This meant that many gardeners suddenly found themselves

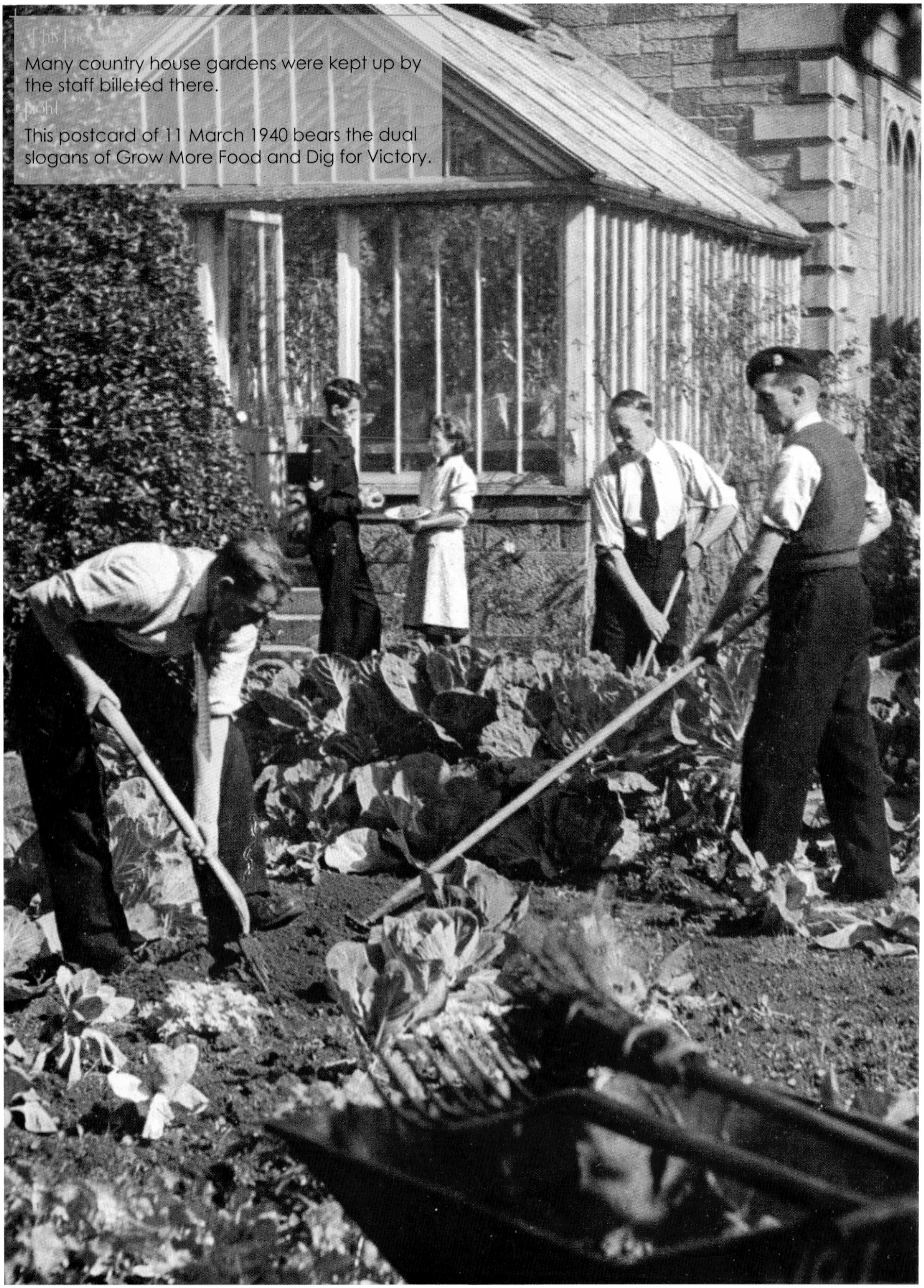

This page

Many country house gardens were kept up by the staff billeted there.

Right

This postcard of 11 March 1940 bears the dual slogans of Grow More Food and Dig for Victory.

liable for immediate call-up. Many of these men had skills and training that would make them valuable in agriculture and they were encouraged to register for agricultural work. Whether they went into the forces or agriculture, they left behind them huge gaps in the country house workforce of gardeners.

Even if a garden was engaged in private food production for the family and surrounding village the gardeners were still liable for call-up. By May 1941 the famous gardens at Bodnant (North Wales) were reduced to advertising for 'Youths of 16–17 with some gardening experience' to replace those called into service. Regulations on reserved occupations and age were constantly changing during the war and both owners and employees had a responsibility to keep up to date for fear of prosecution.

'Sir, My gardener received this morning a week's notice to join an infantry training centre of a county regiment other than his own. He is a skilled gardener, aged 32, height 5ft. 1in., eyesight defective. I know the needs of private individuals, however large and productive their gardens may be, must give way to all other considerations in wartime, but surely there is no sense in making an infantry soldier of a man whose skill, if properly utilised in the public service, could produce extra food for a large number of the population. I do not know if it was a misguided sense of humour that prompted the individual responsible to send out the calling-up notice in an envelope bearing the slogan, 'Dig for Victory – Grow More Food', but I sincerely hope that in future, in calling up gardeners and agricultural workers for service in the Army, this exhortation may be omitted.

I am, Sir, Your obedient servant J.H. Westley (Lieutenant-Colonel).' Letter to the **Times**, 25 February 1941.

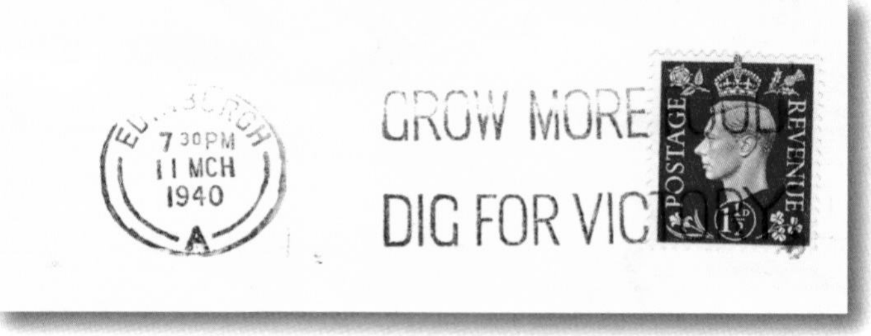
7 30PM
11 MCH
1940
GROW MORE
DIG FOR VIC
POSTAGE
REVENUE

In November 1941 the Minister of Agriculture specifically stated that *'except in the largest of gardens it is expected that the owners and occupiers will themselves undertake the work of cultivating the ground without calling upon the assistance of able-bodied men eligible for national service'*. This must have proved something of a shock for titled and aristocratic estate owners, although perhaps they safely came under the heading of 'the largest of gardens'.

Gardeners and Employment

Despite the restrictions of wartime, or perhaps because of them, there was still an active employment market for gardeners of all sorts in small and large country houses. From advertisements one can track the increasing desperation of many such house owners, and also the shift in availability of gardeners. Almost from the outbreak of war, advertisements for 'Gardeners Wanted' in the **Gardeners' Chronicle** began to specify 'not under 40 years of age', 'over military age', and, even at this early stage 'lady gardener' (although as the last was for a nurses' home it may have been a general rule of the house). There were still many that desired 'improvers' of age 17–18, or did not specify, but these became rarer as time passed. By 1944 advertisements became more desperate, and less numerous, and included a large number wanting men with experience of practical vegetable and fruit production rather than

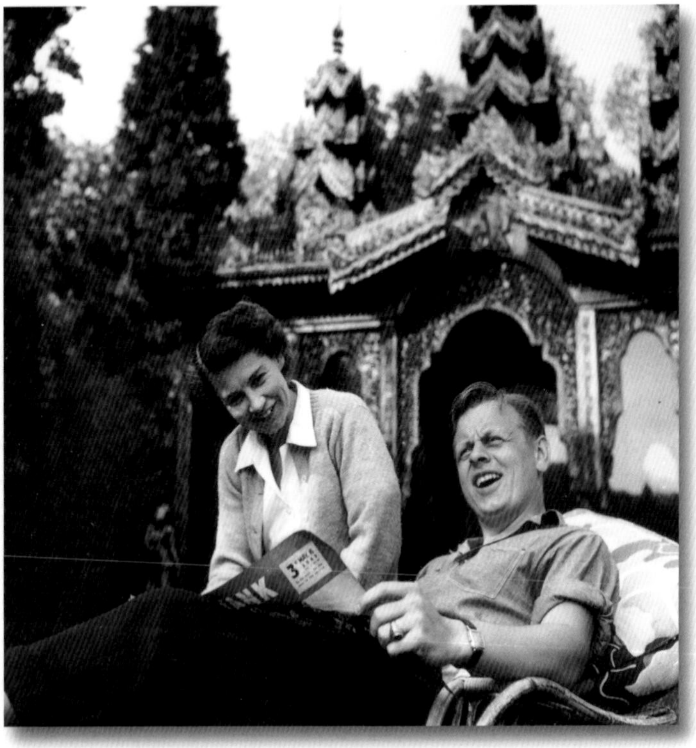

Above
R&R (rest and recuperation) for US airmen, Stanbridge Earls. An unusual garden 'pagoda' can be seen in the background of this picture of Lt M.V. Judas from Illinois. HMSO
Right
This poster is aimed at servicemen, encouraging them to become involved in Digging for Victory. HMSO

the usual peacetime emphasis on 'glasshouses' and shrubs. Those with a pessimistic eye to the future often specified ex-servicemen, or those over conscription age, and there was also a considerable increase in the number of advertisements specifying women gardeners.

Some country houses were fortunate enough to be requisitioned after the introduction of the 'soldier-gardener' scheme. This War Department scheme identified experienced and trained gardeners who had been enlisted in the services, and actually used their skills to maintain productive gardens in requisitioned properties. The scheme's demands had to come second to that of the fighting front, so the men chosen were often those less suited to actual battle, technically termed 'low medical category', but nevertheless several thousand soldier-gardeners were deployed, sometimes supplemented by civilian gardeners taken on to boost production and make the billeted units self-sufficient. In 1943 troops of Southern Command produced 10,400 tons of vegetables by utilising kitchen gardens and parks around requisitioned houses and land surrounding hospitals and encampments, as well as the much smaller plots around AA posts, searchlights and barracks. Much of this was at the expense of the original layout of the parks and gardens, but by the time that tank movements, manoeuvres and mock battles had taken place, there was often little left of this earlier aesthetic design.

Some country house walled gardens were also taken on by nearby farmers or speculative gardeners and run as market gardens, supplying either the local population direct or selling on through government pools. At Aynhoe Park the then gardener Ted Humphris was encouraged to run the greenhouses and kitchen garden on his own account as a market garden. Supported at first only by his wife and son, and later by a 'sturdy girl', he produced fruit and vegetables throughout the war. In order to make the gardens efficient hedges were grubbed up, lawns allowed to grow, fruit trees taken up and paths removed. Fruit and vegetables were sold on two evenings a week and queues formed most evenings. A self-imposed rationing system was introduced when demand for tomatoes was too great. The army, which soon moved into the Anyhoe Park, also

..every available piece of land must be cultivated

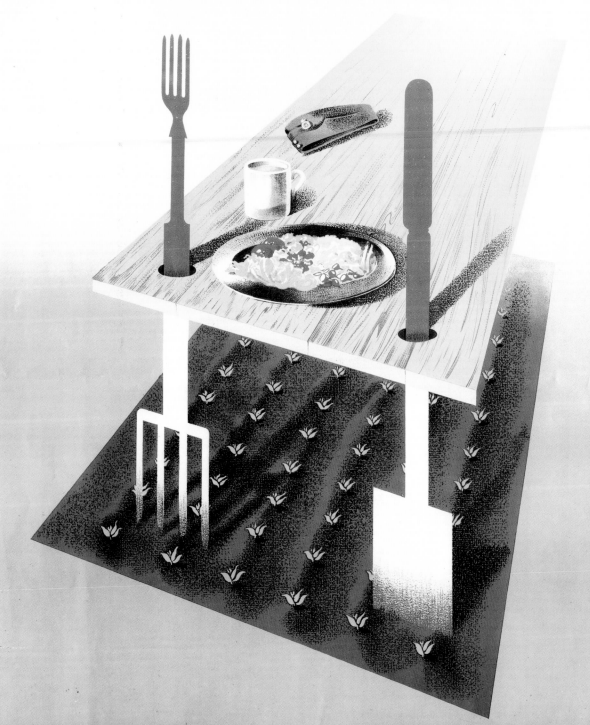

GROW YOUR OWN FOOD
supply your own cookhouse

PRINTED FOR H.M. STATIONERY OFFICE BY J. WEINER LTD. LONDON. W.C.I.   51—4749 purchased produce, although their presence created difficulties. At Wrest Park (Beds) the kitchen garden was also taken on for market gardening, being ideally suited as it lay between the main house and the village of Silsoe, on the main road to Luton.

Scepticism in the Face of Adversity

Enthusiasm among country house owners for the changes imposed upon them or requested from them varied widely. As ever, class divisions arose with suspicions that some owners were not pulling their weight. One lady who went to garden at a country house near Salisbury recalled that *'On Monday we are to be photographed for the press and they want us to be setting out our onion plants for the new bed. We call it "the onion bed" but Lady L. says it is to be known as "the old rose garden" to show what she has sacrificed I suppose.'*

The well-known satirical 'Lady Addle' columns written by Mary Dunn for **Punch** magazine ran throughout the war and included many comical gems on the attitude of the upper classes to the needs of wartime. Regretting the sad decay of the once exquisite lawns and flowerbeds of pre-war houses Lady Addle declared that: *The beautiful clock golf course at Coot's Bladder . . . is now given over to groundsel for the estate canaries, the Duke of Quorn's fernery is a beetery, whilst Lord Sealyham's famous eighteenth century maze was sacrificed to make asparagus beds for his evacuees; an extremely difficult task, involving endless labour digging the beds in all the torturous twists and turns of the maze.'* Lady Blanche Addle's own contributions to the home front in the garden at her 'country estate

at Bengers' included unsuccessful attempts to grow tomatoes in the Weeping Willow walk and cultivating mustard and cress on the statuary on the garden terrace. All were doomed to failure, as were the radishes, which suffered from *'slut weevil'*, and the crop of early parsley *'devoured by fell sod fly'*. *'So ill-fated did we seem in this direction that at one time I thought it might be best to yield to Dame Nature's stern decrees and made all plans for encouraging the woolly aphis in our orchards, as I felt sure there must be some method of gathering and spinning their product to save shipping space for wool.'* Lady Addle also recommends that evacuees be fed a diet of dandelions, groundsel, plantain or even fresh lawn mowings – an extreme form of the diets actually recommended in more serious pieces that appeared in magazines such as the **Tatler**.

Although in most cases scepticism of the contributions made by country house garden owners was unjustified, in April 1944 there were still some country houses that seemed to have maintained hothouses for flowers and rarities. Advertisements in the gardening press included staff wanted for 'well known shrub gardens', 'head gardener experienced in grapes, etc.', 'head working gardener with knowledge of orchid culture,' expert orchid grower', and 'gardener/handyman with experience in greenhouse work'; clear signs that some country house gardens at least carried on as normal. Throughout the war the **Gardeners' Chronicle** included their usual 'work in progress' articles on various aspects of the country house garden including 'The Orchid Houses' (written by the gardener to Lionel de Rothschild), 'Fruits under Glass' (by the gardener to the Earl of Bessborough at Stansted Park), and 'The Flower Garden' (by the gardener to Jeremiah Colman at Gatton Park). Although some of these mention the difficulties of maintaining standards during wartime, others, notably J.M. Richards, in 'The Flower Garden', make no reference to any changes or restrictions in their gardening practices. For Richards *The New Year [1940] brings new hopes and activities . . . the gardener's pocket book will be full of notes made during the year just ended: it should contain ideas that have come to his mind with records of successes or failures of bedding and colour schemes under his own charge and those seen during visits to other gardens or parks'.* March 1940 saw the **Gardeners' Chronicle** carry advertisements such as 'Wanted: large clumps of Blue Agapanthus', alongside offers of cyclamen seedlings and bulbs of *Calanthe Veitchii*, and chrysanthemums – this when many a suburban gardener was busy digging up his bulbs and tender plants and Stephen Cheveley was writing of the sacrifices he made of his entire collection of rare chrysanthemums and dahlias. In the words of the Institute of Landscape Architects, charms were clearly NOT always being sacrificed.

Writing on 'The Vegetable Garden' department, G.F. Hallet (gardener to the Rt Hon. Lord Lilford at Lilford Hall, Oundle) was somewhat more practical, if not enthusiastic, about the role of his garden 'department' in wartime: *the kitchen garden is undoubtedly the most important part of the garden, for supplies must be forthcoming every day of the year. I advise young gardeners to take a more intelligent interest in this department than they seem to do. It is quite necessary that they should, for no small amount of thought is necessary to maintain a regular* supply of vegetables and salads. During the present crisis we shall, no doubt, see an extended interest taken in vegetable cultivation. I will gladly give all the help I can.' Northern gardeners (represented by the gardener at Kilmahew Castle) were also expecting the kitchen garden *'to be worked and cropped to its utmost capacity, which will be an extra responsibility to the "chief".'*

One East Anglian newspaper told the following story. *'A colonel home after four years in Burma, asked his gardener how the lawns were looking. "Well Sir", was the reply, "you are having spuds off the tennis lawn tonight, and cook tells me you are having a special salad from the croquet lawn".'*

Below

The two princesses, Elizabeth and Margaret, digging for victory in a posed publicity photograph, taken at one of the royal estates.

Garden Lover's Calendar, 1941

Enjoying the garden despite it all

Although the common vision of wartime is of gardens devoted to productivity, most gardens still retained some flowers, and keen gardeners ensured that they still had a stock of perennials for replacing their prized borders 'when peace comes'. Even at the outbreak of hostilities flowers were considered an essential element by many, and as the war continued there was often more, rather than less, emphasis on flowers. A need for 'something to brighten the gloom' was the constant refrain even among those who were dedicated victory diggers. Gardens and public parks also became the focus for what little rest and recreation there was. Holidays at home, victory garden shows, weddings, model allotments, outdoor music recitals: all were used as opportunities to relax and enjoy what few pleasures were available on the home front. Birthdays and Christmases were another opportunity to swap plants and enjoy the garden despite it all.

Easter holidays during wartime were no longer a period of Easter eggs and country jaunts. Looking forward to the Easter holiday of April 1941, **Garden Work** envisaged *'everywhere, weather permitting, on gardens and allotments, strenuous efforts will be made to overtake arrears of work'*. Seaside trips were replaced with trenching and manuring, Christmas holidays were full of gardening catalogues and wrapped seed packets.

Flowers could brighten everyone's life: Margaret Gormally (née Brown) recalls that *'I contracted polio in 1940 so up to the age of 9 . . . I spent a lot of time away from school and in dad's garden. My fondest memories are of lounging on a day bed surrounded by glorious flower borders, my dad's favourite being sweet peas. We had a lovely green lawn nearest to the back of the house, with little areas set aside to sit and take in all the lovely colours, flowering currant, lilac, gladioli, roses and the special sweet peas. A cottage garden but beyond was a fence screening off a rougher area where we could play; this was the part that was dug up and became my Dad's War Garden.'*

Mr Charles Graves wrote in **Garden Work**: *'To read "A second sowing of melons should now be made", or "Tulips to flower next January should now be potted" brought back a sense of proportion and reminded one that gardens and other things which made life worth living would survive.'*

FLOWERS IN 1941

Owing to the war, the greater part of your garden will doubtless be devoted to the cultivation of vegetable crops this year. Dig for victory and grow more food by all means, but don't forget to leave some space for flowers as well. In the smallest garden there is usually an odd corner or a neglected patch that can be turned to good account by the addition of a few colourful blooms.

Flowers can play a far more important part in our lives in war-time than you may at first imagine. Not only do they brighten our homes by providing colour and harmony, for table and interior decoration, but they do something more—they stimulate and brighten our mental outlook too !

Remember also, that the tending and growing of flowers soothe mind and nerves as nothing else can in times of stress and strain.

In the following pages Ryders offer the widest possible variety of flower seeds and most of them are available in the standard twopenny packet. From these famous seeds you will get that complete satisfaction which has been the enjoyment of Ryders' customers for so many years.

For a brilliant and profuse floral display sow RYDERS'—THE SEEDS FOR RESULTS.

Left
For many the overflowing herbaceous border was only a fond memory by 1941.
Above
'Flowers can play a far more important part in our lives in war-time than you may at first imagine.'

The Thorny Question of Flowers and Roses

On 30 September 1939 the **Gardeners' Chronicle** discussed the thorny question of flowers and came to the conclusion that: *'A question which presents itself to the mind of every gardener is – What about the flower garden in wartime? Sometimes, alas! There is no question for owner and gardener alike are engaged on war-work and so are the womenfolk also. But where some labour skilled or unskilled, is available for garden work, ought any of it be diverted to the flower garden? In our opinion the answer is an emphatic "Yes". For the time being everyone who can do so should keep up some sort of a flower garden . . . There will be some who dissent from this opinion holding that in such times as these every atom of national energy should be concentrated on work immediately connected with national security. We would answer that relaxation is the nutriment on which exertion thrives.'*

For those who did not feel they could set aside areas specifically for flowers the **Gardeners' Chronicle** suggested that they plant vegetables in decorative style. *'What foliage is handsomer than carrot and seakale, and what purple is more emphatic than that of the garden beet?'* Runner beans had of course long been grown for decorative flowers, and in France were only grown for their flowers. In 1943 **Garden Work** recommended a range of wall plants, shrubs, cut flowers and even the replanting of dwarf dahlias. Favourite flowers might also have been kept to one side when the rest of the borders were dug up. Peonies were the favourite flower of Mr Murphy, a worker at the Derby factory of Rolls-Royce. Although the back garden of the family's suburban semi was given over in wartime to the usual array of vegetables, fruits and ducks, the front and small side passage garden formed a temporary home to his beloved peonies.

Some wartime gardening books ignored flowers altogether. The nearest that the **Daily Mail**'s **Grow It Yourself: Food from the Garden in Wartime** got to flowers was 'a bunch of herbs', and **War-Time Gardening** by John Sydney also avoided any flowering frivolity. **Gardening Made Easy** by the Miall sisters was kinder to the flower gardener, admitting an entire chapter on 'The Flower Garden'. Most popular features of the period were rock gardens, rose gardens, pergolas and arches, and of course the inevitable borders and lawns. A crazy paving path completed the image with perhaps a bird bath or circular pond of the same material. Rockeries were the subject of endless articles and letters in the gardening press, but largely escaped any accusation of lack of patriotism. There were few vegetables that could be grown on a rockery!

In the 1943 edition of their book, **Gardening Made Easy,** Agnes and Beatrice Miall wrote, *'A bird bath is a great joy to all bird lovers, and could be placed in a suitable position, in full view from the windows of the house, so that in winter it can be observed from indoors. Birds are mainly to be considered as the gardener's friends, so you will not be doing any harm in encouraging them.'*

Flower seed continued to be available throughout the war, despite restrictions on the area of land the nurseries were allowed to devote to non-foodstuffs. In 1940 the 'finest strain of early flowering cyclamen seed' could be had for the same price as the 20-packet novice vegetable seed collection

advertised in the same edition of the **Gardeners'**
Chronicle, alongside roses, peonies, calanthe, and
gladioli.

Flowers for cutting were always popular and, as
supplies dwindled at the florists, 'grow your own'
was the obvious solution for celebrations and
events, as well as day-to-day house decoration –
although it was not until the 1950s that flower
arranging really took off as an essential skill of the
housewife. The most common and easiest to grow
were the perennials golden rod (solidago), peonies,
irises, heleniums, coreopsis, Michaelmas daisies,
phloxes, rudbeckias, delphiniums, lupins, gypsophila, galegas, flag iris, and moon daisies. Sweet
peas were a traditional favourite – raised for show
and for their scent. Much-loved varieties included
Gigantic, a white flower with overpowering scent,
Patricia Unwin, Lady Gay, Crimson Emblem, and
Highlander. Unwin Ltd, of Cambridgeshire,
claimed that sweet peas were *The Ideal Flowers for*
wartime growing: easy to grow, adaptable, and
economical in time, space and cost. Bought as
rooted plants they could be hardened off and
transplanted anywhere – garden or allotment.
First-class varieties cost 3s for 36 from Unwin, or
5s 3d for 72 plants, post free. The complete ease
of growing was slightly belied by the inclusion in
Unwin's advert of the offer of a 56-page guide with
culture hints and ideas. Carnations and pinks were
also popular and made long-lasting cut flower
arrangements, and were grown both outdoors and
under glass.

Lupins and phloxes were two of the most
important border plants of the period. **Garden**
Work advised that *'nothing gives greater pleasure*

> **A list of shrubs recommended in Garden**
> **Work magazine in 1943 to brighten the**
> **border and the garden wall.**
>
> Abutilon vitifolium
> Ampelopsis Veitchii
> Berberidopsis corallina
> Camellia japonica
> Ceanothus veitchianus
> Ceanothus thyrsiflorus
> Chimonanthus fragrans
> Clematis Jackmanii (various hybrids)
> Clematis montana
> Clematis rubens
> Clematis macropetala
> Cotoneasters
> Japanese quince (Cydonia Japonica)
> Garrya elliptica
> Jasminum nudiflorum
> Magnolia grandiflora
> Magnolia delavayi
> Polygonum Baldscuanicum (knot weed)
> Prunus triloba
> Pyracanthus rogersiana
> Solanum crispum
> Virginia creeper
> Vitis Coignetiae
> Wisteria chinensis
> Wisteria floribunda

or a finer display than a good selection of lupins'.
Much work had been done on the raising of new
strains in the interwar years and entire nurseries
were dedicated to lupin fanciers. Two-tone lupins
were particularly admired. 'Kenneth Wicksteed'

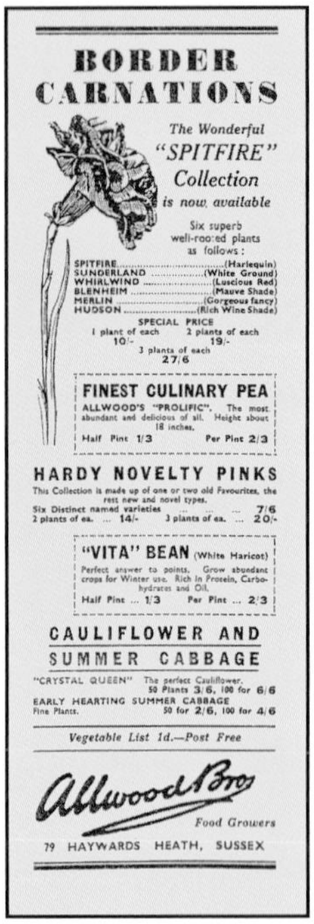
BORDER CARNATIONS
The Wonderful "SPITFIRE" Collection is now available
Six superb well-rooted plants as follows:
SPITFIRE ....(Harlequin)
SUNDERLAND ....(White Ground)
WHIRLWIND ....(Luscious Red)
BLENHEIM ....(Mauve Shade)
MERLIN ....(Gorgeous fancy)
HUDSON ....(Rich Wine Shade)
SPECIAL PRICE
1 plant of each 10/- 2 plants of each 19/-
3 plants of each 27/6
FINEST CULINARY PEA
ALLWOOD'S "PROLIFIC". The most abundant and delicious of all. Height about 18 inches.
Half Pint 1/3 Per Pint 2/3
HARDY NOVELTY PINKS
This Collection is made up of one or two old Favourites, the rest new and novel types.
Six Distinct named varieties 7/6
2 plants of ea. ... 14/- 3 plants of ea. ... 20/-
"VITA" BEAN (White Haricot)
Perfect answer to points. Grow abundant crops for Winter use. Rich in Protein, Carbohydrates and Oil.
Half Pint ... 1/3 Per Pint ... 2/3
CAULIFLOWER AND SUMMER CABBAGE
"CRYSTAL QUEEN" The perfect Cauliflower. 50 Plants 3/6, 100 for 6/6
EARLY HEARTING SUMMER CABBAGE
Fine Plants. 50 for 2/6, 100 for 4/6
Vegetable List 1d.—Post Free
Allwood Bros
Food Growers
79 HAYWARDS HEATH, SUSSEX

was a rich blend of orange and flame, 'Patricia of York' was a combination of pale and deep yellow, while 'York Castle' was a rosy mauve with white standards. Yellows, pinks, mauves, purples, blues, and whites were all used to create a staggering display even in the suburban garden. Where borders were narrow this could give a startling 'children's paintbox' effect, but in more substantial gardens they could be graded at the mid or rear border to give the 'drifts' of colour so loved by followers of Gertrude Jekyll.

Phloxes were also admired when at their most colourful. **Garden Work** declared: *'A carmine eye gives that salmon "Daily Sketch" half its charm, and the white centre to the salmon pink flowers of "Eva Foster" enhance the effect considerably'*, and *'In the case of both Lupins and Phloxes the combination of colours for effect is worth while so that two or more colours may comprise one group. Lavender and pink, orange, scarlet and purple, crimson and white are all effective combinations and easily obtainable from the varieties that are available.'* Considerable care was also lavished on asters, chrysanthemums and dahlias – whether for garden display or showing. Again the larger and more colourful were usually favoured, including the 'pompom' chrysanthemums and 'ostrich plume' asters.

Colour was the order of the day in many front gardens, with an eye-watering display of pinks, oranges and scarlets produced by the favourite annuals. A gardener from West Middlesex wrote in the **Gardeners' Chronicle**: *'Orange Marigolds, Scarlet Pelargoniums, pink and red Impatiens, golden Spartium junceum [Spanish broom] and mauve Heliotrope. What a mixture! I don't care one little bit so long as the colour and perfume please old ladies, young children and the lassies from the factories and first aid posts, and even the stalwart fellows from the A.R.P. and A.F.S. posts – so there!'* If reds and pinks were not your colours then Tulipland's Pedigree Bulbs in Lincolnshire offered the rather more patriotic red, white and blue, although the blue must have been rather more of a purple as the true-blue tulip did not exist.

Not everyone followed the planting advice of the bulb growers and flower lovers. Mr A.G. Symmons of Watford was reported to have turned over his entire garden to vegetables, including his begonia beds, his 'natural aviary of thirty canaries', his rock gardens, and sunken gardens. Previously the exotic plants and birds had been a much-loved view from an adjoining public park, now it was said to be a patriotic example to all. In March 1944 Harrogate Town Council debated the question 'Flowers or Food?' One alderman said that the town was '*a very dull place these days*' and suggested they should plant a few more flowers in the town centre. Another alderman gloried in Harrogate's shabbiness; the fact that it was shabby was to its great credit, he said: *'Harrogate was 100% for the war effort in food production, it was something to be proud of.'*

Garden Work, in November 1940, wrote, *'A Correspondent this week raises the very interesting question of how to beautify a strictly utilitarian*

A.R.P. Post with the amenities of a common garden. Many of these posts have been set up on waste ground amidst drab surroundings. . . . We all trust that there is not a degree of permanency in an A.R.P. Post to justify anything but the most elementary garden. Such wishful thinking however is no valid reason why spring bulbs and the favourite biennials should not be planted now to be followed by a plethora of hardy annuals in their due season. Nor are we certain by any means that suitable quick growing climbers would not serve as camouflage to bare brickwork and divert the inquisitive eyes of those most unwelcome visitors who come to us out of the blue.'

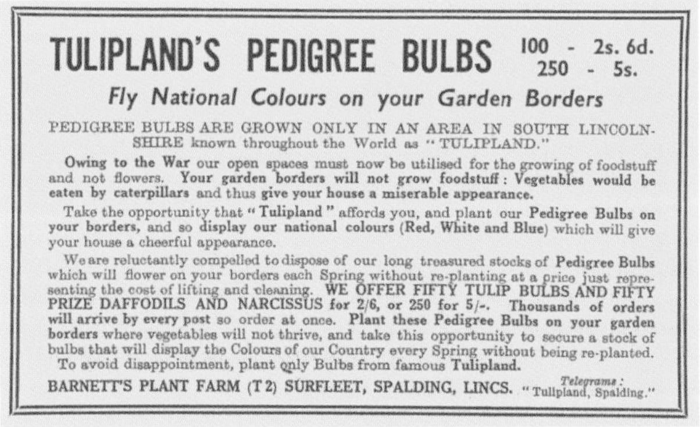

TULIPLAND'S PEDIGREE BULBS 100 - 2s. 6d. 250 - 5s.

Fly National Colours on your Garden Borders

PEDIGREE BULBS ARE GROWN ONLY IN AN AREA IN SOUTH LINCOLNSHIRE known throughout the World as "TULIPLAND."

Owing to the War our open spaces must now be utilised for the growing of foodstuff and not flowers. **Your garden borders will not grow foodstuff: Vegetables would be eaten by caterpillars** and thus **give your house a miserable appearance.**

Take the opportunity that "**Tulipland**" affords you, and plant our **Pedigree Bulbs on your borders**, and so **display our national colours (Red, White and Blue)** which will give your house a cheerful appearance.

We are reluctantly compelled to dispose of our long treasured stocks of **Pedigree Bulbs** which will flower on your borders each Spring without re-planting at a price just representing the cost of lifting and cleaning. **WE OFFER FIFTY TULIP BULBS AND FIFTY PRIZE DAFFODILS AND NARCISSUS for 2/6, or 250 for 5/-. Thousands of orders will arrive by every post** so order at once. **Plant these Pedigree Bulbs on your garden borders** where vegetables will not thrive, and take this opportunity to secure a stock of bulbs that will display the Colours of our Country every Spring without being re-planted. To avoid disappointment, plant only Bulbs from famous **Tulipland.**

BARNETT'S PLANT FARM (T 2) SURFLEET, SPALDING, LINCS. *Telegrams:* "Tulipland, Spalding."

Local and Victory Shows

The enthusiasm for gardening and the general atmosphere of 'community' led to the formation of many gardening societies during the war years. Irlam and Cadishead Garden Society was one of many set up in 1941. Their first annual show was held that year on 6 September. The organisers took pains to make clear that none of the exhibitors had grown with the aim of showing, but had instead joined the society in order to better contribute to the Dig for Victory campaign. Many of the prizes from that first show went to members who had not shown any interest in gardening before the war. Deborah Yates of Cadishead recalls the history of the Cadishead shows. In 1941 the Cadishead Garden Association held their first annual garden show in

"But I CAN'T eat potatoes. I prefer rose hips!"

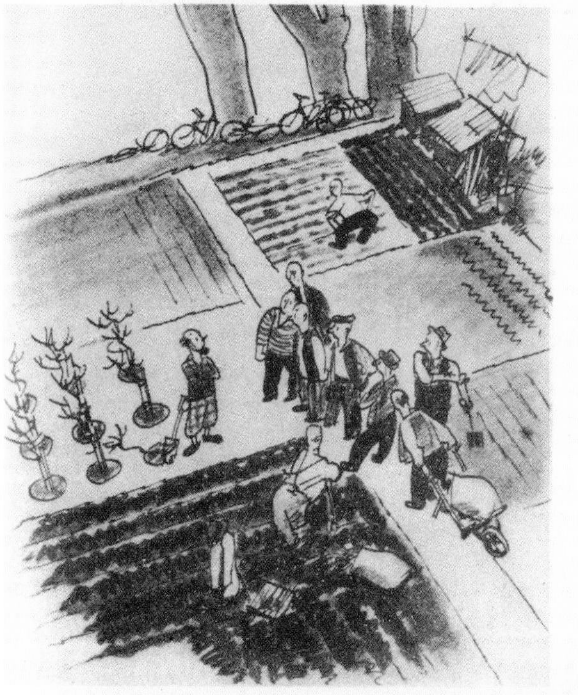

Far Left
It was not only vegetables that were named with a wartime theme. Allwoods' themed 'Spitfire' carnation collection enabled gardeners to feel patriotic, even while planting flowers. They also had a battleship collection.

Left
Tulipland (Barnett's Plant Farm, Spalding) felt that vegetables would give the house a 'miserable appearance' while their own bulbs would display the national colours.

Above
There were clear restrictions on growing flowers on allotments but as rosehips could be used for Vitamin C syrup these might just have got past the regulations.

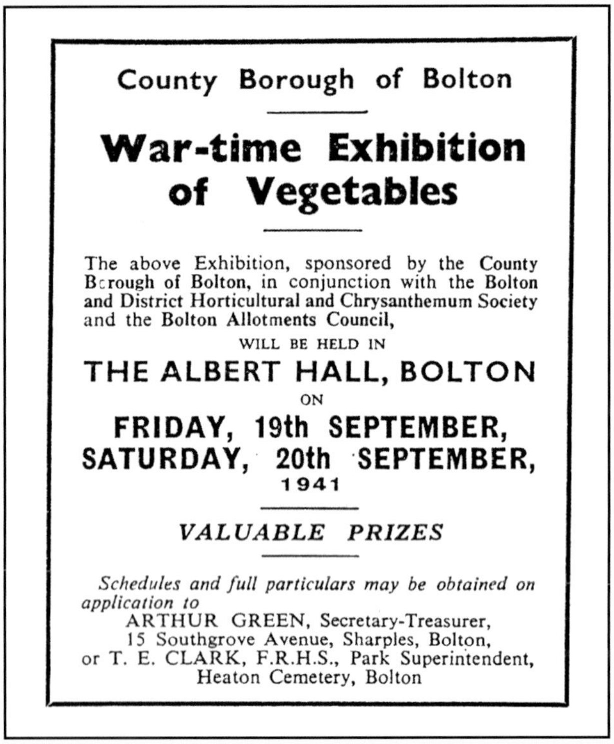

County Borough of Bolton

War-time Exhibition of Vegetables

The above Exhibition, sponsored by the County Borough of Bolton, in conjunction with the Bolton and District Horticultural and Chrysanthemum Society and the Bolton Allotments Council,

WILL BE HELD IN

THE ALBERT HALL, BOLTON

ON

FRIDAY, 19th SEPTEMBER,
SATURDAY, 20th SEPTEMBER,
1941

VALUABLE PRIZES

Schedules and full particulars may be obtained on application to
ARTHUR GREEN, Secretary-Treasurer,
15 Southgrove Avenue, Sharples, Bolton,
or T. E. CLARK, F.R.H.S., Park Superintendent,
Heaton Cemetery, Bolton

the annexe of the Lancashire Steel Employees Recreation Club. '*From the word go the show was an outstanding success. Many of the premier awards went to members who, before the war, took little or no interest in gardening. In addition to the display of fruit and vegetables, there were sideshows and guessing games and during the afternoon a bowling handicap.*' The week after the Young Farmers at Cadishead held their annual show with vegetable displays, livestock, darts, skittles and table tennis!

After the initial shock of autumn 1939, many of the local flower and produce shows resumed in summer 1940 and were held annually throughout the war. Although some made a special effort to encourage more produce than flowers, others gloried in the opportunity of having something normal to look forward to, the chance to think about something other than the war. As the war progressed many of the local shows turned into 'Victory Shows', highlighting the Dig for Victory campaign and including livestock and all kinds of preserves and foodstuffs. In August 1940 the famous Southport Annual Flower Show was mainly devoted to fruit and vegetables, with demonstrations of food production. Only a small space was given to plants and flowers, and 'gardening sundries' were on sale for the growing numbers of amateur gardeners and allotment-holders. For some parishes however the traditional flower show, with its refreshment tent and brass band, was at the heart of it all.

The **Gardeners' Chronicle** of May 1940 stated that '*Planning and preparing for the flower show, admiring other exhibits, and listening to praise of our own, divert the mind from moodily brooding over the troubles in the world outside the tent. Inside the tent, at all events, there is peace on earth and in spite, perhaps, of occasional envy, goodwill amongst men. Furthermore is not relaxation the best of all preparations for a renewal of intense effort? Therefore we say, get on with the flower show and make it gayer with flowers than ever it was and get the local band to play all of the jolly tunes in its repertoire.*'

Some people donated the profits from their gardens to charity; a letter to the editor of **My Garden** magazine, from a Mrs de Robeck, read : '*It may interest you to know I have just handed £11 to the local War Week made from produce of my vegetable garden, collected since February last. I worked it alone and am well over 70, so am pleased. Many thanks for much help from your magazine, to which I look forward.*'

As the war progressed 'produce shows' became increasingly popular. In fact so popular did the various fund-raising shows become that there were not enough weeks in the year. In Wisbech (Cambridgeshire) the Dig for Victory Drive had to be combined with the Warship Week, and the Wisbech Allotment Holders' Association included the Fur and Feather Show. Red Cross Agricultural Shows were among the most popular, with funds being raised for the charity, often combined with the St John War Organisation. In 1941 the Victory Garden Shows were instigated, planned by a special committee of the Red Cross Agricultural Fund. It was hoped that a thousand shows would take place through the summer of 1941, with the emphasis on late autumn shows 'to avoid any waste'. Although the main purpose of the victory garden was to maintain food supplies, that was no reason for there not to be fun, not to mention competitive elements. These shows were enjoyable events, showcasing not only the vegetable and fruit produce, but also with sideshows and livestock demonstrations. In 1941 over fifty local authorities had expanded their garden shows to form 'Victory Garden Week' with dog shows and general entertainments joining the horticulture. The Red Cross Agricultural Fund that organised the weeks hoped that by 1942 every urban and district council would join in, boosting their funds as well as the country's morale. In 1943 over £350,000 was raised for the Red Cross in Victory Garden fetes and shows, and in 1944 the aim was to raise £500,000. Guides were available on how to set up the shows, rules and regulations for the various classes of exhibits, as well as suggestions for 'appealing sideshows'.

The Times in December 1942 told its readers that *'The Horticultural Committee of the Red Cross Agricultural Fund has issued a leaflet entitled "Red Cross Victory Garden Weeks and How to Run Them". [These] are the pre-war horticultural shows in wartime guise, held for the benefit of the Red Cross and St John War Organisation usually with various sideshows to swell the funds. In some districts last year the shows grew into Victory Garden Week, becoming a summer week of entertainment, including horticultural shows, poultry, rabbit and dog shows and other events. . . . This leaflet asks every borough, urban district and rural district council in the country to follow this example next year.'*

All sorts of exhibitions could come under the heading of Red Cross shows. The RHS Orchid committee organised a sale of over 400 specialist and rare orchids in August 1940 in aid of the Red Cross. In 1944 a 'sound movie' was issued to inspire more villages to hold auctions, Victory Garden fetes, poultry and rabbit shows.

As well as the general Victory shows and Red Cross shows, the rather more specialist Royal Horticultural Society shows were for many an essential element of wartime enjoyment. In the First World War the Royal Horticultural Society had their 'Floral Fetes' to raise money for the War Relief Fund. Although the society had temporarily stopped all shows at the outbreak

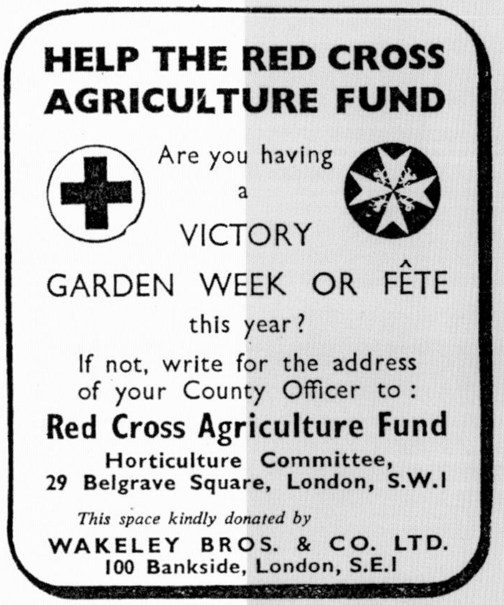
HELP THE RED CROSS AGRICULTURE FUND
Are you having a VICTORY GARDEN WEEK OR FÊTE this year?
If not, write for the address of your County Officer to:
Red Cross Agriculture Fund
Horticulture Committee, 29 Belgrave Square, London, S.W.1
This space kindly donated by
WAKELEY BROS. & CO. LTD.
100 Bankside, London, S.E.1
1944

of war they had soon recommenced on the advice of the government. By April 1940 the RHS was confident enough in its wartime guise to hold its annual 'Spring Floral Meeting', although some might have wondered about the relevance of the Orchid Shows, Daffodil Medals and Rhododendron Awards. In 1943 the RHS May Shrub competitions were taking place 'as normal' for a range of exhibits of 'Shrubs in Bloom'.

Above
Margaret Harber's birthday party in their overflowing garden.
Right
'Rest break for Women War Workers at Walton-on-the-Hill (Surrey)', 1944. HMSO

Enjoying the Garden and Holidaying at Home

As petrol rationing and travel restrictions began to bite, trips to the country or seaside became distant memories and relaxation began to concentrate on the small green space of the garden. Peter Blackburn remembers that even with a large vegetable garden, hens and rabbits: *'We had retained over half of the lawn at the back and this was fully used for play, eating and sitting in the sun with visitors and elderly relatives.'* From 1939 to 1944 Margaret Harber remembers her annual birthday party being held in the family garden in Swindon against a backdrop of runner beans and other vegetables. Her parents had dug up the lawn as part of the Dig for Victory campaign, and also built a dug-out air-raid shelter but there was still room for a family party. Meals out of doors were also a feature of wartime. Magazines such as **Good Housekeeping** promoted the 'carefree' lifestyle of picnic meals and campfire cooking: *'Have every meal out of doors, every day when the summer allows. Children love the casualness of something off a tray, when hopeful sparrows provide the décor; you will appreciate the simplicity of mugs instead of cups and saucers and one knife, one fork, and one spoon for everybody, no frills whatever. Making life sunny, making life easy. . . . It may seem an odd way to help win the war, but remember your health and your children's health are vital to your country.'*

Behind the carefree outdoor life was of course a concern for the health of the nation and providing enough vitamins in a period of rationing at a time when many women were working in offices and factories for the first time. **Good Housekeeping** was aware of this rather more serious element: *'Meals out of doors make a welcome change from routine, and give you an extra ration of Vitamin D because the action of sunlight enables the body to make its own vitamin in addition to that which you get from food. So get out of doors as much as you can this summer, even if it's mostly in the garden, and you will build up health for the winter as well as enjoy this summer more.'*

Gardens were also a recognised therapy for the war weary or those suffering 'nervous strain'. Rest breaks in the country were provided by the government, which requisitioned country houses and gardens to billet war workers as well as the forces. In March 1944 they took on a large modern house in Walton-on-the-Hill in Surrey, naming it 'Rest Break House'. Here women workers of all kinds (inspectors of aircraft, machinists, typists and even bus conductresses) relaxed among the extensive gardens and orchards. The gardens retained many flowerbeds, which the women helped to maintain as therapy from nervous exhaustion.

As well as providing open spaces for creation of allotments, public parks in towns came to play an essential role in the campaign to 'Holiday at Home'. Bandstands resounded with music, seas of deckchairs were squeezed in among vegetables, and a special effort was made to provide colourful bedding and attractions such as the popular floral clocks. In the 1930s public parks specialised in large annual displays, and despite enthusiasm for 'keeping up spirits' it was apparent from the outbreak of war that it would not be possible to keep these going. As the 'Correspondent for Public Parks' in the **Gardeners' Chronicle** noted, *the chief job at the present time is to encourage the new army of allotment-holders. In addition, it is necessary to obey an edict to adopt rigid economy with regard to ornamental horticulture.'* These economies were not just monetary, as he went on to explain, labour shortages also meant that it was simply not possible to continue with the elaborate planting out of annuals, many of which were sensitive to disease and small fluctuations in temperature. Even in the immediate run-up to war labour had become short, *'at the end of August 1939 it was found that twenty-two percent of the [public parks] staff had joined his Majesty's Forces, and forty-five percent had been commandeered for ARP work'.*

Reflecting on 1939, The Correspondent for Public Parks wrote, *'Although there is never a good time for a war to break out, it nevertheless seemed fortunate that the beds and borders had reached the zenith of their display at the end of August (1939) and that the droughts [coming in] September and October obviated the need to water.'*

As well as having to adapt their ornamental displays parks also had to consider whether or not to plough up the tennis courts and bowling greens. In the initial enthusiasm for Dig for Victory, many of these were sacrificed, but as the war dragged on, the government urged instead the need for leisure and recreation areas as a respite from the daily grind. In fact, in many instances digging up tennis courts and suchlike proved unproductive, as they were laid on layers of sand and ash, which gave poor quality crops. Many parks departments had considerable glasshousing for the raising of annuals, and these could be given over to tomatoes and lettuce. In 1940 the Stockport Parks Department grew the lettuce variety Cheshunt Giant through the winter months, and (rather appropriately) Loos Tennis Ball. By the end of February they had over 100 fully grown lettuces ready to use.

Did only men play games in the 1940s? Certainly this piece from Public Park Notes in spring 1940 suggests so: *'As many of our young men are now serving with the colours, or in other important war work, it is obvious, apart from the grass areas which are not regularly mown, that all the football, cricket, hockey and lacrosse pitches may not be required. A proportion of the tennis courts and possibly a few of the bowling greens may not be required either.'*

Public parks had to battle with hazards not usually experienced in peacetime. One London parks department had a conservatory and two glasshouses ruined by bombs in one month, one glasshouse being hit twice. It was no wonder that the head of the department commented in the **Gardeners' Chronicle** that *'some idea may be obtained of the problems involved with regard to the cultivation of stove and greenhouse plants'.* An even stranger hazard to the bedding plants was the digging up of beds and borders by children looking for shrapnel and bullets to sell at 2d each. Many public parks suffered from the construction of air-raid shelters and anti-aircraft gun sites, as well as the tethering of barrage balloons. This was often, not altogether reasonably, resented by the parks superintendents, as were the drastic cuts in budgets for the upkeep of the parks. For many parks the removal of fences and railings led to open public access for the first time ever, and much 'wilful damage' was recorded. One parks superintendent went as far as commenting that many parks were *'scenes of desolation in what were formerly cherished parts of our city'*, and recommended trying to disguise the public air-raid shelters with climbing plants, spiky berberis or turf. While the railings were down some park superintendents suggested that 'ornamental' areas simply be abandoned. It was not the 'usual' culprits of youth that were blamed, but *'folk of all ages and classes ignore the proper footpaths and make ingress and egress at the spot nearest to where they might be travelling'*. In addition, such flowerbeds as were left were being used as a free flower shop.

However, as the **Gardeners' Chronicle** pointed out at the height of the blitz in October 1940, *'Notwithstanding the difficulties of wartime conditions the various London Parks are upholding their tradition in regard to public displays of Chrysanthemums. We are glad to learn this is so because the flowers bring so much pleasure to many people who have little other opportunity of enjoying them. Finsbury Park was the first to open a display this season, followed by Battersea and Victoria.'* St James's Park triumphed over all difficulties to provide what was described as a 'magnificent display' of tulips in the spring of 1944. Twenty thousand bulbs had been planted despite wartime restrictions, in large colour blocks of mauve, salmon, bronze, red, maroon and white, including many Dutch varieties.

Christmas and the Wartime Garden

Gardening-related Christmas presents were a theme throughout the war with magazines such as **Garden Work** suggesting that seeds, fruit bushes, and of course subscriptions to gardening periodicals all made excellent presents. With the increase in gardeners had come a rush of 'how to do it' garden books. Published under wartime restrictions, with low quality paper and few if any photographs, these were not the most attractive of books, but they were relatively cheap and eminently useful as well as being a 'patriotic' present. Reading about what to do in the garden in spring and summer has always been one of the gardener's more popular pastimes in the midst of winter, and, unless the gift of a book was accompanied by a spade, many gardeners undoubtedly spent the holiday season comfortably reading by the fire. By Christmas 1945 the shortage of paper for publishing further diminished the present-giving options, but the Ministry of Agriculture, in its **Allotment and Garden Guide** of December 1945, was quick to suggest that 'practical Christmas cards' might be made of its Dig for Victory bulletins, or if that didn't appeal: *'If you are a member of an allotment or horticultural society, why not make your friend a member by paying his or her first subscription? For knowledge gained from these personal contacts is sometimes more helpful than the written word. Gifts of plants, seeds or bulbs are always appreciated, so what about a collection of vegetable seeds, a few fruit trees or bushes, or perhaps some attractive flowering plants not needing too much attention in these days of scanty leisure. Or a bag of shallot sets, a pinch of a well-guarded strain of onion seed, a few divisions from a clump of chives or other useful perennials, all make timely and acceptable Christmas offerings. Hundreds of thousands have found out during the war the pleasures and excitements of growing plants and tending living things, so it will be in keeping with the spirit of Christmas to give them something that will*

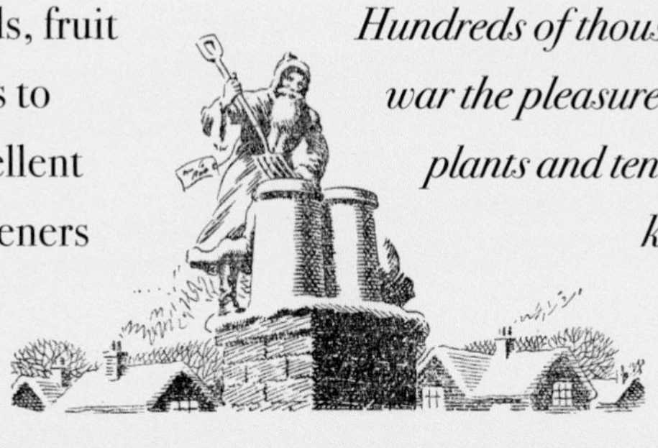

enhance that satisfaction and bind them closer to the most enduring hobby of all.'

Homegrown fruit and vegetables could also be used to decorate the family home during the seasonal festivities. In Christmas 1942 the Ministry of Food suggested that although there were: '*... no gay bowls of fruit, vegetables have such jolly colours. The cheerful glow of carrots, the rich crimson of beetroot, the emerald of parsley – it looks as delightful as it tastes.*' Holly and evergreens from the garden could also be used to decorate the house and the ministry suggested a cheap and easy way to make the decorations that little bit special: '*Christmassy sparkle is easy to add to sprigs of holly or evergreen for use on puddings. Dip your greenery in a strong solution of Epsom salts. When dry it will be beautifully frosted.*'

With a ration of only 4oz of jam or mincemeat per person per week by Christmas 1941 homemade preserves from one's own fruit bushes were especially welcome as Christmas presents. Bottling jars for homegrown vegetables and fruits were popular presents, alongside the seed packets and fruit bushes that would eventually grow food to fill them. A rather unusual approach to 'enjoying' the garden was imagined by Mrs Neal of Luton who, faced with a huge crop of onions from the family allotment in 1940, gave them away as Christmas presents later that year, each one with a small pink ribbon. For those with evacuees billeted on them, making the food and presents go round was especially difficult, although some relief from rationing was made in the winter of 1940/41 when the sugar ration was doubled for the week before Christmas to

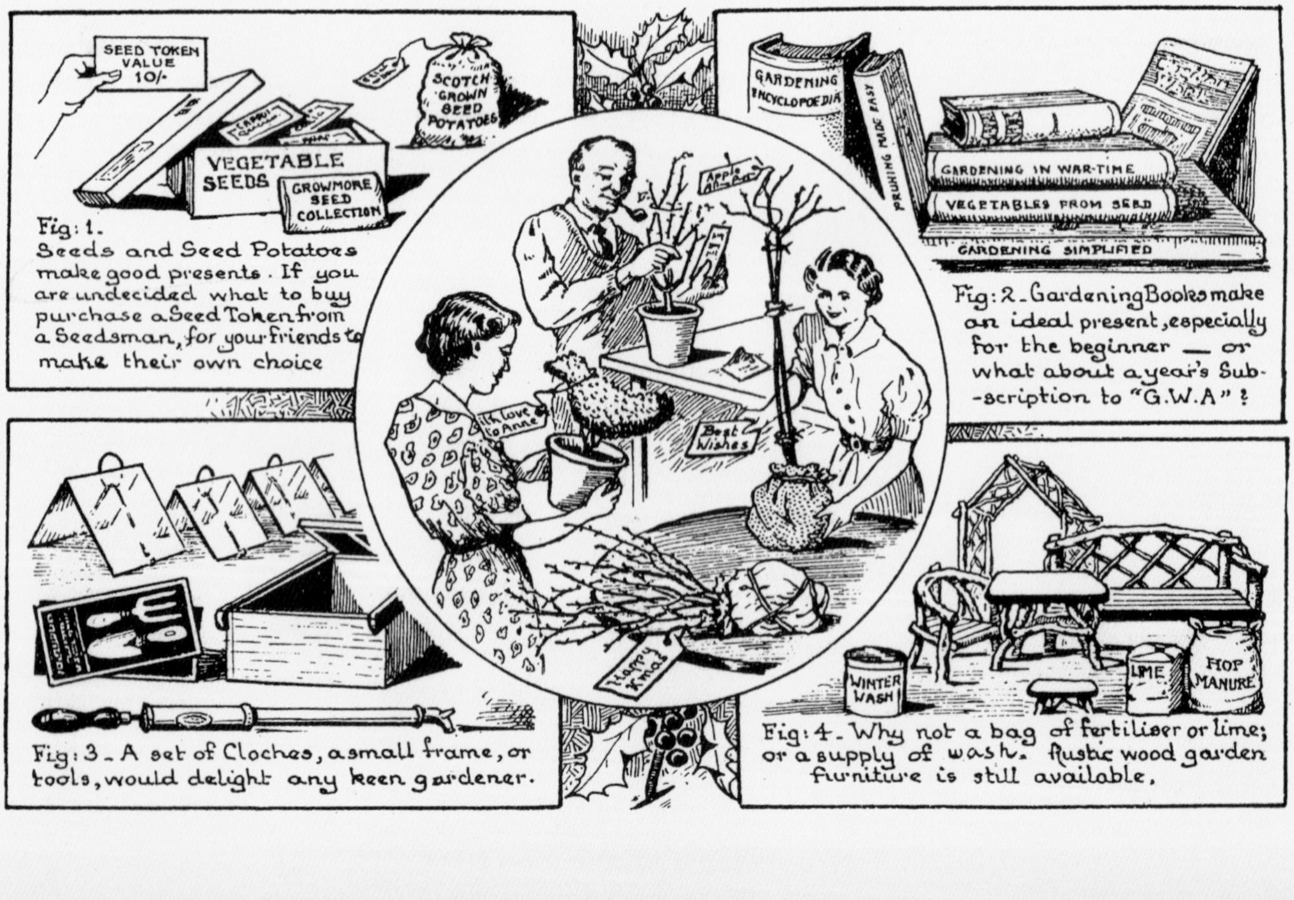
SEED TOKEN VALUE 10/-
SCOTCH GROWN SEED POTATOES
VEGETABLE SEEDS
GROWMORE SEED COLLECTION
Fig: 1. Seeds and Seed Potatoes make good presents. If you are undecided what to buy purchase a Seed Token from a Seedsman, for your friends to make their own choice
GARDENING ENCYCLOPOEDIA
PRUNING MADE EASY
GARDENING IN WAR-TIME
VEGETABLES FROM SEED
GARDENING SIMPLIFIED
Fig: 2 _ Gardening Books make an ideal present, especially for the beginner — or what about a year's Sub-scription to "G.W.A"?
Best Wishes
Happy Xmas
WINTER WASH
LIME
HOP MANURE
Fig: 3 _ A set of Cloches, a small frame, or tools, would delight any keen gardener.
Fig: 4 _ Why not a bag of fertiliser or lime; or a supply of wash. Rustic wood garden furniture is still available.

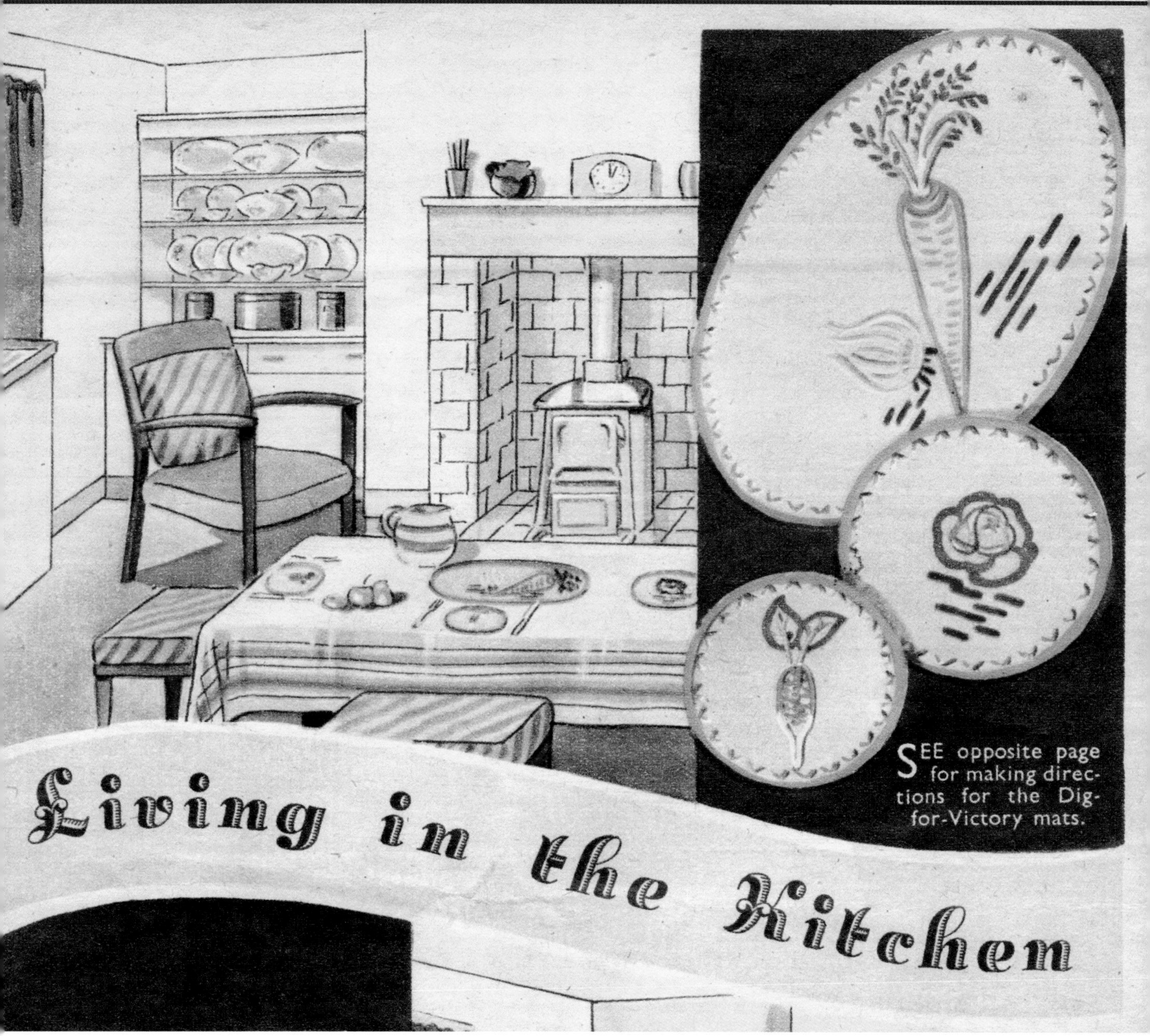
SEE opposite page for making directions for the Dig-for-Victory mats.
Living in the Kitchen

allow more preserves and cakes to be made. Those households which had gone in for raising hens and rabbits in the garden celebrated with an almost 'traditional' Christmas meal, while others made do with 'mock goose' (made from lamb), or 'mock duck'. Rabbit, once despised as the basis of the Christmas family meal, was almost impossible to get in urban areas by the winter of 1943/44, and black market prices shot up. Once again the garden stepped in!

Left

This illustration from *Garden Work* shows a happy family Christmas with everyone giving garden gifts to each other. Rustic wooden furniture was one of the few decorative items still available despite restrictions on metals and better quality timber. The topiary bird is typical of suburban garden fashions leading up to the war.

Above

In 1942 *Home Notes* told you how to create place-mats for your dining table on the Dig for Victory theme.

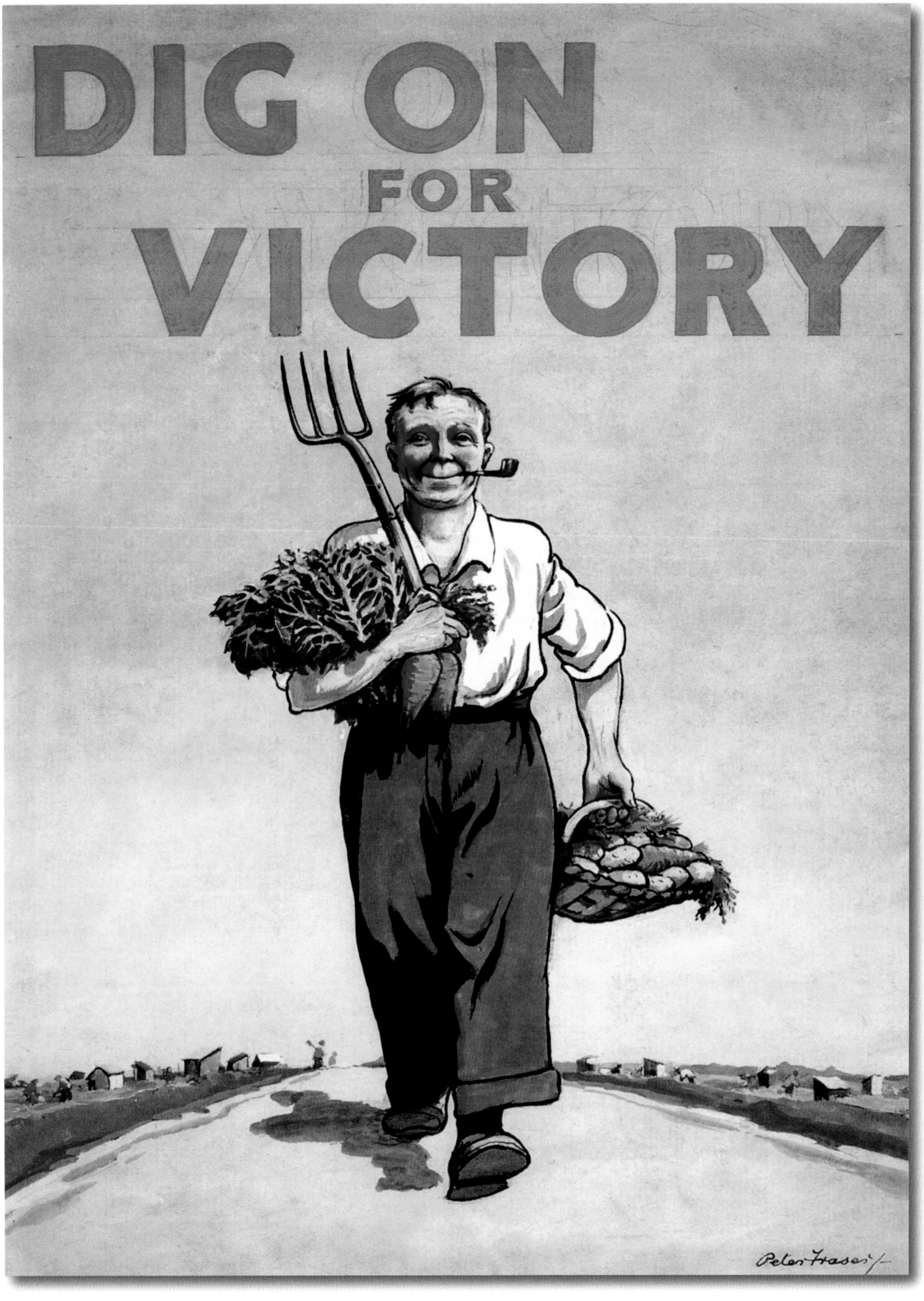
DIG ON
FOR
VICTORY
Peter Fraser

The need is still growing: 1944, 1945 & postwar

At the outbreak of war enthusiasm for the Grow More Food campaign had been more or less instant and through 1940 and 1941 numbers of victory gardeners and members of the Allotment Army rose so rapidly that seed suppliers could not keep up. By 1942 the number of private and allotment gardens Digging for Victory was calculated as almost 5 million.

However by autumn 1943, the fourth anniversary of the outbreak of war, there were distinct signs of slackening. Allied successes in North Africa and Italy, and the entry of the USA and Russia into the war on the Allied side led to a feeling among the general public that the war would soon be over and that as soon as it was food supplies would come flooding through again. In 1944 a Gallup poll revealed that over half the people questioned thought that rations would increase, or rationing cease, immediately after the Armistice. Both assumptions were unfortunately untrue. War was to drag on until May 1945 in Europe, and August 1945 in the Far East. Liberation proved that food was scarcer in many of the countries that used to supply Britain than it was in Britain itself, and rationing continued well into the 1950s, creating what became known as the 'Austerity Years'.

On the Food Front
The Minister of Agriculture warns us that we shall have to maintain Home Food Production to the utmost far into the post-war years.

Left
As the war dragged on new slogans were needed. HMSO
Above
War continued on the Food Front long after the Fighting Front had ended.

The government was well aware that the end of the war on the fighting front was going to mean an intensification of battles on the food front. Rather than importing food, Britain might have to export to Allied countries in Europe as they were liberated, to prevent widespread starvation. It was therefore essential that the enthusiasm and effort seen at the outbreak of war would have to be maintained and even increased . . . the question was, how?

New recruits were always wanted; one advertisement in the **Gardeners' Chronicle** in April 1944 ran, *'As an experienced gardener – an old hand at the game – you know all the wrinkles. But*

In my garden . . .

Looking back, it's difficult to visualise the garden as it used to be: the lawn that was just turning into a respectable bit of turf; the herbaceous border that made a glory of the summer months. Today the lawn is green only in memory but at least the vegetables which have taken its place don't need rolling and mowing: just a good foundation of FISONS GRANULAR VEGERITE to give them a healthy start. The glories of the prewar herbaceous border faded long ago, but tomatoes, fed by FISONS 'TOMORITE' into bright and luscious ripeness, are a nearer and equally colourful memory, and a soft fruit crop raised on FISONS ICHTHEMIC GUANO can be as satisfying a sight, in its way, as the roses it replaced. One thing at least remains unchanged in peace or war: treat the earth generously and it will give back good measure. FISONS IMPROVED HOP MANURE provides humus and feeds, and FISONS CANARY GUANO is a general fertilizer, specially successful on light soils. (*Memo:* Must get in an order for a further supply of FISONS GROWMORE.)

It's Fisons for Fertilizers

From Seedsmen and Stores. *In case of difficulty, kindly send name and address of your most convenient retailer to* FISONS Limited, *(Horticultural Department),* Harvest House, Ipswich. Largest makers of Complete Fertilizers. Pioneers of Granular Fertilizers.

Above
Fisons' fertilisers tried to look on the optimistic side after four whole years of war.
Right
Gardeners with some experience of growing vegetables had been encouraged to help their neighbours throughout the war, as seen in this 1941 advert.

the war "Diggers" don't. Your help can make all the difference. Don't wait to be asked – show them how to go about it, how, for instance, to choose crops and varieties that do best in your district; how to avoid summer glut and winter shortage by careful planning.'

The Need is Growing

Even by 1943 it was not only enthusiasm that was running out: tools, seeds, and even paper for

gardening magazines had all reached a low ebb. Worried that efforts would slacken and allotment plots disappear under weeds, the government renewed its campaign. New slogans appeared; '*Dig on for Victory*' and '*Dig to Keep Well Fed*', the latter an intimation that food supplies were expected to remain low for a long time to come. As spring 1944 arrived with no end to the war in sight, but a general feeling of slackening on the home front, the Ministry of Agriculture came up with the rather more catchy '*The need is GROWING. Dig for Victory Still*'.

These renewed efforts to get, and keep, people digging were accompanied by a series of advertisements and posters encouraging 'old hands' to pass on their experience to those only just joining in the good work. In case there were not sufficient 'old

GARDENERS WHO KNOW—
Help the beginners along!

Already there are over a million wartime gardeners who are new to the game. There will be thousands more, and many of them women. Your advice and encouragement can help them to achieve good results in their gardens and allotments. You help the nation when you help your neighbour to grow more food.

DIG FOR VICTORY
and help others to do so too!

All gardeners should post this coupon NOW
TO MINISTRY OF AGRICULTURE,
HOTEL LINDUM, ST. ANNES-ON-SEA.
Please send me copies of free pictorial leaflets.
NAME
ADDRESS
G.111.

hands' to go round, a series of government Dig for Victory leaflets were recommended (no. 1, no. 23, no. 19, no. 16 and no. 8). Many of the other Dig for Victory leaflets were also reissued to provide fresh encouragement and instruction to those who were wavering. Autumn 1944 saw an influx of requests for these leaflets, providing evidence of a new rush of diggers joining the existing allotment and garden army. Sixteen thousand people wrote in for information following the government's '*Better Planning, Better Gardening, Better Crops*' mini-campaign, and a further 14,000 requests followed the advertisement series '*You Need a Plan*'. This despite the fact, as the gardening press noted, that all leaflets had already had a wide circulation with several reissues. *You Need a Plan* was aimed specifically at those who had a new plot to lay out or garden space for a new vegetable plot.

However, despite all this evidence of vegetable production, there were worrying signs of a return to peacetime habits. Vegetable shows suddenly found themselves lacking in entries, while the flower classes literally bloomed. Increased orders were being placed with the seedsmen and nurserymen for flower seeds and flowering plants, orders which they had trouble fulfilling under the restrictions on flower production. Even the famous Mr Middleton expressed concern at the number of enquiries he was starting to receive about flower growing, and in February 1944 he issued a statement expressing the need for gardeners to concentrate on their vegetables. '*There is nothing I would like better than to put my lawn down again and to refurnish the borders; I should just love to cut bunches of roses and lilac and herbaceous flowers again, but the time is*

not yet. The need for growing food at home is as great, if not greater, than at any time during the war, and we must not relax for a moment, rather should we make still greater efforts for we may yet know what it is to be hungry.' Spring 1944 also saw a new issue of **Mr Middleton's All the Year Round Gardening Guide**. For 2s 6d, it told you what to do every week of the year, leading '*from success to success in your garden or allotment, the Middleton Way*'!

Cecil Middleton was not the only one worried about the public's optimism on the garden and flower front. The Duke of Norfolk (the Joint Parliamentary Secretary to the Ministry of Agriculture) gave a speech in spring 1944 aimed at bringing back to the fold (or the plot) those who had drifted away. Acknowledging that the demands on those at the home front were increasing, leaving less time for the vegetable garden, he urged that: '*We must all try to maintain our physical standard and staying power at the highest pitch*' although demands on people's time had never been heavier. '*Fresh green foods are vital to enable us to carry on our daily tasks under trying conditions. Delays in transport will undoubtedly occur when fresh fronts are opened up; but they will not worry the man or woman who has stuck to the job, carried on with the allotment or vegetable garden and has adequate crops at hand for the gathering.*' This, he told his audience, was their role in the grand strategic plan, helping to feed starving Europe even after the Armistice. This fifth year of war, he ended, was to be the most difficult, the most demanding, and the one for which the nation would most rely on its gardeners. Just as well that in some towns, such as Torquay, allotment provision had increased tenfold since the start of

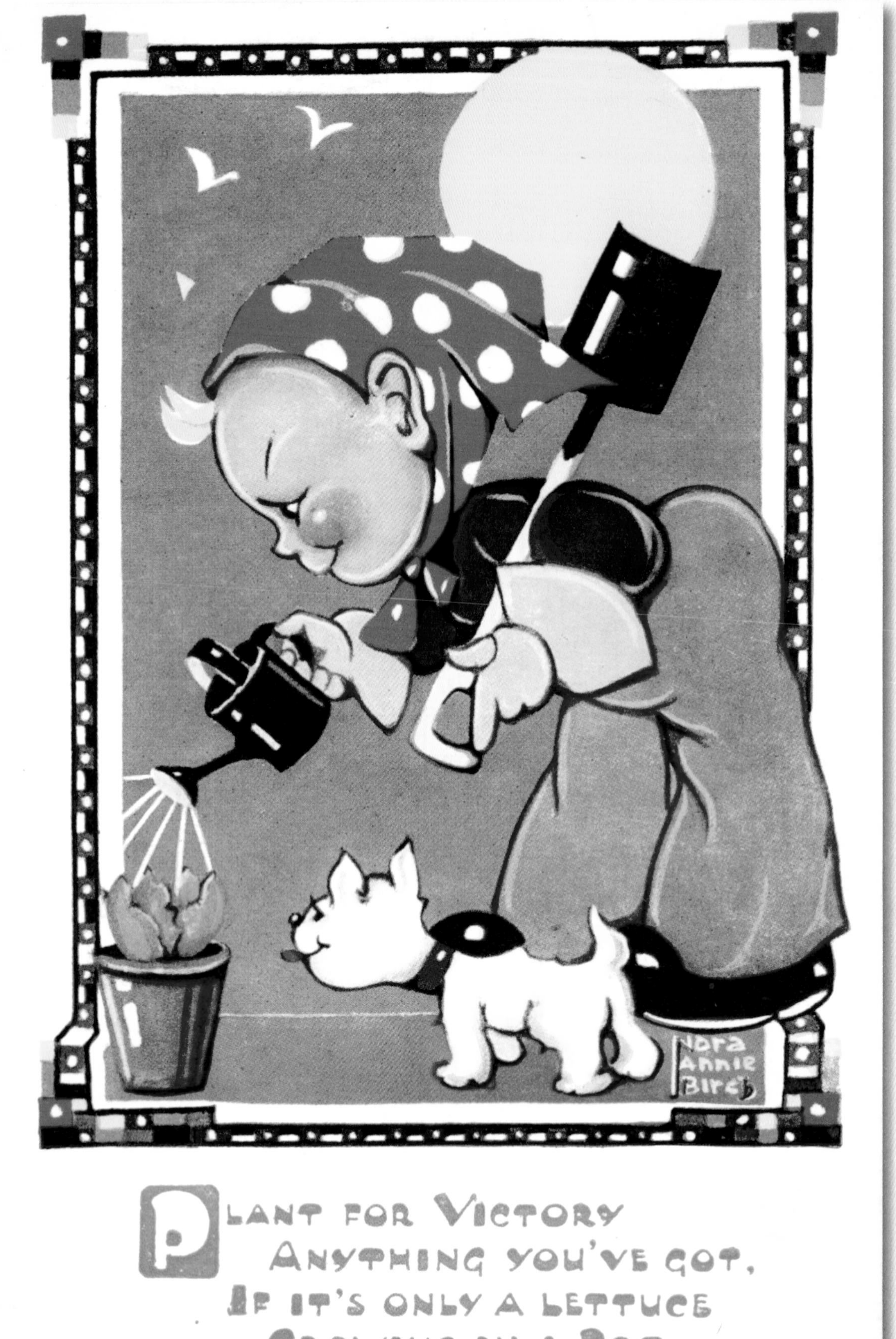
Nora Annie Birch
PLANT FOR VICTORY
ANYTHING YOU'VE GOT,
IF IT'S ONLY A LETTUCE
GROWING IN A POT.

Even the smallest contribution towards the garden front was encouraged, as this postcard shows.

the war. However, resumption of activities by the Committee of the National Sweet Pea Society and the RHS Daffodil Show seem to indicate that the loyalties of the most avid gardener were becoming divided between the call of the home front and the call of floral horticulture.

For those who really didn't have time to tend a full-size vegetable plot as well as their other wartime duties, councils were urged to make an increased number of 5-pole plots available and encourage sharing. In late spring 1944 the government even issued a 'Dig for Victory' leaflet (no. 24) on 'Roof and Window-box Gardening' for those who had neither time nor land! Every lettuce was to count in the last year of war.

At the opening of every Dig for Victory show in 1944 the following telegram from the Minister of Agriculture was read out: *'We have, in the last five years, achieved on the garden and allotment fronts a great deal of which we can be proud. But the war is not yet won, and even when the Nazi gangsters are beaten, food will be scarce. Perhaps scarcer than now. So carry on: do not rest on your spades, except for those brief periods which are every gardener's privilege.'*

The concerns about a postwar starving Europe were certainly justified, and many countries turned to the same campaign of 'Victory' gardens as Britain. In the Soviet Union 11.5 million citizens were tending their own plots by 1944, as opposed to half that number in 1942. A Victory Garden Aid Committee set up by the Trades Unions benefited from seeds and assistance, organising communal areas as well as individual victory gardens. In Moscow alone 1.5 million people cropped 35,000 acres. Men, women and children were said to be in the grip of a gardening 'craze'. Every evening hordes crowded on to the Moscow underground and suburban trains armed with spades, forks and trowels, heading out to the nearest bit of cultivatable ground. Even balconies were being pressed into service.

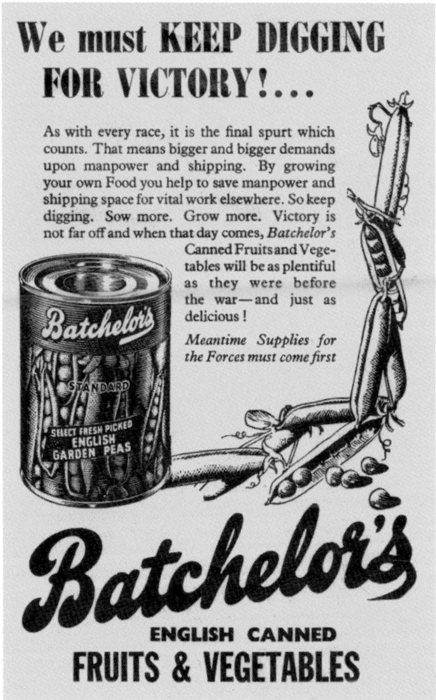
We must KEEP DIGGING FOR VICTORY!...
As with every race, it is the final spurt which counts. That means bigger and bigger demands upon manpower and shipping. By growing your own Food you help to save manpower and shipping space for vital work elsewhere. So keep digging. Sow more. Grow more. Victory is not far off and when that day comes, Batchelor's Canned Fruits and Vegetables will be as plentiful as they were before the war—and just as delicious!
Meantime Supplies for the Forces must come first
Batchelor's
STANDARD
SELECT FRESH PICKED ENGLISH GARDEN PEAS
Batchelor's
ENGLISH CANNED
FRUITS & VEGETABLES

Above
By 1944 everyone was looking forward to the end of the war and a return to 'normality'. In fact cans of peas would be a long time coming back on the shelves and Batchelor's were right in trying to keep people digging.

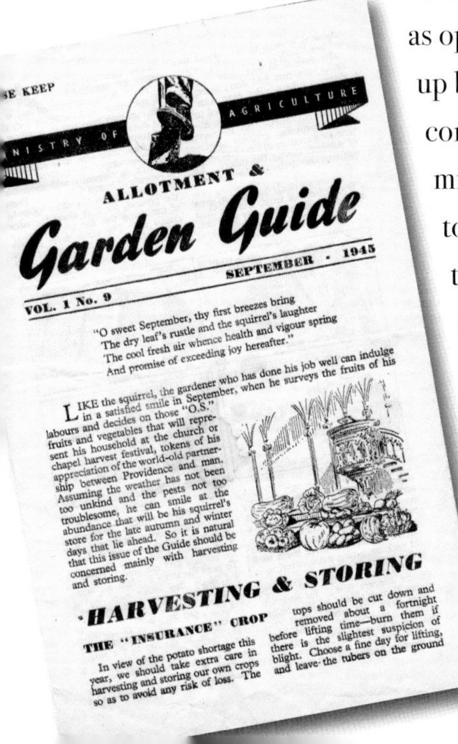
SE KEEP

MINISTRY OF AGRICULTURE

ALLOTMENT &

Garden Guide

SEPTEMBER · 1945

VOL. 1 No. 9

"O sweet September, thy first breezes bring
The dry leaf's rustle and the squirrel's laughter
The cool fresh air whence health and vigour spring
And promise of exceeding joy hereafter."

LIKE the squirrel, the gardener who has done his job well can indulge in a satisfied smile in September, when he surveys the fruits of his labours and decides on those "O.S." fruits and vegetables that will represent his household at the church or chapel harvest festival, tokens of his appreciation of the world-old partnership between Providence and man. Assuming the weather has not been too unkind and the pests not too troublesome, he can smile at the abundance that will be his squirrel's store for the late autumn and winter days that lie ahead. So it is natural that this issue of the Guide should be concerned mainly with harvesting and storing.

HARVESTING & STORING

THE "INSURANCE" CROP

In view of the potato shortage this year, we should take extra care in harvesting and storing our own crops so as to avoid any risk of loss. The tops should be cut down and removed about a fortnight before lifting time—burn them if there is the slightest suspicion of blight. Choose a fine day for lifting, and leave the tubers on the ground

Rationing and Shortages on the Garden Front

Rationing and shortages of materials such as glass, bricks, wood and metals meant that those who were only just starting out as victory diggers

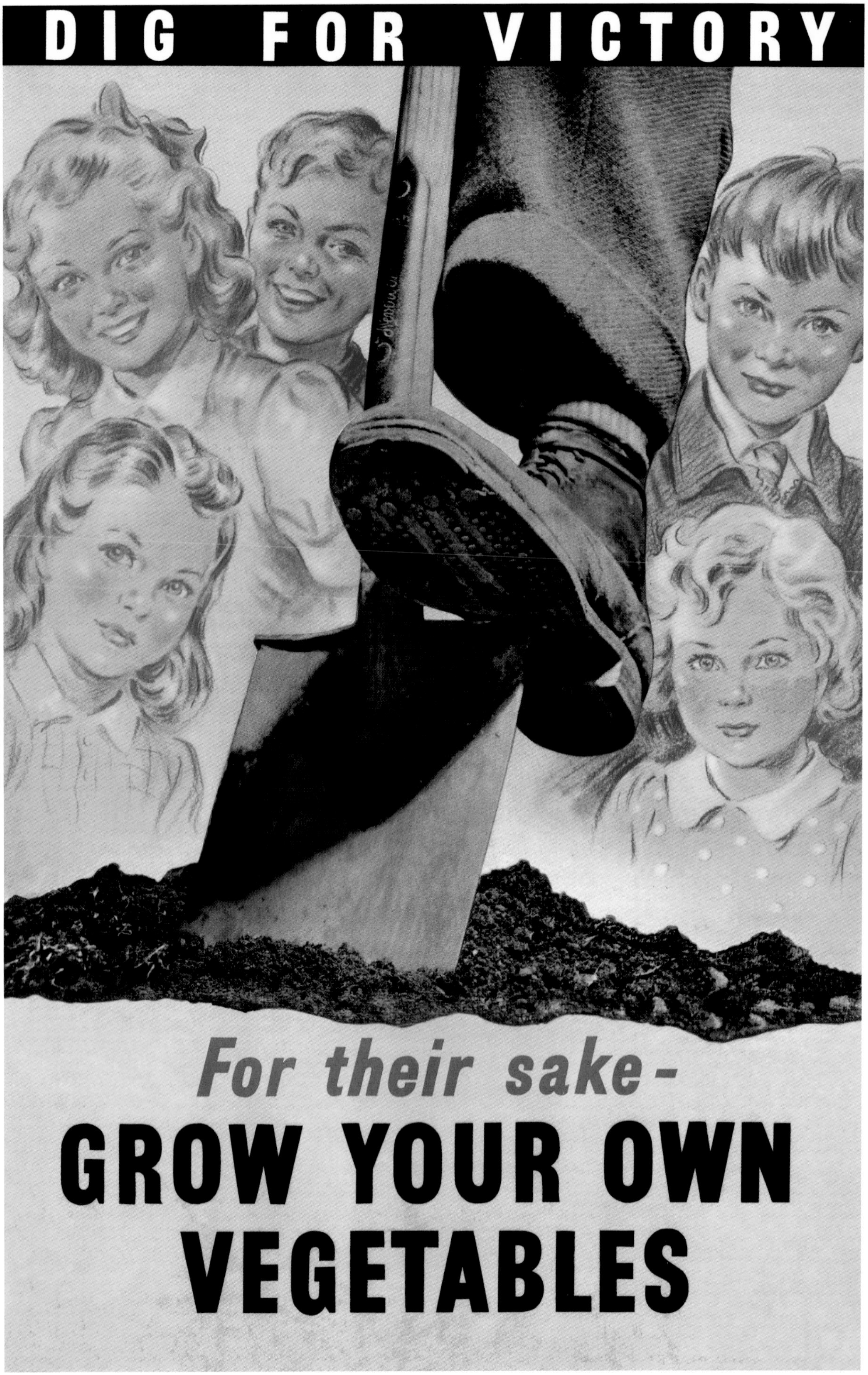
DIG FOR VICTORY
For their sake -
GROW YOUR OWN
VEGETABLES

had to rely on borrowing essential tools and make do without any of the gardening luxuries. The firm of Foster & Pearson Ltd (Beeston, Nottinghamshire) was reduced to advertising that glasshouses would be available 'When Peace Comes', and could only supply replacement parts for boilers and pipes. Boulton & Paul (also makers of glasshousing) had long been requisitioned to turn their factories over to the production of aircraft. In Southport shortages of gardening supplies had become so serious that in July 1944 there was a report that even pea sticks were being pilfered from the town's allotments, alongside entire rhubarb plants ready for replanting elsewhere. Allotment associations suggested that wheelbarrows and tools be shared between plots and that victory diggers try to make as many of their own tools as possible. A wheelbarrow between five plots was thought sufficient. Chicken wire was also in short supply with the increase in numbers of hen keepers and shortage of metals. 'Make Do and Mend' was the watchword in the garden as well as the house.

Even the gardening magazines were encountering difficulties in obtaining sufficient paper, while income from advertisements hit a low point as there was ever less to be advertised. **Smallholder and Home Gardening** magazine complained in their editorial that they were now having to restrict the numbers of copies of their weekly periodical, and stop having photographs on the front page. Instead advertising would cover the front page – if there was anything left to advertise. **Garden Work**, already reduced in format size, had long ago abandoned its photographic cover for cartoon instructions and then advertisements. On 15 April 1944, the **Gardeners' Chronicle** even had to run advertisements asking for advertisers! *'Advertise NOW . . . so as to take immediate advantage of Peace when it comes. Don't let your customers forget you.'* With subscriptions from America and other Allied countries increasingly difficult to collect, the **Gardeners' Chronicle** put out a plea for subscriptions by postal money orders or cheques drawn on a London bank. Fortunately for the gardening press, the Ministry of Agriculture could be relied upon to place an increasing number of advertisements and 'government advice' to bulk out the pages.

Allotment and Garden Guides

In January 1945 the Ministry of Agriculture launched a new series of monthly **Allotment and Garden Guides** (see illustration p.227). Using the logo of the Dig for Victory campaign (the famous foot and spade), they did not actually use the campaign slogan, perhaps for fear of boring people. This new series was aimed at 'helping you get better results from your vegetable plot and fruit garden' and ran for just one year, covering the last months of war and the first months of peace. Every month the guides reminded people of things that should already have been done that month but for whatever reason had been neglected; they then told them what should be done in the coming month, and then they *'looked ahead to the next few months so that all would be in readiness'*. The first of these guides suggested that *'For more detailed week by week information you would do well to take in one of the weekly gardening journals, as soon as the supply situation permits'*.

The guides stressed the need to grow vegetables

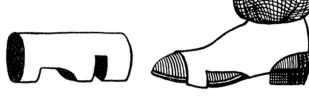

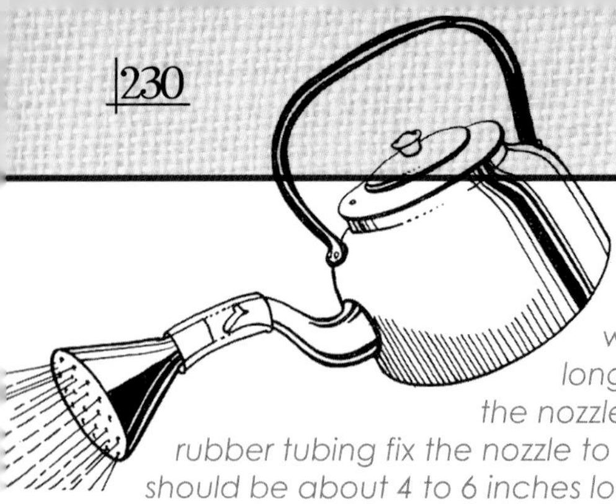

Do-it-yourself tips, from the *House-holder*. 'When the watering-can is no longer any good, cut off the nozzle and with a piece of rubber tubing fix the nozzle to the kettle. The tubing should be about 4 to 6 inches long, and it would be best to tie it to the nozzle of the watering-can and then slip it over the spout of the kettle. Any type of old rubber tubing will do, and the whole gadget will last for years.' and 'How to Enjoy your Hobby without Sore Feet. Here is a good way to prevent dust and earth getting into your boots or shoes when gardening or working on your war-time allotment. Get two pieces of old car inner tube and cut as shown at A. Then slip these over the shoe to cover the lace-holes. Tuck the trouser bottoms into the top and say good-bye to sore feet.'

and not lapse back into flowers. *'Not yet must flowers invade the flat green hinterland of the wartime allotment . . . the man who can grow his own produce. . . will. . . be making an important contribution to a smooth transition from war to peace but will also be looking after his own family interests'* – although flowers were not actually outlawed. An allotment-holder could have a 'happy fringe' of annual bedding round his plot, as long as it was no more than one-tenth of that in peacetime. This was difficult to judge for those who had only taken on an allotment in wartime! With the promise of being able to cheer themselves up with a few flowers and the end of war in sight, it must have been a reality check to learn from the June **Allotment and Garden Guide** that *'The Ministry of Food has told us that this will be the tightest of the war years so far as food supplies are concerned, so the readers of this Guide, who are undoubtedly the "wise virgins" of the parable, will be patting themselves on the back that they did not rest on their spades but continued to Dig for Victory . . . victory in the economic struggle for existence that will be the aftermath of war.'*

War on the fighting fronts may have ended with the surrender of Japan on 14 August 1945, but war on the home front was to continue for many years.

A combination of shortages, continued rationing, severe weather conditions and swingeing cutbacks resulted in the 'Austerity Years'. Lasting from 1945 to 1954 food, clothing, fuel, beer, furniture, housing and even tobacco were variously rationed or un-available. After the initial euphoria of victory morale sank ever lower as rationing increased and the interminable monotony of the daily struggle set in. The best that could be said was that the air raids had stopped and loved ones who had survived slowly came home again in their de-mob suits, although not all homecomings were undiluted joy. Many children failed to recognise fathers who had been away for years, while women used to work and independence had to adapt once again to having a man in the house. Returning men meant more food to find, and they were often critical of the small rations now available. In many ways the garden and allotment now became of even greater importance as women struggled to put enough food on the table and men tried to fit in to homes and families that had been changed by the wartime experience.

Looking back on the wartime efforts of the nation from the vantage point of December 1945, the Ministry of Agriculture (in its **Alotment and Garden Guide**, vol.1 no. 12) reflected that: *'What-*

ever the motive that prompted the man to take on an allotment, he has benefited himself: he is generally better in health because of the exercise, better in spirit because cultivating his plot took his mind off the war or the burdens of office or workshop; he has benefited his family by providing fresh vegetables that kept them fit – and incidentally helped his wife in trying to make ends meet and avoid queues; he and his fellow "Victory Diggers" benefited their country by contributing in every year of the war a substantial and indispensable quantity of food to the national larder, without which the nation might well have had to go short, not only of vegetables but of other food which our farmers have been enabled to grow through the "Victory Diggers'" efforts.'

In a speech as early as September 1943, Mr Hudson, the Minister of Agriculture, had said: *'Let us get rid of the idea that allotments are needed solely to enable folk to Dig for Victory. . . . When the day of victory dawns the need for the little man and his wife to go on producing their own food will be just as pressing. Indeed in many ways it would be true to say that our real difficulties will only then begin.'* With extra mouths to feed as men and children came home, allotments in some areas were more popular than ever and demand reached a peak. But with the end of the war the exceptional defence regulations also gradually lapsed, so requisitioned land began to be returned to private landholders and fewer plots were available. Despite rationing and shortages, public parks, squares and private land were rapidly returned to their original use. Evictions from active allotment plots were unpopular and met with considerable opposition, leaving thousands mourning their leeks and onions. Questions about the security of allotment tenancies had been asked in parliament as early as 1943, but promises had been less than forthcoming. Land on the outskirts of towns would be needed for building, private land would be returned and parks relawned. When the MP Col. Carver asked whether the Minister of Agriculture would be prepared to make provision of allotments permanent he was met

MIDDLETON'S
all the year round
GARDENING
GUIDE
1945
·Spring·Summer·Autumn·Winter·
2/6

Above
Just in case there were a few gardeners who had missed the rush of wartime leaflets, bulletins, books and films, Cecil Middleton brought out a garden guide for 1945.

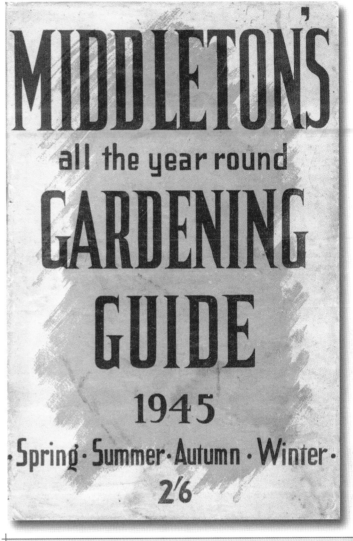

with the evasive reply that *'the postwar position would come up for consideration in all its aspects in the near future'.* In the House of Lords the Minister for Reconstruction was only prepared to suggest that when allotment-holders were dispossessed *'some effort would be made to see that they are accommodated elsewhere'* – an effort which was frequently not to bring results.

In London the council declared that leases on allotments signed at the start of 1945 would hold in force whether or not peace came, but warned that renewals after that year would not be certain. Temporary sites and private sites gave no statutory protection for allotment-holders and no compensation was made when they were taken back. In some areas demand slumped as soon as the war was over, perhaps in part due to the lack of security of tenure. In Birmingham, a city which had always had a tradition of providing allotments for all who wanted one, there was an immediate drop in allotment use. Within just a few months of the end of the war 3,000 of its 22,000 plots were registered as vacant, and sites that had been requisitioned from private landowners were returned. The situation was made worse by the new Town and Country Planning Act (1947) which repealed legislation that had required local authorities to consider reserving land for allotments in their local plans. Over the following years more plots were lost due to building pressure and lack of interest until only 16,600 plots were available in Birmingham in 1953, compared to the 22,000 wartime high.

The Aftermath and Austerity

Perhaps more damaging than any amount of apathy or lack of legislation was the weather! The winter and 'spring' of 1947 were simply appalling. From 21 January to 16 March 1947 the whole country disappeared in a grey blanket of fog, cloud and snow. In parts of the country snow fell on 26 days in this period, parts of Essex and Bedfordshire registered a numbing -21°C (-6°F), while temperatures at Kew in February never topped 5°C (41°F). With no sun at all in some areas during 22 days in February, it was impossible to melt the snow that had fallen, and ice set in. Early March was marked by gales and heavy snowstorms and by the time of the great thaw there was so much water frozen in the soil that rivers burst their banks and entire areas were flooded. In these extraordinary circumstances no gardening was possible in most areas of the country, and crops that were in the fields and allotments largely stayed there. Attempts to use pneumatic drills and pickaxes to remove parsnips expended much energy for little success, and distribution of supplies was almost impossible.

The only winners were those who had supplies of Brussels sprouts, cabbages and leeks in gardens and allotments sheltered from the worst of the weather or sacks of potatoes and onions safely stored in garden sheds. Those who had chosen the traditional earthen 'clamp' to store potatoes and carrots were faced with a frozen mound.

Seedsmen and nurseries took some time to recover from the war. Many had gone out of business or failed to retain sufficient skilled staff to carry on after the war. An exception were the rose nurseries

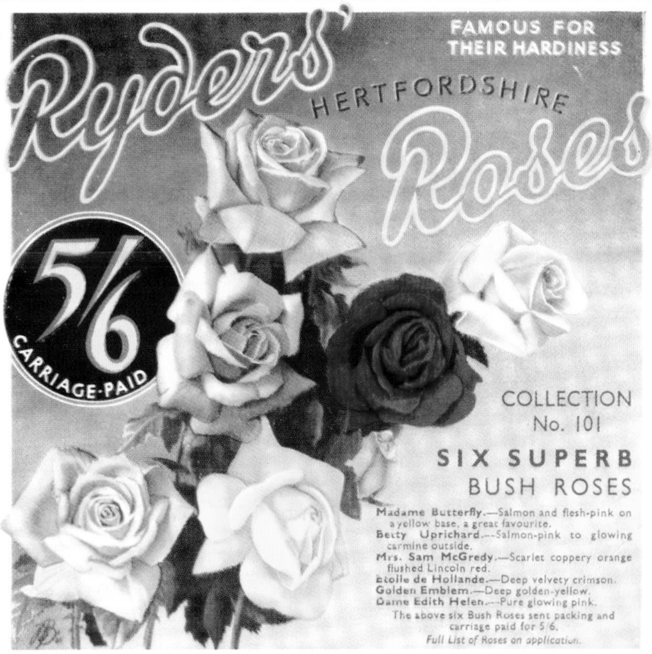
Ryders'
HERTFORDSHIRE
Roses
FAMOUS FOR THEIR HARDINESS
5/6
CARRIAGE-PAID
COLLECTION No. 101
SIX SUPERB BUSH ROSES
Madame Butterfly.—Salmon and flesh-pink on a yellow base, a great favourite.
Betty Uprichard.—Salmon-pink to glowing carmine outside.
Mrs. Sam McGredy.—Scarlet coppery orange flushed Lincoln red.
Étoile de Hollande.—Deep velvety crimson.
Golden Emblem.—Deep golden-yellow.
Dame Edith Helen.—Pure glowing pink.
The above six Bush Roses sent packing and carriage paid for 5/6.
Full List of Roses on application.

of Harry Wheatcroft, who had managed to keep a small supply of their popular roses over the war years. Harry also made contact with rose growers in France, who ironically had not suffered to the same extent as their British counterparts. In Holland enemy withdrawal revealed that up to 60% of the pre-war acreage was still devoted to tulip bulbs, whereas British restrictions had forced acreages down to 20% or less of the 1939 figure. Gandy's roses, the Wheatcrofts' main competitor, had also survived the war and by 1950 was taking out full-page advertisements in **Garden Work**, itself still going strong, although now 6d a copy instead of 3d. Other pre-war nurseries advertising in 1950 included Allwoods with their famous carnations and pinks, Acres of Derbyshire (chrysanthemums) and Woodham Park Nurseries of West Byfleet (Surrey).

British nurseries were forced to introduce new varieties as they rebuilt their stock after the war from European and other sources. Harry Wheatcroft was able to negotiate a business deal with Francis Meilland, a French nurseryman who had bred a rose called 'Peace'. 'Peace' was to be the rose of the future; a cool yellow colour, it arrived at a time when people were ready to replant. The Wheatcrofts initially bought 10,000 specimens for re-sale, but the rose's instant popularity meant that many more were to follow. 'Peace' was planted in thousands of suburban gardens, finally replacing the vegetable beds and air-raid shelters of the wartime garden.

As the austerity years dragged on the Ministry of Agriculture tried to encourage people to keep up their plots and vegetable gardens, supposing they were on public land and not a requisitioned site. In 1948 the slogan 'Dig for Plenty' was launched, admitting that 'plenty' was certainly lacking in most people's lives. '*Sow for Security*', '*Plant for Peace*' and '*Plot for Peace*' were all trialled in the gardening press, as was the less snappy '*Grow for Brighter Days*', but none caught on like '*Dig for Victory*'. Addressing the assembled plot-holders of the National Allotments and Gardens Society the Minister for Agriculture declared that *'Today we are digging for our very lives, for food, for dollars and for our self respect'*. But for many the effort had gone on for too long. They had dug for victory but ended up with austerity.

In a speech given in November 1944, Mr R.W, Haddon, Chairman of the Minister of Agriculture's Publicity Advisory Committee, proudly proclaimed *'We have now completed five years of the Dig for Victory campaign, and I think you will agree that it has been one of the most successful campaigns of the war.'* It was certainly one of the most memorable.

INDEX